Philosophy of Religion

Also available from Cassell:

Christian Ethics: An Introduction
Edited by Bernard Hoose

Philosophy of Religion

A guide to the subject

Edited by Brian Davies OP

GEORGETOWN UNIVERSITY PRESS
WASHINGTON, D.C.

Georgetown University Press,
Washington, D.C. 20007

First published 1998

Library of Congress Cataloging-in-Publication Data
Philosophy of religion : a guide to the subject / edited by Brian
    Davies.
        p.   cm.
    Includes bibliographical references and index.
    ISBN 0–87840–695–6 (pbk.)
    1. Religion—Philosophy.   I. Davies, Brian, 1951–   .
BL51.P5317   1998
210–dc21
                                                98–38312
                                                   CIP

ISBN 0-87840-695-6 (paperback)

Typeset by York House Typographic Ltd
Printed and bound in Great Britain by
Biddles Ltd, Guildford and King's Lynn

Contents

Contents

For Herbert McCabe OP
who will agree with much that he finds in this book
and will have lots to say about the rest

The authors

William Alston, Professor of Philosophy, Syracuse University, New York, USA.

Dominic Balestra, Professor of Philosophy, Fordham University, New York, USA.

David Braine, Honorary Lecturer and Honorary Fellow in Philosophy, University of Aberdeen, UK.

David Burrell CSC, Hesburgh Professor of Philosophy and Theology, University of Notre Dame, USA.

William Lane Craig, Research Professor of Philosophy, Talbot School of Theology, La Miranda, California, USA.

Brian Davies OP, Professor of Philosophy, Fordham University, New York, USA.

John Greco, Associate Professor of Philosophy, Fordham University, New York, USA.

Revd Dr Peter Groves, Curate, St Margaret's Church, Leigh-on-Sea, Essex, UK.

Paul Helm, Professor of the History and Philosophy of Religion, King's College, London University, UK.

Gerard J. Hughes SJ, Professor of Philosophy, Heythrop College, London University, UK.

John Jenkins CSC, Associate Professor of Philosophy, University of Notre Dame, USA.

The authors

Joseph Koterski SJ, Associate Professor of Philosophy, Fordham University, New York, USA.

Julius Lipner, Faculty of Divinity, Cambridge University, UK.

Hugo Meynell, Professor of Religious Studies, University of Calgary, Canada.

Lawrence Moonan, formerly Senior Lecturer in Philosophy at Bolton Institute, UK.

Gareth Moore OP, Prior, Ferme de Froidmont, Rixensart, Belgium.

H. O. Mounce, Senior Lecturer in Philosophy, University of Wales at Swansea, UK.

Gregory Reichberg, Associate Professor of Philosophy, Fordham University, New York, USA.

James Ross, Professor of Philosophy and Law, University of Pennsylvania, USA.

Charles Taliaferro, Professor of Philosophy, St Olaf College, Minnesota, USA.

Peter van Inwagen, John Cardinal O'Hara Professor of Philosophy, University of Notre Dame, USA.

Mark Wynn, Lecturer in Philosophy of Religion, Australian Catholic University, Brisbane.

Introduction

Brian Davies OP

Does God exist? Can God's existence be proved? Can it be defended in some
other way? What is God like? Can we talk sense about God? Does evil
disprove God's existence? Is faith always opposed to reason? Are miracles
possible? Is morality of any religious significance? Is there life after death?
Does Christianity make sense? Can philosophy offer insight when it comes
to the diversity of religious beliefs? What can science tell us when it comes
to religious matters?

   This book is about these questions. Its purpose is to explain how
philosophers have thought about them in the past, and to suggest how we
can think of them today. It is intended for students and teachers of
philosophy and theology. It is also intended for anyone who is seriously
concerned with the puzzles raised by religion. Written by a distinguished
collection of authors from Britain and the USA, it aims to provide a critical
introduction to philosophy of religion. As well as indicating why philosophy might challenge religious belief, its authors are also concerned to ask
what philosophy can contribute to our understanding of such belief
considered as something of importance, something worth thinking
about.

   The expression 'philosophy of religion' is a modern invention whose
users have understood it in different senses. But philosophical thinking
about religious matters (as good a definition as any of 'philosophy of
religion') is something that goes back for centuries. So the book begins
with a brief account of what has been said about philosophy and religion
from the days of the ancient Greeks to the beginning of the twentieth
century. Questions which have always concerned philosophers and theologians include 'What is the relevance of philosophy to religious belief?'
and 'How should philosophers approach religious belief?' Twentieth-
century theologians have had views on the first question. Ludwig
Wittgenstein, considered by many to be the greatest philosopher of the
twentieth century, had views on the second. In recent years, both questions

have been much discussed by a number of writers focusing on a notion they refer to as 'Foundationalism'. So the book continues with accounts of what has been said about philosophy and religion by twentieth-century theologians, by Wittgenstein, and by those with an eye on 'Foundationalism'.

Religious beliefs have been many and various. In Judaism, Islam and Christianity, however, it is taken for granted that the truth on which all else of religious importance depends is the truth that God exists. Yet why suppose that God does exist? This question is what Chapter 2 is all about. Those who have argued for God's existence can be thought of as offering what can fairly be called 'Ontological Arguments', 'Cosmological Arguments' and 'Design Arguments'. It has also been suggested that there is reason for believing that God exists because God can be experienced (rather than argued for). In Chapter 2, readers will discover what 'Ontological', 'Cosmological' and 'Design' arguments have amounted to, and what might be said of them. They will also find an essay intended to help them to consider whether God can be an object of human experience.

In his *Summa Theologiae*, St Thomas Aquinas suggests that, once we have discovered that something exists, we need to ask what the thing is. He goes on to deny that we can know what God is, but he also argues that philosophy can help us to say why certain statements about God (other than 'God exists') are true. Agreeing with the central teachings of Judaism, Islam and Christianity, Aquinas suggests that God can be said to be eternal, simple, omnipotent and omniscient. He also argues that knowledge and will (attributes we ascribe to human persons) can be ascribed to God. The notions of divine eternality, simplicity, omnipotence, omniscience and personality have been central ones for philosophers thinking about the nature of God (what God is, as distinct from whether God is), and these are the focus of Chapter 3.

Talk of God's 'attributes', however, has seemed to some thinkers to be largely nonsense. For how can human language ever succeed in saying anything significant about God? When we say that something exists, or that it is like this or like that, we are normally talking of things in the physical world. But God is not supposed to be a part of this world. He is supposed to be its Maker or Creator. So can we employ any of our usual ways of talking about things when trying to talk about God? Can we talk sense about something which is not a part of the world? These questions are the focus of Chapters 4 and 5. Here readers will find a history of philosophical thinking about 'God-talk'. They will also find a defence of the conclusion that talk about God might indeed make sense.

The defence begins in Chapter 4, where (among other things) James Ross introduces and discusses the theologically influential notion of analogy. It continues in Chapter 5 as William Lane Craig suggests how we might think about the assertion that God is the Creator of a world in which divine providence operates. It is often said that divine providence sometimes arranges for miracles to occur, and the topic of miracles has given rise to much philosophical discussion. For that reason, Chapter 5 also includes a treatment of miracles, one which aims to say what might be meant by 'a miracle' and whether we might ever be right to conclude that a miracle has occurred.

One of the biggest puzzles raised by belief in God's existence is often referred to as 'the problem of evil'. Some have taken this to show that there cannot be a God. Others have taken a different line. With a special eye on contemporary and medieval thinking, Chapter 6 reviews and comments on the major positions adopted with respect to the problem of evil. It concludes with the suggestion that evil is a mystery which, while not counting against God's existence, is not something solvable by philosophy.

Some would say that such a conclusion is best described as a summons to faith. But, though 'faith' is a word much used by religious believers, one might wonder what it means. Some have taken it to be a word designed to throw dust in the eyes of philosophers. On their account, those who appeal to faith are basically trying to block reasonable enquiry. But is that really so? Can faith never be reasonable? These questions are the concern of Chapter 7. And, since 'faith' for millions of people means 'Christian faith', Chapter 8 turns specifically to Christianity. How do the doctrines peculiar to this religion stand up under philosophical scrutiny? What can philosophers say about, for example, the assertion that God became man (the doctrine of the Incarnation), or that God is three persons in one substance (the doctrine of the Trinity). These questions are very much alive in contemporary philosophy of religion, and Chapter 8 addresses them directly.

Chapters 9 and 10 are concerned with two topics frequently connected with each other in the context of religious belief: morality, and life after death. It has often been said that our moral character in this life has consequences for a life to come. Some have implied that religion is needed to safeguard morality. It has even been suggested that religious belief is nothing but a kind of moral belief. But what is the truth of the matter? How might thinking about morality have a bearing on thinking about religion? And is there any reason to think that people somehow survive their death? Chapter 9 turns to the first question. Chapter 10 addresses the second. As well as proposing answers to their questions, both chapters offer accounts of how the questions have been treated in the course of the history of philosophy.

Most philosophers of religion writing in English have concentrated on beliefs to be found by those who subscribe to three of the major world religions. Their concern has mostly been focused on Judaism, Islam, and Christianity. But they have not always paid much attention to the differences between these religions. And they have rarely ventured to philosophize about other religions. Yet such religions exist. There are Hinduism, Buddhism and Sikhism, for example. We might therefore wonder whether philosophy can have anything to say when it comes to the world-wide diversity in religious belief. Chapter 11 is intended as an aid to such wondering. Can Western philosophical thinking help us usefully to reflect on the major world religions? What is a world religion anyway? Can philosophers in one religious tradition fruitfully debate with others in different traditions? These are some of the questions raised and discussed in Chapter 11.

Good though they are, these questions are not much considered in the writings of philosophers living before the twentieth century. And they have not been given the attention they deserve by twentieth-century philosophers. From the nineteenth century onwards, however, questions about religious belief have been raised in the light of the rise of modern science. And these have been much discussed. Many have suggested that science now somehow shows that religious belief is wholly discredited. But are they right to suggest this? This question is Dominic Balestra's specific concern in Chapter 12, which is a brief introduction to the topic of science and religion.

Readers should not be surprised to find that contributors to this book sometimes disagree with each other (by implication if not explicitly). That is because they are philosophers with views of their own, not a group of writers chosen to defend a party-line of some kind. Argument and debate are the life-blood of philosophy, and these cannot be guaranteed to produce a single, unified outcome. In the end, you do philosophy (including philosophy of religion) not just by learning who has said what but also by engaging philosophically with what has been said. So, as well as telling readers something of the history of philosophy of religion, the authors of this book reflect on this history as individuals and thereby encourage their readers to do likewise.

1

Philosophy and religion

(a) Ancient and early medieval thinking

Gregory M. Reichberg

Any serious attempt at determining the position of the ancient Greek philosophers on the meaning of religion must grapple with the indeterminateness of their speech about the divine. Plato and Aristotle, for instance (to restrict our consideration to the two most illustrious philosophers of antiquity), may be found applying the predicate 'divine' to realities as diverse as the intellect, the heavenly spheres, the Olympian gods, the separate Forms (Plato) and the First Mover of the universe (Aristotle). Yet, to the disappointment of modern readers, accustomed as we are to works like Aquinas's *Summa Theologiae*, Hume's *Dialogues on Natural Religion*, and Kant's *Religion within the Limits of Reason Alone*, the ancient philosophers rarely (if ever) saw fit to draft treatises on the existence and nature of divine beings. Nor for that matter do they appear to have troubled themselves very much with composing *systematic* accounts about the ties which might bind people to the realities they so liberally termed 'divine'. Consequently, it is not surprising that the scholarly literature on the Greek philosophers should be so rife with conflicting interpretations of their respective views on religion.

The teaching of Plato (428–348 BC) on religion is a case in point. When articulating his famous doctrine of the separate Forms, Plato often adopts the tone, if not the language, of religious veneration. Philosophy he correspondingly depicts as 'a lifelong quest for salvation' in which knowledge of the divine Forms 'makes the soul more and more like these objects'.[1] Yet, in so doing, Plato never urges his readers to worship these Forms as so many gods. Apparently no cults, prayers or sacrifices need be enacted in their favour. Nor, for that matter, does he portray the Forms as minded beings who might exercise providence over human lives. Hence despite their perfection and transcendence, the Forms are not the sort of entities to which one might direct acts of religious devotion. On the few occasions that Plato terms the Forms 'divine', his intent seems only to underscore their unparalleled excellence, not to assert that they *are* indeed *gods*.

The question of whether Plato did in fact assert the existence of gods (divine beings with personal traits to whom people owe the homage of worship) has long divided scholars of his thought. According to one line of interpretation, Plato's theology may best be understood as a work of demythologization in which (1) the Olympian gods are replaced by the separate Forms, and (2) the traditional cultic practices of ancient Greece are superseded by a rational religion whose principle aim is to unite the human soul with the Form of the Good.[2] By contrast, others argue that Plato never abandoned belief in the deities of ancient Greece, nor did he eschew the traditional religious practices prevalent in his day.[3] Much of this debate concentrates on the interpretation of texts such as the *Laws*, Book 10, where Plato purports to offer a philosophical demonstration of the existence of beneficent gods, the *Republic*, Book 2, where he severely chastises the Homeric poets for their anthropomorphic representations of the traditional deities (the Olympians), and *Phaedrus*, 247 a–e, where he depicts the immortal gods as intelligent beings whose vision of unchangeable truth is for them the source of a perfect felicity. However divergently scholars understand these texts, they generally agree that with Plato a new mode of discourse is inaugurated, one in which the resources of rational argumentation are brought to bear on the question of the divine. Significantly, Plato's works bear witness to the first recorded occurrence of the term 'theology' (in Greek *theo-logia* – speech about God),[4] a term which has since become nearly synonymous with a rational reflection on the divine.[5]

The writings of Aristotle (384–322 BC) on religion give rise to the same sort of interpretive difficulties that we have just encountered in Plato. If anything, the difficulties are even more vexing in Aristotle's case. Although his actual comments on the divine are brief and often elusive, they have nevertheless exercised an enormous influence on the development of Western theism, especially in the medieval period. This in turn has prompted the emergence of a vast body of secondary literature.[6]

Many commentators view Aristotle's thought as subversive to the cause of religion. They point to texts such as the *Metaphysics*, Book 12 (Lambda), chapters 7 and 9, where he allegedly advances a philosophical conception of divinity at odds with traditional religious belief in a provident god (or gods). This interpretation arises apropos of Aristotle's proof for the existence of a First Mover of the universe. Having shown that all motion in the heavens and on the earth depends upon this most primordial of beings, he proceeds to enumerate its attributes. The First Mover is eternal, incorporeal, indivisible and immutable; moreover, it enjoys perfect life and knowledge. Then, pausing to consider the kind of knowledge possessed by this highest being, Aristotle draws a decisive conclusion: the only item worthy of the First Mover's awareness is the First Mover itself; no other object merits the consideration of this self-thinking mind. 'Therefore it must be itself that Thought thinks (since it is the most excellent of things), and its thinking is a thinking upon thinking' (1074b33–34). Eternally engaged in solitary contemplation of itself, the First Mover stands wholly indifferent to all else. Hence the futility of addressing prayers in its direction, leading one historian to conclude that 'with Aristotle, the Greeks had gained an indisputably rational theology, but they had lost their religion'.[7] It was to a deity of this sort that Pascal referred many centuries later when he so sharply distinguished the 'God of the philosophers' from the 'God of Abraham, Isaac and Jacob'.

Against this rationalist interpretation of the *Metaphysics*, other commentators argue that Aristotle never intended to equate the supreme metaphysical principle (the First Mover) with the notion of a god. They point out that for Aristotle (and Greek thinkers generally), the word 'god' did not connote the idea of ultimate perfection. Historically, the association of 'god' with this idea arose only within the context of Christianity; as such it was alien to the Greek mind. Thus the ancient philosophers could assert without contradiction that a level of the divine (be it Parmenides's *One*, Anaxagoras's *Nous*, Plato's *Good*, or Aristotle's *First Mover*) might exist above the gods.[8]

Prima facie, then, Aristotle's postulation of a First Mover should not be construed as a *theological* claim about the existence and nature of *God*. Rather it may best be understood as a *metaphysical* assertion about the first principle of the universe. Accordingly, if for Aristotle the First Mover is not God (on this rendering it is something higher and better than a god), then we need not take his statement that the First Mover thinks only of itself as implying an outright rejection of a divine providence. Indeed, passages in his ethical and political writings indicate that Aristotle believed in superhuman agents (gods) who existed in a realm just below the first (and secondary) movers of the universe, and that he endorsed the traditional acts of worship by which the providential beneficence of these gods was publicly recognized.[9] Aristotle does not appear to have concerned himself very much with elaborating philosophical proofs for the existence of such intermediate divine beings, a matter which he deemed outside the competence of philosophy. The traditional religious teachings conveyed through myth were sufficient in his eyes to assure people that they could depend on the support and guidance of the gods.

Gregory M. Reichberg

Christian monotheists naturally showed little sympathy for the intermediate deities of ancient Greece and Rome. In his monumental work *The City of God*, St Augustine (AD 354–430) took great care to deny the divinity of the pagan gods, arguing that these supposedly divine agents are in reality angels, or demons, or perhaps simply men who have won a reputation of immortality.[10] The principal aim of this polemic was to demonstrate that no religious homage is owed to these beings, since they are mere creatures like ourselves. And attributes which the Greek philosophers had previously assigned to the Good, the One, or the self-thinking First Mover, Augustine now identified with the God of the Hebrew and Greek scriptures. Thus Augustine praises a God who is possessed of mind, eternal, incorporeal, indivisible and immutable. This God differs from the divine of the pagan philosophies in two important respects, however.

First of all, Augustine's biblical God is intimately involved with the world. No longer is the divine absolute so conceived that its perfection entails a detachment from the concerns of human beings. The Christian doctrine of the Incarnation, central to Augustine's thought, forestalls any doubt about God's great love for humanity. This is a God who draws people to himself in friendship, offering to them the promise of perfect felicity (beatitude). Secondly, the biblical God is entirely independent of the world: for even if the world had not been created, this God would still be capable of existing, undiminished in his perfection. By contrast, according to the pagan mind 'the divine, even in its most ultimate form, is never conceived as capable of being without the world. It is divine by being differentiated from what is not divine and by having an influence on what is not divine.'[11]

St Anselm of Canterbury's (AD 1033–1109) famous definition of God as 'that than which nothing greater can be thought'[12] highlights the radical auto-sufficiency which is distinctive of the Christian God. This formula 'implies that God is to be so understood, and the world or creatures are to be so understood, that nothing greater, *maius*, is achieved if the world or creatures are added to God. ... for if the world or any creature were to contribute greatness to God, then God would not be that than which nothing greater would be thinkable'.[13] In other words, central to Anselm's articulation of the Christian notion of the divine is the idea that '(God plus the world) is not greater than God alone'.[14]

If God is 'that than which nothing greater can be thought', Anselm reasons, then we have no choice but to conclude that God's non-existence is impossible. For if God lacked existence, he would not be the greatest being that can be thought, hence God would not be God, which is contradictory. Therefore existence is for God an absolute necessity.[15]

Philosophers have long debated the validity and soundness of Anselm's argument for God's existence. Less often discussed, however, are his very reasons for attempting such a demonstration in the first place. Why would a Christian try to prove God's existence rationally if this truth were already believed as a datum of faith? Did Anselm doubt God's existence and thereby seek to assure himself of it by philosophical reasoning? The answer to these questions lies in Anselm's characterization of the theological project as 'faith seeking understanding' (*fides quaerens intellectum*). A divinely inspired belief in God's existence is on this account the appropriate starting-point for theological enquiry. Nevertheless, the recognition that some people are unable (or unwilling) to endorse this conviction leads the theologian to reflect on the question of unbelief. Is the denial of God's existence rationally tenable? Anselm employs philosophical argument to show that it is not; in doing so he demonstrates 'that faith has nothing to fear from rational inquiry. The God of the Christian faith is such that reason cannot deny his existence. By establishing this security of faith before reason, Anselm opens the door to the reasoned exploration of faith that took place in scholastic theology.'[16]

Taking Anselm's notion of 'faith seeking understanding' as his point of departure, St Thomas Aquinas (AD 1225–74) sought to develop a conception of Christian theology (*sacra doctrina*) which would differentiate this new discipline (a *scientia* or science) from other modes of enquiry. He elucidates this comparison in the terminology of Aristotle's theory of knowledge. A science, on this account, is an acquired mental disposition consisting in the ability to reach true conclusions about some subject through a process of correct reasoning. These conclusions are deduced from true premises (termed 'principles'), which may be known directly, by way of intuitive insight (the grasp of self-evident truths), or indirectly, by recourse to information borrowed from a higher science. It is this latter mode of derivation that obtains in the case of sacred theology. After all, Aquinas reasons, the subject-matter of this science is God himself, whose infinite perfection far exceeds our human capacity for intuitive insight. From what higher science, then, do the principles of theology derive? Aquinas replies that they originate from the very mind of God: 'Theology (*sacra doctrina*)', he writes, 'is a kind of imprint in us of the divine science.'[17]

Thus understood, Christian theology clearly enjoys a special status among the different branches of learning, for in this unique case the guiding principles of the science are imparted by instruction from above (divine revelation). Aquinas quickly tempers this rather grandiose conception of theological science with a caveat, however. Faith in the word of God is an indispensable pre-condition for gaining access to the revealed truths of theology. Yet faith is inherently obscure; it is to our minds 'a ray of darkness' (in the words of Dionysius the Areopagite). Aquinas nevertheless insists that this obscurity does not endanger the certitude of faith, since the witness on whose testimony faith is based is none other than God himself (in the person of Jesus Christ).

However much Aquinas extols faith (and the theology that issues from it) he studiously refrains from asserting that this is our only mode of access to knowledge of divine things. Even without benefit of the revealed teachings set down in the Bible, the pagans were, he thinks, able to enjoy an inchoate awareness of the one true God, an awareness which the great philosophers of Greek antiquity developed into a substantive body of doctrine, a 'natural' (as opposed to a 'supernatural' or divinely revealed) theology. 'There is no reason', he writes in the *Summa Theologiae*, 'why those things which may be learned from philosophical science, so far as they can be known by natural reason, may not also be taught by another science so far as they fall under revelation. Hence the theology included in *sacra doctrina* differs in kind from that theology which is part of philosophy.'[18] Aquinas accordingly recognizes a twofold theology: (1) a philosophical or natural theology, whereby God is known as the first cause of the world, and (2) a sacred theology (*sacra doctrina*), whereby God is known in the light of his self-revelation in the Hebrew and Greek scriptures.

While quick to recognize the legitimacy and value of philosophical theology, Aquinas did not himself write systematic treatises from this point of view. The work for which he is most famous – the *Summa Theologiae* – is by his own admission a project in sacred theology. The same may be said of the vast majority of his other writings. Nevertheless, because Aquinas deemed natural reason an indispensable auxiliary to the work of sacred theology, he took great care to elaborate a philosophy suitable for the accomplishment of this theological task.

Aquinas's contemporary exponents are somewhat divided on the question of how best to present his philosophy. Some contend that because Aquinas developed this philosophy from within the confines of sacred theology, we should remain faithful to his example and never detach his philosophical arguments from their underlying religious context. Conversely, others maintain that the philosophical import of these arguments will never truly come to light unless we remove them from their original (yet extraneous) theological moorings.[19] All agree, however, that Aquinas's writings exhibit a highly original philosophical outlook, one in which the metaphysical implications of the Judeo-Christian revelation receive vigorous articulation against the background of ancient Greek thought.

Notes

1 Michael L. Morgan, 'Plato and Greek religion' in Richard Kraut (ed.), *The Cambridge Companion to Plato* (Cambridge, 1992), p. 232.

2 Morgan observes that not only does Plato characterize philosophical life 'in terms drawn from mystery rites and ecstatic practices; he also develops his account of inquiry and education in part *from* these traditions and in the end takes philosophy to be a form of such initiation rites' (p. 235). 'Platonic learning, then is an ecstatic ritual process because it is precisely organized, religiously motivated by the desire to become divine, and facilitated by the assumption that the human soul, which is immortal, can become divine or nearly divine' (p. 232).

3 Richard Bodéüs defends this interpretation of Plato in *Aristote et la théologie des vivants immortels* (Quebec, 1992). See in particular pp. 149–67 and 171–80.

4 *Republic*, Book 2 (379a).

5 Bodéüs argues (pp. 115–26), however, that Plato (and Aristotle) used the word *theologia* solely to designate a *mythic* or *poetic* discourse about the gods. Only later, in the writings of subsequent philosophers, did this term come to signify a *philosophical* investigation into the divine.

6 See Bodéüs (pp. 337–76) for a bibliography of secondary literature concerning Aristotle's views on the divine.

7 Etienne Gilson, *God and Philosophy* (New Haven, 1941), p. 34.

8 On the distinction in Greek thought between gods and transcendent divine entities, see Bodéüs, pp. 17–52 (especially pp. 36–8).

9 See Bodéüs, ch. 5, 'Les dieux bienfaiteurs: un dogma rationnel', for a list of references and a careful exegesis of these passages.

10 Augustine, *De Civitate Dei*, Book 9.

11 Robert Sokolowski, *The God of Faith and Reason* (Notre Dame, 1982), p. 18.

12 Anselm, *Proslogion*, ch. 2.

13 Sokolowski, p. 8.

14 Ibid.

15 In broad outline this is the argument of *Proslogion*, chs 2–4.

16 Sokolowski, pp. 5–6.

17 Thomas Aquinas, *Summa Theologiae* I, 1, 3, *ad* 2.

18 *Summa Theologiae* I, 1, 1, *ad* 2.

19 For a helpful discussion of this debate, see John F. Wippel, 'Thomas Aquinas and the problem of Christian philosophy', ch. 1 of his *Metaphysical Themes in Thomas Aquinas* (Washington, 1984), pp. 1–31.

(b)   From the thirteenth century to the twentieth century

Joseph Koterski SJ

Relatively few philosophers since the medieval period accept the role of philosophy as *ancilla theologiae* ('handmaid of theology'). The growing predominance of logic within metaphysics that marks late scholasticism leads toward a more autonomous view of philosophy in Renaissance Neoplatonism and Cartesian scepticism. One consequence is to remove the philosophical treatment of religion from consideration as one type of justice, what we owe to God,[1] and to submit religion without privilege to the full range of questions typical of a philosopher's general method. Confidence in the validity and fruitfulness of natural theology has a chequered history in this period, and debates flourish about religion's relation to morality, the mystery of a self-revealing God, miracles, and the interplay of faith and worship with church and world.

Both the late medieval and the early modern periods manifest a strong concern with certain metaphysical questions about religion, a concern which returns to centre-stage with Hegel in a form drastically altered by the perspective of historical consciousness. In between, the strongest philosophical currents run anti-metaphysical, whether in Hume's sceptically driven 'natural history' that traces religion to the passions of hope and fear or in the moral theism of Kant's grounding of religion on the needs of practical reason.

Late scholasticism and early modern philosophy

The road to Descartes's *cogito* and the drastic shift from the objective content of thought to the modes of its subjective production can be traced from figures such as William of Ockham. In the treatment of religion as in much else, the nominalist tradition gradually drew out the consequences of denying that universals have any real existence and are mere names to serve our convenience. Mindful of various good reasons for shifting logic from an ontological division by categories toward a study of intended signification, these early semioticians avoided the presumption that language (which may be construed as we wish) corresponds *prima facie* to objective realities. Yet the unintentional result was to weaken faith in language and logic as a means of arriving at truth. Followers of terminist logic like Richard Billingham or Robert Holcote occasionally voiced doubt over our ability to know any substance whatsoever in the course of professing their scepticism about traditional demonstrations for the existence and unicity of God. It was not that they doubted the truth of propositions like 'God exists' but that their grave, logical reservations about the claims of metaphysics generated doubts about their speculative demonstrations.

Operating from a sophisticated theory of the *suppositio* (the analysis of the various ways in which a proposition's terms can stand for things), thinkers such as Nicholas of Autrecourt tended to accept as absolutely certain only those propositions which could be reduced to the principle of contradiction. But since no proposition about causal relations can be of this sort, an empiricist stance on propositions about causality as at best probable to some degree seemed warranted, even if it entailed doubt about the cogency of the traditional arguments for God's existence. The long-term results of this policy for theology and religion are evident in Descartes's need to postpone consideration of God's existence until he has secured the certainty of his starting-point in the self-referential inconsistency of a performatory contradiction: even to try to doubt his own existence is to affirm what he would doubt. When it comes,[2] the argument for God's existence is an ontological proof about the necessity of divine existence on the basis of the presence of an otherwise unexplainable idea of infinity in the mind of a finite being; but given the frailties of ontological argumentation, one suspects that a wooden horse has been hauled into the Troy of French academic theology. Yet, as in any repair job, the ongoing state of unsettledness during the reconstruction of the philosophical edifice requires that Descartes propose a 'provisional morality' – it is theologically conservative and even pious, but this disarming pacification of morals in his religiously turbulent period brims with the confidence that in due time a more suitable ethics will be devised to join the promised new physics, while the claims about truth that provoked wars over religion will be tamed by policies of toleration.[3]

The larger trend of which Descartes is a part puts greater distance between philosophy and theology by making almost mutually exclusive the distinction between one's own reasoning and divine authority as the source of truth-claims. Not only does there seem to be more a gap than the sort of bridge which someone like Aquinas envisioned in the *praeambula fidei*, but the very notion of authority risks contempt. Responsibility cannot be laid simply at the door of the arbitrary use of political and military powers in the name of religion, although the *Realpolitik* of Machiavelli did usher in regimes whose boldness was restrained only by pragmatic calculation.

The confusion of authority with power and the intellectual resentment provoked in regard to religion also have roots in the late medieval controversies over divine power. Pondering Augustine's queries about whether God's sovereignty could have justly damned Peter and saved Judas, medieval thinkers worked persistently to elaborate some distinction between the *potentia Dei absoluta* and the *potentia Dei ordinata* (God's power considered absolutely and as self-restrained by other divine choices) in order to handle such issues as the permission of evil by an all-knowing God who creates and sustains every being in creation, including free human agents.[4] The difficulties in simultaneously managing all the parameters in questions about divine power, relatively autonomous secondary causes, and human freedom are enormous, but combined with the voluntarist position on divine liberty in Ockham's ethics, these reflections on the logical possibility that God's absolute power could command acts opposed to the demands of right reason and to the natural law began to undermine the distinction between authority and its legitimate power long before kings claimed to rule with the arbitrary sovereignty of divine right or Marsilius of Padua ventured a theory of temporal authority totally divorced from the spiritual in reaction to the sort of claims by Boniface VIII that so bothered Dante.

Before examining the philosophies of religion offered by thinkers who explicitly viewed philosophy as properly autonomous, we should turn briefly to several self-consciously religious philosophers of note. By a generous extension of the term, Nicholas of Cusa (1401–64) may be called a Platonist. Enchanted by the idea of unity as the harmonious reconciliation of differences, he saw the idea of God, the *coincidentia oppositorum*,[5] to transcend and yet include all the distinct perfections of creatures, a metaphysical idea for which he envisioned conciliar applications to settle the quarrels of institutional religion. Cusa's meditations on the incomprehensible infinity of God do not quite carry him into the religious pantheism of John Scotus Eriugena or Giordano Bruno because of his vigorous employment of the *via negativa* to cultivate a 'learned ignorance' in which humility before the *Deus absconditus* is as treasured as the love of Christ, the 'visible' theophany of the 'invisible' God.[6] But his categories open up a philosophically defensible route in mysticism for seeing human nature as a microcosmic mirror of the divine, all the while preserving Christian orthodoxy in religion by refusing to treat philosophy as autonomous. By contrast, the inner logic of this way of thinking in the later period of modern philosophy leads Schelling (1775–1854) to a theory of the Absolute as the vanishing-point of every difference and Hegel

(1770–1831) to see Nature as God in his otherness, the concrete embodiment of the abstract Idea.

The figure in early modern philosophy somewhat comparable to Cusa is Baruch Spinoza (1632–77), who was often regarded as an atheist for openly identifying infinite divine substance with Nature. In the *Ethics*, a work whose structuring by geometrical method exudes confidence in reason's power to construct a world-view from its own resources, Spinoza draws out as the logical implication of Descartes's definition of substance that there can only be one – God. This is not to conceive God as a free, personal, transcendent creator of the world, but as an infinite being whose reality (in order to be truly infinite) must contain all being within itself and not be anything apart from the world. Unafraid of such unusual implications, Spinoza, the careful reader of Bruno's *natura naturans* and *natura naturata*, likewise argues that matter must pre-exist in God, for no being can be the cause of anything it does not already contain, and that our sense of free will is an illusion owing to ignorance of the causes of our wishes and desires.

For Spinoza's philosophy of religion, one must turn to his political theory in works like the *Theologico-political Treatise*. There we find complete religious toleration as a feature of an ideally organized society. It might seem hard to reconcile this with the metaphysical denial of free will, but Spinoza reminds us that the purpose of theological language is not to deliver scientific information about nature but to direct people to adopt certain lines of conduct. Convinced both that human beings are deeply conditioned by nature to pursue their own advantage and that one's 'natural rights' are coextensive with whatever powers and desires nature has given, Spinoza argues for treating political society as a social compact whose welfare rests on the self-restraints imposed by enlightened self-interest. Human beings, after all, are but finite modalities of the one divine substance which alone is ultimately real. Spinoza has had few disciples willing to follow him in detail, but he has had many a successor in political theology willing to subjugate the many to an idea.

Later modern philosophy

Both the anti-metaphysicians of the eighteenth century and the revivers of metaphysics in the nineteenth were deeply attuned to religion as a persistent human phenomenon. Despite wide differences in their treatment of religion, Hume, Kant and Hegel each subject religious belief and practice to the philosophic methods and evidence-tests they used generally. It is not as religious philosophers who privilege truths known by revelation but as practitioners of autonomous philosophy that they enquire about religion, natural and revealed. In the passions of fear and hope Hume finds the genesis of religious belief. He then scrutinizes the reasoned arguments typically offered for these religious convictions. Kant seeks to shift the grounds for religious beliefs from reasoning based in physics and metaphysics to reflection on morality. Hegel binds religious impulses so tightly to philosophical wonder that religion (like art) becomes part of the dialectical path toward philosophizing without alienation or illusion about any objective otherness in the divine principle.

Although raised a believer, Hume (1711–76) gradually fell into scepticism when he found Locke's and Clarke's rational defences for Christianity inconclusive and Bayle's account of the virtuous atheism of the ancient naturalists comforting. But his own estrangement from devotion never diminished his interest in understanding what brought people to religious convictions. The radical views he deleted from *A Treatise of Human Nature* in order to prevent an unfavourable reception earned him the reputation of being an infidel when they appeared in *An Enquiry Concerning Human Understanding*. Although hostile clerics excluded him from a university post, he managed to publish *The Natural History of Religion* (1757) and *Dialogues Concerning Natural Religion* (1779, posthumously).

Resolved to make human nature his central concern, Hume repeatedly examined the proofs for God's existence and doctrines such as divine goodness and providence as religious aspects of human experience. But sceptical of any *a priori* reasoning and insistent on the need to keep morality completely independent of religion,[7] he analysed religious phenomena in terms of the passions of hope and fear[8] (much as Hobbes [1588–1679] had done in *Leviathan*, and Lucretius had done long before) and the psychological forces of association that incline individuals to assign causes outside their experience to what they perceive as affecting their welfare.

As a complement to the *Natural History*'s exposition of the mechanisms by which the human passions generate ideas about the being and nature of God as a powerful, intelligent entity beyond the sphere of our perceptions, the *Dialogues* explore what Hume regarded as the strongest proof theism could muster, the design-argument. Meditation on the mind responsible for the orderliness of nature was popular with the apologists of his day trying to capitalize on the successes of Newtonian science. Even the choice of the dialogue form (discussed at length in the preface) is to stay remindful of religion's passional origins, whatever the value of the arguments debated by the deist Demea, the teleological Cleanthes, and the sceptical Philo. By reflection on the utter uniqueness of the world-making process, Philo forces Cleanthes to back-pedal on claims for an intelligent designer based on insufficiently rigorous analogies. The truncated analogies then permitted in Hume's 'experimental' philosophy of religion (because limited to inferences proportionate to human experience) disappoint believers like Demea and Cleanthes by stripping divinity of such traditional attributes as simplicity, immutability, eternity, and infinity. Further, Philo extracts the admission that analogical reasoning must constantly acknowledge as its weakness the purely probable character of its conclusions.

Hume strategically casts miracles (the 'tolerable reasons' offered in defence of revealed religion) as violations of natural laws, debating not whether miracles can or do occur but whether we could ever know that they occur by experience without recourse to the metaphysics he deems unavailable. Ironically Philo suggests that any successful miracle-claim would harm even a philosophically purified design-argument.

Kant's chief work in the field, *Religion within the Bounds of Reason Alone* (1793), exhibits the application of his trenchant critical method. It also bears the marks of personal religious values (especially joy and tranquillity of spirit based on care for one's duties and tolerance toward others) retained from his Pietist upbringing even after giving up any public expression of religion to avoid any hint of hypocrisy. Kant granted the force of Hume's criticism of the design-argument and followed his lead there in the 1787 edition of the *Critique of Pure Reason*. But on the topic of religion and morality he seems closer to Rousseau's inclination to assess historical religions on the moral traits they foster or hinder, and he ultimately bases his critical philosophy of religion on personal morality.

It would be a mistake to read Kant's thoroughgoing critique of arguments for God's existence as purely deconstructive and better to interpret it as raising what he thought insuperable difficulties in any possible effort at strict, impersonal demonstration and yet as allowing that individuals must seek good evidence for their personal religious convictions,[9] including the moral case for belief which Kant himself favours. The classification he proposes divides these arguments into ontological (based on the ideal of the most real and perfect being), cosmological (employing the distinction between contingency and necessity to reach the notion of God's absolutely necessary being), and physico-theological (arguing for an intelligent designer to explain specific aspects of the phenomenal world). The problem he identifies with the ontological proof is the impossibility in principle of knowing about any being besides those which appear in the phenomenal world of our experience. The argument assumes what it needs to prove if it just stipulates that existence is one of the most real being's perfections. In Kant's view cosmological arguments tend either to drift into the conceptual order (and then fail as ontological arguments) or to fail to reach an unconditioned being existing apart from sensible conditions, for our own ability to distinguish between necessity and possibility, real and logical, can never take place except with reference to sense-experience. The physico-theological proofs also fail, either (as Hume argued) because they only reach back to a finite designer or by making an unwarranted leap to the infinite in one of the two routes described above.

17

Kant's own philosophy of religion assumes this negative verdict about speculative demonstrations as epistemologically defective and ventures that any successful demonstration would obliterate the basis for a moral and religious union with God. In his view this must be a choice in personal freedom, not the result of the compelling cogency possible in the phenomenal realm. But if we may not use the idea of God constitutively to claim metaphysical (trans-phenomenal) knowledge of an unconditioned being, we may use the idea of an intelligent and just God ever beyond our reach regulatively (like the ideas of freedom and world) to unify elusive aspects of the source of moral obligation necessary for practical reason.[10] At this point in the argument Hume warns us of anthropomorphic dangers to theism, but Kant distinguishes between a dogmatic anthropomorphism[11] which proceeds as if we could encompass God's nature in our categories and a symbolic anthropomorphism[12] designed to plumb some of the ways in which the *Deus absconditus* is related to our moral freedom. What the foreclosure of any route to metaphysical knowledge of God from which moral and religious duties might be deduced means for Kant's philosophy of religion is that the reality of God must be treated purely as a practical postulate and that any proposed idea of God must be purified of mythical accretions likely to render autonomous morality heteronomous. One sees here the philosophical roots of theological demythologization, but for Kant this opens up the way for a moral theist to accept God as a holy law-giver, a personal, spiritual being necessary for living out the mystery of human freedom according to the demands of practical reason. The anti-metaphysical reversal of direction between religion and morality at work here also enables Kant to weigh in against Leibniz and Hume on the side of Job when it comes to the problem of evil: the ideal is to rest secure on an untroubled moral conscience, admitting that God remains a mystery not only in himself but in his ways of dealing with the world.[13]

Virtually all of Hegel's books include significant treatments of religion. His theological studies at Tübingen gave him a more systematic knowledge of the field than Hume or Kant received, but his efforts to follow out the Kantian project of presenting Jesus' doctrines in strictly moral terms brought him early to the conviction that philosophy needed a radically different stance toward God and religion. A lifetime of work refining his historical and dialectical method of philosophizing (the root of current theological trends alert to historical consciousness) positioned him to envision religion as an intermediate moment (often simultaneous but conceptually superior) in the stream from art to philosophy that constitutes the unfolding of Spirit in history. Preferring organic terminology to mechanical, Hegel is the sort of thinker who sees religion as philosophy still groping for its answers, and philosophy as the culmination of a lifelong religious searching.

Risking blasphemy to forge a telling allusion, Hegel announces the death of God to testify about the decline of living belief in God, but then explains that philosophically the Good Friday of the theistic conception of God was a necessary prelude to the resurrection of metaphysics. His constant intermingling of very concrete, religious imagery with the very abstract terminology of philosophy is constantly measured to lead his readers, alternately, to *disillusionment* with each of the objects of their attachment (parallel to the cultural progress that unmasks natural religion in favour of polytheism, and that in favour of incarnational monotheism) and to *enlightenment* by a rational comprehension of the more inclusive perspective that lovingly embraces the process rather than turning bitter in scepticism or becoming paralysed in disbelief. For Hegel philosophizing about religion shows the way to engage over and over again in the struggle to reconcile opposites.

Although formal proofs are quite unnecessary in a religious philosophy so all-encompassing, Hegel rescues the beleaguered arguments for God's existence but in the process transforms them into descriptive expressions to grasp the essential openness of human finitude, so that the Kantian objection against any leap to the infinite falls away as one comes to understand the organic continuity of finite and infinite. To regard God as an object over and against the self is a necessary step in recognizing the alienation more familiarly known as sin. But the return of any such particularity separated from universal and infinite reality will be experienced as an individual's participation in salvation and union with God, through worship and ultimately through philosophy.

Whatever one makes of Hegel's claim that Christianity is the absolute form of religion, no one will mistake his multiple historical allusions for Christian orthodoxy. It is the dynamism of a philosophical system which here drives the interpretation of religious phenomena, and yet the system's open friendliness to religion, in contrast, say, to the hostility of Hume or Kant's critical reversals of perspective, has made this philosophy more attractive to many believers temperamentally inclined to use philosophical methods and systems. The situation is not unlike the contemporary attraction of religious minds for the religiously sympathetic Jung in preference to the religiously antithetical Freud, but which one in the long run is not more dangerous for religion remains to be seen.

There are diverse and sometimes virulent reactions to Hegel in the balance of the nineteenth century. Where Hegel's contemporary, Schleiermacher, made the feeling of dependence the ground of religion, Feuerbach (1804–72) countered that our real dependence is ultimately on nature. He found it no surprise that natural religion should deify all sorts of physical objects but deplored Hegel's spiritualization of the absolute. The monotheisms developed by high culture are just the projection of human reason, will, and love, and the danger consists in self-alienation by this idolatry. The only god for man is man, and politics must become the new religion; paradoxically, atheism is the very condition for its theology.

Shifting Feuerbach's reaction against Hegel to the economic plane, Karl Marx (1818–83) inveighed against the Hegelian idea of the state as the source of human alienation and laboured to expose the illusory world of religion as a self-administered opiate to comfort a world in pain rather than to rouse it to praxis. The philosophy of religion needs to generate a theology of liberation to assist the dialectical march of material human progress which philosophy in general abets by disclosing the economic substructures that condition all social superstructures.

Friedrich Nietzsche (1844–1900) found cheer in the Hegelian report that God is dead. Delivered from threat of a slavish God's proactive intervention in the cause of the weak, Nietzsche relished the general decline in religious belief as opening up new paths for creative human energies. Curiously the fatalism of the Stoic idea of an eternal return of the same seemed like fresh air to one suffocating in the Hegelian libraries of historical consciousness and forced to read of the inevitable progress of Absolute Spirit.

On the other bank of the Hegelian current there grew up a fragile reed, often writing anonymously, Søren Kierkegaard (1813–55). He much admired the enormous project of Hegel's system but suspected that in watching the whirlwind this prophet had missed the tiny voice of spirit speaking to individuals in their freedom. Religious existence essentially involves the free choice of self-commitment to God, mindful of the attractions of such real alternatives as beauty and moral respect. The task for philosophy of religion, he urged, is to say very clearly that man is not God and God is not man, and that there is very much a need for the leap of faith.

Notes

1 Cf. Aquinas, *Summa Theologiae* II-II, 80–91 on religion and worship within his general treatise on justice. See especially qq. 81.4 and 85.4.
2 *Discourse on Method*, Part 4 and *Meditations* III.
3 Cf. Thomas A. Russman, *A Prospectus for the Triumph of Realism* (Atlanta, 1987), pp. 93–108. It is interesting to note that Descartes had some first-hand experience of the Wars of Religion, for at the age of eighteen he joined the army of the Protestant Dutch Republic under Maurice of Nassau. Cf. Stephen Gaukroger, *Descartes: An Intellectual Biography* (Oxford, 1995), pp. 63–7.
4 Cf. Lawrence Moonan, *Divine Power: The Medieval Power Distinction up to Its Adoption by Albert, Bonaventure, and Aquinas* (Oxford, 1994).
5 *De docta ignorantia* (On Learned Ignorance), I.4 and II.1.
6 *De visione Dei* (On the vision of God), II, 7.

7 Arguing against the charge that disastrous consequences would follow for morality if relegated entirely to the private sphere, Hume showed a resilient, Enlightenment optimism about secular solutions to social problems and his scandal over the inhumane consequences of religious wars.

8 For example, *Natural History* #2 and *Dialogues* #12.

9 *Critique of Pure Reason* A 829/B 857.

10 *Critique of Pure Reason* A 640–641/B 668–669.

11 Perhaps this is the verdict Kant would have rendered on Newman's moral argument for the existence of God.

12 *Critique of Pure Reason* A 697–701/B 725–729.

13 See, for example, the late essay 'On the failure of all philosophical attempts in theodicy'.

(c) Philosophy, religion and twentieth-century theologians

Peter Groves

Theology at the beginning of the twentieth century bore the heavy imprint of philosophy, especially German philosophy, from the previous two hundred years. The influence of theologians such as Friedrich Schleiermacher and Albrecht Ritschl carried with it the influence of Immanuel Kant, a philosopher in the Idealist tradition. Christian theology was having to come to terms with the realization that certain historical beliefs which it took for granted were not so well grounded in historical fact as had been supposed, and the philosophy of history, particularly the work of another Idealist, Wilhelm Friedrich Hegel, is a significant feature of much German and British theology before the First World War.

That war presents a marked break in the history of theological writing and thinking. Theology since Schleiermacher had tended to focus on the believer and his or her community as the starting-point for understanding Christian doctrine, and had drawn upon contemporary philosophies of the human person, of history and of ethics in order to do this. Christianity was discussed as part of a developing historical process, a route to individual personal fulfilment or the basis of a radical ethical system. Certain younger theologians were concerned that this approach paid insufficient attention to the discontinuity between God and the world, creator and created, infinite and finite. This concern reflected, to some extent, the influence of the

Danish thinker Søren Kierkegaard (1813–55), who stressed the 'infinite qualitative difference' between God and humans, whose very existence God confronts and challenges. The truths of religion, for Kierkegaard, are not rational or demonstrable facts, but are only grasped by those individual human subjects who risk the radical 'leap' of faith. Those theologians who emphasized the 'otherness' of God, and who were disillusioned with a theological establishment which did not condemn the First World War, are often grouped together as advocates of 'dialectical theology', the dialectic being the bringing together, in theology, of subjects which are infinitely different: God and the world.

In 1918 Karl Barth published *The Epistle to the Romans*,[1] often thought of as the watershed of the new theology, and the classic text of the dialectical theologians. But, having made much of the distance between God and humans, the question remained: how can one speak of God at all? For Barth, the answer came in his understanding of the Word of God, set out and developed in his *Church Dogmatics*.[2] God can be known by us, through revelation, in so far as he chooses to make himself the object of our knowledge. Theology should begin, not with any abstract human knowledge of God gained by philosophical enquiry, but with the content of God's revelation of himself in Jesus Christ, and with the witnesses to this revelation provided in Scripture and the proclamation of the Church.

There can be no genuine knowledge of God apart from this revelation, according to Barth. It follows from this claim that one major aspect of the philosophy of religion, natural theology, is dismissed as an activity alien to Christian theology. Natural theology, which asks what humans can know about God from their own rational reflection about themselves and the world, aside from any specific religious or doctrinal claims, was seen by Barth to lie at the root of all that he thought was wrong with the theological tradition he had inherited from his teachers, and could lead to the accommodation of Christianity to political and imperial ends, even to the extremes of National Socialism. His rejection of natural theology was bolstered by his interpretation of the writings of St Anselm.[3] Barth read Anselm not as someone who argues from abstract *a priori* principles to the existence of God, but as a theologian who presupposes the truths of the Christian creeds, and formulates his 'arguments for God's existence' from that presupposition.

Barth's fundamental criticism of natural theology is simple: it cannot be permissible, because if there were any other access to knowledge of God apart from God's revelation of himself, then that revelation must be either less than adequate, or not altogether necessary. Natural theology presents a second, or rival, knowledge of God, which competes with divine revelation. In Barth's own words, natural theology means that 'Instead of finding God where he has sought us – namely in his objectivity – we seek him where he is not to be found'.[4] This is the case because 'God in His incomprehensibility and God in the act of His revelation is not the formula of an abstract metaphysics of God, the world, or religion which is supposed to obtain at all times and in all places'.[5] Natural theology seeks general truths about the divine, Barth thinks. But in fact the only such truths are particular, particular to the Word of God in revelation, in Scripture and in proclamation.

Barth's criticisms of natural theology are often taken as implying that Barth himself saw no place for philosophy within theological study. This is far from true. His work contains detailed discussions and perceptive interpretations of a wide range of philosophical material, particularly from the Cartesian and Idealist traditions, and he also engaged very fully with ideas originating from the loosely defined philosophy known as 'existentialism' (about which more shortly). His emphasis throughout, however, is that philosophy can only serve theology by helping to elucidate the knowledge of God which we already have through revelation. It cannot contribute any such knowledge by itself.

Barth's writings had, and retain, an enormous influence among theologians, and are still used as a stick with which to beat the philosophy of religion. They have also attracted much criticism, however. Defenders of natural theology have observed a number of weaknesses in Barth's position, three of which I shall outline.[6] First, that he misinterprets Anselm (who, in fact, makes explicit claims in his writings to be offering *a priori* arguments for God's existence and nature); second, that he fails to acknowledge that, in certain places, Scripture makes specific reference to knowledge of God which can be obtained by human reflection on the world and its existence; third, that he does not engage sufficiently with one important and traditional claim of natural theology, that philosophers can demonstrate certain general truths about God (for example, that God exists, that God is eternal) without having any ability to establish or prove the claims of a specific religious tradition, such as are made in the Christian doctrines of the Trinity and the Incarnation. It could be observed against Barth, for example, that many practitioners of natural theology (such as Aquinas) held an exceedingly negative view of human knowledge of God. Unfortunately, Barth's attack on natural theology remains an obstacle for many theologians confronted with the sort of philosophy which this book discusses.

A quite different sort of philosophy proved very important for some of Barth's contemporaries. This is the movement called 'existentialism'. A very simple and uninformative definition of an 'existentialist' is that it is someone who believes that 'existence precedes essence', that is that questions about the nature of humanity and the world can only be answered if we think first about the meaning of existence and the experience of living as a human being. Martin Heidegger's work *Being and Time* argued that human existence (*dasein*, literally 'being-there') could be better understood if we recognized the 'concerns' which it involved, particularly our own awareness that we are finite, limited and destined, inevitably, to die. The anxiety which is produced by *dasein*'s proximity to 'non-being' leads to what Heidegger calls 'inauthentic existence', and so the goal of each person should be to overcome the fear and guilt which human life involves.

Rudolf Bultmann, who along with Barth was a leading exponent of 'dialectical theology', was a theologian profoundly influenced by Heidegger. His contribution to New Testament scholarship was enormous, and this specialism is reflected in his emphasis on matters such as revelation, history and the proclamation or message of Christianity. He is well known for his programme of 'demythologizing', by which he attempted to peel away the elaborations of the early Christian narratives to reveal the essence of Jesus' teaching. That teaching contained, Bultmann thought, the path to overcoming the existential problems, and to attaining authentic human existence. Another theologian who made use of existential ideas (though less explicitly of Heidegger) is Paul Tillich. The method of his theology is often described with the word 'correlation', because he attempts to bring together the 'existential' human situation, with its questions and anxieties, and the teaching of Protestant Christianity. God, Tillich thinks, is not an entity or a being, but being itself, or 'the ground of our being'. The 'ultimate concern' of finite human beings is the quest for God, for that which underlies all existence.

Philosophical questions concerning existence also manifest themselves in the writings of many significant Roman Catholic theologians. A revived emphasis on the study of medieval theology, in its historical context and not simply as part of a body of accepted dogma, inspired a generation of widely differing theologians who sought to combine the ideas of St Thomas Aquinas, in particular, with more recent philosophical notions. These 'neo-Thomists' are too numerous to mention, and their work too diverse to summarize. From Aquinas, and often this meant from Aristotle before him, they inherited a helpful philosophical vocabulary. For example, they found congenial the idea that a thing can be thought of as composed of matter (the brute, material stuff of which it is made) and form (that which makes the thing what it is). They also made use of Thomas's idea that God, who does not derive his existence from anything else, can be spoken of as 'being itself' (note the comparison with Tillich); and that, because God does not belong to any class or kind (as natural things do), and because his existence does not differ from his nature (his nature is simply 'to-be'), it is impossible for any finite creature ever to know 'what God is'. Theologians writing in the Catholic tradition drew upon Aristotelian accounts of causation and action when discussing the grace of God, or the theology of the Christian sacraments – the words 'agent', 'patient', 'act', 'potency', 'formal' and 'final' are often much in evidence.

Karl Rahner was a theologian very much in the Thomist tradition, who also claimed to have gained a great deal from Heidegger. He argued that human awareness of being finite, or limited, carries with it a tacit 'pre-apprehension' of God, of that which transcends any limitation.[7] Rahner, however, was not a rationalist. This 'pre-apprehension' does not give us any understanding of what God is. Indeed, only because we are able to argue backwards, as it were, from Christian revelation, are we able to identify the God of Jesus Christ as the source of all being. In the man Jesus, we see one who gives himself over completely to the mystery of being, the divine.

All Catholic theology makes some use, perhaps not always consciously, of the tradition of Aristotle and Aquinas. Another theologian whose work, along with Rahner's, has been given the epithet 'transcendental Thomism' (since it brings Thomas's theology together with ideas associated with Kant) is Bernard Lonergan. Lonergan's studies of Aquinas's philosophy are important in their own right, and they contributed to his enormous and complex work *Insight: A Study of Human Understanding*, and his *Method in Theology*. Perhaps the most important recent Catholic theologian of all is Hans Urs von Balthasar, a thinker whose wide reputation has grown even wider in the years following his death (in 1988). Balthasar's is 'a theology with its roots in meditation and prayer',[8] but his voluminous works include studies of metaphysics, of patristic thought, of idealist philosophy and of Barth's theology. Balthasar's theology draws heavily on an area of philosophy on which theologians have rarely dwelt, aesthetics. He argues that the believer is drawn to faith in God as the beholder is drawn by the beauty of an object: Christ is the form of God's revelation and hence the form of beauty which engages the believer.[9]

Unfortunately for the reader of philosophy of religion, these important theologians, and many others, thought and wrote with little or no awareness of certain philosophers who were their contemporaries. In Germany, Austria and Britain, the early years of the twentieth century saw great advances in logic and the analysis of language in the work of Gottlob Frege, Bertrand Russell and Ludwig Wittgenstein. 'Analytical philosophy' (not a wholly satisfactory term: Wittgenstein, for example, rejected it), which is concerned to give a philosophical account of thought and meaning through a philosophical analysis of language, grew up almost entirely apart from modern theology. Some philosophers even went so far as to dismiss theology as a meaningless enterprise. Theologians wedded to existentialism, for example, are much criticized in the analytical tradition for failing to appreciate the proper logical form of the verb 'to exist', which, Frege argued, could only be a property of concepts, and not of things. There is no such 'thing' as 'being', which all existents share and which can be used to undergird a philosophical argument, many would say. Likewise, those impressed by Wittgenstein's criticism of the Cartesian tradition have posed difficult questions for those who wish to hold on to Rahner's or Lonergan's arguments about the relationship between the human knower and the world.

More recently, this divorce between theology and analytical philosophy has remained a problem. Philosophers continue to influence theologians. Edward Schillebeeckx is another who has combined his interest in medieval thought with a variety of more recent ideas, not least the writings of certain existentialist philosophers, and the philosophy of language, both in its analytical form, and in the hermeneutical schools of continental thought. Jürgen Moltmann built his 'theology of hope' on the ideas of Ernst Bloch, whilst the continuing legacy of Hegel can be found in theologians as different as Wolfhart Pannenberg, Hans Küng and Eberhard Jüngel. Wittgenstein's work has had some effect, in the work of George Lindbeck for example, but his influence among theologians is tiny compared with his importance among philosophers. Contemporary French thought has proved interesting to a number of today's theologians, particularly those in the Catholic tradition, and philosophy is now simply one of a wide range of disciplines on which theologians draw to reflect on their own religious tradition.

In the last twenty-five years or so, analytic philosophy of religion has blossomed, often hand-in-hand with the increase in attention to medieval philosophy. Christian doctrines such as the Incarnation and the Trinity are now being discussed by logicians and philosophers whose equivalents, a generation before, would have dismissed such activity as 'un-philosophical'. But until theology and the philosophy of religion find more common ground, not least in our universities, the gulf between them will remain, and prove extremely unsatisfactory for those theologians who, with much justification, would like to bring them together.

Notes

1 A second edition of the work appeared in 1921.
2 The first part-volume of the *Dogmatics* was published in 1932. Unfortunately, Barth did not live to complete this monumental work.
3 Karl Barth, *Anselm: Fides Quaerens Intellectum* (2nd edn; London, 1960).
4 Karl Barth, *Church Dogmatics* (Edinburgh, 1936–69), II.1, p. 11.
5 *Church Dogmatics*, I.1, p. 325.
6 A recent and excellent critique of Barth's arguments can be found in James Barr, *Biblical Faith and Natural Theology* (Oxford, 1993).
7 Karl Rahner, *Spirit in the World* (London, 1968); also *Hearers of the Word* (London, 1969).

8   John Riches and Ben Quash, 'Hans Urs von Balthasar' in David Ford (ed.), *The Modern Theologians* (2nd edn; Oxford, 1997), p. 149.

9   Hans Urs von Balthasar, *The Glory of the Lord: A Theological Aesthetics* (Edinburgh, 1982–91).

(d)   Wittgenstein and the philosophy of religion

Gareth Moore OP and Brian Davies OP

Ludwig Wittgenstein was occupied with religious questions throughout his adult life.[1] But, though religion was a deep personal concern for him, the philosophy of religion does not occupy a central place in his published philosophical writings. On the surface, these are more concerned with questions of logic and language. It can be argued, however, that Wittgenstein's major works, the *Tractatus Logico-Philosophicus* and the *Philosophical Investigations*, are relevant to the philosophy of religion, and that Wittgenstein meant them to be. As a source for Wittgenstein's religious interests and views, readers may also consult the *Lectures on Religious Belief* and the *Remarks on Frazer's 'Golden Bough'*.[2] There are also scattered remarks throughout other works, particularly the volume published in English as *Culture and Value*.

In the *Tractatus* Wittgenstein is largely concerned with language and meaning, how words have meaning and sentences sense, the way language relates to the world. Towards the end of the book, however, Wittgenstein makes some remarks which might be described as expressing religious thoughts. For example, he says: '*How* things are in the world is a matter of complete indifference for what is higher. God does not reveal himself in the world' (6.432); 'It is not *how* things are in the world that is mystical, but *that* it exists' (6.44).

By 'the mystical' Wittgenstein means seeing or feeling the world as a limited whole (6.45). These religious thoughts are closely linked to Wittgenstein's theory of language in the *Tractatus*. To put this (much too) briefly: words have meaning by being names of objects, and propositions – combinations of names – have sense by picturing a state of affairs in the world. Thus, that words have meaning presupposes the existence of objects, and likewise that propositions have sense presupposes the existence of the world. Since the existence of the world is presupposed in language having sense, language cannot meaningfully assert the existence of the world. The existence of the world lies beyond the boundaries of language. That the world exists rather *shows* itself in the fact that names have meaning and propositions sense: 'There are, indeed, things that cannot be put into words. They *make themselves manifest*. They are what is mystical' (6.552 ['Es gibt allerdings Unaussprechliches. Dies *zeigt* sich, es ist das Mystische']).

For the Wittgenstein of the *Tractatus*, it is in what shows itself, in what cannot be said and must therefore be passed over in silence (7), that true value, the sense of life (see 6.4–6.421) and God are to be found. His view of religion is clearly bound up with what he takes to be the limits of language. To use words like 'God' is to attempt the impossible – to refer to what lies beyond the world. Talk about God is therefore senseless. This is still his view in the *Lecture on Ethics* of 1929.[3] Here Wittgenstein claims that he himself, and all who try to talk about ethics or religion, 'run against the boundaries of language'. He regards this 'perfectly, absolutely hopeless' attempt to speak about the ultimate meaning of life as a human tendency worthy of great respect. (In both the *Lecture on Ethics* and the *Tractatus* there is practically an identification of the ethical and the religious.)

Over a number of years Wittgenstein abandoned his old theory of language and meaning to develop the views on language which find their most mature expression in the *Philosophical Investigations*. Here Wittgenstein directs attention to the use of words and sentences, rather than meaning; one could also say that he sometimes seeks to explain how words get meaning by reference to the way they are used. Words are used, get their meaning, in countless ways, and the task of philosophy is to describe these. Philosophical problems stem from deep misunderstandings of the ordinary uses of words, and clarity is gained, the problems dissolve, when we have a clear view of the ways words are used. This involves describing the 'language games' in which the words are used. Words and sentences function as parts of larger linguistic complexes which may be likened to games, in that they are normally rule-governed and have a point; we use words as we use chess pieces. Understanding the point of the game in turn means understanding the 'form of life' in which the language game functions, the kind of human practice in which the language game has its home and which gives it its sense.

It is central to Wittgenstein's thought at this time that there is a great multiplicity of language games, that there is no one way in which language works. If one understands the way one word works, which Wittgenstein calls its 'grammar', one must be careful not simply to assume that another, superficially similar word works in the same way. One must always look and see. From this point of view, all words are on an equal footing; all have a use that can be described. 'God' is a word like any other. It does not lack meaning, because it does not refer to an object in the world – as the *Tractatus* would have it. It gets its meaning by being used, along with other words, in a variety of language games, and these games are to be understood by reference to the forms of life in which they are embedded. If it is the philosopher's task to carry out grammatical investigations, this applies to religious words as much as to any other. Investigation of the word 'God', as of other words, will involve asking how we are taught to use it (cf. *Culture and Value*, p. 82 and *Lectures and Conversations*, p. 59).

In most of his work Wittgenstein concentrates on an investigation of words like 'intention', 'pain', and 'thought'. Though much of his general approach is important for a philosophical understanding of religion, he does not carry out a systematic investigation into the grammar of religious words, such as 'God', 'prayer', 'soul', and 'grace'. It is, however, possible to see what his major preoccupations were when thinking philosophically about religion.

One of the ideas that Wittgenstein seems to wish to combat is the philosophical idea that God is a kind of person – a person like you and me, except that he is immensely more powerful and knowledgeable and has no body. Thus, he writes: 'The way you use the word "God" does not show *whom* you mean – but, rather, what you mean' (*Culture and Value*, p. 50). We may add straight away that for Wittgenstein the way you use the word 'God' includes the way it is integrated into your behaviour: '*Practice* gives the [religious] words their sense' (*Culture and Value*, p. 85).

We can get a further glimpse of what he means from a remark at the end of *Zettel*: ' "You can't hear God speak to someone else, you can hear him only if you are being addressed." – That is a grammatical remark' (para. 717). One purpose of this comment is to show that the word 'God' functions differently from the way words referring to individual persons function, that the language games in which they figure are used differently. Some of the ways in which 'God' is used, both in the Bible and by modern believers and non-believers, do make it look as if it purportedly referred to a person. One might say, for example, 'God freed Israel from Egypt' just as one might say 'Moses freed Israel from Egypt'; or one might say 'God is dead' just as one might say 'Nietzsche is dead'. But these similarities should not blind us to the differences, one of which is that we cannot overhear God speaking, whereas we can, if suitably positioned, overhear one person speaking to another. The point here is not that it is extremely difficult or even impossible to overhear God speaking to somebody else (one of the difficulties being, perhaps, that God is a *bodiless* person), but that *we have no use* for sentences such as 'I just overheard God speaking to Margaret'. While such sentences form part of the language games we play with names of persons, they do not enter into the language games we play with the word

'God' — just as picking up one's king and throwing it at one's opponent does not form part of the game of chess. It would of course be possible to invent a use for such a sentence, but its use would be different from the use of a sentence like 'I just overheard Herbert speaking to Margaret' (for which we do not have to invent a use). We would use it in different circumstances, do different things with it. In the same way, 'God is dead' is used differently, and to different ends, from 'Nietzsche is dead'. Grammatical differences such as these (and there are many more) show that 'God' is not to be construed as referring to a person (cf. *Lectures and Conversations*, p. 59).

A related idea of Wittgenstein is that *belief* in God is very different from other kinds of belief. In particular, belief in God is not like the belief that a hypothesis is true. To believe in God is not to have, for example, a hypothesis about how the world came into existence, or a hypothesis that a certain being exists. Hypotheses are adopted, perhaps tentatively, tested, and confirmed or perhaps rejected according to the evidence. We use the word 'believe' differently in connection with God, and belief in God plays quite a different role in a believer's life.

> If the question arises as to the existence of a god or God, it plays an entirely different role to that of the existence of any person or object I ever heard of. One said, had to say, that one *believed* in the existence [of God], and if one did not believe, this was regarded as something bad. Normally if I did not believe in the existence of something no one would think there was anything wrong in this. Also, there is this extraordinary use of the word 'believe'. One talks of believing and at the same time one doesn't use 'believe' as one does ordinarily. You might say (in the normal use): 'You only believe – oh well. . . . ' Here it is used entirely differently. (*Lectures and Conversations*, pp. 59f.)

Wittgenstein also claims that Christianity (and it is normally Christianity he has in mind when speaking of religion) is not based on historical evidence, and this again affects the nature of religious belief.

> Christianity is not based on a historical truth; rather, it offers us a (historical) narrative and says: now believe! But not, believe this narrative with the belief appropriate to a historical narrative, rather: believe, through thick and thin, which you can do only as the result of a life. *Here you have a narrative, don't take the same attitude to it as you take to other historical narratives!* Make a *quite different* place in your life for it . . . This message (the Gospels) is seized on by men believingly (i.e. lovingly). *That* is the certainty characterising this particular acceptance-as-true, not something *else*. (*Culture and Value*, p. 32)

Related to these remarks are Wittgenstein's view that it is life, not rational proofs, that can teach a person to believe in God (*Culture and Value*, p. 86), and his belief that when believers in God ask where everything came from they are not seeking a causal explanation of the world's existence (*Culture and Value*, p. 85).

If belief in God is not the belief appropriate to a causal or historical hypothesis, it is a misconception to reject religious belief on the grounds that belief in God, or other religious beliefs or practices, rests on a *mistaken* hypothesis. So, in his *Remarks on Frazer's 'Golden Bough'*, Wittgenstein wholly rejects Frazer's attempt to represent 'primitive' religion as a series of mistaken pre-scientific hypotheses. Religious believing is simply different from the kind of believing associated with a hypothesis, however well or badly established. Religious belief is therefore misrepresented if it is made to look reasonable by ordinary canons, based on sound argument and premises any reasonable person would accept, as is sometimes done by believers themselves. Not that religious belief is unreasonable either; reason simply does not play the same role in this kind of belief as in scientific hypotheses (cf. *Lectures and Conversations*, pp. 56–9).

Wittgenstein's reputation as a major philosopher (arguably the greatest of the twentieth century) is now well established and has given rise to much literature exploring his life and ideas. Most of those writing about Wittgenstein have avoided the question of his interest in religion and have ignored the significance of his thinking for religious matters. But some have tried to explain what he had to say about religion while others have made serious attempts to develop and apply his thinking with a focus on religion.

Two notable attempts to document how Wittgenstein thought of religious topics are Cyril Barrett's *Wittgenstein on Ethics and Religious Belief* (Oxford, 1991) and Norman Malcolm's *Wittgenstein: A Religious Point of View* (Ithaca, 1994). According to Barrett, Wittgenstein's views on ethics and religious belief formed a consistent whole, which can be expounded as such. He also argues that Wittgenstein regarded matters of value (including religion) as of supreme importance. Malcolm, a close friend of Wittgenstein, holds that there is discontinuity between Wittgenstein's earlier and later views when it comes to religion. But he also shows how religion was important in Wittgenstein's thinking. Having noted Wittgenstein's reported remark 'I am not a religious man, but I cannot help seeing every problem from a religious point of view' (Rush Rhees [ed.], *Ludwig Wittgenstein, Personal Recollections* [Oxford, 1984], p. 94), Malcolm pays special attention to Wittgenstein's tendency to be amazed at the existence of something and to his stress on action as prior to intellectual understanding and reasoning. Wittgenstein's amazement at existence is something also stressed by Herbert McCabe OP, a notable defender of the teachings of Thomas Aquinas, who, with evident delight, finds similarities between what Wittgenstein says of the 'mystical' at the end of the *Tractatus* and what Aquinas says about *esse* in works like the *Summa Theologiae* ('The logic of mysticism – I' in Martin Warner [ed.], *Religion and Philosophy* [Cambridge, 1992]).

With an eye on philosophers influenced by Wittgenstein in their thinking on religious matters, one should note that Wittgenstein's philosophy of mind and language is very much present in Anthony Kenny's study of Aquinas's teaching on the human soul (*Aquinas on Mind* [London, 1993], chapters 11 and 12) and in Fergus Kerr's *Theology After Wittgenstein* (Oxford, 1986). Kenny, though critical of Aquinas for various reasons, finds in Aquinas congenial thoughts which may be compared with what Wittgenstein had to offer. Kerr, as well as providing an exceptionally clear account of Wittgenstein on mind and language, compares and contrasts what he had to say with what can be found in the writings of theologians both ancient and contemporary. Kerr's verdict, defended with much reference to the writings of theologians, is that students of theology have much to gain from reading Wittgenstein. The same verdict (albeit delivered for different reasons from those offered by Kerr) can be detected in the work of Elizabeth Anscombe (another friend of Wittgenstein who came, like him, to be Professor of Philosophy at Cambridge University). Wittgenstein's *On Certainty* is evidently an influence on what she has written with an eye on the topic of faith (cf. 'What is it to believe someone?' in C. F. Delaney [ed.], *Rationality and Religious Belief* [Notre Dame, 1979] and 'Faith' in G. E. M. Anscombe, *Collected Papers*, vol. III [Oxford, 1981]). In a famous discussion of miracles (chapter 10 of his *Enquiry Concerning Human Understanding*) David Hume asserts that one's beliefs should always be based on evidence. Anscombe, drawing on Wittgenstein, reminds us that 'the greater part of our knowledge of reality rests upon the belief that we repose in things we have been taught and told'.[4]

The most significantly sustained attempt to make use of Wittgenstein for purposes of philosophy of religion comes in the work of D. Z. Phillips, who has been writing on Wittgenstein and religion since the 1960s. Drawing on the thinking of Wittgenstein as outlined above, Phillips has paid special attention to the question 'What is the role of philosophy with respect to religious belief?' Many would say that its role is to adjudicate between believers and unbelievers with an eye on such notions as 'evidence' and 'reasons'. For Phillips, however, these notions are context-relative. What counts as 'evidence' or 'reason' may vary depending on our object of enquiry. There is no absolute position outside specific human concerns from which to demand evidence and reasons. So it is inappropriate to ask, in the abstract, for 'evidence' and 'reasons' for or against religious beliefs. We need to start by examining such beliefs and by trying to see what they amount to in practice. If we do so, says Phillips, we shall see (as Phillips thinks most philosophers of religion do not see) that religious beliefs are significantly different from other kinds of belief and that many traditional philosophical approaches to them (coming from both believers and non-believers) fail to do them justice. Phillips is especially hostile to attempts to prove or disprove the existence of God. We should not, he argues, assume that the reality of God (like, for example, the reality of such physical objects as planets) is, for those who believe in it, something to be thought of as possible not to be, or as something arrived at on the basis of inference.

Echoing Wittgenstein, Phillips insists that 'philosophy leaves everything as it is'. In his view, the chief task of philosophers of religion is to examine the nature of religious belief as it exists in the field (so to speak) and not as it exists in the minds of philosophers. These, so Phillips often argues, offer a false and theoretical account of religion quite oblivious to its nature as expressed in the talk and behaviour of believers.

> One will never understand what is meant by belief in God if one thinks of God as a being who may or may not exist ... let us assume, for a moment, that the reality of God is akin to the reality of a physical object. It will then make sense to assume that one day we will be able to check whether our belief is true. Let us assume, further, that such a day comes, and that we find that there is a God and that He is as we had always thought Him to be. What kind of a God would we have discovered? Clearly, a God of whom it would still make sense to say that He might not exist. Such a God may, as a matter of fact, never cease to exist ... A God who is an existent among existents is not the God of religious belief. (*The Concept of Prayer* [London, 1965], p. 81)

Readers trying to understand Phillips and his use of Wittgenstein will be helped by reading texts such as Richard Swinburne's *The Coherence of Theism* (Oxford, 1977) and *The Existence of God* (Oxford, 1979). Swinburne's view is that there is something called 'theism' espousers of which believe that there is a person, called 'God', who can be inferred to exist by reasons on a level with those employed by scientists. Swinburne's attempt to explain and defend this view is a good example of what Phillips regards as deep philosophical confusion when it comes to the study of religion. So it may be taken as an example of what Phillips, in the name of Wittgenstein, is chiefly out to oppose. For a negative reaction to the kind of philosophy of religion exemplified in the writings of Swinburne, one much indebted to Wittgenstein, readers might also consult Gareth Moore's book *Believing in God* (Edinburgh, 1989). Moore attempts to follow Wittgenstein's general philosophical approach, as expressed in the *Philosophical Investigations*, by trying to understand the functioning of some of the things Christians say by setting them in their context in the lives of believers. His central concern is to show that 'God' is not the name of a thing. That is to say, the way in which the word is used shows that the relationship between 'God' and God is not to be conceived on the model of a name and the object to which it corresponds. Thus, Moore follows the ideas expressed in the early sections of the *Philosophical Investigations* and applies them to the word 'God' as used in the Christian tradition. In particular, according to Moore, Christian use of 'God' shows that the Christian God is not to be conceived as a *personal* individual, rather like a human being, albeit much more knowledgeable, powerful and moral – God is not a 'bodiless person'.

Notes

1 See M. O'C. Drury, 'Conversations with Wittgenstein' in Rush Rhees (ed.), *Recollections of Wittgenstein* (Oxford, 1984). Also see the references to 'religion' and 'Christianity' in Ray Monk, *Ludwig Wittgenstein: The Duty of Genius* (London, 1990).
2 (1) Cyril Barrett (ed.), *Wittgenstein: Lectures and Conversations on Aesthetics, Psychology and Religious Belief* (Oxford, 1966), pp. 53–72. (2) Ludwig Wittgenstein, *Remarks on Frazer's 'Golden Bough'* (trans. A. C. Miles, rev. Rush Rhees; Retford, 1979). (1) is a transcript of a course given by Wittgenstein in 1938. (2) consists of notes made by Wittgenstein in 1930.
3 Reprinted in *Philosophical Occasions*, pp. 37–44.
4 'What is it to believe someone?' in C. F. Delaney (ed.), *Rationality and Religious Belief* (Notre Dame and London, 1979).

(e)   Foundationalism and philosophy of religion

John Greco

Before discussing foundationalism in the philosophy of religion it will be helpful to consider foundationalism in general. Accordingly, we begin by discussing foundationalism as an answer to the sceptical problem of an infinite regress of reasons. Next we look at foundationalism in the context of several issues regarding faith and rationality. These include the evidentialist objection to religious belief, the role of natural theology in providing evidence for God's existence, and the Calvinist position that belief in God can be rational without evidence. Finally, we will consider whether Aquinas was a foundationalist.

Foundationalism and the regress problem

First and foremost, foundationalism is a solution to the regress problem. The problem arises because it seems that one must have good reasons for whatever one claims to know. But not any reason is a good reason; one must have reasons for thinking that one's reasons are true. Accordingly, it seems that knowledge requires (*per impossibile*) an infinite regress of reasons. Both the problem and the foundationalist solution are articulated by Aristotle.

> Some people think that because you must understand the primitives there is no understanding at all ... [These people,] supposing that you cannot understand in any other way, claim that we are led back *ad infinitum* on the ground that we shall not understand the posterior items because of the prior items if there are no primitives. They are right – for it is impossible to survey infinitely many items. And if things come to a stop and there are principles, then these, they say, are unknowable since there is no *demonstration* of them and this is the only kind of understanding there is ...

> We assert that not all understanding is demonstrative: rather, in the case of immediate items understanding is indemonstrable. And it is clear that this must be so; for if you must understand the items which are prior and from which the demonstration proceeds, and if things come to a stop at some point, then these immediates must be indemonstrable.[1]

Aristotle speaks in terms of 'understanding' and 'demonstration', but neither of these concepts is essential to the regress problem. First, the problem can be formulated for any variety of positive epistemic status. Aristotle talks about understanding, but we could frame a similar problem for rational belief, knowledge, or other kinds of positive epistemic status. Second, the regress problem trades on the demand for good reasons, and not on a demand for demonstrative reasons in particular. Thus if some variety of positive epistemic status requires only inductive reasons, the threat of an infinite regress looms just as large.

Accordingly, the regress problem is captured by the following sceptical argument, this time stated in terms of knowledge.

1. To know that something is true one must believe it on the basis of good reasons, or reasons that indicate that the thing is likely to be true.
2. But not any reason is a good reason. Good reasons themselves must be

35

backed up by good reasons for thinking that they are true, which reasons will in turn be in need of further good reasons.
3. Therefore, to know that something is true one must believe it on the basis of an infinite number of good reasons. (1, 2)
4. No humans are capable of basing their belief on an infinite number of reasons.
5. Therefore, knowledge (for humans) is impossible. (3, 4)

A foundationalist theory of knowledge answers the regress argument by denying premises (1) and (2). Specifically, foundationalism asserts that (a) not all knowledge is based on inferences from further reasons, and (b) knowledge in the foundations can act as good reasons for other beliefs. The foundationalist also holds that (c) all non-foundational knowledge ultimately rests on knowledge in the foundations. These three theses define foundationalism as a theory of knowledge. Analogous theses define foundationalist theories of understanding, rational belief, etc.[2]

Foundationalism is therefore characterized by a two-tier structure of belief and/or knowledge. Some beliefs are properly basic, meaning that they have some relevant positive epistemic status even though they are not inferred from other beliefs that act as their evidence. All other beliefs are non-basic, meaning that they depend on proper inference from evidence for their epistemic status. Different versions of foundationalism specify different criteria for properly basic belief and for proper inference. For example, Descartes and Hume are often interpreted as accepting only self-evident beliefs about simple necessary truths and incorrigible beliefs about one's own mental states as properly basic. The same philosophers are also commonly interpreted as accepting only deductive reasoning as proper inference. But nothing about foundationalism *as such* requires these strictures; the defining characteristic of the position is its two-tier structure of belief and/or knowledge. Again, this structure is posed as a solution to the sceptical argument from an infinite regress of reasons.

In this context we can see that many of the usual objections against foundationalism are misguided. For example, it is often objected that foundational beliefs are impossible because no beliefs are irrevisable. But in so far as foundationalism is an answer to the regress problem this objection plainly misses the mark. The reason is that foundationalism need not posit irrevisable beliefs to stop the infinite regress of reasons. What is required is that some beliefs having a relevant epistemic status are not inferred from other beliefs, and therefore do not issue in the need for further justifying reasons. Similar things can be said against the objections that no beliefs are infallible and that no beliefs are indubitable. In general, foundationalism should not be saddled with theses that are unnecessary for its characteristic answer to the regress problem.[3]

Foundationalism and evidentialism

In the philosophy of religion foundationalism is most relevant to issues of faith and rationality. Alvin Plantinga and Nicholas Wolterstorff see foundationalism behind the evidentialist objection to religious belief, and also behind evidentialist apologetics.[4] The evidentialist objection states that belief in God is not rational unless it is based on good arguments or evidence; but since no good arguments are forthcoming, belief in God is not rational. A common response to the evidentialist objection is evidential apologetics. The apologist accepts the premise that rational belief in God needs evidence and tries to provide it. Plantinga and Wolterstorff argue that both the evidential objector and the evidential apologist assume foundationalism – both assume that some beliefs are rational even though they are not based on further reasons, while other beliefs are rational only if they are properly inferred from what is properly basic.

Furthermore, both sides of the evidentialist debate assume that belief in God is not properly basic; if belief in God is rational at all then it must be based on good arguments or evidence. Accordingly, both are assuming a form of foundationalism that restricts belief in God from being in the foundations. Plantinga and Wolterstorff suggest that what is assumed is 'classical foundationalism'. This version of foundationalism asserts that a belief is properly basic only if it is self-evident, incorrigible or evident to the senses. Since belief in God has none of these properties, it is rational only if it is based on reasons that do have these properties.

Belief in God as foundational

Plantinga argues that the Reformed objection to natural theology is best understood as a rejection of classical foundationalism. More specifically, it is a rejection of classical foundationalism's criteria for properly basic belief. Reformed theologians reject natural theology because they reject the idea that one cannot rationally start with belief in God. The following passage from Herman Bavinck asserts this position.

> We receive the impression that belief in the existence of God is based entirely upon these proofs. But indeed that would be 'a wretched faith, which, before it invokes God, must first prove his existence'. The contrary, however, is the truth. There is not a single object the existence of which we hesitate to accept until definite proofs are furnished. Of the existence of self, of the world round about us, of logical and moral laws, etc., we are so deeply convinced because of the indelible impressions which all these things make upon our consciousness that we need no

arguments or demonstration. Spontaneously, altogether involuntarily: without any constraint or coercion, we accept that existence. Now the same is true in regard to the existence of God.[5]

The Reformed theologian, Plantinga argues, holds that belief in God can be foundational; i.e. it can be rational, or even known, even though it is not inferred from other beliefs acting as its evidence.

Plantinga endorses this position and develops a general epistemology to explain how it could be so.[6] The main idea is that a belief has positive epistemic status in so far as it is produced by our cognitive faculties functioning properly in an appropriate environment. Plantinga explains proper function in terms of a design plan: our faculties function properly when they function as they were designed, and in an environment for which they were designed. A theist will attribute such design to God, but Plantinga argues that non-theists can accept the same framework, attributing design to evolution or some other natural process rather than to God.

The next step is to argue that some of our cognitive faculties are inferential and some are non-inferential. Sometimes we form beliefs by inferring them from other beliefs we already hold. But we also have the ability to form beliefs via faculties like sensory perception, memory, introspection and logical intuition. Plantinga argues that these are non-inferential faculties; they properly function so as to form beliefs in some way other than inference. For example, when I see a bird in my yard I do not typically form the belief that there is a bird on the basis of inference from other beliefs. I do not, for example, base the belief on beliefs about my visual experience. In the typical case I do not even *have* beliefs about my experience, much less use them as grounds from which I infer beliefs about material objects. Whether or not one accepts this example, the important point is that some beliefs are properly formed by inference and some are properly formed by non-inferential faculties. But given Plantinga's general criteria for positive epistemic status, this explains how some beliefs can be properly basic.

We are now in a position to see how beliefs about God could be properly basic. Specifically, such beliefs are properly basic if they are formed by a non-inferential cognitive faculty functioning properly in an appropriate environment. This is in fact the case if we are fitted with a *sensus divinitatis*, i.e. a divine sense that gives us a direct (meaning non-inferential) awareness of God. The idea that we do have such a sense is suggested by Calvin.

'There is within the human mind, and indeed by natural instinct, an awareness of the divinity.' . . . To prevent anyone from taking refuge in the pretense of ignorance, God himself has implanted in all men a certain understanding of his divine majesty . . . [M]en one and all perceive that there is a God and that he is their maker . . .[7]

Many objections might be raised against the idea that belief in God is foundational. Here we will consider only two. First, one might object that the position makes belief in God dogmatic. But if 'dogmatic' means impervious to reason then the objection is misguided, for we have seen that nothing about foundationalism implies that basic beliefs are irrevisable or otherwise immune to evidence against them. A second worry is that the position is a form of fideism. But this too is a misunderstanding if fideism is opposed to rationality. Foundationalism is a theory *about* rationality (or other positive epistemic status); the claim is that some beliefs *are rational* even though they are not based on inference from further reasons. Another way to put the claim is that inference from reasons is not the only source of rationality.

Aquinas and foundationalism

Since Aquinas seems to follow Aristotle in his solution to the regress problem, it is reasonable to think that Aquinas was a foundationalist.[8] However, Eleonore Stump argues that Aquinas was not a foundationalist regarding knowledge.[9] Two of her reasons for this conclusion are (1) Aquinas held that one's acceptance of something as a first principle need not be certain and does not guarantee the principle's truth, and (2) Aquinas held that first principles proper to a specific subject are arrived at by induction from particulars, and so are not even basic. But neither of these considerations shows that Aquinas was not a foundationalist. First, we have seen that foundationalism is not committed to the thesis that foundational beliefs are certain. Neither must foundational beliefs be guaranteed to be true, since neither of these properties is necessary to stop the regress of evidential reasons. Second, even if proper first principles are known by inductive inference this only shows that *these principles* are not foundational. It leaves open the possibility that the inductive evidence for the principles is foundational. For example, knowledge of particulars might be foundational because it is evident to the senses.

A third reason Stump gives against the position that Aquinas was a foundationalist regarding knowledge is that Aquinas's *scientia* cannot be equated with knowledge; therefore, even if Aquinas were a foundationalist regarding *scientia* this would not entail that he was a foundationalist regarding knowledge. However, we have seen that neither the regress problem nor Aquinas's answer to it trades on any special characteristic of *scientia*. The regress problem arises because an infinite number of reasons is threatened, and Aquinas follows Aristotle in replying that some states get their positive epistemic status in ways other than inference from further reasons. Since nothing here depends on special characteristics of *scientia*

John Greco

(such as demonstration or certainty), it is reasonable to conclude that Aquinas was a foundationalist for all kinds of positive epistemic status.

Was Aquinas a *classical* foundationalist? In particular, did Aquinas require that knowledge and rational belief concerning God be based on evidence that is self-evident, incorrigible, or evident to the senses? Plantinga answers both questions in the affirmative, citing Aquinas's natural theology as evidence. But here we must respect distinctions between *scientia*, rational belief and knowledge. It is true that Aquinas required demonstration from evident truths for *scientia* about God, but he required no such thing for rational belief; beliefs about God are rational because they are based on good testimony, the authority of which is confirmed by miracles and other aspects of the history of Christianity.[10]

Moreover, Stump argues that Aquinas's conditions for knowledge are close to those suggested by Plantinga: 'human knowledge is a function of our using the cognitive capacities God created in us as God designed them to be used in the world God created them to be used in'.[11] If that is correct, then for Aquinas the foundations of knowledge are broader than those of *scientia*, and therefore Aquinas was not a classical foundationalist regarding either rational belief or knowledge.

Notes

1 *Posterior Analytics*, Book Alpha, Chapter 3.
2 Coherentist theories answer the problem by denying the inference from (1) and (2) to (3), holding that reasons can be mutually supportive. The coherentist alternative to foundationalism will not be considered here.
3 A question arises regarding why, historically, some foundationalists have required very high standards for properly basic belief and for proper inference. One answer is that these are extra requirements of *scientia*. See N. Wolterstorff, 'The migration of the theistic arguments: from natural theology to evidentialist apologetics' in Robert Audi and William Wainwright (eds), *Rationality, Religious Belief, and Moral Commitment* (Ithaca, NY, 1986).
4 See Alvin Plantinga, 'Reason and belief in God' in Alvin Plantinga and Nicholas Wolterstorff (eds), *Faith and Rationality* (Notre Dame and London, 1983). Also see: Nicholas Wolterstorff, 'Can belief in God be rational if it has no foundations?' in Plantinga and Wolterstorff, op. cit., and Nicholas Wolterstorff, 'The migration of the theistic arguments: from natural theology to evidentialist apologetics' in Audi and Wainwright, op. cit.
5 Herman Bavinck, *The Doctrine of God* (trans. William Hendricksen; Grand Rapids, 1951), pp. 78–9. Quoted in Plantinga (1983), p. 64.
6 Plantinga's general epistemology is set out in Plantinga (1993).
7 John Calvin, *Institutes of the Christian Religion* (trans. Lewis Battles Ford; Philadelphia, 1960), pp. 43–4. Quoted in Plantinga (1983), p. 65.
8 *Commentary on the Posterior Analytics of Aristotle*, esp. I. 7.
9 Eleonore Stump, 'Aquinas on the foundations of knowledge', *Canadian Journal of Philosophy*, Supplementary Volume 17 (1992).

10 See Scott MacDonald, 'Theory of knowledge' in Norman Kretzmann and Eleonore Stump (eds), *The Cambridge Companion to Aquinas* (Cambridge, 1993), and Wolterstorff (1986), esp. pp. 63–5.
11 Stump (1992), p. 148.

2
Arguments for God's existence

(a) Cosmological arguments

David Braine

The term 'cosmological argument' was introduced by Immanuel Kant to refer to (in his view, mistaken) arguments for the existence of God starting from the existence of some thing or things whose existence is contingent (oneself, the world, experiences, events, substances, or whatever). Contingency has been taken to mean or imply some kind of dependency, i.e. as requiring a cause or causal background, or reason for existence. Such arguments have, roughly, the following general form:

1. Experience tells us that there exist things of some sort or sorts whose existence is not necessary but 'contingent'.
2. Because their existence is not necessary, but contingent, each of them must have a cause or causal background or reason for existence, and this will be itself either contingent or else necessary.
3. If it is the former, then it must have cause or reason, and, if this cause or reason is also contingent, the same dilemma will arise again unless we arrive at something which has necessary existence in some way which excludes having cause or reason.
4. But such a series, or series of series, cannot be endless, since, if it were, nothing will have been explained, or since such causal order is accidental unless grounded in some underlying cause.
5. Therefore, there must be some first cause which is intrinsically necessary.

Terminology

The words 'contingent' and 'necessary' are used in so many different ways that we need to make careful distinctions before assessing the argument outlined above.

Applied to propositions, the word 'contingent' means 'possibly true and possibly false'. Applied to realities of some sort – substances, states of affairs, or goings-on – it means 'could have not existed, obtained or gone on' and 'could cease to exist, obtain or go on'. If attention is limited to the true or the actual (i.e. setting aside the impossible), its proper opposite in either case is called 'the necessary'. In relation to propositions, 'necessary' means 'necessarily true' (inescapable in thought), whereas in relation to realities it means 'necessarily existent or necessarily actual' (inescapably having and/or having had real existence or actuality). A complication arises with the knowledge of propositions: 'it is certain' means 'it is not possible that it not be true' even when the knowledge depends on experience, whereas philosophers have come to use the word 'necessary' in narrower ways, either as meaning knowable *a priori* (the opposite of the empirical), or as meaning knowable through mere logic (Frege's 'analytic' or the 'logically necessary') as opposed to not being determinable by logic alone.

In connection with causal explanations, the terms 'contingent' and 'necessary' need to be understood in the way they apply to the states of affairs, situations, events, activities, processes, fields, substantial objects, etc. – in sum, to the 'realities' and/or 'actualities' (past, present or future) of which propositions tell us, rather than as they apply to the propositions themselves. Aquinas distinguishes (1) 'being' (*esse*) as signifying a thing's 'activity' (*actus*) of being or existing from (2) 'being' as 'signifying the composition of a proposition' – i.e. between *esse* as something fully actual, an 'actuality', and *esse* as merely what is expressed in some positive predication or positive existential proposition, e.g. 'Socrates *is* wise', 'Socrates *is* blind', 'Socrates *is*' (as stated in 400 BC) and 'God *is*' (stated at any time).

Aquinas's word *actus* here means the same as Aristotle's *energeia* (envisaging 'existing' as analogous to the 'living' spoken of in 'is living an active life', as distinct from 'living' as 'being of the genus living being' or 'being alive rather than dead'). Plainly, in the cosmological argument, our concern is with the necessity of God's existing as an actuality, and the status of the proposition 'God exists' is irrelevant.

Ordinarily, modern philosophers ascribe real necessity to that which the natures of natural things makes necessary, either because it belongs to their natures or because their natural action makes it necessary. However, if God underlies nature, then what is thus naturally necessary will not be absolutely necessary – only what belongs to or arises from the existence and nature of God will have absolute real necessity.[1]

Kant on cosmological arguments

Kant's primary objection to any cosmological argument is that it involves proving the existence of an intrinsically necessary being. However, his notion of an intrinsically necessary being is the notion of a being, X, such that the proposition 'X exists' is unconditionally necessary in virtue of some concept contained in the concept of 'X'. But this kind of unconditional necessity is a property of propositions – not at all what cosmological arguments aim to prove. As we saw earlier, these argue for an intrinsic or unconditional ('absolute') necessity of a kind applying, not to propositions, but to actualities or realities – a necessity analogous to natural necessity, not to being logically necessary or knowable *a priori*. Cosmological arguments rely on their objections to the notion of an infinite regress to show that there is an intrinsically necessary being, but to show this only *a posteriori*. They do not provide us with any concept of this being, or of its essence such as would allow us to see how it is possible for a thing to exist with intrinsic necessity or what could make it intrinsically necessary. They imply no concept of God allowing us to see these things.

The confusion in Kant and many others between the idea of the absolutely necessary in reality and the ideas of the logically necessary and of the *a priori* which have to do with our knowledge of propositions, in fact, has its historical origin in the theological principle that, apart from what is excluded by his existence and nature, God can do anything which is logically non-contradictory. Thus, paradoxically, it is only theology which provides any excuse for the rationalist and empiricist doctrine that nothing 'conceivable in idea' is absolutely impossible in reality.

Objections and kinds of cosmological argument

We can present the other common objections to cosmological arguments in the course of distinguishing the three different types of such argument.

The first kind argues from the universe's having had a beginning in time. In this, it is quite unlike any of the traditional arguments, none of which assumed that time had a beginning.

Aristotle thought the universe had no beginning. While refuting Aristotle's arguments for this conclusion, Thomas Aquinas (whose famous 'Five Ways', to be found in *Summa Theologiae* I, 2, 3, are often taken as paradigmatic examples of cosmological arguments) thought it impossible to prove the opposite. Aquinas saw no problem in time having no beginning, despite its involving many infinite series of causes. In his view God causes the coming to be of Jacob by Isaac, of Isaac by Abraham, and so on, so that there would be no philosophical difficulty in an infinite series of human ancestors – it would be like an infinitely long-lived blacksmith getting through an infinite series of hammers, using each in succession until it was broken. There is no difficulty in these cases because the action of each father or each hammer does not depend on the continuing operation or even the continued existence of the earlier members of the series (cf. *Summa Theologiae* I, 46, 2). For Aquinas, any knowledge that the universe had a beginning depends on revelation. Leibniz (a notable figure in the history of cosmological arguments) proceeds on the same assumption. He argues that there must be some cause external to an infinite series of the kind Aquinas thinks possible. And, for him, this external cause does not act by temporally preceding the whole of the supposed beginningless time. It acts by operating contemporaneously with each member of it. For Leibniz, like Aquinas, God is omnipresent in space and time.

However, the scientific acceptance of the idea of cosmological expansion, and of the universe's originating in a so-called 'Big Bang', has suggested a novel modern non-theological basis for thinking that the universe had a beginning and therefore a cause. Also, the idea that conceiving God as cause of things implies a beginning has become very common since it is often presumed that the only intelligible notion of cause we can have involves the supposition that a cause precedes its effect. Yet none of the traditional cosmological arguments (e.g. arguments found in Aquinas) assumed this. It is typical of causal agents that they should exist contemporaneously with their action and that their action should be contemporaneous with their effect, as when a man breaks a stick (the action) and the stick breaks (the effect). This has been the model for considering God's causing of the existence of the universe. And this model has been thought equally applicable whether God does this causing by firstly creating the universe out of nothing and then upholding it in existence (thereby continuing the same action) or by simply continuing this action of causing this existence over a beginningless time.

The argument from the Big Bang hypothesis, taken as showing that the universe had a beginning, has been powerfully presented by William Lane Craig. And, with Craig's argument in mind, it should certainly be said that the freedom with which modern physicists (not to mention Aquinas) treat questions about the whole universe as objects of scientific enquiry and possible knowledge suggests that we should dismiss the second peculiarly Kantian objection to cosmological arguments, namely that the universe should not be regarded as an object of science. None of Kant's four proofs that contradiction follows if one treats the universe as an object (the 'Antinomies') seems actually valid. In each case either only one or neither of the pairs of supposedly contradictory propositions seems provable.

Nonetheless, taken by itself, this science-reliant form of the cosmo-logical argument seems open to most of the same obstacles as the argument in its traditional forms.

Firstly, however plausible it may seem that the universe's having a beginning shows that it must have a cause, this cannot be considered as a strict proof. Quentin Smith's suggestion[2] that it originated by some quantum variation does not seem very coherent, since the very idea of quantum variation seems to require some context – a background which is actual, in some way available to be open to quantum variation. But we can say that, if the universe has no causal background, it makes no more sense to speak of its existing by chance than by a cause, since the very word 'chance' suggests a causal background, one leaving it open whether the chance thing arise or not. In that case, it could be suggested, especially in view of its intensely integrated and unitary character, that the universe itself has necessary existence, but only a necessity *de facto*, not intrinsic. (This might perhaps be a necessity somewhat analogous to the necessity of the past, i.e. the necessity of being already established, by contrast with the future.) Therefore, this argument cannot be considered a proof: it does not show that a regress cannot stop with something necessary merely *de facto*, rather than intrinsically – i.e. something for which there is no reason why it should not have a causal background, but which merely happens not to.

Secondly, and in fact a mere symptom of this problem, this kind of argument, taken by itself, still leaves untouched the problem of excluding an infinite regress. For, if Craig's argument only supplies a God which might have a merely *de facto* necessity, it is still unclear why we couldn't leave God out and be content with the universe as the underivative *de facto* necessary first thing. Therefore, some argument excluding an infinite regress is still needed as the only argument which would justify regarding the necessity of a first cause as intrinsic to it, not merely *de facto*.

Thirdly, almost all the argument required if the universe did not have a beginning is still required even if it be granted that it did have a beginning. Moreover, until we have this further argument, the science-dependent cosmological argument by itself can tell us nothing about God except that he is cause of the universe, at least as unitary or integrated as the universe itself, and not physically related to it. If time and space are both equally inseparable from the physical system of this universe, then he is atemporal (or at least no reason has been given for supposing that any ordered succession in him has any relation to our time). No reason has been given for supposing him omnipresent either in being or in capacity to act in this universe, once it has begun. And no reason has been given to prove his transcendence in nature, his infinity or his uniqueness.

Nonetheless, this apparent scientific evidence that the universe had a beginning does constitute a very strong reason, even though not a proof, for the conclusion that it arose by the action of some agent or agents, whether animate or inanimate, exercising active causal power. An event is something we may want to explain without invoking the action of such an agent. The explanation of a rocket's premature explosion, for instance, may be a chance loose wire rather than the appropriate exercise of active power by technicians. The explosion is probably an exercise of the active power ('potential energy') of the mixture of gases which explodes, although we do not give this as 'the cause' in our summary report (this picks out the factor which differentiates the case from the 'normal'). However, the present question is not of an event's coming to happen within a field within which some events are determined and some happen by chance, but of an extraordinarily highly ordered system or whole coming to exist with no physical background. If a full-grown rabbit suddenly came into existence in front of us with no connection of origin with its immediate physical background, then we would surely look for some cause; viewed as caused, e.g. by a magician or spirit, it might seem a unitary effect; viewed as uncaused, it seems an incredible coincidence. Likewise, viewed as uncaused, the universe's having a beginning would seem to involve an infinite coincidence; either way, for the universe to have a beginning except by the action of some agent or agents would seem much more extraordinary. In thinking this, we rely on a principle much less extravagant than the principle of sufficient reason, or even the principle that every event has a cause – it is much closer to Aristotle's original conception that every ordered natural system ('substance') which comes to be must have an efficient cause.

And certainly, the universe's having a beginning can serve with other things already suggesting belief in God, if these exist, to add strength to a cumulative argument for the existence of God. In addition, it reinforces the Jewish, Christian and Muslim perspective whereby cosmology is embraced within a history, rather than history being a mere incident within cosmology.

* * *

The other two types of cosmological argument are distinguished according to whether (1) they rely upon a principle that everything of a certain sort requires a cause as a condition of its existence, an agent or agents with active power or powers adequate to cause the existence concerned, or (2) they rely on Leibniz's principle of sufficient reason, 'that every contingent truth or truth of fact must have a sufficient reason' (*Monadology*, §36), or some equivalent requirement that every such matter of fact should have an explanation making it intelligible why it should be. Germain Grisez (*Beyond the New Theism* [Notre Dame and London, 1975], Part III), and David Braine (*The Reality of Time and the Existence of God* [Oxford, 1988], pp. 234–49) provide different refutations of Kant's *a priori* arguments against any use of such principles beyond the sphere of experience. Thomas Aquinas (in the 'Five Ways' and elsewhere) relies on the first principle, followed recently by David Braine and Barry Miller, while Leibniz and in modern times Bernard Lonergan, Hugo Meynell, Germain Grisez, and sometimes John Haldane, rely rather upon the second.

Henceforth, I shall speak of 'cause' when an agent with active power is being sought, and of 'reason' when one is seeking an explanation making it intelligible why something or other. There is an interplay between the two types of argument. Thus Leibniz's approach always ends by giving God's causing of the existence of things as the ultimate reason for the existence of the universe. And the principle that infinite coincidences must have explanations appears in Aquinas as well as Leibniz. Thus, Leibniz argues that if one copy of a book arises by copying an earlier copy, and this by copying yet another, and so on endlessly, we still need an explanation of the origin of the text and content of the book. And Aquinas argues that if every being is contingent, even if it may happen that when one contingent being ceases afterwards always by accident another comes to be, nonetheless if this is always truly accidental, so that this constancy is mere coincidence, then over an infinite time everything would have ceased to be and there would now be nothing; therefore something must be necessary. (No real disagreement with modern thinking is involved here: for example, in Newton's thought mass, momentum and energy are by their nature conserved, but this simply makes either these or the universe comprising them into necessary things, though all these might be necessary only derivatively.)

However, the principle of sufficient reason is questionable on three counts.

Firstly, it is unprovable. As Kant recognized, it serves admirably as a methodological principle, an ideal of reason. But there seems no *a priori* reason to suppose that 'being is as such intelligible', even if there is a God to whom all things are presumably intelligible (a supposition we cannot invoke as part of an argument for God's existence).

Secondly, the principle seems to be invalid within the sphere of natural explanation. The received view of empirical scientists includes the Heisenberg indeterminacy principle, integral to quantum mechanics, as an established part of physical science. This principle as customarily understood implies that the principle of sufficient reason actually fails within physics, and not because of anything wrong with our physics – there are 'why'-questions which naturally arise within our received modes of scientific description, but to which quantum theory requires that there be no answer. Furthermore, although human action is not called 'accidental' (this word's meaning excludes both being caused and being intentional), commonly nothing determines which of two motives will move us to action.

Thirdly, the way that it brings the supposed regress of causes of contingent beings, or of reasons for their existence, to an end (i.e. in a being whose reason for existence lies in its own essence or nature) is unsatisfactory. For, it is not just that from a nominal definition of God (i.e. what the word 'God' means) we cannot deduce his existence (as Kant and Aquinas agree). That is a matter of our human modes of knowledge of God. What is relevant to cosmological argument is the quite different matter of the explanation or cause, if any, of God's existence. Here, Aquinas argues that God's essence (his 'nature', or, in later language, his 'real essence') cannot be reason for God's existence. If God's nature or essence explained his existence (or its necessity), the two would have to be sufficiently distinct for one to be able to conceive God's existing as an exercise of his nature. But having a nature presupposes the existence of the thing having the nature, and therefore essence cannot explain existence ('existence cannot be derived from essence'). It is in this sense that Aquinas says that in God existence and essence are identical, because it is only thus that neither can be prior to the other.

Attempting a cosmological proof by means of the principle of sufficient reason seems therefore a failure.

Aquinas and cosmological arguments

This brings us to consider Aquinas's very different approach. He looks for a cause in the sense of a causal agent exercising active power. And he argues that what God causes is the existing of things in their natures. Let us first explain this conception, today so unfamiliar, considering its justification later. It appears most vividly when Aquinas discusses God's upholding of existence (*Summa Theologiae* I, 104, 1). There he tells us: 'Nor can the being of a thing continue after the action of the agent has ceased, if the agent is the cause of the effect not only in respect of becoming but also in respect of being. This is why hot water retains heat after the cessation of the fire's action, whereas the air does not continue to be lit up even for a moment when the sun ceases to act upon it, because water is a matter susceptive of the fire's heat in the same way as it exists in the fire ... whereas the air is not of such a nature as to receive light in the same way as it exists in the sun, which is the principle of light.'

Aquinas has no particular interest in God as causing things to come to be as such. The cause of things coming to be is commonly something natural.

David Braine

Thus, it is the potter who causes a pot to come to be. But in this process, the potter does nothing to give existence to the clay, nor to secure its continuance in existence and in its usual properties while being moulded in his hands, nor to secure its continued existence after being made and after being put on the shelf to be sold later. Of course, he may act to protect it from ceasing to be by natural causes, but he does not and cannot do anything to prevent it simply disappearing into nothing. This is unsurprising, since there is no particular risk of its simply disappearing into nothing (not from natural causes), any more than there was particular risk of the earlier-mentioned rabbit simply coming into existence in our midst out of nothing. However, whereas the non-existence of something where there is no reason to expect it to exist scarcely needs explanation (let alone the exercise of causal power), not being an example of real existence or positive existence of any kind, the case is quite different with continuing to exist and not disappearing into nothing. It is the real existing of those things which have real existence which constitutes that which is positive in the existence of the universe. It might therefore seem the principal thing for which causal power needed to be exercised. But the existence of created things cannot be explained by their nature for the reason given earlier to the effect that God's existence cannot be explained by his nature (i.e. having a nature presupposes the existence of the thing having the nature).[3]

Rather it is God that causes the existence or being (*esse*) of every real[4] being (*ens*) except himself. And this is Aquinas's basic conception. God gives all the real existence which is given, there being no role for any instrument or intermediate cause (*Summa Theologiae* I, 45, 5; cf. *De Potentia* 3, 4). The creation of things out of nothing is the initiation of this action. The upholding of things in existence is the continuance of the same action. For the reason given at the end of my discussion of the principle of sufficient reason above, God's essence is identical to his existence, there being no priority between them. God is therefore intrinsically underivative, there being no room for his existence's having a cause. Where a thing is such that there is room for a cause, the same internal conditions of possibility must be satisfied as if there were actually a cause (cf. Aristotle, *Metaphysics*, Theta, 4, 1047b 14ff.). Therefore only God exists intrinsically and with absolute necessity, since with everything else, its essence being prior to its existence, this essence might not be actualized. Therefore, in Aquinas's view, its existence requires a cause.

Aquinas raises the objection (later pressed by David Hume) that whatever is possible in the understanding must be possible in reality, so that since neither the existence of a thing nor its having a cause belongs to the concept of a thing, it follows that it is possible for the thing to exist in reality without a cause. His only answer is that existence is external to the concept of a thing and the question is of the possibility of existence, not of the possibility of a concept (*Summa Theologiae* I, 44, 1; cf. *De Potentia* 3, 5). He considers that, since it is not logically contradictory or self-evidently false, someone might think this (this is why he rejects the ontological argument). But he would reckon the only reason for thinking that everything logically possible is really possible within creation (unless it is in the past) is that God could bring it about, since possibility in reality depends on the powers of the natures at work in the universe from God downwards. But this still leaves Hume's problem that the principle that the real existence of things needs a cause is unproven.

Here, Braine argues that, if time is real, it follows that what is now past has a *de facto* necessity, and the future is only open because it is not yet existent. This is the only way there can be genuine free choice and real chance; and if things were already coexistent in an already established four-dimensional world, rather than causes determining things (making them naturally necessary), the things would be already *de facto* absolutely necessary. And there is no doubt that Aquinas conceived the world in this way with time as real,[5] even though today viewing time as real and even viewing causal action as real require some philosophical justification (cf. Braine, 1988, pp. 25–51; cf. 55–6, 77; cf. also David Braine, *The Human Person* [London, 1993], pp. 204–15; cf. 131–3).

Now, it belongs to the very nature of temporal things that they have some persistence (otherwise, their natures would be never exercised). Yet, the same principle which Aquinas insisted on in the case of God, that a thing's nature can never explain its existence, applies just as much to ordinary things and to the universe as to God (Braine, 1988, pp. 10f., 14f., 340–2). So, what is at stake is not just the beginning of a universe of an extraordinarily integrated nature, but at each juncture the ultimate contingency of the continuance of things in the same nature (not a continuance from one moment to the next as if time was discontinuous, but from the period from the past to the present on into the future). The existence of the system of things into the future needs a cause just as much as its coming into existence from nothing (Braine, op. cit., pp. 219f.). And it is less easy to dispute that the future has to have a causal background than to dispute this about the beginning.

Braine considers that the *only* sense in which the distinction between A's existing and A itself is a real distinction in the case of creatures but not in God, other than in our way of speaking, is that the internal conditions for having an existence which has the absolute contingency implied by temporality are satisfied.

Aquinas argues as follows. Unless existence and essence are identical, (1) essence stands to existence as potentiality to actuality (here he goes beyond Aristotle). In this case, since any potentiality presupposes some prior actuality (cf. Aristotle, *Metaphysics*, Theta, 8), (2) existence will need a cause

51

David Braine

(*Summa Theologiae* I, 3, 4; cf. *De Potentia* 7, 2). Therefore (3), if infinite regresses are excluded, the first cause must be pure actuality (and its existence and essence identical).

The first of Aquinas's Five Ways argues from movement or change (*motus*) to a first and unchangeable cause of change (an unchanged changer or unmoved mover). Aquinas called this argument 'the most obvious' when it comes to arguing that God exists (*Summa Theologiae* I, 2, 3) for two reasons. Firstly, its closeness to Aristotle's physics, which treats it as obvious that moving is always a being moved by something, supplemented by his cosmology (presented in *Metaphysics*, Lambda and *Physics*, VIII, 4–10), served his purpose to his hearers. Secondly, he envisaged it as showing that we have experience firstly of potentiality and secondly of the actual causing the potential to be actual, and that we experience the second in a way which intuitively exhibits the truth of the general principle that potentiality always presupposes some prior actuality.[6] The very next article (*Summa Theologiae* I, 3, 1) shows that, for him, the principles by which the First Way demonstrate the existence of an unmoved mover suffice to show the existence of an actuality without non-active potentiality.

As to the exclusion of any infinite regress, the Third Way (from contingency) refers back to the Second (to a first 'efficient cause'). There the intended argument is solely to the impossibility of a *per se* series of causes, as when A causes B, C and D, B causes C and D, and C causes D, so that when he says we experience an 'order of efficient causes', and refers to 'all efficient causes following in order', he is referring to *per se* series in which all the causes are of the same thing (this is made plain by the parallel in Aquinas, *Summa Contra Gentiles* I, 13, §33). Likewise, the argument of the First Way was intended to prove the impossibility of a *per se* series of movers, i.e. so that all the movers are of the same thing (compare *Summa Contra Gentiles* I, 13, §14, and note how §13, 15–19 confirm his parallel understanding of the First and Second Ways, while I, 13, 21ff. deal with a difficulty raised by Aristotle's *Physics*, VII). Neither argument is concerned with accidental (= non-*per se*) causes at all – these are regarded as independent in operation, each operating independently even of the continued existence of its predecessor.

It is these first three of the Five Ways which are commonly thought to be Aquinas's main cosmological arguments. As we have seen, his real understanding appears better elsewhere, and the Five Ways are just its Aristotelian formal dress.[7]

Notes

1 Conceivably, Aquinas follows Aristotle so that 'necessary' applied to substances means 'by nature imperishable'. So understood, 'being necessary derivatively' would mean having imperishable existence derivatively, like angels or human souls, and would be compatible with having a cause of existence – by contrast, the first cause has to exist imperishably of itself (be necessary *a se*). This would mean that Aquinas's expression of our idea of intrinsic and absolute necessity is rather in terms of the absence of non-active potentiality, than of some kind of 'necessity'.

2 William Lane Craig and Quentin Smith, *Theism, Atheism and Big Bang Cosmology* (Oxford, 1993).

3 Braine here thinks of existence as an actuality referred to by a complete proposition. Barry Miller has a more abstract argument thinking of A's existence as a 'property' referred to by the 'predicate' '. . . *exists*' as applied to A, using the fact that A had a beginning as evidence that this property is a real thing, and arguing that A and this property have to be 'co-constituted' in order for A to exist at all.

4 Aquinas's concern is not with abstract objects such as numbers or colours, nor with the being of things such as holes and blindness which consist in the absence of something positive, nor even with positive accidents such as Socrates' wisdom. He conceives this to consist in Socrates being wise, and to be a matter of Socrates' existing more fully in some accidental respect. By 'real beings', I mean things which are grammatical subjects of existence in their own right (only for these is existence an *actus*).

5 He conceived even the angels as created in relation with the world, and as having a succession of acts though not at dividing points in our continuous time (*Summa Theologiae* I, 61, 3 and 62, 5).

6 The usual argument against him that it presupposes Aristotelian physics, and that in Newtonian physics motion does not presuppose a mover, would be irrelevant to his main concern. Newton still thought that inertial movement presupposed actualities, viz. mass, momentum and energy. And in every physics, some motions seem due to violence (the action of a mover) and some to nature as something in some way actual.

7 It is a common objection, that if the first three ways established anything, *they would still* not establish God as personal, great, good, holy, etc. But *Aquinas* never supposed that it did – his argument extends at least to *Summa Theologiae* I, 26. From the first argument, he argues that the first mover must be in no respect in passive potentiality (q. 3, arts 1 and 4). From this, he concludes that it is simple and unique (qq. 3 and 11). As cause of all the positive attributes (things in respect of which things have actuality, especially when integral to the natures their existence is realized in), it must possess these attributes in a pre-eminent way, possessing each unrestrictedly; since it is only attributes in virtue of which things exist positively that make them good, and vice versa, it must be alone pre-eminently good (qq. 4 and 6). As alone capable of causing being, it must be immediate to every being and to every place and time where something could be. As simple, wherever it is present it must be present whole and undivided, and must therefore be not just everlasting but eternal. As cause making things able to act, cause of life, love, and (always inseparable) intellect

and will, this being must have active power, life, love, intellect and will; and must have intellect, perfect not just in power to understand and know, but in actually understanding and knowing. Its power being unrestricted (except that it cannot bring about what involves a contradiction), whatever it loves unqualifiedly it possesses and enjoys, not just desires; and knowing itself perfectly it must have supreme beatitude. Since it is personal it has a personal love towards creation, which towards created persons is called mercy (*misericordia*, Latin translation of the Greek *eleos* and Hebrew *cheçed*; 'loving kindness' in the Revised Version of 1841), and this mercy has respect for man's dignity as a consequence, so that divine justice is a consequence, not the context, of divine mercy (q. 19, art. 6; q. 21). Aquinas attempts to show all this not in q. 2, but in qq. 3–11, qq. 14–26. The preceding and intermediate questions, qq. 1, 2, 12 and 13, concern our knowledge of God. qq. 29, 39–41, 44–48, 103–105 supply key further clarifications.

(b)   Ontological arguments

Peter van Inwagen

The label 'the ontological argument' was invented by Immanuel Kant,[1] who used this phrase as a name for an argument he knew from the writings of Christian Wolff. Wolff's argument was derived, via Leibniz, from an argument in the fifth of Descartes's *Meditations* (1635). The argument of the Fifth Meditation may well have been original with Descartes, but it is possible that he had heard some account of a similar argument that had been devised in the eleventh century by Anselm, monk of the Abbey of Bec in Normandy (and later Archbishop of Canterbury).

In a work called *Proslogion*, written about 1080, Anselm argued that if one denies the existence of 'something a greater than which cannot be conceived' one must thereby contradict oneself. For, Anselm argued, if one holds that this 'something a greater than which cannot be conceived' exists in the mind alone – that it does not exist in reality as well as in the mind – one has, in effect, claimed to be able to do the impossible: to be able to conceive of something *greater* than something a greater than which cannot be conceived. All one would have to do to accomplish this would be to think of that same 'something' as existing in reality, for existence in reality is greater than existence in the mind alone. Therefore, this 'something' must exist, since it cannot consistently be thought of as not existing.

This argument was immediately attacked by a monk called Gaunilo, and philosophers have been attacking it ever since. (Schopenhauer called it a 'charming joke'.) Gaunilo argued, very acutely, that Anselm's reasoning, if it were valid, could be used to prove the existence of a greatest conceivable *anything* – an island than which no greater could be conceived, for example. Anselm replied to Gaunilo, but many of the crucial points in his reply are very hard to understand, and this is particularly true of his reply to the 'greatest conceivable island' difficulty. Two hundred years later, St Thomas Aquinas presented a refutation of Anselm's argument, but his 'refutation' does not seem to do justice to the argument, and it is in fact unlikely that he actually had access to the text of *Proslogion*. Nevertheless, the authority of Thomas was so great that his refutation of the argument became more or less standard in the Middle Ages. (It is therefore entirely possible that Descartes had heard something of Thomas's statement of Anselm's argument from his Jesuit schoolmasters at La Flèche.)

Descartes's version of the argument proceeds as follows. Consider the concept of a supremely perfect being, or a being that possesses every perfection. (The concept of a supremely perfect being plays the role in Descartes's argument that is played by the concept of a greatest conceivable thing in Anselm's.) But existence (Anselm's 'existence in reality') is a perfection. (Cf. Anselm: Existence in reality is greater than existence in the mind alone.) Therefore, just as shape is a part of the concept of a body, existence is a part of the concept of a supremely perfect being: just as one cannot conceive of a body that lacks a shape, one cannot conceive of a supremely perfect being that lacks existence. Therefore, a supremely perfect being exists.

Kant claimed to have found a logical flaw in Descartes's argument,[2] and his criticism of the argument immediately became more or less the standard one and remained the 'textbook' refutation of the argument for two hundred years. (But essentially the same criticism had been communicated to Descartes by at least two of his contemporaries, Caterus and Pierre Gassendi.) Kant makes several points against the argument. The remainder of this paragraph is an adaptation of one of them.[3] Let us grant that Descartes's argument establishes that one cannot consistently think of a supremely perfect being that does not exist – or, to speak impersonally, that the idea of a supremely perfect being that does not exist is not a consistent idea (just as the idea of a body that has no shape is not a consistent idea); from this it does not follow that a supremely perfect being *exists*. That this does not follow is easy to see, for the idea of an X that does not exist is an inconsistent idea, no matter what X may be. The idea of a non-existent angel is an inconsistent idea, for nothing could possibly be a non-existent angel: the description 'non-existent angel' could not possibly apply to anything. But this does not constitute a proof that there are angels, and neither does the fact that 'non-existent supremely perfect being' is an inconsistent description constitute a proof that there is a supremely perfect being.

Interestingly enough, however, there is a logically unobjectionable argument that can be expressed in words very close to those of Descartes's argument.[4] (Many modern commentators claim, and with considerable justification, to have found *two* versions of the ontological argument in Anselm's *Proslogion*, the argument discussed above and another. It is interesting to note that the argument that will be discussed below is in many ways very similar to the 'second' Anselmian argument.)

In order to state this argument, we require some technical terms. A property or attribute is *essential* to a thing x if x could not exist without having it. Thus, snubnosedness and intellectual honesty are attributes of Socrates, but ones that do not belong to him essentially, since he might have had a long, straight nose or have enjoyed a successful career as a sophist. But creaturehood and animality are essential attributes of Socrates, since, no matter how the world might be, if Socrates exists at all, he must be a created being and an animal. Once we have noted that an attribute of an object may or may not belong to that object essentially, it becomes plausible to suppose that Descartes was mistaken in defining a perfect being (from now on, we shall omit the qualification 'supremely') as a being that possesses every perfection. Rather, one should define a perfect being as a being that possesses every perfection *essentially*. Suppose for the sake of the illustration that wisdom is a perfection. We should not want to count a being as perfect if, although it was wise as things stood, it *might have been* foolish: a perfect being must be one that is not only wise but one the very nature of which is inseparable from wisdom. And so for all other perfections. It is, moreover, implausible to suppose that existence is a perfection, for existence belongs to everything, even the lowliest worm, the most ephemeral bubble, and the most rebellious fallen angel. It is much more plausible to say that *necessary* existence is a perfection, for if a thing exists necessarily − if its non-existence is impossible − then its existence is a consequence of its nature alone, and is entirely independent of the actions of other beings and the accidents of history.

If we define a perfect being as a being that possesses every perfection essentially, and if we suppose that necessary existence is a perfection, then the existence of a perfect being follows from a single premise: that a perfect being (so defined) is possible. (That is, that a perfect being is not intrinsically impossible, in the sense in which a round square or shapeless body is intrinsically impossible.) Or, at any rate, it follows given the set of rules for reasoning about necessity that logicians call 'S5'. There are weaker sets of rules on which this conclusion does not follow, but most philosophers and logicians regard it as at least extremely plausible to suppose that S5 comprises the correct set of rules for reasoning about necessity.

That the existence of a perfect being follows from the possibility of a perfect being may be proved as follows. If a perfect being is possible, then a perfect being exists in some possible world (that is, at least some among the intrinsically possible ways for reality to be include the existence of a perfect being). If a perfect being exists in some possible world, then in that world it is not only existent but necessarily existent – necessary existence being a perfection. Necessary existence, however, is the same thing as existence in all possible worlds: a necessarily existent being is just a being whose non-existence is impossible, and the impossible is just that which is not included in any of the possible ways for reality to be (which is not included in any possible world). A being that exists necessarily in some possible world *w*, however, must exist in *this* world, our world, the actual world – for if that being did not exist in the actual world, it would not be *necessarily* existent in *w*; that is, it would not be true in *w* that it existed in every possible world. This being, moreover, must not only exist in this, the actual, world, but it must have all perfections in this world – for if it lacked some perfection in this world, it would not have that perfection *essentially* in *w*. If, for example, wisdom is a perfection, a being that was foolish in the actual world could not be *essentially* wise in *w*, for the inhabitants of *w* could say truly of that being that it *could have been* foolish (our world being, from their point of view, one of the ways reality could have been). If, therefore, there is a possible world *w* in which there is a necessarily existent being that has all perfections essentially – that is to say, if a perfect being is possible – there must *actually* be a being that has all perfections. It is not difficult to show, by extending this line of reasoning, that this being must not only actually exist and actually have all perfections, but that it must actually be *necessarily* existent and actually have all perfections *essentially*. In sum, given only that it is not intrinsically impossible for a perfect being to exist, a perfect being actually does exist.

But what about the antecedent of this conditional? Is it true? Is it so much as possible for a perfect being to exist? Such questions, questions concerning the possibility of concepts remote from the uses of everyday life, are not easy to answer. One way to see why this is so is to reflect on the fact that for any such concept, it is usually easy to find a second concept so related to the first that it is demonstrable that exactly one of the two concepts is possible – although neither of the two concepts bears any obvious mark either of possibility or impossibility. This is certainly the case with the concept of a perfect being. For consider the concept of a 'correct atheist', the concept, that is, of someone who believes, and rightly, that there is no perfect being. If the concept 'correct atheist' is a possible concept, the concept 'perfect being' is an impossible concept. (For if 'correct atheist' is a possible concept, then in some possible world there is no perfect being; and, as we have seen, if 'perfect being' is a possible concept, then in no possible world is there no perfect being.) And if 'perfect being' is an impossible concept, 'correct atheist' is obviously a possible concept. One of these two concepts is therefore possible and the other impossible.

But which is which? There seems to be no way to answer this question. At any rate, no one knows how to answer it. Our conclusion must be that, although there is a version of the ontological argument that is without logical flaw, the argument proceeds from a premise such that there is no way to decide whether it is true. Or no way other than this way: someone may somehow know that there is a perfect being; that person will, of course, know that a perfect being is possible. It would seem, therefore, to be impossible to know that the premise of the ontological argument is true without first knowing that its conclusion is true. The ontological argument, therefore, cannot serve as a means by which someone can pass from not knowing whether a perfect being exists to knowing that a perfect being exists.

Notes

1 *Critique of Pure Reason* (1781 and 1787), A591/B619.
2 *Critique of Pure Reason*, A592–602/B620–630.
3 A595–596/B623–624.
4 The argument that will be discussed in the sequel is based on an argument presented in chapter 10 of Alvin Plantinga's *The Nature of Necessity* (Oxford, 1974).

(c) Design arguments

Mark Wynn

In the course of human history, few ideas have proved more deeply fascinating than the claim which stands as the conclusion of the argument from design: the world is the product of benign contrivance. Of course, there are other arguments which also seek to establish the existence of a beneficent deity, on *a posteriori* grounds,[1] but the design argument enshrines this claim more clearly by virtue of its starting-point: it is the apparent order and purposiveness of the world which the argument sets out to explain, and in consequence it is the intelligence and benevolence of the divinity, rather than for example his self-sufficiency, which provide the argument with its basic explanatory resource.[2]

Such arguments are as old as Western philosophy. They are found in the works of the pre-Socratics,[3] and receive clear expression in the writings of Plato. For instance, in Plato's work *The Laws*, it is suggested that the existence and beneficence of the gods may be inferred from the regular movement of the heavenly bodies.[4] Aristotle has also been taken as a source for the argument from design. Of course, the God of the *Metaphysics* is not a providential deity; but Aristotle does maintain that nature is ordered teleologically, and his thinking on this point was to exercise a profound influence on the natural theology of later, Christian authors. For instance, in Aquinas we find a clear association between the thought that individual things, including inanimate things, act for a purpose, and the thought that these things are guided by an intelligence. Thus he writes: 'Goal-directed behaviour is observed in all bodies obeying natural laws, even when they lack awareness. Their behaviour hardly ever varies and practically always turns out well, showing that they truly tend to their goals and do not merely hit them by accident. But nothing can tend to a goal except it be directed by someone with awareness and understanding.'[5] Here two sorts of consideration are cited in support of the idea of design: the fact that things act regularly, and the fact that they act for what is best. These same considerations are evident in *The Laws*, in so far as the regularity of the world is taken as a mark of the benevolence of its source.

In the seventeenth century, in the wake of the new, mechanistic physics. of Newton and others, the design argument entered a new phase. Where the ancients had tended to consider the universe by analogy with an organism, it now became common to think of it as a machine, so providing the argument with a new analogical foundation.[6] After all, in the case of human activity, it seems clear enough that mechanisms result not by chance but from the purposeful exercise of intelligence; and by analogy we might suppose that the universe derives from an extra-mundane intelligence. Thus in Hume's *Dialogues*, the figure of Cleanthes urges his interlocutors to compare the universe to 'one great machine' and to marvel at the 'curious adapting of means to ends, throughout all nature'.[7] The same sort of appeal to a mechanical analogy is evident, famously, in William Paley's proposal that the world resembles a watch.[8] Despite this change in the scientific basis of the argument, it retains its basic structure. Thus, in these remarks of Hume there is an appeal once more to regularity and teleology. And in Paley's writings, too, we find reference both to the regular movement of the heavenly bodies and to the intricate structure, apparently teleological, of individual organisms.

In the view of many commentators, Hume's arguments in the first *Enquiry* and, above all, in the *Dialogues* have decisively refuted this form of the design argument.[9] Through the character of Philo, Hume argues variously that the analogy between the universe and the products of human agency is weak (like any comparison between the parts of a thing and the thing as a whole, where the parts comprise an insignificant portion of the whole);[10] that even if the analogy should work, there are other, competing analogies which are at least as persuasive (perhaps the universe is more akin to an animal or vegetable?);[11] that this sort of argument is misconceived in principle (above all because we have no experience of the origin of worlds, and therefore have no experiential basis for the thought that worlds like ours are more likely than not to derive from design);[12] and that the analogy is anyway of no use to theology, since it invites an anthropomorphic conception of the deity (indeed, Hume suggests, if we persist with the analogy, we ought to postulate a number of such deities, since human artefacts are generally made in collaboration).[13] Hume also explores the thought that a merely random exploration of possibilities will hit upon an orderly outcome given sufficient time,[14] so removing any need for the design hypothesis. And he suggests that while the world, with its imperfections, may be compatible with belief in beneficent design, it can hardly provide a secure basis for that conviction.[15]

Later commentators have argued that, even if the design argument is able to resist Hume's criticisms, the work of Darwin and his successors has put an end to whatever plausibility it may have had. Darwin's theory, together with subsequent elaborations, threatens the argument at a number of levels. First of all, the theory proposes that certain species have become extinct, a view which appears to undermine decisively the idea that in general creatures have been contrived so that they can flourish in their respective environments. Next, the theory argues that new species emerge over time, and that maladapted variations on existing types are eliminated, on account of their inability to compete effectively for scarce resources. Such a view implies that the neat fit between creatures and their environments which we observe in the present may reflect, not so much the working out of a beneficent purpose, but rather the extermination of weaker, less competitive forms of life, and the survival of their 'fitter' counterparts. Moreover, given the development of genetic theory, it now seems that the generation of new creaturely types is in large part a random process. So, from the perspective of evolutionary theory, we may wish to say that the adaptedness of creatures to their environments, which so impressed Paley and others, is best understood not as a matter of contrivance, but in terms of a random exploration of possibilities, coupled with a selection mechanism which ensures the elimination of any emergent characteristic which lacks survival value.[16]

Not surprisingly, modern discussion of the design argument has concentrated on the question of whether it can be plausibly reconstructed in a post-Humean, post-Darwinian form. Some scholars point towards alleged lacunae in the Darwinian account, but more commonly it is argued that there are certain general facts about the world which are suggestive of design, but necessarily elude Darwinian kinds of explanation, since they are presupposed in the processes described by Darwin. In particular, it has been said that Darwinian kinds of mechanism cannot account for the over-arching framework of natural law which undergirds the process of evolution. This sort of broadening of the design argument's focus is evident in the writings of, for instance, Tennant, Hambourger, Swinburne, and Walker.[17] As we have seen, this sort of interest in the regularity of the world has clear antecedents in earlier versions of the argument.

As Kant anticipated, developments in science have continued to prompt new formulations of the argument.[18] Most notably, a range of new design arguments have been formulated in response to the proposal of cosmologists that there is a delicate connection between the character of the cosmos as a whole and its suitability for the development of life.[19] It seems for instance that life would not have emerged in a universe with a rather different expansion rate, or rather different ratio of hydrogen to helium in its early moments, to name just two examples from many. There are two widely canvassed explanations of this 'fine-tuning' of the universe to the possibility of life. Some commentators suggest that we should postulate many universes. In that case, even if the conditions required for life are unlikely to be found in any one universe, it may be that they are likely to arise at some point within such an ensemble of universes. (Our presence in this special sort of universe then follows from the tautology that we can only exist in a universe consistent with our own existence.[20]) On the other side, it is said that this sort of 'explanation' is unacceptable, above all because it violates, in spectacular fashion, Ockham's Razor, and that we should therefore explain the phenomena of fine-tuning in terms of design. This debate continues.[21]

The fine-tuning idea provides another way of evading Darwinian kinds of criticism. For its basic claim is that Darwinian evolution, which is enacted on this planet, presupposes a broader process of cosmological evolution, which in turn points towards design. The idea also sheds interesting light on another enduring criticism of the design argument, whose precursor is evident in Hume. It is sometimes said that the argument from design requires the use of *a priori* probabilities — since we have not observed the origins of universes, the relevant probabilities cannot be of the relative frequency type, or grounded in some other way in the empirical data. But then, it is said, in the absence of some empirical reference point, are we not left merely with competing intuitions, and no real basis for making any judgement of probability?[22]

This is perhaps the single most important issue in contemporary debate concerning the design argument. Swinburne's proposal that simplicity can serve as an overriding measure of *a priori* probability has provided the principal focus of this discussion.[23] Whatever the merits of this suggestion, the fine-tuning argument seems to point towards a relatively unproblematic way of introducing *a priori* probabilities. For the adjustment of cosmological conditions to the possibility of life which forms the basis of the argument is spelt out in numerical terms. In turn, this enables us to say, for example, that the various possible expansion rates of the universe at the time of the Big Bang have the same probability *a priori*, which suggests that there is only a low probability that the right expansion rate will arise by chance. Analogously, we might suppose not merely that we cannot think of any reason for distinguishing between the *a priori* probabilities of a square whose sides are 1.2 cm in length and one whose sides are 1.3 cm, but that there cannot be any such reason. The possibilities in cases of this kind are so closely alike that any consideration which is relevant to the *a priori* probability of the one seems bound to be relevant in just the same degree to the *a priori* probability of the other.[24]

Of course, this leaves unresolved the *a priori* probability of a designer. But unless there are good reasons for supposing that this probability is exceptionally low, we should allow relative predictive power to determine the relative overall probability of design and various competing hypotheses.[25] Notice that at this point the argument also seems to be freed from another Humean-style criticism, concerning the availability of alternative analogies. For if an animal or vegetable should have an inherent tendency to produce a universe with such an expansion rate, then we will merely have replicated the fact which we wanted explained; and if such a thing should have the ability to produce other expansion rates as well, then we will want to know why it should have hit upon the particular rate which is required for the development of life, granted that it lacks the intelligence we associate with personal agents.

No doubt theological sceptics will continue to question the argument's relevance, saying that at most it can establish the existence of a finite artificer, not an agent who would be worthy of worship (although interestingly, Swinburne's argument aims to establish the infinity of the designer). And it is certain that philosophical criticism of the argument will also persist. In my own view, the argument's difficulties are in the end external to the argument itself. They have to do with the thought that evil makes the idea of benevolent design at best implausible, and at worst offensive.[26] And they have to do with the risk that an apologetic strategy which rests on the design argument will result in a distorted piety, not because the argument's understanding of God is simply mistaken, but because it needs to be supplemented, by other, religiously richer ways of conceiving of God.[27]

Notes

1 That is, by reference to our experience of the world.
2 Notice too the suggestion that the 'intelligence' here might not be an individual mind but creatively efficacious evaluative ideals. See for instance John Leslie, *Universes* (London, 1988) and S. Clark, 'Limited explanations' in Dudley Knowles (ed.), *Explanation and Its Limits* (Cambridge, 1990).
3 See Anaxagoras, in J. Barnes, *Early Greek Philosophy* (Harmondsworth, 1987).
4 *Laws*, Book X.
5 Of course, this constitutes Aquinas's 'Fifth way'. For discussion, see Anthony Kenny, *The Five Ways* (London, 1969), ch. 6.
6 For a description of these developments see R. H. Hurlbutt, *Hume, Newton, and the Design Argument* (Lincoln, NE, 1965). For a discussion of the resulting deism see P. Byrne, *Natural Religion and the Nature of Religion: The Legacy of Deism* (London, 1989).
7 Hume, *Dialogues Concerning Natural Religion*, ed. Martin Bell (Harmondsworth, Penguin, 1990), p. 53. First published 1779.
8 See the opening of Paley's *Natural Theology*.
9 See for instance J. C. A. Gaskin, *Hume's Philosophy of Religion* (2nd edn; London, 1988) and G. Doore, 'The argument from design: some better reasons for agreeing with Hume', *Religious Studies* 16 (1980).
10 Hume, op. cit., p. 58.
11 Ibid., pp. 86–91.

12 Ibid., p. 60.

13 Ibid., pp. 77–8.

14 Ibid., pp. 92–5.

15 Ibid., p. 121.

16 For a modern statement of the Darwinian view, and its implications for the design argument, see R. Dawkins, *The Blind Watchmaker* (Harlow, 1986).

17 F. R. Tennant, *Philosophical Theology*, vol. II (Cambridge, 1930), ch. 6; R. Hambourger, 'The argument from design' in Cora Diamond and Jenny Teichman (eds), *Intention and Intentionality: Essays in Honour of G. E. M. Anscombe* (Brighton, UK, 1979); R. G. Swinburne, *The Existence of God* (revised edn; Oxford, 1991), chs 8–10 and appendices.

18 Hence Kant remarks that the argument 'enlivens the study of nature, just as it itself derives its existence and gains ever new vigour from that source' (*Critique of Pure Reason*, A623/B651).

19 See J. D. Barrow and F. J. Tipler, *The Anthropic Cosmological Principle* (Oxford, 1986). See also I. G. Barbour, *Religion in an Age of Science* (London, 1990), ch. 5 and Leslie, op. cit.

20 For contrasting interpretations of the significance of this fact, see Barrow and Tipler, op. cit., as reviewed in William Lane Craig, 'Barrow and Tipler on the anthropic principle vs. divine design', *British Journal for the Philosophy of Science* **38** (1988).

21 For contrasting readings of the simplicity requirement, see Swinburne, op. cit., pp. 314–22, and W. Drees, *Beyond the Big Bang: Quantum Cosmologists and God* (La Salle, IL, 1990).

22 For sceptical reviews on the value of *a priori* probabilities, at any rate in this context, see R. Prevost, *Probability and Theistic Explanation* (Oxford, 1990), ch. 5, and D. H. Mellor, 'God and probability', *Religious Studies* **5** (1969).

23 For critical responses see J. L. Mackie, *The Miracle of Theism* (Oxford, 1982), pp. 146–9; Anthony O'Hear, *Experience, Explanation and Faith* (London, 1984), pp. 131–43. See also Mark Wynn, 'Some reflections on Richard Swinburne's argument from design', *Religious Studies* **19** (1993).

24 For more extended discussion, see Mark Wynn, '*A priori* judgments and the argument from design', *International Journal for Philosophy of Religion* **39** (1996).

25 Bayes's Theorem states that:

$$P(h/e.k) = \frac{P(h/k) \cdot P(e/h.k),}{P(e/k)}$$

where e, h, and k are respectively the evidence, the hypothesis, and background knowledge, and $P(h/k)$ is read as 'the probability of the hypothesis on background knowledge'. In calculating the relative explanatory power of the design and other hypotheses, $P(e/k)$ will cancel out.

26 But notice the possible relevence of fine-tuning considerations for a theodicy. See A. Olding, *Modern Biology and Natural Theology* (London, 1991).

27 See M. J. Buckley, *At the Origins of Modern Atheism* (New Haven, CT, 1987).

(d)   God and religious experience

William P. Alston

An argument from religious experience that is parallel to the cosmological and design arguments would start with a kind of experience that is specified purely subjectively, in terms of its qualitative character, and then argue that it can only be adequately explained in terms of divine agency. But that is not the way people who base a belief in God's existence on experience typically think of the matter. Rather than supposing they need this, or any other, *argument* for the existence of God, they take themselves, or others, to have been directly aware of God. And just as actually perceiving a certain tree is the best way of knowing the tree exists, so it is here. This is the kind of basis for belief in God's existence that I will be considering.

The term 'religious experience' can be applied to any experiences one has in connection with one's religious life, including a sense of guilt or release, joys, longings, and a sense of gratitude. But the usual philosophical concern is with experiences taken by the subject to be an awareness of God. To cast the net as widely as possible, let's understand 'God' to range over any *supreme reality*, however construed.

Here is an anonymous report of such an experience, taken from James (1982).

> All at once I . . . felt the presence of God – I tell of the thing just as I was conscious of it – as if his goodness and his power were penetrating me altogether . . . Then, slowly, the ecstasy left my heart; that is, I felt that God had withdrawn the communion which he had granted . . . I asked myself if it were possible that Moses on Sinai could have had a more intimate communication with God. I think it well to add that in this ecstasy of mine God had neither form, color, odor, nor taste; moreover, that the feeling of his presence was accompanied by no determinate localization . . . But the more I seek words to express this intimate intercourse, the more I feel the impossibility of describing the thing by

any of our usual images. At bottom the expression most apt to render what I felt is this: God was present, though invisible; he fell under no one of my senses, yet my consciousness perceived him. (pp. 67–8)

This report is typical in several respects.

1. The awareness of God is *experiential*, as contrasted with thinking of God or reasoning about God. Like sense experience it seems to involve a *presentation* of the object.

2. The experience is *direct*. It seems to the subject that she is *immediately* aware of God rather than through being aware of something else. It seems to be analogous to seeing another human being in front of you, rather than seeing that person on television. But there are more indirect experiences of God. For example:

There was a mysterious presence in nature ... which was my greatest delight, especially when as happened from time to time, *nature became lit up from inside* with something that came from beyond itself. (Timothy Beardsworth, *A Sense of Presence* [Oxford, 1997], p. 19)

3. The experience is lacking in sensory content. It is a *non-sensory presentation* of God. But there are also experiences of God that involve sense perception.

I awoke and looking out of my window saw what I took to be a luminous star which gradually came nearer, and appeared as a soft slightly blurred white light. I was seized with violent trembling, but had no fear. I knew that what I felt was great awe. This was followed by a sense of overwhelming love coming to me, and going out from me, then of great compassion from this Outer Presence. (Beardsworth, op. cit., p. 30)

4. It is a *focal* experience, one in which the awareness of God attracts one's attention so strongly as to blot out everything else. But there are also milder experiences that persist over long periods of time as a *background* to everyday experiences.

God surrounds me like the physical atmosphere. He is closer to me than my own breath. In him literally I live and move and have my being. (William James, *The Varieties of Religious Experience* [New York, 1982], p. 71)

This discussion will be limited to *direct*, *non-sensory*, *focal* experiences, since they involve the most striking claims to be experientially aware of God.

Much of the literature on this subject concentrates on *mystical experience*, understood as a state in which all distinctions are transcended, even the distinction between subject and object. The person is aware only of a seamless unity. This falls under our general category, for it is typically taken by the mystic to be a direct non-sensory awareness of supreme reality. But experiences like this pose special problems of their own. In what follows I will be thinking of more moderate cases like the ones I have cited, in which the subject does not seem to lose her own identity. Nevertheless, I will use the term *mystical experience* to designate what is taken by the subject to be a direct experience of God. And since these subjects suppose themselves to be aware of God in a way analogous to that in which one is aware of things in one's environment through sense perception, I will also use the term *mystical perception* in this connection. (See William Alston, *Perceiving God* [Ithaca, NY, 1991], ch. 1 for a defence of the use of term 'perception' in this application.)

Our specific concern here is with the idea that mystical experience is a source of knowledge about God, more specifically the knowledge that God exists. Since the subject of the experience takes herself to be perceiving God, she naturally takes it that God exists. One cannot genuinely perceive something that does not exist. But, of course, the fact that she supposes this does not guarantee that it is so. Even with sense experience one can be deceived as to what, if anything, one is perceiving. One can suppose that one saw, at dusk, that there was a car in the distance when it was actually a cow that one saw. And one can even be subject to complete hallucinations, as when Macbeth falsely takes there to be a dagger in front of him. With both sense experience and mystical experience contradictions between reports prevent us from taking all of them to be veridical. Reports of automobile accidents provide many examples for sense experience. As for mystical experience, there are cases of someone supposing that God told him to murder as many people of a certain sort as possible, in contrast to awarenesses of God as supremely loving. The people in question can't be genuinely perceiving God in both cases. Thus the main issue to be addressed in assessing the claim that mystical experience enables us to know that God exists is this. *Are mystical experiences ever, or significantly often, genuine experiences of God?*

In discussing this question I will first look at reasons there are for a positive answer, and then consider reasons for a negative answer together with responses to those reasons by supporters of mystical perception.

The most important philosophical positive reason is this. Any supposition that one perceives something to be the case – that there is a zebra in front of one or that God is strengthening one – is *prima facie* justified. That is, one is justified in supposing this unless there are strong enough reasons to the contrary. In the zebra case these would include reasons for thinking that there is no zebra in the vicinity and reasons for supposing oneself to be subject to hallucinations because of some drug. According to this position, beliefs formed on the basis of experience possess an initial credibility by virtue of their origin. They are innocent until proven guilty.

This position has been widely advocated for sense perception, e.g. in Roderick M. Chisholm, *Theory of Knowledge* (2nd edn; Englewood Cliffs, NJ, 1977), chapter 4. (See the references there to other advocates.) It is applied to mystical perception in Richard Swinburne, *The Existence of God* (Oxford, 1979), chapter 13, where it is termed 'The Principle of Credulity'. In Alston (op. cit.) it is given a more social twist. The claim is that any socially established belief-forming practice is to be accepted as a source of (generally) true beliefs unless there are sufficient reasons against its reliability. The main argument for the 'innocent until proven guilty' position is that unless we accord a *prima facie* credibility to experiential reports, we can have no sufficient reason to trust *any* experiential source of beliefs. This is the only alternative to a thoroughgoing scepticism about experience.

On the negative side a number of arguments have been put forward, most of which turn on alleged differences between sense experience and mystical experience. They are critically discussed in Alston (op. cit.), chapters 5–7 and William Wainwright, *Mysticism* (Brighton, UK, 1981), chapter 3.

1. Most obviously, there are many striking differences between sensory and mystical experience. (1) Sense experience is a common possession of mankind, while mystical experience is not. (2) Sense experience is continuously and unavoidably present during all our waking hours, whereas for most people mystical experience is, at best, enjoyed rarely. (3) Sense experience, especially visual, is vivid and richly detailed, while mystical experience is meagre and obscure. These differences certainly show that mystical experience provides much less information than its sensory analogue, but why suppose that it does not give one knowledge of the existence of God?

2. A frequent charge is that since mystical experience can be completely explained in terms of this-worldly factors, we cannot suppose that it constitutes a genuine awareness of anything supernatural. It is a basic principle of perception that we cannot be perceiving anything that does not make a causal contribution to the experience involved. If a dog is on the other side of a solid wall from me, then I can't actually see the dog, whatever my experience is like. But if mystical experience can be completely explained without mentioning God, then God is not among the causes of the experience.

There is more than one response to this. (1) We are not actually in possession of any purely naturalistic explanation of mystical experience. At most there are programmatic suggestions of the form such explanations might take. (2) The strongest response is this. The case of sense perception shows us that the object perceived need not be among the *proximate* causes of experience. Those causes are all within the subject's brain, which is not itself perceived. What we sensorily perceive is located further back along the causal chain leading to the experience. Hence even if the proximate causes of mystical experience are all within the natural world, the possibility remains that God figures further back among the causes of the experience in such a way as to be perceived in having that experience.

3. An important difference between sensory and mystical perception is that there are effective intersubjective tests for accuracy for the former but not for the latter. When someone claims to have seen a certain person at a party at a certain time, there are procedures that can, in favourable cases, yield a conclusive verdict on that claim. We can look into whether qualified observers who were at the party at that time saw the person. If guests signed a guest register, we can check that. But nothing like this is available for mystical perception. There *are* checks that are commonly applied in mystical communities, e.g. conformity with the background system of religious doctrine and conducivity to spiritual development. But they are far from yielding comparable results. And there is nothing like the check of other observers we have for sense-perceptual reports. If I claim to have been aware of God's sustaining me in being, there are no conditions such that if someone else who satisfies those conditions is not (at that time or at any other time) aware of God's sustaining her in being, I will take that as showing that I was mistaken. The critic argues that this discredits the claim of the mystic to be aware of an objective reality. If my claims to perceive something objective cannot be validated by intersubjective agreement, they have no standing.

The best response of the mystic is to charge the critic with *epistemic imperialism*, subjecting the outputs of one belief-forming practice to the requirements of another. The critic's complaint is that a mystical perception cannot lay claim to putting its subject into effective touch with objective reality because she cannot validate this status in the way she can with sense perceptions. Note that there are unproblematic sources of belief that work quite differently from sense experience in this respect. Consider introspection, one's awareness of one's own conscious states. My report that I feel upset cannot be validated by considering whether someone else, who satisfies certain conditions, feels upset (mine or his). But it would be absurd to reject introspection as a source of knowledge because of the unavailability of such tests. Unless the critic can give a convincing reason for supposing that the criteria available for sense perception constitute a necessary condition for *any* experiential access to objective reality, he is guilty of epistemic *chauvinism* (to change the metaphor) in rejecting mystical perception for this reason. Epistemic chauvinism is also exhibited by criticism 1, as I, in effect, pointed out in asking why one should suppose that a mode of experience different from sense experience in the ways specified should be less likely to be a source of knowledge.

3

The attributes of God

(a)   Simpleness

David B. Burrell CSC

Since the very idea of divine simpleness has come under scrutiny of late, usually with a strong odour of incomprehensibility, it behoves us to sketch the origins of this teaching of classical philosophical theology. For like many other such teachings, it represents a strategy on the part of thinkers in the Jewish, Christian and Muslim traditions to employ the philosophical tools available to them to express the utterly unique relation of the universe to its free creator, and thereby to gain some insight into that One from whom all-that-is freely comes. In the early medieval period, when the rediscovery of Hellenic philosophy under the aegis of faith made such a recasting imperative, thinkers of the three Abrahamic faiths were faced with a common task, and some of them were in literary contact with the others.[1] The task was twofold: first, accounting for the origin of the universe itself, when a thinker as formidable as Aristotle had simply presumed it to be everlasting; and then to parry the emanationist account of Plotinus, which seemed more elegant philosophically than the apparently anthropomorphic picture of a creator willing the universe into being. The first was less difficult on the face of it, because Neoplatonic thinkers had recognized that the 'natural desire to know' which Aristotle had identified in human intelligence would have to push his own metaphysics to some account of origins. It was this which Plotinus brilliantly supplied, perhaps as a direct counter to the assertions of the Hebrew scriptures, introduced into the Hellenic world assertively with Christianity. If the one God of Jews and Christians presented itself as the origin of all-that-is, Plotinus's One would be such a transcendent source as well.[2]

The key word is 'transcendent', for Plato's *Good*, which provides the background for Plotinus's *One*, recommended itself to thinkers from the two scriptural traditions of Bible and Qur'an as a way of conveying this God whose very presence in Torah, Jesus, and Qur'an signalled that same God's utter 'distinction' from the universe itself, which in some fashion emanated from God. Like Plotinus's One, the God of Abraham and free creator of all cannot be part of creation.[3] When thinkers in these scriptural traditions sought to characterize such a divinity, however, they could not have immediate recourse to Plotinus's One, since the emanation of the universe from this One, though imaging an overflow of goodness, was also modelled on logical deduction so as to forge a necessary link between creator and creation. So the demands of revelation required adapting the resources of this intellectual tradition to characterize a relation between the universe and its origin which respected both the transcendence and the freedom of the creator.

The Muslim thinker Ibn Sina (Avicenna) introduced a distinction at the heart of being itself, between *necessary* and *possible* being, which he proposed to do justice to the Qur'an's insistence that God alone is uncreated and all else comes from this one creator. On Avicenna's account, God alone is *necessary*, for only God simply *is*, while everything else is at best *possibly* existing. An infelicity of his account (which his Muslim critic Ibn Rushd [Averroës] was to exploit) lies in its stark essentialism: *existing* is said to 'come to' possible beings, which grammatically suggests that 'possible beings' in some sense must *be* for existing to come to *them*.[4] Moses Maimonides (1135–1204) was content to endorse Avicenna's account in his *Guide of the Perplexed*, allowing the assertion that essence and existing are identical in God to offer an adequate philosophical expression of the divine transcendence.[5] It fell to Aquinas (in his *De ente et essentia* [*On Being and Essence*]) to recast Avicenna's argument in a way designed expressly to overcome this infelicity. He deliberately enhanced Aristotle's metaphysics by expanding his basic distinction of potency/act to locate *esse* as the act to which *essentia* (essence) is in potency, thereby removing any hint of *esse* (or 'act of existing') being an *accident* which 'comes to' an essence.[6]

It is this distinction of *being* (or *esse*) from *essence*, suitably recast, which provides Aquinas with the philosophical tools to characterize divinity in a way that distinguishes it from everything else that is, yet derives from it, giving us the teaching of divine simpleness. Yet everything turns on our understanding of God as creator, since any other route to God will end up postulating a divinity which is either part of the universe or pictured over against it after the fashion of an additional being. Robert Sokolowski introduces his celebrated 'distinction' of God from the universe to counter the first alternative, which he descriptively dubs 'pagan', while Kathryn Tanner shows the ineptness of the latter by noting how it violates the rules for discourse about God implicit in the nominal definition of Aquinas which we have seen.[7] Indeed, they come to the same thing, for to picture God as an additional being over against or parallel to the universe itself will be to treat God similarly to objects within the universe, related to the universe itself as objects within the world are related to each other. So to be consistent with our assertion that God is the free creator of all-that-is, presupposing nothing, either from the side of things or in God, we must find a way of uniquely characterizing divinity which escapes having to identify God as we identify objects within the created universe.

That, I submit, is the role of the metaphysical construction of divine simpleness. I prefer the constructed English rendering of *simplicitas* as 'simpleness' to 'simplicity' to remind us that we are dealing with a metaphysical construction.[8] For *simpleness* is not a common notion which we can comprehend other than by attempting to stretch our metaphysical categories to identify this One uniquely. In that sense, 'simple', said of God, is like 'eternal': they are each used of divinity in a way that they cannot be used of anything else; hence 'eternal' cannot be rendered here as 'timeless'. (Aquinas treats such predicates in *Summa Theologiae I*, questions 3–11, setting them off from his treatment of 'divine attributes' in question 13, as if to signal their 'formal' character.[9]) So we cannot say what *simpleness* comes to other than to indicate how it must be said of divinity to identify it uniquely, although that very process will give us some understanding of what we are saying.[10] For to say that God is *simple* (in this metaphysical sense) is to say that this One cannot be located as any other object in the universe can: by spatio-temporal parameters, as an instance of a kind, by genus or species, or finally, by its existential point of origin. And the last negation logically contains all of the preceding negations, as well as assuring us that this divinity is neither part of the universe nor can be pictured over against it. For everything which we know to exist substantially must have come to be, and so cannot itself offer an account of its own existing.

The heart of divine simpleness, then, is the assertion that God's very essence is to exist. There is nothing else we can say, by way of ontologically locating this One in whom Jews, Christians, and Muslims believe, except that 'to be this God is to be to-be'.[11] If we are to call God 'the First', this is what we mean, and not that God can be assimilated to the initial premise in a logical chain of reasoning. If we are to call God 'necessary being', this is what we mean: that God's very essence is to-be, and not that God '"exists" in all possible worlds', or whatever other construction one might give for *necessity* as we try to understand it.[12] All of this should remind us that divine simpleness trumps all other statements about God, including all of the biblical attributes, for it reminds us that whatever is said of God will be said differently from the way it is said of any creature. That is what I mean by insisting on *simpleness* as a 'formal feature': one which governs all discourse about God because it offers a unique characterization of divinity, at least as Jews, Christians and Muslims have traditionally understood God.[13] What interests us here is the way in which this unique characterization functions not only to set off divinity in a way that respects 'the distinction', but also the way it sets off the universe as a new kind of whole. For this may be the most salient fruit which we can realize from what looks to be – and has been taken to be – an abstruse metaphysical quibble.

Here again we shall be rehearsing, in a metaphysical idiom, the doctrine of free creation. That is, if God is uniquely identified as the One whose very essence is to-be, then everything else has been given existence, has been caused to be by God. This assertion has the effect of relating each existing thing to God as the cause of its being, which is to say that divine creating causality is ingredient in the ontological constitution of everything which is. And what this assures, paradoxically enough, is that while each created thing is 'really related' to God as the cause of its being, God is not related in a reciprocal fashion to anything at all. This is the apparently infamous thesis that God is 'not really related to the world' which has been misconstrued by less metaphysically adept readers as signifying God's indifference to the universe.[14] What it rather states is that God and the universe are related by a 'non-reciprocal relation of dependence', which at once blocks naive pictures of God as standing over against the world and at the same time suggests a profound immanence to the world.[15] And the vehicle of that immanence will be the *esse* (or 'act of existence') which is freely bestowed by the One whose essence is to-be on each thing which exists. For the fresh sense of the whole which redounds to the universe from reflections on divine simpleness is precisely that the universe as a whole might not have been, and that this fresh sense of contingency gives a correspondingly fresh valence to *existing* as the free gift of a creating and preserving God.

My focus on Aquinas with his Islamic and Jewish interlocutors has been more strategic than substantive. One may have other metaphysical predilections, as current philosophers who question 'divine simplicity' do indeed have. Their objections to the teaching, as they construe it, turns on ways in which assertions of its proponents, like Aquinas, fail to square with their philosophical 'intuitions'.[16] Yet they expend little effort querying why someone as astute as Aquinas would make what appear to be such logical howlers. But his concern to stretch the philosophical categories inherited from Aristotle via Avicenna was motivated by the preoccupation endemic to all Abrahamic faiths: to avoid idolatry. How can we adapt a set of philosophical categories to characterize the One who is the free source of all-that-is? Whatever one's metaphysical commitments, a philosophical theologian operating from any of those traditions must attend to that demand. The God of whom philosophers pretend to speak cannot simply be

73

reducible to an item within the universe, however large; the God who is free creator of all cannot simply be the greatest of things that we know. So whatever one might make of Aquinas's recasting Avicenna's distinction of essence from *esse*, as a way of characterizing both the transcendence and immanence of creator to creation, if the God of whom one hopes to speak is to be faithful to the revelations of Bible or Qur'an, one must find a way of characterizing divinity which does so uniquely and transcendently. That, I submit, has been the function of the 'doctrine of divine simplicity', and anything which purports to replace it must meet those challenging parameters.

Notes

1 See my *Knowing the Unknowable God* (Notre Dame, 1986).
2 See Lloyd Gerson, *God and Greek Philosophy* (London, 1990), ch. 5: 'Plotinus on the God beyond God', and Pierre Hadot, *Plotinus: The Simplicity of Vision* (Chicago, 1993).
3 For an astute use of 'the distinction' of this God from the world, see Robert Sokolowski's genial *God of Faith and Reason* (Washington, DC, 1994); see also my 'Christian distinction celebrated and expanded' in John Drummond and James Hart (eds), *The Truthful and the Good* (Dordrecht, 1996), pp. 191–206.
4 See Fazlur Rahman, 'Essence and existence in Avicenna', *Mediaeval and Renaissance Studies* 4 (1958), pp. 1–16. For Averroës' critique, see Simon Van Den Bergh (ed. and trans.), *Averroës Tahafut al-Tahafut* (Cambridge, 1978).
5 *Guide of the Perplexed*, trans. Schlomo Pines (Chicago, 1963), 1.62. See my 'Aquinas' debt to Maimonides' in Ruth Link-Salinger et al. (eds), *A Straight Path: Studies in Medieval Philosophy and Culture* (Washington, DC, 1989), pp. 37–48.
6 See my 'Essence and existence in Avicenna and Greek philosophy', *Mélanges Institut Dominicaine d'Etudes Orientales* [Cairo] 17 (1986), pp. 53–66.
7 Sokolowski (see note 3 above), and Kathryn Tanner, *God and Creation in Christian Theology* (Oxford, 1988).
8 Timothy McDermott introduces this term in his translation of *Summa Theologiae* I, 2–11: *Existence and Nature of God* (New York, 1964).
9 This structural point has been made by Mark Jordan in his 'Names of God and the being of names' in Alfred Freddoso (ed.), *Existence and Nature of God* (Notre Dame, 1983), pp. 161–90; it guides my presentation in *Aquinas: God and Action* (Notre Dame, 1979).
10 For an extensive and constructive treatment of this issue, see Barry Miller, *A Most Unlikely God* (Notre Dame, 1996).
11 See my *Aquinas: God and Action*, ch. 2.
12 Robert Adams acknowledges this in 'Divine Necessity' in his *The Virtue of Faith* (New York, 1987), pp. 209–20: 'I believe the most plausible form of the doctrine of divine necessity is the Thomistic view' (p. 209). He mis-states that view, however, as asserting 'that God's existence follows necessarily from his essence'. As Brian Davies notes, what Aquinas 'says is that God is neither made to be by anything nor able to be made by anything. And, in spite of what writers like Penelhum argue, this is not to hold that the fact of God's existence

is deducible from his nature': see 'Classical theism and the Doctrine of Divine Simplicity' in Brian Davies (ed.), *Language, Meaning and God* (London, 1987), p. 64.

13 Eddy Zemach, 'Wittgenstein's Philosophy of the Mystical' in Irving Copi (ed.), *Essays on Wittgenstein's 'Tractatus'* (New York, 1966), pp. 359–76.

14 See my *Aquinas: God and Action*, ch. 7, for an exposé of the critique of 'process theologians'.

15 See the Teape lectures by Sara Grant RSCJ, *Towards an Alternative Theology: Confessons of a Non-dualist Christian* (Bangalore, 1991), p. 48; or a summary in David Burrell CSC and Elena Malits CSC, *Original Peace: Restoring God's Creation* (New York, 1997), ch. 7: 'The Creator and creation'.

16 For example, see Alvin Plantinga, *Does God Have a Nature?* (Milwaukee, 1980); Christopher Hughes, *On a Complex Theory of a Simple God* (Ithaca, NY, 1989); and William Mann, 'Divine Simplicity', *Religious Studies* 18 (1982), pp. 451–71.

(b)   Eternality

Paul Helm

In the history of thought during the Christian era about God's relation to time there have been two contrasting, *prima facie* incompatible views, and this divergence is reflected in contemporary debate on the issue. According to the first view, God exists in timeless eternity; in the classic words of Boethius,

> It is the common judgement, then, of all creatures that live by reason that God is eternal. So let us consider the nature of eternity, for this will make clear to us both the nature of God and his manner of knowing. Eternity, then, is the complete, simultaneous and perfect possession of everlasting life; this will be clear from a comparison with creatures that exist in time. (*The Consolation of Philosophy* V.vi)

This has been the dominant view in Christian thought at least until the twentieth century; the position of Augustine, Anselm, Aquinas, the Reformers and countless other thinkers. It has two sources: the data of Scripture, for example the thought that 'from eternity to eternity, thou art God'; and *a priori* reflection on the ideas of the divine fullness and self-origination and on the creator–creature distinction.

Paul Helm

Eternalists reckon that a God who had an irretrievable past and a future that is yet to be enjoyed would lack fullness of being, since at any time part of his existence would be over, and part yet to be. In what is sometimes referred to as 'Perfect Being Theology' eternality implies and is implied by divine simplicity (God is without parts, including temporal parts). It also implies immutability (God cannot change; any such change would be for the better or the worse, and would imply an absence of perfection), and it implies impassibility (God is not subject to spasms of emotion, though this is not to say that God does not care for his creation, or that he does not possess love).

It has been argued that the eternalist view is incoherent, since if God's timeless life is simultaneous both with, say, the Battle of Hastings and with the Battle of Arnhem, then these battles must occur at the same time, since simultaneity is a transitive and symmetrical relation, and this is absurd. But timelessness is only incoherent if it is supposed that timeless eternity is a kind of time which could be (temporally) simultaneous with the times of true temporality.

Attempts have been made to explain and refine eternality by claiming, for example, that though timeless eternity is not a kind of time, yet it has some of the features of temporal duration. For example, in an important article Eleonore Stump and Norman Kretzmann articulate the timelessness view in terms of presentness which is in some sense simultaneous with the events of the creation. In order to avoid the earlier problem about simultaneity they distinguish between eternal simultaneity and temporal simultaneity. They introduce the idea of simultaneity ('ET-simultaneity') that can obtain between what is eternal and what is temporal; any eternal event is ET-simultaneous with any temporal event. But unlike simultaneity *simpliciter*, ET-simultaneity is not transitive, since in order for ET-simultaneity to apply there must be either an eternal or a temporal standpoint from which such simultaneity is observed. This view requires the obscure claim that an eternal observer should observe an event as temporally present, that eternity should have some of the features of temporality, but it appears to stipulate the absence of transitivity, and hence the absence of the *reductio ad absurdum* of the idea of timelessness, rather than offering an account which explains why such transitivity cannot occur in these circumstances.

Rather than attempt to explicate eternality in such a way, it is perhaps wiser, though intellectually less satisfying, to think of divine timeless eternity as a piece of negative thinking about the divine being, of negative theology; divine eternality is time*less*ness, and it cannot be expected that human analogies and models will throw much light on it. Nor is it a requirement of a satisfactory articulation of the doctrine that one can say what it is like to be timeless.

According to the second view, God is in time; unlike ourselves, he exists at all times, he is sempiternal, or everlasting; like ourselves, he has a past, a present and a future. This view, which has come into its own in the twentieth century, has earlier proponents, for example William Ockham (1285–1347), who in his treatment of the problem of divine omniscience and human freedom refers to what God presently knows and will come to know. The modern popularity of this view is due to support from arguments allegedly contrasting biblical and particularly Hebraic modes of thought with Greek and Platonic thought forms; by the desire (in the post-Holocaust world) for the portrayal of a God who can readily identify with the pains and other needs of humankind; to do greater justice to the idea of a divine personality; and by the desire to provide an account of God's relation to time that is more in accord with religious practice (e.g. petitionary prayer) than the eternality account is presumed to be.

Such temporality has been taken further by some (e.g. by process theologians, but not only they), who have argued that not only does God change (and is therefore in time) but that such change as is implied by God's creation of the universe and his interaction with it is essential to the achieving of the divine fullness. Without a creation to react with in time God himself would be impoverished.

Each of the dominant views may be said to pick up one element in the scriptural account of God and time; as noted, the eternalist stresses that God exists from eternity to eternity (Psalm 90), and that a day with him is as a thousand years, a thousand years as one day (2 Peter 3:8); the temporalist stresses that God acts in time, in judgement and redemption, in the Exodus and the incarnation of the eternal Son, and that he hears and answers the cries of his people; things which, *prima facie* at least, a timelessly eternal God cannot do.

Attempts to mediate between the two apparently exclusive positions of temporalism and eternalism fail to carry conviction. For example the theologian Karl Barth has argued that eternity is not God's independence of time and space but it is his time, his authentic temporality, his holding together of past, present and future in pure simultaneity. God's eternity contains past, present and future. Such a position teeters on the brink of incoherence, though it is best resolved in favour of an eternalist understanding of God. The failure of such mediating views suggests that the positions of eternality and temporality are also exhaustive of the question of God's relation to time.

Does the difference in view of God's relation to time matter? It matters in two respects. A thinker's preparedness to consider that God is in time is a criterion of his general approach to thought about God. If God's temporality is upheld, this signals a general willingness to think of God more anthropomorphically than if he is thought of as timelessly eternal. For if God is in time, then he is much more human-like than otherwise; he has memories, expectations and intentions of a readily recognizable kind; on some accounts his will may be thwarted, and he is vulnerable, experiencing disappointment and frustration, even though his powers of thought and action are infinitely more powerful than any human being's. By contrast, God's eternality signals a stress on the divine incomprehensibility; we cannot say what God's eternal existence is like, only what it does not imply.

The second respect in which the controversy matters is that each view produces a different range of problems and solutions to problems in philosophical theology. Three such problems may be noted here:

The creator–creature distinction

For the eternalist, temporality is an essential feature of creatureliness; the universe is created by God with time, not in time; 'all at once' only in the sense that the creation is the product of a divine timeless decree. The universe could not have begun with an event such as the 'Big Bang' thought of as temporally preceded by something or other; to suppose so is to confuse science with metaphysics. God is before the creation not by virtue of existing at a time when the universe was not yet in existence, but by virtue of his necessity and the creation's contingency. Everything created is necessarily in time, mutable and (so) corruptible; anything not created is necessarily eternal, immutable and incorruptible. By contrast, for the temporalist the creation has a beginning in time, even though before the regularities of the creation became apparent such time was un-metricated. God's necessity is everlastingness, and such changefulness as he possesses does not imply corruptibility.

Divine omniscience and human freedom

If divine omniscience is temporal, then God's knowledge of what is as yet future to us is foreknowledge for God. This has led to the much-discussed argument that if God's knowledge that Jones will wear a red tie tomorrow is past, it is necessary; and so what that knowledge entails, that Jones will wear a red tie tomorrow, is likewise necessary; a result incompatible with libertarian views of freedom. This has led some temporalists who favour libertarianism (and the desire to uphold libertarianism has frequently motivated temporalism) either to deny that even an omniscient being can know future free acts, or to maintain that God voluntarily curtails such knowledge in the interests of upholding creaturely freedom.

If God is timelessly eternal, then he cannot, strictly speaking, *foreknow* anything; he knows everything at once; Boethius and also, for example,

Aquinas held that this does not present problems for libertarianism, on the grounds that God's knowledge and will do not temporally precede the events of the creation. God's knowledge 'sees things present to it exactly as they will happen at some time as future events . . . in Him they are present things, but under the condition of time they are future things' (*The Consolation of Philosophy* V.vi). 'Things which are brought to the state of actuality in the time-series are known by us in time successively, but by God in eternity, which is above time. Hence future contingents cannot be certain to us, because we know them as future contingents; they can be certain only to God whose act of knowledge is in eternity, above time' (Aquinas, *Summa Theologiae* I, 14, 13).

Divine action and interaction

Miracles, petitionary prayer and the Christian account of human redemption appear to require not only that God acts in time, but that he reacts upon learning of the actions of his creatures. The action of God in time can be accounted for by the eternalist; in Augustine's words, God can will a change without changing a will. But the idea of interaction, of dialogue, of the idea of God 'repenting' of some previous deed or declaration, is better accounted for by the temporalist understanding of God, since it is consistent with this account to suppose that God can change by responding. The eternalist has to say that such occasions and expressions either are metaphorical (Aquinas) or are cases of God accommodating himself to human space-bound and time-bound patterns of thought and action (Calvin).

The question arises as to whether divine eternality is an attribute of God, as wisdom and goodness (say) are attributes. The foregoing discussion suggests that eternality or temporality are not so much attributes as modes of possessing attributes; God's wisdom is eternal (or everlasting) wisdom, his knowledge eternal (or everlasting) knowledge, and so on.

(c)   Omnipotence

Lawrence Moonan

Scope

Under 'omnipotence' (*omnis* = 'all'; *potens* = 'powerful') philosophers may treat less, or more, than the word suggests. Puzzles are raised in a wide range of questions – 'Can an omnipotent being (or, can God) _____?', 'Does omnipotence (or, divine omnipotence) entail _____?', 'Is it compatible with _____?' – whose superficial form can mislead. Some of the problems concern, not ascription of powers, but limits of coherent formation, or necessary relations between concepts. 'Can that which is omnipotent bligs blags blugs?' need not be about omnipotence at all. It could be asking: Is 'bligs blags blugs' significant in English?; or, from an anthropologist, whether the form 'That which is omnipotent can _____' is believed, in a given culture, to have the marvellous property of making gibberish put in the slot to become significant.[1] Even with a significant filler, it could be open to more than one type of analysis.

By contrast, we may restrict consideration to powers ascribable not to just any omnipotent being, but to God: understood either as something which exists, but not in any determinate manner (a 'simply existent'), or as something possessed of determinate attributes. For convenience, I call the former understanding 'existence-theism', and the latter 'character-theism' (for it implies that God has a specifiable character, whether or not we can know all or any of the specifications). On either understanding God may, in addition, be identified (or not) with the object of worship within some religious tradition.

'Loading' picked up by 'omnipotence' and its cognates

Pantokratōr, a Greek cognate, conveyed to early Christian writers both the sense of (1) 'all-ruling' (as in *kratein* + the genitive case) and (2) 'all-upholding' (as in *kratein* + the accusative case). Sense (1) carried associations from Jewish and Christian scriptures.[2] Sense (2), as in *kratein* + accusative, or in the adjective *ktistēs*, reflected rather a philosophical tradition reaching back to the divine, sustaining 'environment' of the Greek philosopher Anaximenes (*sugkratei, periechei*), and forwards to the 'enveloping' (*das Umgreifende*) of the twentieth-century philosopher Karl Jaspers. Any preference for relational 'almightiness' to the exclusion of a power not necessarily carried into execution in this or any possible order of things cannot claim support from early Christian readings of 'Almighty' in the first article of the Creeds.

Latin *omnipotens*, in the sense of 'master of all things' was cheerfully applied to deities whose wills could quite evidently be thwarted. *Potens* itself had conveyed both 'power over' and 'capacity not necessarily exercised'. In St Augustine's writings, *omnipotens* moved towards the sense of 'divine power, exercised or not',[3] which (with complications from Peter Abelard [1079–1142] and Plato's *Timaeus*) medieval schoolmen picked up.[4]

Modes of analysis

At bottom, attributions of omnipotence can be analysed in either of two ways. In one, a 'deadpan' analysis, omnipotence is understood as an attribute in the strict sense: that which the significant predicable '_____ is omnipotent' designates. In the other type of analysis attributions of omnipotence are treated as 'systematically misleading'. This can be seen in the 'deployed omnipotence' canvassed by the contemporary author Richard Swinburne, which is nonetheless ascribed to a God endowed with at least some essential attributes.[5] Some medieval schoolmen used analyses of this sort more radically, in conjunction with supposing a strictly infinite God, a 'simply existent'. If there is a simply existent, there logically cannot be more than one of it: its reference (*suppositio*) is fixed non-arbitrarily, without room for vagueness or indeterminacy. But if nothing we can understand can properly and absolutely be affirmed of it, no 'deadpan' analysis is a possibility.

To say that things can be done by a simply existent is to say of things considered abstractly (*absolute*), i.e. prescinding from whether or not they are (ever to be) instantiated, that either they (are going to) exist in an order compatible with a simply existent (for medieval schoolmen: 'God can do them within option-tied, "ordained" power [*de potentia ordinata sua*]'); or they are possible to exist in such an order ('God can do them within option-neutral, "absolute" power ([*de potentia absoluta sua*]').[6] To say thus that a simply existent is omnipotent is to say either that whatever counts as a determinate kind of thing, and is instantiated, is instantiated in an order compatible with a simply existent, or that whatever counts as a determinate kind of thing is – when abstractly considered – possible to be instantiated in an order compatible with a simply existent. The kind of order needed excludes the world-view in which ultimately there is no imposed order but only a sum of things. The existence-theist 'theology' resulting does not entail commitment to worship in any familiar sense. Neither does it exclude it. To say that things come under the omnipotence of the God of Judaism, say, or catholic Christianity (identified with a simply existent) may need more. It need not be that 'our ordinary human concept of omnipotence may be subverted by encounter with God's revelation'.[7] It is rather than whatever concepts we can use may have to be used under 'pragmatics' respectful of revelation: e.g. the understanding that 'God has sworn and will not repent' (Psalm 110:4).[8]

Puzzles

Recent discussion of omnipotence – nearly always under a 'deadpan' analysis – focuses on the question of definition, on the 'paradoxes', and on matters involving theodicy. Inspection shows that the basic issue is that set by J. L. Mackie and Antony Flew as long ago as 1955.[9] Attention, however, is more often on intra-scholar refinement of pro-theist responses. At the same time, a wide variety of other topics has received at least some attention.

Omnipotence itself

A unitary concept of omnipotence, covering a comprehensive range of desired attributions and exclusions, may not be definable and may not be expressible without incoherence.[10] If that is so, it may be beside the point if our logical resources are still not up to the task of precise formalization. Yet definitions of omnipotence are still sought. A common strategy is spelled out by G. van den Brink, who examines a variety of leading attempts and who concludes that 'proposals to define omnipotence (though proliferating) . . . tend to get entangled in . . . a mass of technicalities' and ' . . . the very claim that an unambiguous definition of the concept of omnipotence is possible is in danger of dying the death of a thousand qualifications'.[11]

Paradoxes

Mackie distinguished a Paradox of Omnipotence and a Paradox of Sovereignty (of particular importance to those who hold to relational 'almightiness' only).[12] The first runs: 'Can an omnipotent being make things which he cannot control?' If we answer 'Yes', it follows that the being is not, in fact, omnipotent; there are things which it cannot do. If we answer 'No', then the being is again not omnipotent.[13] Mackie's response was to jettison either the concept of omnipotence or the theist's concept of God. Nearly everyone who writes about this paradox believes that there is a solution, but the solutions differ widely. Many have taken Mackie's first way, retaining only 'almightiness'. Some have argued that Mackie's paradox was beside the point in that the 'omnipotence' needed by theologians cannot be contructed from our ordinary notions of power. It has also been argued that, rephrased, the 'paradox' is no paradox or that it can in some way be dissolved.[14]

Extent

Does omnipotence extend even to necessary truth or logical laws? Some recent philosophers have urged that it does. Others have taken the opposite view. Is bringing about the past within the scope of omnipotence? Is undoing the past? Again, answers have differed.[15] Other questions recently discussed with an eye on omnipotence include 'Can God tell the time?' If God is non-temporal, then he cannot, presumably, occupy any 'now' in which he can say 'It is now such a such a time'. With this thought in mind some have denied that telling the time falls under God's omnipotence. Others, however, have found it unproblematic to think of God occupying time and knowing what time it is at any time.[16]

Compatibilities

If a coherent concept of omnipotence survives – whether a unitary concept of omnipotence-in-general, or a strategically ordered pair (of 'almightiness' and 'divine infinite power'), or 'almightiness' only – we can ask: does it satisfy the intuitions of particular philosophers, or of bodies of worshippers? We can also ask: is it compatible with the goodness, wisdom, immutability, etc. of the theist's God?

With respect to divine goodness, it has been argued that if God cannot abolish evil, he is not all powerful, and that, if God does not will to abolish evil, he is not all good.[17] In replying to this charge, some, such as Alvin Plantinga, have invoked the 'free will defence'. According to this, it is good that there should be a world containing free creatures, and the fact that they sometimes do wrong counts neither against God's omnipotence nor against God's goodness since God cannot determine them to do only what is right.[18] Rejecting the free will defence, however, philosophers such as Antony Flew have claimed that there is 'no contradiction in saying that a particular ... choice was both free, and could have been helped ... ; and ... foreknown, and explicable in terms of caused causes', so that the free will defence, which requires a contradiction of the sort, will not stand.[19] Flew's position, in turn, has been contested, e.g. by Plantinga and Swinburne.[20]

On the topic of omnipotence and omniscience, Anthony Kenny concluded a detailed exploration by saying: 'Omnipotence may ... be capable in isolation, of receiving a coherent formulation; but ... is inadequate as a foundation for divine foreknowledge of undetermined human conduct'; and 'There cannot ... be a timeless, immutable, omniscient, omnipotent, all-good being'.[21] Even if so, some would preserve compatibility by narrowing the range of either concept – e.g. by denying that God knows future free acts, or counterfactuals with consequents implying free will.

Why bother?

The highly professional arguments of the character-theists during the last twenty years or so do not seem to me to have overcome the difficulties raised by Mackie, Flew and Kenny. Comparable arguments from the perspective of existence-theists are not yet in evidence. The philosophical study of omnipotence forces decisions: and if the final issue to be decided is between existence-theists, and sum-of-things atheists, it really will be over how the world ultimately is, or is not.

Notes

1 Cf. P. T. Geach, *Providence and Evil* (Cambridge, 1977), p. 13 (on C. S. Lewis) and Antony Flew and Alasdair MacIntyre (eds), *New Essays in Philosophical Theology* (London, 1955), p. 145 (on J. McTaggart).
2 The name *kurios pantokratōr* in the Septuagint (Greek translation of the Old Testament) translates, with rare exceptions, *Yahweh Sabaoth*. *Pantokratōr* by itself indicates other names of God. *Yahweh Sabaoth* was a name given to God first as commander of the armies of Israel (more often, of the whole people; and never as a mere warrior-God), then generalized to mean orderer of all the arrays of the universe.
3 Augustine opposes *omnitenens* ('master of all things') and *omnicreans* (same, in creational contexts) to *omnipotens* (taken as attributable to God, even had there

been no creation): explaining (away) the case where *omnipotens* translated *pantokratōr* in the Creeds by its translators having taken it as coextensive (*tantum valere*) with *omnitenens*. To oppose the Manichees he moved to emphasizing universality: 'Who is *omnipotens* if not the one who can do all things?' (*De Trinitate* 4, xx, 27).

4 So whereas *pantokratōr* had earlier emphasized 'master of the universe' as in popular or civic religion, warmed by scriptural associations, *omnipotens* tended to lead in the direction of the transcendent God of negative theology, with debts to more learned, philosophical Greek sources (cf. A. de Halleux, 'Dieu le Père tout-puissant', *Revue théologique de Louvain* 8 [1977]). The medieval schoolmen, who owed some central relevant notions (on existence, and on the abstract way – *consideratio absoluta* – of considering things) to the Arabic thinker Avicenna (980–1037), had some debts beyond both Athens and Jerusalem. We may note then that of the two roots used in the Qur'an, the adjectival *qadir* overwhelmingly conveys relational 'almightiness', while adjectival *qadhar* is almost invariably used in parallel with 'the One', and contrasted with 'creator of everything'. Related verbal forms – perhaps only because recorded ones are active – have a relational sense. Cf. H. E. Kassis, *A Concordance of the Qur'an* (Berkeley, 1983), pp. 896–7 and 902.

5 Richard Swinburne, *The Coherence of Theism* (Oxford, 1977).

6 Cf. Lawrence Moonan, *Divine Power: The Medieval Power Distinction up to Its Adoption by Albert, Bonaventure, and Aquinas* (Oxford, 1994).

7 G. van den Brink, 'Descartes, modalities and God', *International Journal for Philosophy of Religion* 33 (1993), p. 118.

8 Cf. Geach, *Providence and Evil*.

9 Cf. J. L. Mackie, 'Evil and omnipotence', *Mind* 64 (1955) and Antony Flew, 'Divine omnipotence and human freedom' in Flew and MacIntyre (1955).

10 Geach argues this in *Providence and Evil*. For some related discussion, see Anthony Kenny, *The God of the Philosophers* (Oxford, 1979), ch. 7.

11 G. van den Brink, *Almighty God: A Study of the Doctrine of Divine Omnipotence* (Kampen, 1993), p. 140.

12 The Paradox of Sovereignty asks: 'Can a legal sovereign make a law restricting its own future legislative power?' If the answer is 'Yes', we should be admitting the validity of a law which, if it were actually made, would mean that the legal sovereign was no longer sovereign. If the answer is 'No', we should be admitting that the legal sovereign is not now a legal sovereign.

13 Mackie (1955).

14 Cf. G. B. Keene, 'Capacity-limiting statements', *Mind* 70 (1961); B. Mayo, 'Mr Keene on omnipotence', *Mind* 70 (1961); G. Mavrodes, 'Some puzzles concerning omnipotence', *Philosophical Review* 72 (1963).

15 Cf. Michael Dummett, 'Bringing about the past' in Michael Dummett, *Truth and Other Enigmas* (London, 1978); T. J. Holopainen, *Dialectic and Theology in the Eleventh Century* (Leiden, 1996); Anthony O'Hear, *Experience, Explanation, and Faith* (London, 1984).

16 Cf. Kenny, *The God of the Philosophers*; Norman Kretzmann, 'Omniscience and immutability', *Journal of Philosophy* 63 (1966); A. N. Prior, 'The formalities of omniscience' in A. N. Prior, *Papers on Time and Tense* (Oxford, 1968); Swinburne, *The Coherence of Theism*.

17 Cf. Mackie (1955) and Flew in Flew and MacIntyre (1955).

18 Cf. Alvin Plantinga, 'The free will defence', reprinted in Basil Mitchell (ed.), *The Philosophy of Religion* (Oxford, 1971).

19 Flew, op. cit.
20 Alvin Plantinga, *The Nature of Necessity* (Oxford, 1974); Swinburne, *The Coherence of Theism.*
21 Kenny, *The God of the Philosophers*, p. 121.

(d) Omniscience

Gerard J. Hughes SJ

Philosophers and theologians alike have traditionally been agreed that God must know everything. Differences of opinion have centred round two questions. Exactly what is meant by 'everything'? And how does God come by this knowledge? The view one takes about God's omniscience will, as is the case with all the attributes of God, depend on the way in which God's nature is conceived quite generally. In what follows, I shall assume what may broadly be said to be a traditional conception of God as an eternal, spiritual, and personal being.[1] Thus, since God is a spirit and not a bodily being, God does not have sensations (since he does not have sense organs); and it was at least commonly held that God does not have emotions either, since emotions too are at least in part bodily states.[2] It was, and still is, a matter of disagreement whether God's eternity is to be construed as timelessness, or whether it is better to say that God is everlasting, existing through the whole of time. But if God is eternal in the sense that his existence is not extended in time, then he is changeless, since to change requires a time before it took place and a time after which it has taken place; and if he is changeless, then there can be no *processes* in God, such as coming to know something, or reasoning something out. And if God is not in time, then neither can his knowledge be located at any moment in time. And finally, if nothing in God is dependent on creatures, then God's knowledge cannot in any respect be produced by creatures; it must belong to God as he is in himself.

These apparently rather bland traditional statements are less straightforward than they might at first sight appear. Exactly what they imply, and whether they are mutually consistent, are the issues which have provoked most discussion from the time of Aristotle until the present. Nor have they been finally resolved.

God knows everything

It is natural for us humans to express our knowledge in statements. We know that Paris is the capital of France, and that the sun is many millions of miles distant from the earth. Even in those cases in which what we know is some entity rather than a statement (as in 'I know John very well'), it is not entirely clear that we are saying more than that we know the truth of many statements about John. In this respect, 'know' behaves rather differently from 'to be aware of'. At least in many instances, our awareness of things is the basis of our knowledge of truths about those things. Thus, it is in being aware of the position of my body that I know that I am sitting down with my legs crossed. It is in being aware of sensations that I know that the dog is barking outside the door. We typically 'fix' our awareness of things by formulating statements about those things, and this process of 'fixing' is at least the commonest, and is perhaps the only, way in which we form beliefs, or attain to knowledge.

This 'fixing' of our awareness is a *process*, and the formulation of sentences takes time. If God is timeless, then his knowledge cannot require any such process, and cannot consist of sentences. His knowledge must be something like a perfect self-awareness, which does not require to be formulated in order to be fully grasped.[3] So, though it is natural for us to describe God's knowledge in terms of the truths which God knows, God's knowledge is of things rather than truths about those things.[4] A grasp of this point dispels some of the puzzles about whether God knows that I am now writing this essay. The sentence 'I am now writing this essay' is a tensed statement, which I can truly make only because my assertion is contemporaneous with my writing. But God, being outside time, cannot truly make any assertion, nor know any truth, which depends on his being contemporaneous with my actions. 'Gerry Hughes is now writing an essay' would be false as said by God (so to speak) since the 'now' can have no function in God's experience; and what is false cannot be known.[5]

For just the same reasons, though God can indeed know the birth of Jesus and the Battle of Hastings, and the temporal relation between them, he cannot know that both events happened a long time ago; *that* true statement is true only when said by someone appropriately situated in time, and God is not situated in time at all. On the other hand, God is aware of my writing, and of the fact that it takes place at a particular date in time. God's knowledge of time, like his knowledge of human emotions, sensations or other bodily activities, is an understanding of these features of our experience rather than an experience of them. A rough parallel might be a man's understanding of childbirth, or our understanding of how bats navigate by a kind of sonar detection.[6] God's knowledge is the perfect awareness and understanding that is proper to a being like God; we should be wary of taking literally our natural human ways of describing God's knowledge, or of seeing it as a limitation in God that his way of knowing is so very different from ours.

On the traditional view, God knows not merely himself and all the things he has created; he is also aware of his own creative powers to have created other things than these; and he is aware of the possibilities inherent in creation for things to have worked out differently. This is sometimes, and somewhat misleadingly, expressed by saying that God knows not merely actual things and states of affairs, but all possible things and states of affairs as well. Of course 'possible things and states of affairs' are not a special class of things which are 'there' to be known, and to speak of them is to speak simply of the powers of actual things.

In short, God's omniscience was traditionally interpreted, at least usually, to mean that there is nothing of which God does not have a perfect understanding. But it was not held to include the ways of knowledge that are proper only to timebound beings (such as what time it is now, or how long ago the Battle of Hastings took place); nor was it taken to include the kinds of awareness that only material beings can have. So God has a perfect understanding of what sensations or emotions are, but does not have those experiences.

Omniscience, necessity, and freedom

The really controversial questions about omniscience concern the source of God's knowledge of things, and, in particular, how God has knowledge of our free choices. Aquinas, along with the whole of the medieval tradition, held that God knows all things, actual and possible, by his awareness of his own causal activity in bringing them about, or his own causal powers to bring them about. He was emphatic that God does not obtain his knowledge of things by being aware of them, since that would imply that they had a causal effect on God. It was taken as axiomatic that, though creatures are causally dependent upon God, God is in no way causally dependent on creatures. But this position had a history.

Aristotle, in a famous passage,[7] enquires whether, if it is true now that someone will do something in the future, then they must be going to do it; for, if they must be going to do it, it does not seem that they could possibly do otherwise. This puzzle had its application also within Christian theology: if the all-knowing God knows what I am going to do, is there any sense in which I can *freely* choose to do it?

The problem involves several different strands. Some of them, though they require care, can be teased out reasonably easily.

First, some distractions can be eliminated. We talk, in human terms, of God's *fore*knowledge. But God does not *in advance* know what I am going to do, since that would imply that God's knowledge temporally precedes my action. God's knowledge is not in time. Still, it is true that God eternally knows all my actions, and that might seem to pose problems enough. For if God knows that I am to do something, must it not be true that I will do it? Of course it must. It is impossible to have knowledge of what is not true.[8] Notice, though, that in just the same sense it also follows that if I see that you are sitting down, then you must be sitting down. The 'must' here is the 'must' of logical consequence, not of causal necessity. If someone knows something, it follows of necessity that what they know is the case. It does not follow that it was *unavoidably* the case, any more than my seeing that you are sitting implies that you could not have avoided sitting down. It is also true that, if I decide not to go to Scotland in the summer, God eternally knows that I will not go: and if I decide to go, God eternally knows that I will go.

The Christian writer Boethius (*c.* 484–*c.* 524) addressed this problem, and answered it along the lines I have given:

> Why therefore do you insist that things which are surveyed by the divine sight should be necessary, when not even men make the things that they see necessary? Surely, when you see present things, your gazing does not impart any necessity to them? Certainly not. But, if it is right to compare the divine present with the human, then, just as you see some things in this temporal present of yours, just so does God see all things in his eternal present. And for this reason this divine foreknowledge does not change the nature and character of things, and sees things present to itself in the same way as they are going to come to be at some future time.[9]

The elements in this solution are three: (1) God's knowledge is not in time, and the whole of temporal creation is equally accessible to him; (2) God's knowledge, and indeed any knowledge which is properly so called, knows things *as they truly are*: if they are free choices, then God knows them as free choices; (3) the truth that anything known must be so is a logical truth, and says nothing about the causal inevitability ('necessity' in that sense) of what is known. Nothing in any of these arguments runs counter to the doctrine that God is unchanging. His knowledge eternally and unchangingly corresponds to the way the history of the world – from beginning to end – in fact is.

Thomas Aquinas (*c.* 1225–74) took over the main outlines of this solution.[10] But he introduces an additional complication. In his commentary on Aristotle's discussion, he points out that it is not only God's omniscience which might have been thought to be problematic. Divine

Providence is more than a detached knowledge of the world; it is a will that things in the world work out well.

> It would look as though everything happens of necessity, first on the part of his knowledge . . . and secondly on the part of the will, for the will of God cannot be inefficacious; it would seem, therefore, that everything he wills happens of necessity.[11]

Aquinas's answer to the knowledge problem is along the same lines as those proposed by Boethius; and his comment on the problem about God's will runs as follows:

> He disposes necessary causes for the effects that he wills to be necessary, and he ordains causes that act contingently (that is, are able to fail) for the effects that he wills to be contingent. And according to the condition of these causes, effects are called either necessary or contingent, although all depend on the divine will as on a first cause which transcends the order of necessity and contingency.[12]

The approach is clear enough. If God wills that some things should happen of necessity (for example, the movements of the heavenly bodies, or, as we might put it, the interactions between things in the material world) he achieves this result by creating things which act in a physically determined way, according to the laws of nature. If he wills to achieve something which happens contingently, for example, that Saul should be converted on the road to Damascus, then he achieves this outcome by Saul's free decision. God, as first cause, sustains the whole universe, heavenly bodies and Saul alike; his sustaining activity underlies both contingent and necessary causes. But, as was to become evident in subsequent controversies, the central difficulty with this approach is whether Aquinas can successfully claim both that God's providential will is always efficacious, while at the same time leaving human beings free in their actions. In what sense can God *efficaciously* will that Saul will freely come to believe in Jesus of Nazareth? And if God's knowledge of what Saul decides is derived not from Saul's decision, but from God's own activity in sustaining Saul's free choice, then God's knowledge will be guaranteed only if God's activity is in fact efficacious. On the other hand, if God's action does *not* determine Saul's choice, how does God know what Saul chooses unless (which no medieval philosopher would have accepted) God knows what Saul chooses only because Saul chooses it? This was the problem which subsequent writers believed Aquinas had not clearly solved.

William Ockham (1290–1349) thought that the notion of eternity, conceived as atemporality, did not make sense, and construed God's eternity as everlasting existence in time. He seems to have held that, although what God knew at any given point would be different, since different things would be true at different points in time, this still allowed God himself to be changeless, since it was the world that changed over time, not God. God always knew what would in fact take place, although he cannot know that it *is* taking place until it actually does.[13] In commenting on the same passages in Aristotle already mentioned, Ockham repeats the by now standard point that from the mere fact that it was always true that I would be writing this now, given that I am, it does not follow that I am not writing freely, nor that I could not have chosen not to write now. On the other hand, Ockham objected to Aquinas's description of God's knowledge as 'eternal' and as 'necessary',[14] preferring instead to say that it is necessary only after the events known to God have actually occurred, since up until that point some things could in fact turn out otherwise. It seems clear that Ockham and Aquinas are using 'necessary' in somewhat different senses, rather than straightforwardly disagreeing with one another on this point, though they do indeed disagree about the proper understanding of God's eternity. Aquinas holds that God is timelessly eternal, Ockham that God exists everlastingly in time. It is therefore more difficult for Ockham to explain God's knowledge of the future, since it really is future for God; a difficulty which he freely admits. Aquinas also holds that, since God's knowledge is one with God's essence, it is necessarily as it is (though he does not clearly explain how to reconcile this view with his view that God could have created, and therefore known, a different world from this one). Perhaps by 'necessary' Aquinas here means no more than 'unchangeably'? Ockham, on the other hand, refuses to use 'necessary' of God's knowledge until the events known have actually occurred, after which point they are, unavoidably, the way they are.

The more intractable problem remained the source of God's knowledge. Aquinas believed that the ground of God's knowledge of all created things, including our free choices, just is his perfect awareness of his own creative activity upon which those choices depend for their existence. There is no contradiction, he argued, in God creating beings like ourselves who can act freely, even though everything about us exists dependently on God.[15] Ockham, though admitting that he had no positive solution to offer, still believed that Aquinas's view was incompatible with human freedom. And indeed it is hard to see how God's creative power suffices to give him knowledge of our free choices, if that power is compatible with us being free and so does not force us to do one thing rather than another. If God's input does not determine human choice, how is knowledge of that input alone sufficient to guarantee knowledge of the choice a human being makes?

The Jesuit theologian Luis de Molina (1536–1600) agreed with the criticism, but thought that, with some modification, Aquinas's view could be defended. What is needed, Molina argued, is that God should have knowledge which was halfway between the two kinds of knowledge ascribed to him by Aquinas. He would know what was possible or inevitable in any conceivable creation, independently of any creative activity, simply by his comprehensive grasp of his own causal powers; he would also, in creating, know what was actually taking place in this creation; but crucially, he would also have *scientia media*, 'Middle Knowledge'; God knows, independently of his actually creating anything at all, what people *would* freely choose to do in any circumstances in which some choice were open to them, even if they were never to exist, or never to find themselves in such circumstances.[16] So even if, Molina argued, God 'already' knew what we would freely do, he still does not need to derive this knowledge from his creative involvement in the free choices people actually make.

> It falls under his immense and altogether unlimited knowledge, by which he comprehends in the deepest and most eminent way whatever falls under his omnipotence, to penetrate created free choice in such a way as to discern and intuit with certainty what part [human choice] is going to turn itself to by its own innate freedom.[17]

This, Molina hoped, would reconcile freedom, providence and omniscience. Now, it is true that many of the choices people make can, perhaps, be predicted on the basis of their characters and education, thus giving colour to Molina's suggestion that even we often know what people would or would not do in hypothetical situations, and God can be presumed to understand people's character and circumstances much better than we do. But it is far from clear that people always act in character or predictably; and even less clear that, if they did, they would genuinely be able to do otherwise. Many philosophers have concluded that there is no basis on which such knowledge of possible free actions can rest, and hence to be known about them 'in advance' even by an omniscient God.

Other philosophers (and theologians) have argued that freedom does not require that one could do otherwise, but simply that what one does one willingly and spontaneously does; and some have argued that this is all that Aquinas would have claimed. To this the counter-argument is that actions which are determined, even if spontaneous and in that sense uncoerced, are still not free in the sense required for moral responsibility. A further possibility is to argue that God's knowledge of our free actions derives from the occurrence of those actions themselves. This view runs quite counter to the traditional view that nothing in God is dependent upon creatures in any way (though of course it would remain true that he is not dependent on creatures for his existence or his creative activity). All three possibilities have their contemporary defenders, and none has won general acceptance.

Notes

1 That God is eternal is indeed the almost universally held view of the great monotheistic religions. However, 'eternity' is sometimes understood as 'standing totally outside time', and sometimes as 'everlasting, without beginning or end'. In the Western Christian tradition, Thomas Aquinas understood it in the former way, while William of Ockham understood it in the latter. Some of the implications of this difference of interpretation will become apparent later in our discussion.

2 See, for example, Thomas Aquinas, *Summa Theologiae* I, 3, 2, reply to the second objection: 'anger and other such things are attributed to God because of a similarity in effect; since punishment belongs to anger, divine retribution is metaphorically termed anger'. The article itself is concerned with whether God is a bodily being; and since he is not, he cannot literally be said to have emotions.

3 Perhaps the famous passage in Aristotle, *Metaphysics* XII, 9, 1175a4–11, where God's knowledge is described as *gnōsis gnōseōs*, is an attempt to capture some such idea. Though the phrase is usually translated as 'a thinking upon thinking', it might perhaps mean something more like 'a grasp of awareness'.

4 Aquinas is willing to say that God knows all true propositions, but not in a propositional way (*Summa Theologiae* I, 14, 15). I think the best interpretation of this somewhat obscure remark is that God knows all the states of affairs which true propositions express, but does not need to, and in any case could not, spell this knowledge out, so to speak, by making statements.

5 There is comparatively little difficulty about saying that God knows the event which consists in my writing this essay in 1996; and in general, that there is no timebound event of which God is unaware. But that is quite different from saying that he is aware *now* of my writing: only a being in time can be aware of something taking place now. More detailed discussion of these issues can be found in: W. A. Alston, 'Does God have beliefs?', *Religious Studies* 22 (1986), pp. 287–306; Nelson Pike, *God and Timelessness* (London, 1970); Alvin Plantinga, 'On Ockham's way out', *Faith and Philosophy* 3, pp. 235–69; Arthur Prior, 'The formalities of omniscience' in his *Papers on Time and Tense* (Oxford, 1968).

6 It is common enough in English to say that nobody can really know what something is like unless they have experienced it for themselves. Of course a mother has had an experience of childbirth and a male gynaecologist has not, and there is a clear difference between the two. It is perhaps less clear that this is a difference in *knowledge*. The issue, I think, is a purely verbal one; but if it is thought appropriate to describe the having of such experiences as a form of knowledge, then in that sense of 'knowledge' God does not know experiences which God cannot have, just as he cannot know those true statements which we, situated in time as we are, can know.

7 *De Interpretatione*, ch. 9. It is still a matter of controversy whether Aristotle in the end denies that there are any true statements which can be made now about what someone will freely do in the future. He takes as his example whether a general will give orders tomorrow for a sea-battle to take place.

8 This, at least, was the common assumption about how the word 'know' was to be used. Most recently, some philosophers have been inclined to weaken the requirements upon knowledge so that it is sufficient to have a rationally warranted belief, even if, as a matter of fact, that belief is false.

9 Boethius, *De Consolatione Philosophiae*, V, 5, 18–21 (trans. R. W. Sharples, in *Cicero 'On Fate' and Boethius 'The Consolation of Philosophy' IV, 5–7, V* [Warminster, 1991]). When Boethius says that 'divine foreknowledge does not change the nature and character of things' he means that contingent things remain just that, contingent, whether they are known or not; and things which happen of necessity happen of necessity whether they are known or not. Aquinas was later to make the same point, using as his illustration that, though knowledge is not a physical activity, it is still possible to know physical objects, which remain physical objects whether they are known or not.

10 *Summa Theologiae* I, 14, 13–15.

11 Aquinas, *Commentarium in Aristotelis Peri Hermeneias (De Interpretatione)*, 14, 17.

12 Ibid., 14, 22. This problem is discussed at greater length in the *Summa*, I, 22–23, on providence and predestination.

13 Ockham discusses these points in his *Expositio super primum librum Peri Hermeneias*, and in his *Tractatus de praedestinatione et de praescientia Dei et de futuris contingentibus*. Both texts are most easily found in the translation and commentary by Marilyn McCord Adams and Norman Kretzmann: *Ockham's 'Predestination, God's Foreknowledge and Future Contingents'* (New York, 1969).

14 Aquinas, *Summa Theologiae*: God's knowledge is eternal (I, 14, 8, reply to second objection) and necessary (I, 14, 13, reply to first objection). Aquinas, of course, insists that, though eternal, God's knowledge includes knowledge of timebound things, and, though necessary, it includes knowledge of contingent things. It is important to remember that, following Aristotle, the medieval philosophers were also willing to describe as 'necessary' something which, though contingent, is now unchangeable. That I was in London yesterday is in this sense necessary (there is nothing I can now do to change that fact), even though I need not have been. It is important to note that the issue is further complicated that since, on Aquinas's view, God did not have to create this world, or indeed any world at all, there is an important sense in which God cannot be said of necessity to know *this* world, even though his knowledge is eternal and unchanging. So here, too, there is a sense of 'necessary' in which, since God is unchanging, even God's free decisions (to create this rather than some other world) are unalterable and thus necessary.

15 See *Summa Theologiae* I, 19, especially art. 6; I, 22–23; I, 83; *De Malo*, 6. The argument in these texts is difficult, and much depends on the sense in which Aquinas holds that, though nothing in the world operates without the action of God as First Cause, human beings are still capable of acting freely.

16 Luis de Molina, *Concordia Liberi Arbitrii*, Part IV. This text is perhaps most conveniently to be found in the translation and commentary by Alfred J. Freddoso, *Molina 'On Divine Foreknowledge'* (Notre Dame, 1988).

17 *Concordia*, IV, 50, 15.

(e)   Personal

Charles Taliaferro

What does it mean to claim that God is personal? The term 'personal' has been used in a variety of ways. Here are four that have been at work in the claim that God is personal.

'Personal' may be used (a) to designate things that belong to persons (as in 'personal property'), (b) to characterize events or things that affect persons (as in 'personal tragedy'), (c) to refer to conditions or places that are amenable to private exchanges (as in 'a personal atmosphere') and (d) to refer to a person's acting intimately or in an engaged way with other people (as in 'a personal relationship'). When persons act personally as opposed to impersonally they may be affectionate or spiteful, but they reveal their individual characters, their beliefs and desires. Each of these four meanings of 'personal' have been used in what we might call 'talk about God'.

(a*) Some henotheists have held that God belongs to individual persons or groups. A *henotheist* acknowledges and reverences God but, unlike a *monotheist*, does not deny that other gods exist. Because henotheists hedge an unqualified acknowledgment of the omnipresence and uniqueness of God, there has been an analogous hedge on the conviction that God is the God of all people or the whole cosmos. While God has been thought of as belonging to people, people have been thought of as belonging to God. The ownership of all creation by God is upheld in the Hebrew and Christian Bibles (see 1 Chronicles 29:11–18; Psalms 24:1, 50:12; and Ezekiel 18:4) and in the Qur'an ('To God is the personal ownership [*mulk*] of the Heavens and the earth', from the chapter 'The Light').

(b*) Judaism, Christianity and Islam have also depicted God as demanding our love and obedience. According to these religions, our deepest pleasures are to be found in God and our sorrows are to be transfigured in a relationship with God.

(c*) God has also been thought of as the reality in which one's life unfolds, both public and private. 'In God we live and move and have our being' (New Testament, Acts 17:28).

95

(d*) In Judaism, Christianity and Islam, God is described as not only creating the cosmos, but caring for it intimately. On this view, God knows created persons better than we know ourselves. Moreover, God's character and intentions are disclosed in historic events, involving miracles, prophecies or God's incarnation.

Not all proponents of Judaism, Christianity and Islam uphold the personal nature of God. Some philosophers and theologians permit personal descriptions of God only if these are understood to be metaphorical. But a wide range of philosophers treat monotheistic tradition as committed to the supposition that God is literally personal. The claim that theists believe God is a person is so prevalent that it is often assumed in philosophical texts and not independently argued. Belief in a personal God extends beyond Judaism, Christianity, and Islam. Hinduism has important traditions in which God is non-personal, but it also has strands that depict God or Brahman as a person or like a person. A wide array of indigenous religions envisage God as a powerful, good person or person-like reality.

In the twentieth century many philosophers and theologians who hold a high view of the personal nature of God have been classified as 'personalists'. E. S. Brightman, one of the Boston personalists, writes: 'To be God is to enjoy the highest possible degree of . . . personality, creativity, control, and development' (E. S. Brightman in P. Bertocci [ed.], *Persons and Reality* [New York, 1958], p. 201). The movement of process philosophy and theology also has representatives who give pride of place to a personal God. A. N. Whitehead refers to God as 'the great companion – the fellow-sufferer who understands' (cf. A. N. Whitehead, *Process and Reality* [New York, 1978], p. 351).

Persons

The English term 'person' is derived from the Latin *persona*. Originally it referred to a mask used in a theatre. Coming from a context in which it defines a dramatic role, the term evolved to refer to roles of a broader social and legal kind. It had important uses in Roman law, referring to an individual's liabilities and privileges, and the term altered in meaning as law developed. From the third century onward, the term came to have a specific, religiously significant use as philosophers and theologians articulated their understanding of the substantial nature of God. In the sixth century Boethius in his *Consolation of Philosophy* (and elsewhere) defined 'person' as 'an individual substance of a rational nature'. This definition proved highly influential in medieval thinking, and it contributed to attempts to explain how humans, as it says in the book of Genesis, are made in the image of God.

The development of the term 'person' in the history of ideas has not been uniform; it is no more stable than the concepts 'soul', 'spirit' and 'human being' which have gone through countless revisions. I note two topics of perennial importance about the nature of persons: the *constitution* of persons and the *value* of persons.

Constitution

Are persons essentially biological or can there be a person that is not constituted by matter? If 'person' can *only* be used to designate animals such as human beings, then it appears that God, not being an animal, is not a person.

The ancient Stoics thought of God as the world-soul or very much like an animal, and Thomas Hobbes in the seventeenth century described God as corporeal, albeit this corporeality is pure, simple, and invisible. For an interesting contemporary defence of the belief in the personal and material nature of God, see Grace Jantzen's *God's World, God's Body* (London, 1984). But the majority of theists in Judaism, Christianity and Islam have been reluctant to adopt such a picture of God's materiality, and this has led some either to argue for the legitimacy of using the term 'person' to apply to non-animals (God) or simply to forgo describing God as resembling a person. In these debates it is pivotal to note when the disagreement is merely verbal and when it rests on substantial philosophical assumptions.

The case for the essential materiality of persons can be traced to materialists like Democritus (fifth–fourth century BCE), but also to Aristotle, though he was not a thoroughgoing materialist. In Aristotle's philosophy, the person is profoundly embodied in an organic unity of form and matter. Persons are materially constituted and, because of this, an individual life after the disintegration of a person's body is doubtful. In the thirteenth century Aquinas sought to make Aristotle's philosophy of human nature consistent with Christian beliefs (individual afterlife, etc.), and while many are convinced that he succeeded, some critics believe there is unresolved tension in Aquinas's version of Aristotelianism. Those who hold that persons are *not* essentially material often trace their lineage to Plato. Plato held that a human person has a material body and contains an immaterial soul, the bearer of one's identity. He therefore thought himself able to conceive of an afterlife in which the soul survives the destruction of the body. If the soul is the very same thing as the body, it appears that the fate of body and soul must be the same. Platonic dualism (as Plato's view as just reported is sometimes called) was refined by Boethius and Augustine, and has its defenders today. An important dimension of this thesis is that the concept of person is not inextricably wedded to biology or the human species.

Modern opponents of the Aristotelian, bodily criterion of personal life may align themselves with Plato, Augustine or Descartes, but they also receive considerable support from the eighteenth-century empiricist John Locke. Locke defined the person as 'a thinking, intelligent being, that has reason and reflection, and can consider itself as itself, the same thinking thing, in different times and places' (*An Essay Concerning Human Understanding* II, XXVII, 9). A popular, contemporary analysis of persons that similarly does not explicitly require that persons be materially constituted has been advanced by Harry Frankfurt. According to Frankfurt, a person is a subject that has beliefs and desires about his or her beliefs and desires. In some respects this position continues the legacy of Boethius for it defines 'person' in terms of being a subject that is capable of a certain level of rationality. If Locke's or Frankfurt's depiction of persons is plausible, then at least one obstacle has been removed that would otherwise block belief in a personal God.

One of the problems with defining 'person' in specific, exclusively biological terms is that it appears to be easy to imagine persons who are profoundly different from ourselves. Perhaps there are persons whose biology is not remotely like our own (extraterrestrials) or possibly even persons who are not biological at all (advanced, super-computers). The biological definition of person as 'human being' has been challenged by many advocates of animal rights who claim that there are persons in other animal species, cetaceans for example. (For a defence of an open-ended concept of 'person' see William Alston, 'Functionalism and theological language', *American Philosophical Quarterly* 22 [1985].)

Another debate concerning constitution that has considerable importance concerns the substantiality of persons. According to most forms of Buddhism, persons are best viewed as composed of a collection or system of desires, beliefs, sensations and so on. In the West, David Hume is considered one of the best-known proponents of a similar, non-substantial picture of persons; his view is sometimes called 'the bundle theory'. This stance contrasts with the conviction that persons are substantial, concrete individuals. Advocates of this later position include Thomas Reid, Joseph Butler (eighteenth century), and today Richard Swinburne and Roderick Chisholm. This debate affects the philosophy of God in several respects. On a bundle theory of persons, God may be conceived of as a vast network of beliefs, desires, sensations and the like. On a substantialist account, God and humans are subsistent, distinctive individuals.

Value

Another relevant debate concerns the value of persons. On one view, to think of a person *as a person* is already to suppose that the individual has worth. 'Treat me as a person' is analysed by some philosophers as a request to be treated with dignity and respect. Immanuel Kant held a related stance. 'Rational beings . . . are called persons because their nature already marks them out as ends in themselves – that is, as something which ought not to be used merely as a means – and consequently imposes to that extent a limit on all arbitrary treatment of them (and is even an object of reverence)' (*Groundwork of the Metaphysic of Morals* [trans. H. J. Paton; New York, 1964], p. 96). On another view, 'person' functions as a value-free description. It may be that persons deserve dignity and respect, but this is not, as it were, built into the very concept of 'being a person'.

The philosophy of God has reflected parallel developments. For some theists the term 'God' refers to a person who is omnipotent, omniscient and, along with the other divine attributes, essentially and supremely good. On this view it would be incoherent to suppose that God could do evil or should be treated as a mere means to an end. Alternatively, theists have treated 'God' as a proper name or as standing for a description that does not require God's essential goodness and worth. To these theists, it is not conceptually absurd to claim that God does evil.

Some religious implications of belief in a personal God

The belief that God is a person has an impact on a wide range of religious beliefs and practices.

In petitionary prayer requests are made to God for guidance or assistance. This appears to require the belief (or hope) that God is aware of petitions and has the power to respond to them. Peter Geach argues: 'It makes sense to approach God in the style of a petitioner only if one conceives of God as a rational agent who acts by free choice' (*God and the Soul* [London, 1969], p. 87).

The philosophy of religious values seems profoundly affected by whether they are informed by the belief in a personal God. Thus, one's ethic can be shaped by the thesis that the cosmos belongs to God in which God is a person with desires and feelings about welfare and justice. On this view, God's desires can intensify moral requirements, as when the duty to act justly is acknowledged both for its own sake as well as for the sake of responding in gratitude to the God who made all things. If God is thought of as passionately present to the world's goods and ills this can also result in a magnified view of the values at stake. Some ethical systems explicitly focus on divine–human interaction; this is true in covenantal ethics, some forms of theistic narrative ethics, and ethical systems that incorporate concepts of divine mercy and salvation. An exploration of the religious consequences of believing in a personal God has been especially fruitful in twentieth-century Jewish philosophy. The personal nature of God is dramatically represented in work by Martin Buber (1878–1965), particularly in his book *I and Thou* (sometimes translated *I and You*). The emphasis here is on the personal character of God as an eternal Thou; God cannot be talked about but can be talked with or to. Following Buber, Emmanuel Levinas (1906–95) has produced important work on how God may be revealed in and through our encounters with other persons.[1]

Nine arguments for a personal God

The following nine interrelated arguments have been advanced to defend the thesis that God is a person or personal.[2]

(1) Arguments from religious experience

Reports of experiencing God as a person or person-like being appear in a wide range of cultures over time. In so far as an argument from religious experience carries evidential weight it can be used to provide a reason for thinking of God as a person.

(2) Teleological, design arguments

These may be considered arguments for a personal cause or ground of the cosmos.

(3) Cosmological arguments

These arguments use various principles of explanation to advance the conclusion that the existence and continuation of our cosmos is best explained by the sustaining causation of a God-like being (self-existing, necessarily subsisting). Maimonides and others have defended accounts of creation that appeal to the volition or intentions of this being, and not its bare existence and power. If cosmological arguments are designed to secure belief in a being with intentions and will, they may be used to offer partial support for the belief that God is a person or like a person.

Standard cosmological arguments take the existence of the cosmos as their point of departure, but forms of the argument have been cast to explain the existence of abstracta like necessary propositions ($1 + 1 = 2$ and so on). Descartes and Leibniz appealed to the mind and preferences of God to explain the existence of these objects. This argument may also be explicitly formulated to support the thesis that there is a personal God.

(4) Arguments from miracles

It has been argued that certain historically important events provide evidence that God cares for humanity.

(5) Ontological arguments

If there is reason to think that the greatest possible being would be a person or personal, then ontological arguments for a greatest possible being may be read as arguments for a personal God.

(6) Theistic accounts of ethics

Some philosophers argue that objective moral laws are best explained as reflections of the preferences of God. A being with such approval and disapproval would presumably have traits that are personal.

(7) Kantian moral arguments

It has been argued that in order for ethics to be intelligible to us, we must assume that the universe is just. The most likely way in which the universe may be just (virtue and happiness are brought together) is if there is a powerful judge who will put things right. This appears to require presupposing the existence of a personal God. (The roots of such an argument are in Kant's *Critique of Practical Reason*, Book II, chapter II.)

(8) Wager arguments

Blaise Pascal and William James argued that it is prudent and good to cultivate the belief that theism is true even if we do not have strong evidence for it. A similar argument can be constructed for cultivating the belief that God is personal. (For a review of wager arguments see Nicholas Rescher, *Pascal's Wager* [Notre Dame, 1985].)

(9) Arguments from other theistic convictions

If certain beliefs about God are reasonable and it is reasonable to believe that they require God's being a person, then they can come into play in bolstering belief in God's personal nature. For example, if one has reason to think that there was an incarnation of God as the person of Jesus Christ, and the best way to describe and explain this is on the basis that God is a person, then this may provide added reasons for the belief that God is a person.

Other arguments can be constructed on behalf of the belief that God is a person. Another option is to bypass arguments altogether and simply rely on faith in a personal God rather than reason.

Nine counter-arguments

Belief in a personal God has been challenged systematically.

(1*) Arguments from religious experience

Consider two arguments. The aim of the first is to defeat the earlier argument from religious experience and holds that the supposed experience that God is personal should be explained away as mere projection and wish-fulfilment. The second is more aggressive. According to John Hick, the experience of the divine is so broad that it extends beyond the personal. Hick invokes the notion of 'the Real' to refer to the object of religious awareness; 'the Real' transcends both personal and non-personal notions of the deity (*Disputed Questions in Theology and the Philosophy of Religion* [New Haven, 1993]). While Hick retains personal notions of the deity as reflections of the divine, one may develop arguments that an altogether non-personal portrait of God is better secured experientially. In Advaita Vedanta forms of Hinduism, God or Brahman is conceived of as a non-personal reality. Confucianism and Daoism may both be interpreted as nature-oriented and capturing a religious experience that does not uphold God as a transcendental person.

(2*) Teleological, design arguments

These may be formulated with the conclusion that God is a non-personal force or that the earth is self-perpetuating and self-sufficient (cf. M. Martin, *Atheism* [Philadelphia, 1990]).

(3*) Cosmological arguments

As with teleological arguments, these may be formulated to argue that the cosmos has an impersonal cause. Rather than appeal to the intentions of a supreme cause, one may invoke the notion that the creation involves an impersonal emanation.

(4*) Arguments from miracles

If there have been some miracles, why haven't there been more? The following argument has been deployed: If God is a person that is all-good and all-powerful, miracles would be more widespread. If there are not as many miracles as we should expect from an all-good, all-powerful person, it is unreasonable to believe God is a person.

(5*) Ontological arguments

It has been argued that to think of God as a person is not to think of the greatest possible being.

(6*) Theistic accounts of ethics

This counter-argument has been the most influential historically. On this view, the difficulty with believing God is a person is that this opens the door to conceiving of God as a morally capricious individual. A personal God is one that may have a personality and thus idiosyncratic preferences like a favourite colour; it is relatively harmless to suppose God prefers blue for the sky but another thing to suppose God favours a specific race or gender. The promotion of ethically unstable pictures of God and the gods was a key element in the early philosophical opposition to the poetry of Hesiod and Homer. In their poems, gods rape, steal and murder. Plato credits the philosophical opposition to this view as pivotal in 'the ancient quarrel between poetry and philosophy' (*Republic* 10.607b5). The argument against a personal God may be formulated on the basis of the thesis that God is essentially good and thus impersonal, or as part of the wager argument below, viz. the cost of such a belief in a personal God is too high.

(7*) Kantian moral arguments

Here one might use Kant against himself. While Kant argues for a presumption of theism in the *Critique of Practical Reason*, elsewhere he appears to prize following one's duty with no thought of ultimate happiness or the final concord between virtue and happiness brought about by God (cf. early sections of *Groundwork of the Metaphysics of Morals*).

(8*) Wager arguments

In one version, Jean-Paul Sartre may be placed against Pascal and James. If Sartre is correct, then God's existence is a challenge or threat to one's subjectivity. Sartre contends that to believe there is a personal God is to envisage an encompassing divine gaze that locks and freezes one's otherwise free subjective life. (See his reflections on 'the look' or *Le regard* in *Being and Nothingness*.) If the belief that there is a personal God comes with such a cost, perhaps one should wager that it is false.[3]

(9*) Arguments from divine attributes

Insofar as one has reason to believe each of the following pairs, then it seems reasonable to conclude that God is not a person:

(a) God is eternal and nonspatial; persons are temporal and spatial.
(b) God is omnipresent, simple, indivisible and without parts; persons are finite, complex, divisible and composed of parts.
(c) God is essentially omniscient and omnipotent; persons are limited in knowledge and power.
(d) God is incorruptible, necessarily existing, without origin, immutable, and impassible; persons are corruptible, contingent, have a beginning, changeable, and subject to passion.
(e) God is essentially good; persons are not essentially good.
(f) God is ineffable; persons are comprehensible.

Other arguments against the thesis that God is a person may be forged on the basis of an appeal to Christian doctrine. Arguably, the Fathers and Councils of the Church did not advance the view that God is a person consisting of three persons. When a member of the Trinity is referred to as a person, this has a technical use that should not be interpreted as a univocal attribution between God and creation (e.g. 'person' is used in the same sense in these two sentences: 'The Father is a person' and 'John Doe is a person').

In defence of the personal nature of God

There is not space for a systematic reply, so I note two strategies and offer a final suggestion.

The first move in a rejoinder may involve arguments for a more elevated picture of persons and a more immanent view of God. Thus, one may argue that it is not a necessary truth that persons are such that they have origins or are corruptible or subject to wickedness. And, on the other hand, one may argue that God is temporal, subject to change and passion.

A second move may involve developing a conception of the personal nature of God that incorporates some of the precepts used in the counter-arguments above, e.g. perhaps God may be a person *and* essentially good and thus not such that God would ever act unjustly. By forging the link between persons and goodness, theists may reply that views like Sartre's rest on a mistaken view of 'the gaze of God'. God's gaze is liberating, and not suffocating.[4]

A suggestion

Belief in a personal God may have an impact on how one approaches the debate outlined in this entry. That is, the prospects of believing in a personal God may affect one's methodology and overall assessment of the strengths and weaknesses of the arguments at hand. C. S. Lewis sought to position debates about God's existence in a framework that takes the personal character of God seriously. 'What would, a moment before, have been variations in opinion, now become variations in your personal attitude to a Person. You are no longer faced with an argument which demands your assent, but with a Person who demands your confidence' (*The World's Last Night and Other Essays* [New York, 1960], p. 26).[5]

Notes

1 The belief that God is a person or personal has an impact in other areas I simply note for readers to explore further: concepts of meditation and religious experience, the concept that God is omnipresent, the philosophy of history, the notion of providence and tradition, belief in the beauty of God, the sacraments. Questions to be considered: Does it make sense to think of God having a personality? To what extent does the belief that God is a person rest on a theory of gender? Those interested in a philosophical or theological investigation of the Christian doctrine of the Trinity will need to address the belief that God is personal. Consider the Creed of the Council of Toledo: 'Each single Person is wholly God in himself and . . . all three Persons together are God.'

2 These arguments and the arguments in the next section are not exclusive and may be developed in either a cumulative or serial fashion.

3 Related arguments may be developed that involve puzzles addressed in other areas of the philosophy of God and human nature. Thus, one might argue that God's omniscience involves a threat to human freedom.

4 Indeed, Sartre seemed to suggest that the threat of the other's gaze might have a different value if one were spiritually in harmony with God.

5 I explore some of the ways in which philosophy may be carried out personally in 'Taking philosophy personally', *The Cresset* 57 (1994). A neglected but very fine treatment of a personal view of God is Clement C. J. Webb's *God and Personality* (London, 1971).

4

Religious language

James Ross

1. What is it? and what is the problem?

Religious language is the portion of natural language people use in
religious talk, whether stating their beliefs or unbelief, explaining a belief,
telling religious stories, interpreting their life events religiously ('God
answered my prayer'), disputing about the meaning of a sacred text,
writing hymns or even popular religious songs (Gospel music), praying,
performing liturgy or religious rituals, asking divine forgiveness for sins or
transgressions and so on. It is not just 'God talk', that is, talk about God,
pro or con, though that turns out to be a central element of religious
discourse and presents one of its central problems, namely, how we can use
words devised to apply to things we can see, hear, touch, smell or feel, to
describe a wholly transcendent being that cannot 'be seen with bodily eyes'
and is, apparently, vastly (some think wholly) unlike anything we can
experience.

I shall for the most part substitute the words 'religious discourse' for
talk, whether written or spoken, of matters religious. That is because I find
the common phrase 'religious language' infelicitous. Its nearest analogues
would have to be 'bad language', 'obscure language', 'smutty language',
'obscene language' and the like. For there really is no language that, as
such, is religious. Religious talk can go on in any natural language. The
basic syntax (grammar) and semantics (meaning relationships) of French,
German, Attic Greek, Latin or Arabic are unchanged when the languages
are used in religious discourse. It is true that there is specialized vocabulary
in religious talk, with expressions like 'almighty', 'creator', 'sin', 'salvation', 'grace', 'predestination' and the like being characteristic of Western
Christian discourse, and other expressions being characteristic of Jewish
ritual discourse, and still others characteristic of Islam, and so on. And
within Christian sects, as in Jewish and Islamic sects, there are further
vocabulary peculiarities. Among some Christian groups, for instance, the

notion that Jesus is 'my personal saviour' is a central idea, not emphasized as much by other groups.

Notice also that religious discourse does not have to be monotheistic (expressing belief in one supreme being) as it is for Jews, Christians and Muslims. It can be polytheistic (many divine beings), as was the discourse about the gods in ancient Greece and later Rome and in German mythology (cf. the operas of Wagner). It can be polytheistic and pantheistic (everything is in some sense divine), as in many African animist religions and many oriental religions such as forms of Hinduism. It can even be atheistic (i.e. religious without acknowledging any supreme or otherwise divine being, as in some forms of Buddhism and Unitarianism). It is parochial to think that religious talk has the vocabulary and concepts peculiar to Western monotheism (though some of the philosophical problems to be discussed below arise only in the monotheistic contexts). And most of the other religious traditions mentioned above do not intersect with the Western philosophical tradition in which the meaningfulness of religious discourse and the origin of religious knowledge are systematically discussed.

So, what is the problem? Let us consider talk about the existence and nature of God, first, putting the rest (which includes talk of sin, judgement, resurrection, eternal life, the kingdom of God, and the like) aside for a while.

Anaxagoras (around 450 BC) observed that if sheep and oxen had hands and could paint they would render the gods in their own likenesses. For that and other sentiments he was accused of impiety and had to flee from Athens to avoid prosecution (which ended in death for Socrates on a similar charge). But what Anaxagoras said highlights the basic options when talking about divinity. For either:

(a) What we say about divine beings who are not sensibly perceptible, either because they are invisible and immaterial, or because they dwell in some inaccessible part of the world (Mount Olympus, Valhalla or wherever), is no more than a projection of our own images, imaginations, feelings and features of our experienced world (*anthropomorphism*: making things in the image of humans);

or

(b) we know nothing whatever about such beings, even whether there are any, and what we say about them makes as little sense as the ravings of a madman about the objects of his delirious experiences. For if the words we use to attribute things (e.g. being, power, wisdom, intelligence) to the gods do not mean what they mean when we talk about humans and our world, then from where do they get their meanings?

107

It seems as if the basic problem is an unhappy choice between anthropo-morphism (thinking of divinity in human terms) and full-blown agnosticism (knowing nothing about divine things at all).

As to that choice, most of us now would say that the entire religion of the Greek and Roman gods was anthropomorphic and false, regardless of how fruitful the myths of Greek and Rome may be. And, perhaps incautiously, we would say something similar about the animistic myths of various African and Native American religions (stories that attribute active spirits to trees, rocks, mountains, etc.). Some great philosophers have opted for fairly strong versions of the second, agnostic, option noted above. An example is the Jewish thinker Moses Maimonides (1135–1204). He said that, outside negations like 'God is not a body', and some very general things like 'God exists', 'God is the first uncaused cause of all change', and a few other things we can establish with the help of Aristotle's philosophy, there is nothing both literal and positive that we can say about God on the basis of any reasoning not prompted by divine revelation in the Scriptures. And, even then (so Maimonides suggests), most of what we can say informatively is metaphorical, allegorical and untranslatable into literal positive truths. Various strains of agnosticism about the meaning of God-talk (some even denying there is any literal, meaningful, positive truth about God) recur throughout later history right to the present time.

The first option just noted has the result that what is said is false. The second option seems to imply that what is said does not mean anything literally, and that we have no genuine knowledge about any divine being, or even of the existence of any divine being. All the major discussions of religious language (religious discourse) either adopt one of these options or propose one or another way through the dilemma – some by systematic qualification of the options, and others by the introduction of new options, like that of Aquinas, both about meaning and about knowledge. In what follows I shall describe the twentieth-century Anglo-American positivist attack on religious discourse as meaningless. I shall also try to explain the medieval analogy theory of St Thomas Aquinas (a theory designed to preserve the cognitive content of religious discourse in general). I shall conclude with a contemporary elaboration of Aquinas's basic position based on phenomena that I call 'semantic contagion' (i.e. the automatic adapta-tion of word-meanings to their verbal environments when discourse is in traction – when it is being used to modify thought and action, as in 'She dropped her books' and 'She dropped her eyes').

2. What happened?

There was a very long tradition beginning early in the Christian era (when Jewish and Christian religion first encountered Greek and Roman philosophy) and repeated again when Islam encountered Greek philosophy, of having to determine which parts of the Bible were to be taken literally and which metaphorically, or allegorically, and so forth. One of the earliest major books on the matter, St Augustine of Hippo's *On Christian Teaching*, tries to arbitrate regarding some conflicts between the Neoplatonic philosophical world-view and the Bible. It also proposes a 'fullness of truth' attitude toward the words of the Bible. Augustine suggests that, in addition to the narrative, historical or legal content of a given passage, the divine author of Scripture also intended to convey any true thing that can be expressed by the words of the text, whether taken literally, figuratively (prophetically), allegorically (as carrying another message besides the surface story) or metaphorically.

Augustine, the first great Christian philosopher, was simply not troubled by the dilemma I described above because, like Neoplatonists in general, he thought we could transcend the world of sensation once we get by the childish idea (which, so Augustine reports in his *Confessions*, blocked him a long time until he read some philosophy) that a divine being is some sort of a material or physical thing, more or less the way the Romans thought of their gods and as many people nowadays think of movie stars and sports heroes, as if they are larger than life, models of how things really are, somehow more real than things around us, but still physical things. Once he accepted the Neoplatonic idea that the material is less real than the immaterial, and that no genuine knowledge comes through the senses anyway, he had no problem with the question of where our words get their meanings (he wrote a dialogue specifically on that, *On the Teacher*) or where we get our knowledge of such spiritual things as the Bible conveys: it is by divine illumination. In fact, all knowledge comes from God just as all seeing is in the light of day or other illumination.

Another Neoplatonic contribution that had immense historical influence came from an otherwise unknown author now commonly referred to as 'Pseudo-Dionysius'. In medieval times, his work (consisting of several treatises focusing on how humans can know and talk about God) was regarded as having great authority because it was (wrongly, as we now know) believed to have been written by an associate of St Paul. And, so he says, there are three states of knowledge and meaning in what we can know and say about God. The first is the way of negation, where we deny that God in a body, in a place, can be seen, and the like. The second is the way of affirmation, in which we say affirmatively, but very inadequately, things like 'God is alive', 'God is wise', 'God is loving', all of which, though true, fall short of saying anything really significant. The third is the way of eminence or superlatives, where we say such things as 'God is beyond being', 'God is beyond goodness', and where we say 'God is super-being, super-good', and so on – using superlatives as a way of expressing what is really true about God. Neoplatonist Christians and Jews characteristically rejected the dichotomy of anthropomorphism versus agnosticism by rejecting the idea that any genuine knowledge comes through the senses or from material things. They held that we have another source of all genuine knowledge with which we can express many and deep truths about God and can interpret the revelation in the Scriptures.

Neoplatonist philosophy was a very important influence on Western Christianity for 1,100 years. And it has never been extirpated from Western philosophy. Consider, for instance, the Augustinian dualism of Descartes, the Neoplatonism of Leibniz, and the many forms of Platonism to be found even among contemporary, supposedly physicalist, philosophers. Note, for instance the dualism (actually trialism) of Karl Popper (1902–94) and John Eccles. Also note the materialists who are Platonists about logic and mathematics, not to mention the determinedly Augustinian dualism in which body and soul are distinguished in popular religious discourse in which Jesus is said to save souls and in which prayers ask for the passage of souls into heaven.

3. Aquinas's analogy theory

Once Aristotle's philosophy came to replace Neoplatonism (which, of course, was never entirely accomplished, as Bonaventure, Scotus, the Renaissance Platonic revival, and Descartes's Augustinian dualism illustrate), and once it was interpreted and adapted by St Albert the Great and St Thomas Aquinas, Aristotle's three-part doctrine of analogy of being, thinking and meaning not only served for metaphysics in general, philosophy of nature, moral philosophy and philosophical psychology, but was particularly applied by Aquinas to the study of God and religious doctrines in general. And there it untied the anthropomorphism/agnosticism knot, and provided a means for a general account of knowledge of God through God's effects, the creation, and through the scriptural revelation of God's action within history that, taken together and explicated together, were called 'divine science' (*scientia divina*), by analogy to the science of nature.

Among statements about God, Aquinas distinguished between (a) those that are true independently of any spatio-temporal vantage (e.g. 'God is one, almighty, all-knowing, eternal and simple'), and (b) statements vantaged in the human standpoint (like 'God knew before the Earth began to be that humans would fall into sin', 'God knows what will happen throughout the rest of human history' and 'God knows everything I will ever think or do'). Among the vantaged truths (that is my phrase not his), Aquinas distinguished those to be taken literally (like 'God has always loved me' and 'God will forgive my repented sins') from those to be taken metaphorically (such as 'God repented ordering the complete destruction of the enemies of the Israelites'). And he distinguished allegorical, symbolic and prophetic statements, including statements expressing the 'spiritual' meaning of Scripture and of the Mosaic Law. Among vantaged truths, Aquinas also distinguished truths (these are his phrases) according to the appearances of things (e.g. 'The stars are the ornament of the heavens') from truths according to the reality of things (e.g. 'The stars are the substance of the heavens').

While those distinctions are very important to Aquinas's overall treatment of religious discourse and are constantly used by him (for example, to reconcile the truth of popular piety that God knows the future with the 'scientific' truth that God is eternal and unchangeable), they do not form part of the analogy of meaning theory. Rather, they use it, often involving cases of words used analogically. For instance, in certain vantaged truths the words function both allegorically, analogously and metaphorically – for instance: 'The kingdom of God will be established on Earth with the return of the Messiah and will last until the end of the world.'

Aquinas used the analogy theory to escape the dilemma that if our words, applied to God, mean the same thing they mean applied to creatures, the resulting descriptions are anthropomorphic and thus false (though some evangelicals and process theologians disagree about that even today), whereas, if the words have not the same meanings they have when applied to things of our experience, then they are used merely equivocally and there is no content to what is said because there is nothing to determine which concepts attach to the words. If the words are cut loose from anchoring in our experience, they lose all content and religious talk becomes mostly meaningless.

The basic assumption of the theory adapted from Aristotle was that *the meaning of a word is a concept derived by abstraction from things*, so that *analogy among words reflects analogy among things* (*analogia entis*). Meaning-differences for the same word in different occurrences that are not mere homonyms track reality-differences in the things named or predicated. And metaphorical thinking is an application of analogous thinking.

I shall now outline Aquinas's account, noting that the organization and divisions within his theories are contested among scholars and that my explanation is heavily influenced by Cajetan's (1498) work *On the Analogy of*

Names (*De Nominum Analogia*) not only by the names of the classifications he imposed on Aquinas's texts, but also by the theoretical priority, both in metaphysics in general and in theology particularly, that he assigned to 'analogy of proper proportionality', holding, in brief, that when we think 'God is intelligent' our judgement is not just an extrinsic attribution, as when we say of food that fosters health 'That's healthy food', nor even one of intrinsic attribution alone, as when we say of the author of a brilliant book 'He's brilliant' – though such judgements are for Aquinas the beginning of our natural knowledge of God through God's effects, the creation. Rather, from a platform of knowledge of God through God's effects, such as the intelligence manifested in creation, we get into a position of recognizing analogies of proper proportionality by our recognizing the *participation* of creatures in the being of God.

In other words, the groundwork for judgements involving notions (and words) that apply by proper proportionality to creatures and to God is the real relation of participation by which creatures have their being and everything that is real about them from God. This ontological basis for key analogical judgements is usually not explained clearly enough by commentators, though some like Norris Clarke SJ have been emphatic about it.

The order of knowledge Aquinas develops is that we first come to know the existence and something of the nature of God by considering the origin of the material world in a first mover, first productive cause, an uncaused necessary being, a source of all perfection, and a designer of the goal-directed nature of the universe. Thus knowledge of God begins with knowledge of the cause of the being of what we perceive. But by further philosophical reflection, we recognize that the relation in being of creatures to God has to be participation, a notion Aquinas adapted for his own use, partly reminiscent of Plato's and Plotinus's notions, but in no way suggesting sameness of being between creatures and God; instead, participation involves constant causation of the finite by God, complete derivativeness of finite from infinite being, real reflection of divine being in finite perfections, and enough likeness for God to be present both by likeness and by constant causation everywhere in his creation, though most perfectly, among material things, inwardly among humans, by causing the light by which they understand, just as he causes the daylight in which the sighted can see.

Another useful metaphor for participation is a mirror reflection. In the presence of light the surface of the mirror reflects whatever it faces. The being of the mirror image, while its own, is entirely caused, and constantly caused, by whatever it faces that is illuminated. So the content and the being of the mirror image is entirely derived, entirely caused. You can see that for yourself, just by turning a small mirror in your hand and watching the image change by what it faces. The image exists by participation in the being that causes it.

Once that relationship is recognized, especially that everything about the creature is constantly caused by God, one can, Aquinas thinks, make many judgements that are not just based on inference from effect to cause, but are based in universal metaphysical and evaluative principles that apply analogously to everything that is, in any way whatever, adjusted according to the manner and perfection of its being. Thus the intelligence of God is understood not only as required of the cause of intelligent creatures and of the order of nature, but as an intrinsic pure perfection of being, that is, the kind of feature (like 'to be', 'to live', 'to understand', 'to love') that involves no limitation (no unfulfilled capacity) in itself and excludes no other feature that involves no limitation (all pure perfections being compatible). Thus God is understood to possess all pure perfections without any entitative plurality or real distinction among them at all.

And since there is no composition of matter and form or of capacity and activity in God, God's essence is said to be identical with his existence, not in the sense that by knowing that God exists one can know what God is (for the essence of God is unknowable to creatures), but in the sense that, unlike all other real things, there is no real distinction (no real difference) between God's being and what God is, while with all other things, *what* they are is related to their *being* as a *capacity* to its *realization* (a potency that limits act). So, for any other thing, *what-it-is* limits its being: a dog can only be a dog, not a lion. A created thing, a thing that does not exist necessarily, has its being as if it fills a limited container, namely, what-it-is, which is its potentiality to be.

With the relation of participation understood, the infinitude of divine perfections grasped, the absolute simplicity and the lack of real distinction between essence and being in God, understood, the philosophers can then go on to figure many other things out about God, ranging from what creation involves, to divine omniscience, omnipotence, providence, governance, omnipresence, immensity, impassibility, and care for the whole cosmos, besides being by nature love. That is the way Aquinas constructs the first part of his *Summa Theologiae*.

The problem that emerges by question 13 of *Summa Theologiae* is what determines the content, the meaning, of all those terms that are applied to God. In particular, Aquinas is concerned to ask how univocation (with its consequent anthropomorphism and falsity) is avoided on the one hand, and the vacuity of mere equivocation avoided on the other. That is where Aquinas responds, first, with the easily understood analogy of attribution (where a common term is used to designate an intrinsic property of an effect, and then by attribution designates an appropriate feature of the cause, sign, symptom, etc., of that effect, as is the case with 'healthy', 'medical' and 'legal' applied to the processes and then to the accoutrements). But Aquinas is also concerned to make clear that, with things related by participation, whatever words designate perfections in the dependent thing can without limitation of the concepts be used to designate perfections in the participated being – otherwise there would be no genuine participation. So I suggest that the foundation for analogy of proper proportionality for Aquinas is the participation of the creature in the being of its cause, the creator. It is better to formulate the basic A:B :: C:D expressions in such a way that the analogous term is the common *predicate that makes a true statement out of the fragments*, as I will indicate in section 5. Thus: As Socrates was to the practicalities of his life, so God is to the order in nature: namely 'wise'. Thus both 'Socrates was wise' and 'God is wise' are true but 'wise' is not univocal, because the manner of being for the participating and the participated are different, though the concept, the conception (the *res significata*), is the same: that can be seen from the common linguistic affinities and oppositions of the two predicates. Plato was to philosophy as God is to everything knowable: namely, 'understanding', and so forth. The analogy of meaning is consequent on the analogy of being, mediated by analogous thinking (*analogia rationis*) by which the relevant sameness of *res significata* (conceptual content) and difference of *modus significandi* (proportional to the participated vs. participating perfection) is recognized.

People have tried to co-ordinate Aquinas's varying divisions of kinds of analogy into a single table. I think the general division of multiple occurrences of the same word into (a) univocal, (b) merely equivocal (homonymous), and (c) analogous, with analogous terms divided into (1) analogous by attribution (what Aquinas calls 'by proportion' where he means 'by a relation' of cause/effect, sign, symptom, representation, etc.), (2) analogy of proper proportionality, and (3) analogy of improper proportionality (metaphor), is the most comprehensive.

There is another co-ordinate division of analogous terms into 'of one to another' and 'of many to one', applying to all analogous terms, regardless of type. Thus, the terms belonging to the ten Aristotelian categories (substance, quantity, quality, relation, action, passion, time, place, position and disposition) are ordered 'many to one' because the sense in which individual substances are said to exist is prior to the sense in which anything in any of the other categories (a colour or a quart, say) is said to exist. Another example of an order 'of many to one' is the multiple senses in which 'medical' is ordered by attribution to 'medical' applied to the art of the practitioner. Similarly, the analogous order of 'of one to another' is exhibited in the sense in which a creature is said to be (e.g. by participation), in comparison to the sense in which God is said to be (by subsistent being: *ipsum esse subsistens*), and it is also illustrated by the analogy of attribution by which both an author and his book are called 'brilliant'. The dispute about the best classification is not important, whereas that about what is the fundamental sense in which words are applied as divine predicates is, in my opinion, central. If the sense in which 'wise' applied to God has no more content than 'so disposes of the order of nature as to be similar to what a wise engineer or ruler does', then the content of statements about the divine being is vastly less than that supposed when analogy of proportionality based in real participation in being is treated as fundamental. In sum, the basic idea of Aquinas is that meanings (which are concepts, and habits of judgement associated with words, naming, predicating or affirming or denying being) adjust to the mode of being (*modus essendi*) of what we are talking about. And that extends everywhere, not just to religion, and includes all the basic notions of metaphysics including 'cause', 'exists', 'knows', 'acts', 'desires', 'loves', 'understands', 'matter', 'form', 'substance', 'accident', and every other general notion with which we do philosophy.

In sum, there are two ways in which positive literal truths can be stated about God by analogy of meaning. The first is that of attribution, where a term that attributes something intrinsically present in something (e.g. health in a dog) is also used to characterize something related to it as cause, effect, sign, symptom or representation, as 'the dog's coat is healthy', and in reasoning about, say, change in the physical world, one concludes there is an unmoved mover, by attribution, though once the participation relation is recognized, then there is further content by analogy of proportionality to the statement that there is one unmoved mover of the entire cosmos. Thus, there is a second kind of analogy in which a word occurs in related senses when applied to suitably different subjects. For instance, 'collected' applies, with differentiation, to 'he collected books' and 'he collected dues'. Similarly, 'knows' applies to both Socrates and God, but whatever Socrates knows is through abstraction and judgement from sense perception, whereas nothing God knows involves any material process or animal process at all. Yet the common word 'knows' is neither merely equivocal nor merely metaphorical; nor is it applied merely by extrinsic attribution. Rather, the common predicate applies literally and intrinsically to both subjects, but differentiated according to the manner of being of each.

The manner of being for things is very varied: there really are planets, eclipses, days, books, fields, furniture, and even privations like blindness and lameness. None of these things exists in the manner of any of the others, yet the reality commitment is the same in each case, its mode or modality differing with the ontological status of the subjects. That is also true when we say substances (e.g. cats) exist, as do shapes and amounts and locations. Similarly when we say God is intelligent and Plato is intelligent, the manner of intelligence differs but what intelligence is remains the same in both cases – that is what Aquinas called 'sameness of *res significata*' and 'difference of *modus significandi*' where the mode of signifying tracks the manner of being (*modus essendi*) of the subject.

That is what Aquinas's solution to how we can make true, literal, positive statements about God and other things religious comes to. His account involves many acute observations about meaning-relationships among same-terms in natural languages, and, of course, is inextricably tied to two theses about language: that the meanings of words are concepts abstracted through our acquaintance with perceived things, and that our conceptions differentiate in response to the diversity of the manner of being of things, even things otherwise similar and described with the same words. And there is the underlying metaphysical theory about the relationship of creatures to the cause of their being: that creatures participate in the being of the creator so that there is therefore a basis for conceptions to apply analogously by proportionality to both creatures and creator. There is a further, unexpressed commitment, that there is great cognitive efficiency in analogy, just as there is in metaphor, an efficiency that would be totally lost if whenever things were analogously differentiated we had entirely different words for them. Thus, although the manner of perception between humans and higher animals, say horses and cats, is importantly different because all human perception is intelligent, involving conception and judgement to some degree, if we used different words to name the process by which animals are aware of themselves and of their environments, the analogous community of consciousness and real presence of things through perception might permanently escape notice. Besides, we would not have any words to describe God in that case. So analogy is not a substitute for a more elaborate vocabulary; it cannot be replaced by adding more words. Rather, the carry-over of meaning is cognitively essential.

Of course, if animals are not really conscious and aware, then to use the common term 'perceive' would just perpetuate an error of judgement, just as the use of the word 'adds' applied to an adult who understands a sum and to a calculator without any awareness at all tends to confuse some students as to just what a machine is doing. A recent illustration of that point is in the description of Deep Blue (the IBM computer) that 'won' a chess match with Kasparov, the world champion at the time. Many people erroneously supposed the machine was playing chess, rather than just simulating chess-playing. That kind of case gives us the first warning that something may be missing in Aquinas's assumption that our differentiated concepts track the real differences in things. For if you do not recognize the real difference (between adding and simulating adding) you won't think the words differentiate, and you will falsely conclude that the machine and the person are doing the very same thing: adding. But if recognizing analogy, especially of proportionality, is a fallible process, one where we may easily think that because the same word applies to quite different things it still means the same thing, and thus denotes the same reality in both (as might be the case for a person who thinks that 'see' in the two statements 'He could see the tug towing the barge out on the horizon' and 'He could see the interior angles of a triangle had to be 180 degrees' has the same meaning and denotes the same reality, rather than analogous but different realities), then the question will arise how to bring others to recognize analogous predication. Now Aquinas did not discuss that. But I think that as people are made aware of semantic contagion, they will become more attentive. Still, Aquinas made a lot of progress, eliminating both the anthropomorphic and the mere equivocation options on very plausible linguistic, conceptual and ontological grounds. And a genuine basis for knowledge of things related causally and also by participation has been proposed.

4. The non-cognitivist attack

David Hume (1711–76) launched the first modern version of non-cognitivism at the end of his *Inquiry* (1748) where he said that when we come across any book that contains metaphysics we should consign it to the flames. But it was the development of logical positivism in the twentieth century that put a new curve on an otherwise old pitch. The philosophers like Bertrand Russell and his Austrian-born colleague Ludwig Wittgenstein in England and the members of the Vienna Circle (Rudolf Carnap, Moritz Schlick, and other followers like A. J. Ayer and R. B. Braithwaite) wanted to make philosophy clearer, more like science; so they adopted the view that anything we say that is meaningful, that expresses something, whether true or false, that has cognitive content, has to be either a mere relation of ideas (of meanings) or verifiable directly or indirectly. By cognitive content they meant something intelligible that, at least in principle, we can find out to be true or false, either by formal manipulations that we do mathematically and logically, or by experimentation and observation that we do through perceptual experience. Anything else falls below the level where truth or falsity can be ascribed to it, resembling poetry, painting, and even the mumbling of madmen, amounting, cognitively, to nonsense. That general attitude was refined into particular tests of meaningfulness (which in this context really means accessible cognitive content), one of which was the verifiability principle, with which Ayer became so well known: that an utterance is meaningful only if it is directly or in principle verifiable through observation. That led Ayer to say loudly and iconoclastically that none of the religious talk that expressed belief in God, or in any of the transactions of God with the perceptible world, had any cognitive content at all – that, just like moral and aesthetic discourse, it could be completely dismissed from the realm of the meaningful. That led to various versions of emotivism: that such utterances are nothing more than expressions of our attitudes, not suitable for appraisal as true or false, but more like sighs, gasps and groans, as poetry and music were taken to be.

Two things happened. The philosophers reacted very critically and by 1933 it was pretty clear that no formulations of the verifiability test for meaningfulness could pass the test of being verifiable. The only other option was that the principle was, if true, true on account of a relation of ideas or a meaning relation. But, in that case, it was trivial, because it was a cardinal principle of positivist thinking that so-called *a priori* truths (truths not derived from experience) were mere tautologies, lacking any content beyond connecting ideas. As a result, verificationism was evidently self-refuting. Nevertheless, a lot of religious thinkers, including Braithwaite, hopped onto the bandwagon and started offering empirical interpretations of religious doctrines – culminating in John Hick's idea that credal beliefs are 'eschatologically verifiable' (for instance, if the dead will rise, you just have to wait long enough to see it). Now I mention that only to indicate a recurrent tendency of theologians to 'buy into' the prevailing philosophical views and to re-tailor their religious commitments to fit. But the verifiability attack and the theological surrender to finding empirically verifiable truths in the Creed were, to us now, obvious and horrendous mistakes. In fact, one lesson to be learned from the long history of attacks on the meaningfulness of religious discourse (a lesson that applies to Continental attacks on language in general today) is that they all end up clearly defeated, and usually by self-refutation. So, for instance, what does the Continental cry that language is unfit for the expression of knowledge, because it is so corrupted by the political and paternalistic prejudices of dominant males, come to but a claim that is incompatible with its own truth?

5. Updating classical analogy theory

By 'the classical analogy theory' I mean the account as first explained and used by Aristotle and then further developed especially by Aquinas and further by his commentators, like Cajetan, John of St Thomas (1589–1644), Francis Suarez (1548–1617) and many later writers.

There are three parts of the classical analogy theory: analogy of meaning (a linguistic phenomenon), thinking analogously (a mixture of epistemology and psychology), and analogy of being (a metaphysical aspect that I call analogous reality). Each needs an updated explanation, and so do the ways they are connected. For in the classical theory the connections were simpler, in principle anyway, than we can suppose now. The meaning of a word was thought to be a concept derived by abstraction from perceptual experience of things (including oneself), so that conceptual differences, and therefore word-meaning differences (for example 'sees' applied to a ship's lookout and to a bird), were thought to track the real difference between intelligent sight and animal perception. Similarly, when one thinks metaphorically that Jesus is the king of peace or the lamb of God, the concept of 'king' is adjusted to leave out the limitations of human kingship, while retaining the notion of supreme authority aimed at peace, and the element of unprotesting innocent sacrifice is retained without the element of mute uncomprehending dumb animality. As I explained above, once one recognizes the participation in being between the creature and God, and keeps in mind that everything about the creature is derived causally and by finite representation of the infinite, one has found the basis in reality for the common but adapted conceptions that are the meanings of the words for perfections attributed both to creatures and to God.

That neat mapping of words and their meanings, and differing but related concepts, onto real differences among proportionally similar things has to be updated for at least four reasons. First, because we now know that meanings of words are not simply concepts-in-the-mind. Second, we know that differentiation in meaning does not always map real differences in reality (there are mistakes). Third, we know that there are differences in realities that are not tracked by our meaning differentiations (again, there are mistakes). And fourth, we know, or some of us do, that words differentiate in meaning depending upon what other words are used with them (e.g. drop/eyes; drop/pen). We also know that contextual adaptation can happen while a speaker insists, mistakenly, that the word continues to have the same meaning. Lots of philosophers, like W. V. Quine, think there is a basic sense of 'exists' that applies univocally to whatever really exists. But, when I say 'there really are galaxies, protons, accidents, traffic jams, concerts, pauses, misunderstandings, conflicts, appointments, monetary supplies and money as well', I expect the notions of 'really are' to adapt according to what the completion words mean, just as 'govern' does in 'He governed himself and he governed his province'.

So meanings are not just 'in-the-head'. They have publicity and objective interpersonality. And while you can mean anything you like, up to a point, by your words, that is *your* meaning, not *the* meaning, which itself may be vague and vacillating – as are the meanings of 'valid', which for students can range from 'relevant' to 'worthwhile', to 'true' to 'convincing', to 'conclusive' (students, when asked, can rarely articulate the contrasting senses of the word or the exact sense in which they meant it). But that, with thousands of other cases, only displays that the meanings of words are entirely determined by use (of which an individual speaker may have an inchoate grasp) and follow semantic regularities that differentiate meanings by context: compare 'He collected debts' with 'He collected china dolls'.

So, updating classical analogy of meaning has to take into account the linguistic phenomena of analogy. That will still leave Aquinas's basic division of the material intact, though we will find that 'attribution' has many other forms, better called denominative analogy (my late friend, yesterday's dinner), and that paronymy (difference of related word forms: healthy/healthful) in one language is analogy in another (*sanus* for both in Latin), and that what comes out as many words in one language can be a single polysemous word in another: *dare* in Italian can mean 'to give, hand, grant, permit, commit, appoint, announce, produce, yield, show, tell, stroke, dart, incline to, sell, buy'. And *levare* means 'to raise, lift, take away, remove, carry, take off, raise up, get out, buy (a large quantity), prohibit, levy'. At least in the latter case we can discern a continuity across many of the meanings; in the former, continuity is less obvious in English but clear in Italian.

And the updating, while not denying that it is by notions, concepts, conceptions and ideas and other abstractions that we understand both words and things, will not *equate* meaning with concepts and will not claim that analogy of things is accurately or adequately reflected in analogy of meaning, though to a great extent it is, or claim that we can inherently detect or discern analogies because, in fact, they are often very hard to discern and it may require extraordinary intelligence to grasp some of them, and we can often be mistaken as well.

The accounts of analogy of meaning, of thinking and of being, like Aquinas's account, have to be made *general*, to encompass the whole of thinking, meaning and reality, so that the solution to the cognitive content of religious discourse, like that of any other, including morality, metaphysics and science, will simply drop out as a particular case within the semantic and other regularities, though I will urge that traditional talk about God does linguistically presuppose the metaphysical doctrine of participation as Aquinas understood it.

Before I go on to explain the linguistic phenomenon that I call 'semantic contagion', one might very well ask whether *differences of meaning* caused by contrasting completion expressions ('the news *shook* him'/'the bouncing truck *shook* him') is a reflection or resonance of *reality differences* between information and a vehicle. Are we not going to get the same sort of parallelism between language and reality, mediated by thought, that Aristotle and Aquinas supposed, just made more complex by the fact that analogy of meaning among occurrences of the same words is virtually everywhere in natural languages? In the end, yes, but not item by item by abstraction, but by a more complex account of how discourse is a medium of thought modulating human action, with plenty of room for meaning-relationships that embed false, as well as true, beliefs about the world. Then, what about linguistic metaphysics, the activity of mapping ontology from the grammar and meaning relationships within natural languages? The short answer to that is that it is a very unreliable enterprise because meaning relationships, including oppositions, do not infallibly parallel the real relationships of things and, often, the names we use are quite arbitrarily related to the objects that bear them. So you cannot reliably extract the ontology of the world from the presuppositions of meaning and grammar.

There is no neat parallel among differentiated meanings, differentiated conceptions and differentiated reality. Meanings are not just concepts, and we can form contrasting concepts and conceptions that do not reflect really contrasting realities. So there are some quite difficult aspects to 'updating' Aquinas's analogy theory to give it a larger linguistic component while trying to preserve the general outline of his ideas about analogous meaning, analogous thinking and analogous realities. Some of those issues require a lot more work than has been done yet. But enough has been done to get us started, anyway, first to show on linguistic grounds that analogy of meaning, as contextual adaptation of meaning, really does have a universal basis, and that it is not some mysterious and cognition-defeating peculiarity of religious discourse, and that analogous differences of meaning often do reflect differences in the manner of being (*modus essendi*) of things: for instance, we say 'there really is [are]' money, mountains, stone walls, hills, bushes, forests, pathways and individual mice. They are all existents, objects of thought, spatio-temporal and historical entities; yet the term 'really exists' applies differently to different items.

The most useful start, I think, is to contrast analogy of meaning with univocity of recurring words, where the spelling is the same and the meanings are the same, in contrast to mere equivocation (e.g. *bank* = repository for money; *bank* = verge), where the spelling is the same and the meanings are unrelated. And within the class of same-terms related but differentiated in meaning, we distinguish between words that, taken in pairs of occurrences,

(1) express sign, cause, effect, symptom, representation, or other relationships to an intrinsic case, as with 'medical' applied to the physician's art and applied to medical facilities, medical licences, medical smells, medical books, medical school, etc. (Those are all cases of what Aquinas calls analogy of attribution [analogy of relation].)

(2) are used to express a proportional similarity: 'He *sought* a new job'; 'He *sought* learning'. Within that class, there are words used to express a

121

likeness among very different things, metaphors: He was the Lion of Judah; He was the Lamb of God.

The foundation of all metaphor is analogy of proportionality, as I will explain. Then we can move on briefly to analogous thinking and analogous reality. But notice, in each case, the fundamentals for the solution of the problem about religious discourse are to be provided by a *general* account of some aspect of language, thought, or reality, not in some features peculiar to religion alone.

The positivist/empiricist enemies of religion, metaphysics, art criticism, poetry and moral discourse, in section 4 above, thought there was an infirmity of meaning, thinking and reality, peculiar to those subjects, as I have explained. But a further grasp of meaning, cognition and reality shows there is none; they are all cases of questions and answers that apply to everything at every level of abstraction. So, let us turn to the language aspects of analogy of meaning.

Language

Reading Aristotle and Aquinas you might suppose analogy to be a feature of just some words, particularly those used in philosophy and religious discourse. So the first novelty is to notice that analogy is a general feature of words depending upon their verbal context and larger environment of use. Analogy is adaptation of meaning to contrast of context and environment. It comes about by semantic contagion. It does not involve changed meaning, though it may appear so when we interchange completion words, like 'books', 'eyes', 'jaw', 'courses', in a sentence frame like 'She dropped her . . . '. But rather, 'dropped' just has different meanings in the different sentences; the appearance of change is illusory.

Now suppose we have an ordinary disambiguating use in which each of those sentences is used to modify belief or action, and thus the discourse is *in traction* with life: it is evident that 'dropped' does not have the same meaning in each pair of cases. What accounts for the differences of meaning is the dominance of the completion expressions over the pliant common verb. Similarly with 'he collected . . . ' completed by 'stamps/debts/tickets/donations/his wits'. (I will explain the dominance phenomenon shortly.)

That you may call some of those cases metaphors only reinforces the claim that analogy of meaning is a general linguistic phenomenon, to be explained by general features of natural language, because metaphor is just a family of usages within the linguistic phylum of analogy. The other two main families of analogy are analogies of attribution (the 'medical' examples above) and the analogies of proper proportionality, as in 'He read philosophy'/'He read magazines'. The adjustment of meaning is so smooth most people do not even notice the difference of meaning in the two cases.

The differentiation of words used to attribute a feature to things (brilliance, intelligence, health, wealth, power, and so on), and to characterize the cause, effect, signs, symptoms and representations, is so common and orderly that we seldom notice it either. For instance, we speak of *business* practice/schools/ethics/methods/services/theory/experience/history/ and so on. Some people think these differences and the other analogy differences are a matter of the speaker/hearer's intention. But you can see that all you have to do is combine the words and the differences are made. A story goes: 'He reached way down, to recover the pearls that fell down the back of her dress, and suddenly felt a perfect ass.' Dennis the Menace (the American cartoon boy) says 'I thought I'd call you early while the phone lines are fresh'. Looking at a hatchery, he says 'Look at all the chicklets'. Looking at tangerines, he says 'They're loose leaf oranges'. At twilight he says 'Boy, we sure wore this day down to a stub'.

If I say 'He has money in the bank', the fact that you might want that to mean he has currency in a river bank will not be sufficient to ensure that it does; the linguistic and thought/action environment settle the matter. Sometimes meaning is settled by law. So if in a will I say 'I leave my piano to my children' the law settles the ambiguity among natural children, children by adoption, acknowledged illegitimate children and unacknowledged illegitimate ones. Those examples merely illustrate that the meaning of what you say is not entirely a matter of what you intend but is subject to objective forces, some of which are linguistic forces. Sometimes we are quite surprised by what we have said, embarrassed too, and sometimes delighted with a happy phrase, as when Quine said a line of reasoning has to 'wind down'.

Now I will explain analogy of proportionality before going on to the general principles of linguistic inertia, and universal linguistic force and others, that may explain the analogy phenomena. Then I will apply the results briefly to reflections on analogous thinking and analogous reality.

Both Aristotle and Aquinas explained analogy of proportionality, by comparisons to mathematical proportionality, e.g. A:B :: C:D; 2:4 :: 8:16 (i.e. half). But the later commentators missed the point that very many proportionalities are true or false just *because* the common predicate that corresponds to 'half' in the above example is *not univocal and is not merely equivocal either*. For example: 'Dentist:cavity :: doctor:disease.' Various words will make that come out true, e.g. 'fixes', 'cures', 'gets rid of'. But none will apply to both the parts in exactly the same sense, but rather in related senses. So too 'Asylum:refugee :: destination:traveller.' You fill in the words that work; they will all differentiate. 'A horse:herd :: mountain:

range.' Suppose we picked 'belongs to' as the common predicate; it will not mean exactly the same thing in both cases; for one thing, a horse can wander off and be separated from its herd, but it would be strange, even unacceptable, to say that a mountain wandered off from its range (except in geological aeons).

Aristotle said (*Topics* I, 17, 108a, 7–10): 'Likeness should be studied first in the case of things belonging to different genera, the formula being A:B :: C:D, as sight is in the eyes, so is reason in the soul, and as calm is in the sea, so is windlessness in the air.' It is one thing to grasp the analogy after it has been formulated and another to find a common term that differentiates to make both parts true. The ability to recognize the analogy in the first place is a matter of both intelligence and training. Although most of the cases I call analogy of proportionality do not involve explicitly formulated four-part formulas, it is clear that Aristotle and Aquinas wanted to emphasize that genuine insight can come from comparing things that appear quite unlike, as I will further illustrate with the analogous thermal, electrostatic and mechanical properties of solids, below. In particular, for Aquinas, it would be acceptable to say things like 'as Plato was to some of the intelligible things of philosophy, so God is to whatever is intelligible at all', namely, 'understanding', where the common term is analogical. But to get this sort of analogy we need only talk in single sentences, leaving the comparison to other uses of the word implicit. 'Looking for that book I wandered all over the study.' 'Talking about meaning, he wandered all over the subject.' You can see the analogy of 'wandered', metaphor in the second use. We do not even need the first sentence, the comparison need only be implicit.

Differing meaning, say of 'understanding' in the case above, is not to be reduced to a difference of truth-conditions (conditions under which the statement would be true) though such differences can often effectively indicate differences of meaning. But meaning and truth-conditions are not binary stars. We can understand the analogy, often, without knowing the truth-conditions, and we can understand many, many sentences without an articulate knowledge of their truth-conditions or even of the meaning-relevant truth-conditions (i.e. the conditions such that a difference among them amounts to a difference of the meaning of some component word, compared to another typical use). So, we might believe the statement 'At the Second Coming the dead will rise and be publicly judged' without having any secure grasp of non-trivial truth-conditions for it.

Instead, sameness of meaning, in contrast to difference, is better thought of as sameness of the particular meaning-network in which the word occurs, that is, sameness of the affinities (like near synonyms, appropriate modifiers, paraphrases, etc.) and of oppositions (like contraries, negations, incompatibilities, etc.). So difference of meaning for a pair of occurrences of the same word comes down to difference of local meaning-network. And when the network for one occurrence is definite and filled in from experience or reflection and another is indefinite or opposed in various respects, there is a difference of meaning even though there may be a large carry-over of cognitive content from one to the other. That is prominent where the analogy is literal ('He collected the tickets'; 'The workers collected the garbage') and is usually pretty obvious even in cases of metaphor: 'He stomped his foot'; 'He stomped his opponent's argument'.

Since everything said positively of any creature implies participated being (in talk about God within the discourse framework of Aquinas), and nothing said of God implies anything but the opposite of that, then nothing, whether it be 'is wise', 'exists', 'knows everything', or whatever, is positively true in the same sense in which it might be said of a creature. (Oddly enough, Duns Scotus [c. 1265–1308], who accepted the participation framework, still thought that 'exists' [being] applies univocally to creatures and to God.) Aquinas's whole metaphysics depends on his claim of both real analogy and analogy of meaning.

Now what do we do when someone like Richard Swinburne (cf. *The Coherence of Theism* [Oxford, 1977], p. 71) says that when he says God is good, he is using 'good' in the 'perfectly ordinary' sense in which he would say his grandmother was good? There are two options: either he is talking within a discourse framework like Aquinas's, and thus his predicate is semantically captured without his noticing it, so that 'good' does not occur in the same sense in which he speaks of his grandmother, or he is explicitly presupposing a meaning-network derived from some opposing beliefs, the way some process theologians talk (like Whitehead, Hartshorne and Schubert Ogden). In the latter case, he may mean exactly what he says he does, and the reply of Aquinas would be that what he says is false, for God is not good in the same sense in which the grandmother is. For, within the meaning-network Aquinas is using, and among the suppositions Aquinas believes to be true as well, the word 'good' is captured by its semantic context where predicates that stand as affinities for the good grandmother, like 'exists materially', 'acts numerically discretely', 'exists contingently', and the like, are all *opposed* to what is meant when one says God is good. So even though there is a large meaning carry-over (what Aquinas called the *res significata*) there is an enormous difference (of what Aquinas called *modus significandi*) which tracks difference in the manner of being (which Aquinas called *modus essendi*). Another example: the goodness of Swinburne's grandmother is a separable quality, not the same as her wisdom or knowledge or being; not so in God. And those are meaning-relevant differences.

To say those differences are meaning-relevant is the nub of the dispute because Swinburne's surrogate may try insisting that the senses of the word 'good' are in neutral with respect to the manner of being of the things talked about. But that does not seem very plausible. For if I say 'I want a lot of money, as much as Bill Gates has', I am definitely not in neutral as to whether that is to be currency, gold or accounting entries; for where could I keep the currency or the gold? It would cover the earth. I am obviously talking about money in the more abstract sense in which we say that the US national debt is 5 trillion dollars. The words we use belong to meaning-networks that include belief-elements of meaning, and therefore, general presuppositions, even though we may never notice them. So, if I say 'In the US money is green', I obviously cannot be talking of money in the same sense in which I talked of it when describing the national debt.

We usually fail to notice analogical adjustments of meaning, as I have said: for one thing, they are adjustments comparatively to other putative utterances, usually, not to actual others as I usually illustrate them; secondly, the adjustments of meaning-network are so fluid, like automatic transmission, that no jolt of difference is felt: 'He *saw* the trees'; 'He *saw* he was going to hit them'; 'He *saw* how to prove his innocence'; 'He *saw* how to prove the theorem'. That is as smooth as great Scotch. Most of the time we do not even notice a difference of meaning – after all, who but writers, editors, philosophers and lexicographers pays much attention to word meanings, anyway? If you reread this chapter, looking for the various analogies and metaphors that are used, not just given as examples, I think you will be surprised at how many you simply did not notice.

Suppose that earlier debate with the surrogate continues. 'Why', he says, 'do you contend that religious beliefs are part of word-meanings?' Well, I say, as Wilfrid Sellars pointed out, there are belief-elements of meanings. I add: everywhere! Just look at a dictionary: 'a lichen is a cryptogamous plant formed by symbiotic association of a fungus and an alga'. Is that definition not made of belief-elements? Look up the definition of 'iron', 'soldier', and so on. The reason you cannot put words into neutral as to their semantic networks is that natural languages function in traction with our activities, for which we need the networking: 'The stove smoked every time I lit it'; 'The priest smoked while praying'!

When you say something that belongs, as a working element in a thought/action process, like traditional religious teaching and theologizing, the words are *semantically captured* by the context. So, when I say 'My dog, Gus, loves me', 'loves' cannot mean the same thing as it does when I say 'My mother loves me'. And obviously the same again, when I say 'God loves me'. For a creature to be is to be loved by God, just as for a tree to be visible is to be illuminated. God's knowing and loving *causes* being (*cognitio Dei causa rerum*, as Aquinas put it). So on linguistic grounds alone, if we talk within the framework of belief-elements of meaning characteristic of Aquinas and even the Neoplatonist tradition from the early Fathers of the Church, we can simply dismiss the claim that we can even *say* something positively of God, whether true or not, in the *same* sense in which we can say the same thing of some creature.

Now notice: I have said nothing disparaging about the meaningfulness of metaphorical descriptions of God as contained in expressions like 'The Lord is my Shepherd', 'The Hound of Heaven', 'Our Father who art in heaven', 'Father, let this cup pass away'. They can be marvellously revealing. Aristotle said: *'But the greatest thing by far is to be a master of metaphor.* It is the one thing that cannot be learned from others; and it is also a sign of genius, since a good metaphor implies an intuitive perception of the similarity in dissimilars' (*Poetics* 22, 1459a, 5–9). Nor do I disparage the anagogical, allegorical, prophetic, spiritual, typical or figurative meanings that Aquinas attributes to various parts of the Scriptures and to other writings. They all have their uses, and not just in religious discourse, either, but for literature in general: who could understand *Moby Dick*, or *Peter Grimes*, or even *Rabbit at Rest*, without such interpretations?

Rather, along with Aquinas, while allowing vast scope for such talk and interpretation, especially in religious discourse, I hold that the foundation for all those modes of meaning and for all the figures of speech (which I explain elsewhere) is in analogy of meaning, which is a universal linguistic regularity, with a multiplicity of component laws, that is part of all natural languages. I will explain some of the laws briefly, next.

But first let me warn you: do not fall into the widespread mistake that it is only with language that we do intelligent thinking or recognize analogies or even think metaphorically. Just look at the intelligence in Bach's music, the metaphor in Picasso's bicycle (bull), the metaphors in modern dance, and Joel Grey's mime. Humans are so intelligent, even the more limited ones, that they can think with their fingers (cf. making knots). Humans are so intelligent they can think with their faces (pouting, smiling, kissing, grieving). They can think with their lungs (astonishment) and with their bowels (in fear). All other sorts of meaning, expressible in natural languages, are built out of analogy, semantic contagion of many sorts, and modes of reference, e.g. naming the whole with the name of the part (as in 'my blade').

General linguistic principles

I can only outline what deserves detailed consideration. There are two universal regularities that will explain semantic contagion, though sub-regularities are needed to explain sub-cases: (1) words recur in the same sense unless something differentiates them (that is linguistic inertia); (2) words resist combining unacceptably in the environment unless forced to (that is linguistic force, akin to gravity). In a word, sentences make what sense they can. Sometimes, they just cannot (as in 'Thingness evokes

essential being' and comparable sentences to be found in print). Philosophers, and preachers, and sometimes lawyers, and doctors as well as
salesmen and appliance repairers, are very good at making nonsense by
exsanguination, by combining abstractions so that all the meaning is sucked
out. Take 'Time is imperfect double negation'. Here there is no resistance
to any reading. Each word is a blur with a tattered semantic network. The
words have bled to death. There is another kind of nonsense, too, caused by
conflicting dominance, where the utterance is superficially grammatical,
but one of the words behaves like a duck–rabbit picture[1] to make the
appearance, belonging to one meaning-network to hook up with one word
and jumping to another network to hook up with the rest. Take 'Saturday
follows Mary'. 'Saturday' hooks up with 'Friday' to fit 'follows' and then
with 'Fido' to fit 'follows Mary'. And nothing stabilizes the whole as the
story's environment does for 'Friday followed Crusoe'.

It is by linguistic force, resistance to unacceptability, along with weak,
defeasible, resistances to commonplace falsehood, vulgarity, taboos, trivial-
ity and public offence, that the expressive power of languages, prominently
English, evolves so rapidly. 'Betwixt my sheets [he] has done my office',
growls Iago. 'Every lover is a thief, all want, no friend . . . No wonder every
love, with want, will end' sings a singer. Here, items far apart lexically
('love' and 'thief') get closer together. Items closer ('lover' and 'friend') are
pushed apart. But quote St Paul (Romans 13:10): 'Love is the one thing
that cannot hurt your neighbour', and space reshapes. The world-line of
'love' veers toward 'friend' and streams along near 'want'. It wobbles nearer
'loyal' and sharply veers toward and away from 'ends', time after time. It is
as if the culture moved its knee in bed and the blanket of meaning
reshaped.

The inertia-resistance structure of words generates endless expansion of
expressive capacity, depending only on how words are combined. Think of
contrasting adaptations as the suppressing of affinities and oppositions to
other words – relations that, if maintained, would make the resulting
string unacceptable as an utterance in the language, the way I thought
'Night sings posts' must be until I encountered it in a novel. It turns out
that for any grammatically well-formed utterance, we can, with imagination, devise a context where it will mean *something*, though probably
nothing anyone would be likely to want to say. Still, philosophers and
others get trampled by their words, caught in a stampede of verbosity to
express themselves: what I take to be the fate of much European philosophy
recently.

Think of a word's being dominated as the suppression of what, among
other words and phrases, are its opposites, near-synonyms, appropriate
modifiers as adverbs and adjectives, or paraphrases (etc.) in some other
characteristic use. Suppressing affinities and oppositions to some words is

typically the same as acquiring such relations to still other words and phrases. Unacceptability is variously based depending on the area of discourse, as 'He lubricates his fallacies' indicates: there are contexts that would make sense of it. Unacceptability variously based is variously resisted, as I have said. There is strong resistance to failure to acquire an overall meaning; there is weaker and defeasible resistance to commonplace falsehood, impropriety, and so on as mentioned, but particularly, to meanings that conflict with the belief-elements incorporated into the meaning. Though the effects of weak resistance are local, it is, like the cosmic weak force that deflects neutrinos, a starbuilder.

The resistances exert dominance over the less resistant, more flexible words, especially utility words like 'run', 'fix', 'see', 'work', 'grow', 'die', 'hold', 'drop', 'climb', 'race' and thousands of others. It is easy to combine them with various nouns and watch their differentiation, relatively to other uses, reshaping the meaning network: the car wouldn't run; the thief tried to run; the road runs along the shore; he ran off a few copies, and so on. I shall not go into a more detailed explanation of how this all works (*there's* adaptation for you!); you can read about it by following up the bibliography to this book.

The point of it all for religious discourse is that adaptation of meanings to one another to make discourse with cognitive content is the norm for natural language and nonsense the episodic by-product (though it seems like constant static in philosophy and religion). So religious discourse, moral, metaphysical, astrological, and other neighbourhoods, though they can have abandoned blocks of empty meaninglessness, normally function effectively to express and convey what is believed, and where appropriate, what is known. That does not mean that there is no religious knowledge possessed by the enlightened, the mystics and other adepts, that cannot be effectively conveyed in words; there may indeed be some very important understanding like that, just as there is musical understanding that even the greatest performers and conductors cannot describe but only display.

The linguistic community among religious, scientific, historical, political, moral, legal and other craft-bound discourse is so obvious that there is no point to the claim that such discourse is cognitively impaired. If such talk fails to convey meaningful belief it will not be because the discourse has something wrong with it, but because of some failure in the associated processes of knowledge, as I think is the case with astrological discourse; it is not unintelligible, for the most part, just entirely unjustified. So it is not only that positivists and verificationists were mistaken about religion and science and offered a criterion that could not pass its own test. They additionally failed to understand the general linguistic phenomenon of meaning-adaptation and like many philosophers, even now, supposed the vocabulary of natural languages to be made up of thousands of fixed and static meaning units, many with several or more different meanings, and supposed that sentences are composed of word-meanings stacked up, grammatically, the way stones are fitted to make a stone wall. It totally eluded them, even good philosophers like Donald Davidson, that sentences are not made that way at all. Instead, word-meaning decomposes from sentence-meaning, so that comparatively, from one sentence to another the same words have adjusted in semantic network, to fit with more dominant (resistant) units of their environments. Sometimes it looks like backwards causation because the sense of an uttered word is determined by what comes after it, as 'He governed himself and his province'. But the sentence meaning is *prior* to the meanings of the components.

It is not only that there are specialized craft-bound vocabularies for cod-fishing, brain surgery, obstetrics, religion and philosophy. Words common to several craft-bound discourses differentiate from one another, particularly the utility words. 'Run' in sailing is different from 'run' in baseball or in manufacturing. To those knowing the language, and understanding one or another craft, or parts of many, as most of us do, adaptation of meaning is second nature from childhood; we are no more aware of it than we are of our accent.

Semantic contagion is present everywhere in discourse and it is principled. The identity of the lexical components of a sentence is, thus, dependent on the items that are combined. That dynamic feature of meaning cannot be explained by any account that supposes a fixed vocabulary or a fixed categorical nesting of lexical fields, or even a finite stock of lexical markers that retain their original affinities and oppositions no matter how they are arranged. The two key features of lexical organization, adaptation to context and pragmatic traction (words work to modify thought and action), are consequences of the engagement of discourse with endeavour. When you put talk into gear, to do something, from simply lying, sighing or crying to 'telling how it happened', to talking a non-pilot down to a safe landing, or an enraged friend from walking out, the necessities and niceties of the task explain the ramification (and often the simplification – as in talk to small children) of the vocabulary and the polysemy (many senses) of the words, just as they do in the practical crafts of boat-building, plastering, sailing and instrument-flying. To see the gears and levers of adaptation working, look at some craft-talk you know well; it is a planetarium for the whole language.

The whole of the data, the rioting waves of opposition, overlap, contrast and clash of meaning, are whipped around by the winds of our doings, shaping discourse to action and making acts out of talk, in a sea of semantic relativity explained by harmonious and elegant symmetries.

A conclusion

Two central points can be established linguistically:

(1) Religious discourse is just another among endlessly differing neighbourhoods of talk, all governed by the same semantic regularities, and in no way made deficient or expressively impaired by its subject matter, any more than any other craft-bound discourse is.

(2) The semantic presuppositions, including belief-elements of meanings of words like 'God', 'all-powerful', 'wise', 'good', 'eternal', 'simple' and even 'exists' in Judaeo-Christian and classical Islamic God-talk, differentiate, sometimes denominatively (by attribution) and sometimes by proportionality (and sometimes both at once) compared to applications to contingently existing things.

Thomas Aquinas was right to say that nothing positive is said univocally of both God and creatures, but that the words used in accepted beliefs are related in meaning to applications to creatures. Unlike that of Aquinas, my account of the meaningfulness and of the analogy involved in mainstream talk about God makes no supposition that the orthodox religious beliefs and explanations are true, though it is compatible with their being true, and also compatible with one's saying lots of things about God that are not true as well. Which linguistically acceptable statements about God are true and which false is settled by means other than the features of the language.

Thinking analogously

Everybody can do it, from early childhood, as my examples from Dennis the Menace illustrate. I know from observation that the belief of many psychologists, that children do not understand metaphors until they are about five years old, is false. As soon as a child begins to talk on his/her own, adaptation to diverse contexts is already mastered: 'fix' occurs in the first elementary readers in dozens of senses: 'fix dinner', 'fix my wagon', 'daddy will fix you', etc. Thinking analogously (a child with a comb says 'Look daddy, I'm raking my hair') is as natural as thinking at all, though, of course, some can do it better than others. Analogical visual perception is also natural, and yet differently expert, as the Visual Analogies Tests show.

When you have become skilled at putting words together to say something in a new way, you are thinking analogously. Sometimes that thinking is effortless and unnoticed as in 'He *missed* the appointment', 'He

James Ross

missed his dog', 'He *missed* the ball', 'He just *missed* that post', 'He *missed* the right answer'. And sometimes the thinking is deliberate, as when, elsewhere, I explained adaptation of meaning as ratcheting of one meaning network to fit with another, but so automatically that it seems continuous, like a movie.

So we can certainly all think analogously. And we can understand such thinking. And it is clear that metaphorical thinking is nothing but a special case of analogical thinking, though, for mastery of metaphor, as Aristotle said, insight into the similarity of dissimilar things is required. Sometimes that happens automatically too: we can think of a writer fastidiously picking words, like a child picking the hated peas out of the mixed vegetables; or we can think of a writer smashing words together, like a machinist bending rods with a hammer, to make them fit together into the shape of his idea. Those metaphors just flow off the pen. You only need to be a genius to see and fashion important metaphors habitually. All of us can make brand new little ones.

No one, that I know of, has ever written anything explanatory about how we do analogical and metaphorical thinking. Maybe there is nothing to explain, once we explain how judgement is done at all.

Analogical realities

The claim that what exists, even in the sublunary world, is analogically various is peculiar to the metaphysics of Aristotle and Aquinas, and is pretty much left out of metaphysics, and therefore theory of knowledge, as offered by writers in the last three centuries. However, there is a tantalizing footnote in Kant's *Prolegomena to any Future Metaphysics* that shows an interesting but misleading understanding. Kant says: 'Thus there is an analogy between the juridical relation of human actions and the mechanical relation of moving forces. I can never do anything to another man without giving him a right to do the same to me on the same conditions; just as no body can act with its moving force on another body without thereby causing the other to react equally against it. Here right and moving force are quite dissimilar things, but in their relation there is complete similarity. By means of such an analogy I can obtain a relational concept of things which are absolutely unknown to me.' Unfortunately Kant supposes the common relation to be one of 'complete similarity' while I have been contending that it is what is analogical.

Whatever the defects of modern metaphysics, it takes only a little reflection to see real analogies of proportionality, not just in the variety of reality things have (from people to diseases, dreams, nations, coincidences, heart attacks, trains, crowds, concerts, pauses, noises, invisible light, gases, oceans, sounds, coves, shipyards, money and debts). They all 'are' but not in the same way, nor in a definite order to one primary way of being, unless one means the being of God.

Even among the physical properties of solids there are some analogous properties: the thermal, the mechanical and the electrostatic, so that a change in the thermal can cause a mechanical change: a drawbridge sticks open after a hot day increases its length; and mechanical change can cause thermal change: bending a piece of metal back and forth heats the bend, as everyone knows, and applying a magnetic (electrical) charge can bend a piece of metal; that is how we can have a magnetic switch or a solenoid. There is a lot to say about the communities among those kinds of properties: for instance, that they are reversible. But that is enough for now.

Mechanically, electronically and logically equivalent things are often analogous. So the three different processes for automatic focusing of still cameras, though differing somewhat in their outcomes, are analogous. I presume that an automatic transmission is analogous to a manual transmission, and that a quartz watch is analogous to a spring-wound one. I suppose a word processor is analogous to a typewriter. Is word-processing analogous to handwriting? In both cases we would say 'I wrote that out yesterday'. Is the programmed machine analogous to a pencil?

That raises a question that I shall leave to the reader: can things be *really* related metaphorically as well as analogously? However one answers it, the question calls attention to the fact that when things are analogous, that relationship holds whether or not we ever think of it. And this truth is important when we turn to the idea that there is something which might be called a real analogy of being between God and the world and that what can be truly said of God is enabled by the real analogy, just as in the case of things that bear predicates univocally.

In the basically Aristotelian metaphysics of many Latin and Arabic medieval writers causation is at most analogous even among creatures: for there is efficient, formal, final and material causation and those notions are also applied differentially to substance causation and to event causation. So sometimes the cause must precede the event, like striking a match to start a fire, and sometimes the cause must be co-present with the effect, as the soul is the cause of the life of a living thing. So those notions differ, but analogically. It is not surprising, then, that in general metaphysics, stemming from Aristotle, causation, being, form, matter, act, potency and all the other general explanatory notions are applied analogically. Aquinas just carries that idea further by emphasizing the analogy of being between creatures and God which is explained, as I said above, by his participation theory. For although both the creature and God exist, the creature is caused, contingent, continuously dependent in being, and is a limited reflection of divine perfection. Creatures are destructible, changeable, complex, composite, and in endless ways different from God. But they chiefly differ from God by having participated being. Of course, one's figuring out the last point produces an analogous notion of God, the unparticipated, pure perfection, simple, independent, uncaused, etc., whose existence can be deduced as a causal necessity for the being of anything else, and whose being can then be understood to be that in which we participate (in the sense defined above) and imperfectly reflect. To think about God we put on intellectual glasses to adapt the conceptions arising from unaided perception of material things.

Once one thinks in a general metaphysical framework of real analogies and develops the conception of God as part of that general ontology, the key positions become incorporated as belief-elements of the meanings of the words used to describe God and are built right into the discourse, right into the meaning-network of the words we use to talk about God.

That, of course, has what might appear to be an uncomfortable consequence, that people who have never heard of metaphysics, but who have been taught how to talk about God, whether as believers or not, are using words whose full meaning-network is unavailable to them, and further, whose meaning network changed when the Neoplatonic assumptions of the first millennium were replaced with the more Aristotelian assumptions of the second. Now it is not much of a problem that people use words whose meaning-network is not fully accessible to them; that happens all the time: how many people can explain in detail what they mean by 'execrable' or even by 'ripe' or 'finish', or describe the network of affinities and oppositions for such words? Yet the second facet does present a problem. For it seems that there was a change in what Christians meant by 'God', and thus by many other expressions, with the development of the analogy and participation doctrines. If we regard the changes as additions to what was unspecified earlier, then, strictly, there was no change of belief, in the sense of rejection of anything that went before. That is probably the better account. So the change of meaning, great as it was, was not like the change in the conception of physical matter that happened in the seventeenth century, as compared with what prevailed in the thirteenth, and has undergone radical changes since (e.g. micro-matter is now understood to lack the primary qualities by which it was defined in the seventeenth century).

In any case, even if one does not consider the analogy-of-being theory true (though for what reason could one doubt it?), one can still easily see that the meaning-networks of words applied to creatures and to God have to differ because the substitutable modifiers, paraphrases, etc., have to differ and are importantly opposed. And so, it stands on linguistic grounds alone that terms applied to God, even terms applied falsely, like 'is evil', have to apply analogously to what they mean applied to humans and other creatures. And there is no doubt that when there is carry-over of meaning, as indicated by the similarity of meaning-networks, despite key differences in supposition, there is carry-over of belief-content, as is obvious in all the ordinary cases of analogous differentiation that I have illustrated. Thus, the basic 'cognitivity' problem is dissolved because it turns out that religious discourse is like any other neighbourhood of discourse in natural language, and that within it, as within any neighbourhood of discourse, there can, of course, be vacant tracts of utter nonsense, even a lot of them. But that is only possible because the discourse on the whole makes sense, whether or not it succeeds in telling us the truth.

Note

1   A figure that can be seen either as a duck or as a rabbit, developed by the psychologist Joseph Jastrow about 1900. Cf. J. Richard Block and Harold E. Yuker, *Can You Believe Your Eyes* (New York and London: Gardner Press, 1989), p. 16.

5

Creation, providence and miracles

William Lane Craig

Creatio ex nihilo

'In the beginning God created the heavens and the earth' (Gen 1:1). With majestic simplicity the author of the opening chapter of Genesis thus differentiated his viewpoint, not only from that of the ancient creation myths of Israel's neighbours, but also effectively from pantheism, panentheism and polytheism. For the author of Genesis 1, no pre-existent material seems to be assumed, no warring gods or primordial dragons are present – only God, who is said to 'create' (*bara*, a word used only with God as its subject and which does not presuppose a material substratum) 'the heavens and the earth' (*et hassamayim we et ha ares*, a Hebrew expression for the totality of the world or, more simply, the universe). Moreover, this act of creation took place 'in the beginning' (*bereshith*, used here as in Isaiah 46:10 to indicate an absolute beginning). The author thereby gives us to understand that the universe had a temporal origin and thus implies *creatio ex nihilo* in the temporal sense that God brought the universe into being without a material cause at some point in the finite past.[1]

Later biblical authors so understood the Genesis account of creation.[2] The doctrine of *creatio ex nihilo* is also implied in various places in early extra-biblical Jewish literature.[3] And the Church Fathers, while heavily influenced by Greek thought, dug in their heels concerning the doctrine of creation, sturdily insisting, with few exceptions, on the temporal creation of the universe *ex nihilo* in opposition to the eternity of matter.[4] A tradition of robust argumentation against the past eternity of the world and in favour of *creatio ex nihilo*, issuing from the Alexandrian Christian theologian John Philoponus, continued for centuries in Islamic, Jewish and Christian thought.[5] In 1215, the Catholic Church promulgated temporal *creatio ex nihilo* as official church doctrine at the Fourth Lateran Council, declaring God to be 'Creator of all things, visible and invisible, ... who, by His almighty power, from the beginning of time has created both orders in the same way out of nothing'. This remarkable declaration not only affirms that God created everything *extra se* without any material cause, but even that time itself had a beginning. The doctrine of creation is thus inherently bound up with temporal considerations and entails that God brought the universe into being at some point in the past without any antecedent or contemporaneous material cause.

At the same time, the Christian Scriptures also suggest that God is engaged in a sort of on-going creation, sustaining the universe in being. Christ 'reflects the glory of God and bears the very stamp of His nature, upholding the universe by his word of power' (Heb 1:3). Although relatively infrequently attested in Scripture in comparison with the abundant references to God's original act of creation, the idea of continuing creation came to constitute an important aspect of the doctrine of creation as well. For Thomas Aquinas, for example, this aspect becomes the core doctrine of creation, the question of whether the world's reception of being from God had a temporal commencement or not having only secondary importance.[6] For Aquinas creation is the immediate bestowal of being and as such belongs only to God, the universal principle of being; therefore, even if creatures have existed from eternity, they are still created *ex nihilo* in this metaphysical sense.

Thus, God is conceived in Christian theology to be the cause of the world both in his initial act of bringing the universe into being and in his on-going conservation of the world in being. These two actions have been traditionally classed as species of *creatio ex nihilo*, namely, *creatio originans* and *creatio continuans*. While this is a handy rubric, it unfortunately quickly becomes problematic if pressed to technical precision. As Philip Quinn points out,[7] if we say that a thing is created at a time *t* only if *t* is the first moment of the thing's existence, then the doctrine of *creatio continuans* lands us in a bizarre form of occasionalism, according to which no persisting individuals exist. At each instant God creates a new individual, numerically distinct from its chronological predecessor, so that diachronic personal identity and agency are precluded.

Rather than reinterpret creation in such a way as to not involve a time at which a thing first begins to exist, we ought to recognize that *creatio continuans* is but a *façon de parler* and that creation needs to be distinguished from conservation. As John Duns Scotus observed,

> Properly speaking . . . it is only true to say that a creature is created at the first moment [of its existence] and only after that moment is it conserved, for only then does its being have this order to itself as something that was, as it were, there before. Because of these different conceptual relationships implied by the words 'create' and 'conserve' it follows that one does not apply to a thing when the other does.[8]

Intuitively, creation involves God's bringing something into being. Thus, if God creates some entity e (whether an individual or an event) at a time t (whether an instant or finite interval), then e comes into being at t. We can explicate this notion as follows:

E_1. e comes into being at t iff (1) e exists at t, (2) t is the first time at which e exists, and (3) e's existing at t is a tensed fact.

Accordingly,

E_2. God creates e at t iff God brings it about that e comes into being at t.

God's creating e involves e's coming into being, which is an absolute beginning of existence, not a transition of e from non-being into being. In creation there is no patient entity on which the agent acts to bring about its effect.[9] It follows that creation is not a type of change, since there is no enduring subject which persists from one state to another. It is precisely for this reason that conservation cannot be properly thought of as essentially the same as creation. For conservation does presuppose a subject which is made to continue from one state to another. In creation God does not act on a subject, but constitutes the subject by his action; in contrast, in conservation God acts on an existent subject to perpetuate its existence. This is the import of Scotus's remark that only in conservation does a creature 'have this order to itself as something that was, as it were, there before'.

The fundamental difference between creation and conservation, then, lies in the fact that in conservation, as opposed to creation, there is presupposed a subject on which God acts. Intuitively, conservation involves God's preservation of that subject in being over time. Conservation ought therefore to be understood in terms of God's preserving some entity e from one moment of its existence to another. A crucial insight into conservation is that unlike creation, it does involve transition and therefore cannot occur at an instant.[10] We may therefore provide the following explication of divine conservation:

E_3. God conserves e iff God acts upon e to bring about e's existing from t until some $t^* > t$ through every sub-interval of the interval $[t, t^*]$.

Creation and conservation thus cannot be adequately analysed with respect to the divine act alone, but involve relations to the object of the act. The act itself (the causing of existence) may be the same in both cases, but in one case may be instantaneous and presupposes no prior object, whereas in the other case it occurs over an interval and does involve a prior object.

The doctrine of creation also involves an important metaphysical feature which is rarely appreciated: it commits one to a tensed or, in McTaggart's convenient terminology, an A-Theory of time.[11] For if one adopts a tenseless or B-Theory of time, then things do not literally come into existence. Things are then four-dimensional objects which tenselessly subsist and begin to exist only in the sense that their extension along their temporal dimension is finite in the *earlier-than* direction. The whole four-dimensional, space–time manifold is extrinsically (as opposed to intrinsically) timeless, existing co-eternally with God. The universe thus does not come into being on a B-Theory of time, regardless of whether it has a finite or an infinite past relative to any time. Hence, clause (3) in E_1 represents a necessary feature of creation. In the absence of clause (3) God's creation of the universe *ex nihilo* could be interpreted along tenseless lines to postulate merely the finitude of cosmic time in the *earlier-than* direction.

Since a robust doctrine of *creatio ex nihilo* thus commits one to an A-Theory of time, we are brought face to face with what has been called 'one of the most neglected, but also one of the most important questions in the dialogue between theology and science', namely, the relation between the concept of eternity and that of the spatio-temporal structure of the universe.[12] Since the rise of modern theology with Schleiermacher, the doctrine of *creatio originans* has been allowed to atrophy, while the doctrine of *creatio continuans* has assumed supremacy.[13] Undoubtedly this was largely due to theologians' fear of a conflict with science, which *creatio continuans* permitted them to avoid by operating only within the safe harbour of metaphysics, removed from the realities of the physical, space–time world.[14] But the discovery in this century of the expansion of the universe, first predicted in 1922 by Alexander Friedman on the basis of the General Theory of Relativity, coupled with the Hawking–Penrose singularity theorems of 1968, which demonstrated the inevitability of a past, cosmic singularity as an initial boundary to space–time, forced the doctrine of *creatio originans* back into the spotlight.[15] As physicists Barrow and Tipler observe, 'At this singularity, space and time came into existence; literally nothing existed before the singularity, so, if the Universe originated at such a singularity, we would truly have a creation *ex nihilo*'.[16]

Of course, various and sometimes heroic attempts have been made to avert the initial cosmological singularity posited in the standard Big Bang model and to regain an infinite past. But none of these alternatives has commended itself as more plausible than the standard model. The old steady-state model, the oscillating model, and vacuum-fluctuation models are now generally recognized among cosmologists to have failed as plausible attempts to avoid the beginning of the universe.[17] Most cosmologists believe that a final theory of the origin of the universe must await the as yet undiscovered quantum theory of gravity. Such quantum gravity models may or may not involve an initial singularity, although attention has tended to focus on those that do not. But even those that eliminate the initial singularity, such as the Hartle–Hawking model, still involve a merely finite past and, on any physically realistic interpretation of such models, imply a beginning of the universe. This is due to the peculiar feature of such models' employment of imaginary, rather than real, values for the time variable in the equations governing the universe during the first 10^{-43} second of its existence. Imaginary quantities in science are fictional, without physical significance.[18] Thus, use of such numbers is a mathematical 'trick' or auxiliary device to arrive at physically significant quantities represented by real numbers. The Euclidean four-space from which classical space–time emerges in such models is thus a mathematical fiction, a way of modelling the early universe which should not be taken as a literal description.[19]

Now it might be said that so-called 'imaginary time' just *is* a spatial dimension and to that extent is physically intelligible and so is to be realistically construed. But now the metaphysician must surely protest the reductionistic view of time which such an account presupposes. Time as it plays a role in physics is an operationally defined quantity varying from theory to theory: in the Special Theory of Relativity it is a quantity defined via clock synchronization by light signals, in classical cosmology it is a parameter assigned to spatial hyper-surfaces of homogeneity, in quantum cosmology it is a quantity internally constructed out of the curvature variables of three-geometries. But clearly these are but pale abstractions of time itself.[20] For a series of mental events alone, a succession of contents of consciousness, is sufficient to ground time itself. An unembodied consciousness which experienced a succession of mental states, say, by counting, would be temporal; that is to say, time would in such a case exist, and that wholly in the absence of any physical processes. I take this simple consideration to be a knock-down argument that time as it plays a role in physics is at best a measure of time, rather than constitutive or definitive of time. Hence, even if one were to accept at face value the claim of quantum cosmological models that physical time really is imaginary prior to the Planck time, that is to say, is a spatial dimension, that fact says absolutely nothing at all about time itself. When it is said that such a regime exists timelessly, all that means is that our physical measures of time (which in physics are taken to define time) break down under such conditions. That should hardly surprise. But time itself must characterize such a regime for the simple reason that it is not static. I am astonished that quantum theorists can assert that the quantum regime is on the one hand a state of incessant activity or change and yet is on the other not characterized by time. If this is not to be incoherent, such a statement can only mean that our concepts of physical time are inapplicable on such a scale, not that time itself disappears. But if time itself characterizes the quantum regime, as it must if change is occurring, then one can regress mentally in time back along the imaginary time dimension through concentric circles on the spherical hyper-surface as they converge toward a non-singular point which represents the beginning of the universe and before which time did not exist. Hartle–Hawking themselves recognize that point as the origin of the universe in their model, but how that point came into being (in metaphysical, that is, ontological, time) is a question not even addressed by their theory.

Hence, even on a naive realist construal of such models, they at best show that that quantity which is defined as time in physics ceases at the Planck time and takes on the characteristics of what physics defines as a spatial dimension. But time itself does not begin at the Planck time, but extends all the way back to the very beginning of the universe. Such theories, if successful, thus enable us to model the origin of the universe without an initial cosmological singularity and, by positing a finite imaginary time on a closed surface prior to the Planck time rather than an infinite time on an open surface, actually support temporal *creatio ex nihilo*.

But if the spatio-temporal structure of the universe exhibits an origination *ex nihilo*, then the difficulty concerns how to relate that structure to the divine eternity. For given the reality of tense and God's causal relation to the world, it is very difficult to conceive how God could remain untouched by the world's temporality. Imagine God existing changelessly alone without creation, with a changeless and eternal determination to create a temporal world. Since God is omnipotent, His will is done, and a temporal world begins to exist. (We may lay aside for now the question whether this beginning of a temporal creation would require some additional act of intentionality or exercise of power other than God's timeless determination.) Now in such a case, either God existed temporally prior to creation or he did not. If he did exist alone temporally prior to creation, then God is not timeless, but temporal, and the question is settled. Suppose, then, that God did not exist temporally prior to creation. In that case he exists timelessly *sans* creation. But once time begins at the moment of creation, God either becomes temporal in virtue of his real, causal relation to time and the world or else he exists as timelessly with creation as he does *sans* creation. But this second alternative seems quite impossible. At the first moment of time, God stands in a new relation in which he did not stand before (since there was no *before*). We need not characterize this as a change in God; but there is a real, causal relation which is at that moment new to God and which he does not have in the state of existing *sans* creation. At the moment of creation, God comes into the relation of *causing the universe* or at the very least that of *co-existing with the universe*, relations in which he did not before stand. Hence, even if God remains intrinsically changeless in creating the world, he nonetheless undergoes an extrinsic, or relational, change, which, if he is not already temporal prior to the moment of creation, draws him into time at that very moment in virtue of his real relation to the temporal, changing universe. So even if God is timeless *sans* creation, his free decision to create a temporal world constitutes also a free decision on his part to enter into time and to experience the reality of tense and temporal becoming.

The classic Thomistic response to the above argument is, remarkably, to deny that God's creative activity in the world implies that God is really related to the world. Aquinas tacitly agrees that if God were really related to the temporal world, then he would be temporal.[21] In the coming to be of creatures, certain relations accrue to God anew and thus, if these relations be real for God, he must be temporal in light of his undergoing extrinsic change, wholly apart from the question of whether God undergoes intrinsic change in creating the world. So Thomas denies that God has any real relation to the world. According to Aquinas, while the temporal world does have the real relation of *being created by God*, God does not have a real relation of *creating the temporal world.* Since God is immutable, the new relations predicated of him at the moment of creation are just in our minds; in reality the temporal world itself is created with a relation inhering in it of *dependence on God.* Hence, God's timelessness is not jeopardized by his creation of a temporal world.

This unusual doctrine of creation becomes even stranger when we reflect on the fact that in creating the world God does not perform some act extrinsic to his nature; rather the creature (which undergoes no change but simply begins to exist) begins to be with a relation to God of *being created by God.* According to this doctrine, then, God in freely creating the universe does not really do anything different than he would have, had he refrained from creating; the only difference is to be found in the universe itself: instead of God existing alone *sans* the universe we have instead a universe springing into being at the first moment of time possessing the property *being created by God,* even though God, for his part, bears no real reciprocal relation to the universe made by him.

I think it hardly needs to be said that Thomas's solution, despite its daring and ingenuity, is extraordinarily implausible. 'Creating' clearly describes a relation which is founded on something's intrinsic properties concerning its causal activity, and therefore *creating the world* ought to be regarded as a real property acquired by God at the moment of creation. It seems unintelligible, if not contradictory, to say that one can have real effects without real causes. Yet this is precisely what Aquinas affirms with respect to God and the world.

Moreover, it is the implication of Aquinas's position that God is perfectly similar across possible worlds, the same even in worlds in which he refrains from creation as in worlds in which he creates. For in none of these worlds does God have any relation to anything *extra se*. In all these worlds God never acts differently, he never cognizes differently, he never wills differently; he is just the simple, unrelated act of being. Even in worlds in which he does not create, his act of being, by which creation is produced, is no different in these otherwise empty worlds than in worlds chock-full of contingent beings of every order. Thomas's doctrine thus makes it unintelligible why the universe exists rather than nothing. The reason obviously cannot lie in God, either in his nature or in his activity (which are only conceptually distinct anyway), for these are perfectly similar in every possible world. Nor can the reason lie in the creatures themselves, in that they have a real relation to God of *being freely willed by God.* For their existing with that relation cannot be explanatorily prior to their existing with that relation. I conclude, therefore, that Thomas's solution, based in the denial of God's real relation to the world, cannot succeed in hermetically sealing off God in atemporality.

The above might lead one to conclude that God existed temporally prior to his creation of the universe in a sort of metaphysical time. But while it makes sense to speak of such a metaphysical time prior to the inception of physical time at the Big Bang (think of God's counting down to creation: . . . , 3, 2, 1, *fiat lux!*), the notion of an actual infinity of past events or intervals of time seems strikingly counterintuitive. Not only would we be forced to swallow all the bizarre and ultimately contradictory consequences of an actual infinite, but we would also be saddled with the prospect of God's having 'traversed' the infinite past one moment at a time until he arrived at the moment of creation, which seems absurd. Moreover, on such an essentially Newtonian view of time, we would have to answer the difficult question which Leibniz lodged against Clarke: why did God delay for infinite time the creation of the world?[22] In view of these perplexities, it seems more plausible to adopt the Leibnizian alternative of some sort of relational view of time according to which time does not exist in the utter absence of events.[23] God existing alone *sans* creation would be changeless and, hence, timeless, and time would begin at the first event, which, for simplicity's sake, we may take to be the Big Bang. God's bringing the initial cosmological singularity into being is simultaneous (or coincident) with the singularity's coming into being, and therefore God is temporal from the moment of creation onward. Though we might think of God as existing, say, one hour prior to creation, such a picture is, as Aquinas states, purely the product of our imagination and time prior to creation merely an imaginary time (in the phantasmagorical, not mathematical, sense!).[24]

Why, then, did God create the world? It has been said that if God is essentially characterized by self-giving love, creation becomes necessary.[25] But the Christian doctrine of the Trinity suggests another possibility. Insofar as he exists *sans* creation, God is not, on the Christian conception, a lonely monad, but in the tri-unity of his own being God enjoys the full and unchanging love relationships among the persons of the Trinity. Creation is thus unnecessary for God and is sheer gift, bestowed for the sake of creatures, that we might experience the joy and fulfilment of knowing God. He invites us, as it were, into the inner-Trinitarian love relationship as his adopted children. Thus, creation, as well as salvation, is *sola gratia*.

Providence

The biblical world-view involves a very strong conception of divine sovereignty over the world and human affairs, even as it presupposes human freedom and responsibility. While too numerous to list here, biblical passages affirming God's sovereignty have been grouped by D. A. Carson under four main heads: (1) God is the Creator, Ruler, and Possessor of all things, (2) God is the ultimate personal cause of all that happens, (3) God elects his people, and (4) God is the unacknowledged source of good fortune or success.[26] No one taking these passages seriously can embrace currently fashionable libertarian revisionism, which denies God's sovereignty over the contingent events of history. On the other hand, the conviction that human beings are free moral agents also permeates the Hebrew way of thinking, as is evident from passages listed by Carson under nine heads: (1) people face a multitude of divine exhortations and commands, (2) people are said to obey, believe and choose God, (3) people sin and rebel against God, (4) people's sins are judged by God, (5) people are tested by God, (6) people receive divine rewards, (7) the elect are responsible to respond to God's initiative, (8) prayers are not mere showpieces scripted by God, and (9) God literally pleads with sinners to repent and be saved.[27] These passages rule out a traditional deterministic understanding of divine providence, which precludes human freedom.

Reconciling these two streams of biblical teaching without compromising either has proven extraordinarily difficult. Nevertheless, a startling solution to this enigma emerges from the doctrine of divine middle knowledge crafted by the Counter-Reformation Jesuit theologian Luis Molina.[28] Molina proposes to furnish an analysis of divine knowledge in terms of three logical moments. Although whatever God knows he knows eternally, so that there is no temporal succession in God's knowledge, nonetheless there does exist a sort of logical succession in God's knowledge in that his knowledge of certain propositions is conditionally or explanatorily prior to his knowledge of certain other propositions. In the first, unconditioned moment God knows all *possibilia,* not only all individual essences, but also all possible worlds. Molina calls such knowledge 'natural knowledge' because the content of such knowledge is essential to God and in no way depends on the free decisions of his will. By means of his natural knowledge, then, God has knowledge of every contingent state of affairs which could possibly obtain and of what the exemplification of the individual essence of any free creature could freely choose to do in any such state of affairs that should be actual.

In the second moment, God possesses knowledge of all true counterfactual propositions, including counterfactuals of creaturely freedom. Whereas by his natural knowledge God knew what any free creature *could* do in any set of circumstances, now in this second moment God knows what any free creature *would* do in any set of circumstances. This is not because the circumstances causally determine the creature's choice, but simply because this is how the creature would freely choose. God thus knows that were he to actualize certain states of affairs, then certain other contingent states of affairs would obtain. Molina calls this counterfactual knowledge 'middle knowledge' because it stands in between the first and third moment in divine knowledge. Middle knowledge is like natural knowledge in that such knowledge does not depend on any decision of the divine will; God does not determine which counterfactuals of creaturely freedom are true or false. Thus, if it is true that *If some agent S were placed in circumstances C, then he would freely perform action a*, then even God in his omnipotence cannot bring it about that S would freely refrain from *a* if he were placed in C. On the other hand, middle knowledge is unlike natural knowledge in that the content of his middle knowledge is not essential to God. True counterfactuals are contingently true; S could freely decide to refrain from *a* in C, so that different counterfactuals could be true and be known by God than those that are. Hence, although it is essential to God that he have middle knowledge, it is not essential to him to have middle knowledge of those particular propositions which he does in fact know.

Intervening between the second and third moments of divine knowledge stands God's free decree to actualize a world known by him to be realizable on the basis of his middle knowledge. By his natural knowledge, God knows what is the entire range of logically possible worlds; by his middle knowledge he knows, in effect, what is the proper subset of those worlds which it is feasible for him to actualize. By a free decision, God decrees to actualize one of those worlds known to him through his middle knowledge.

Given God's free decision to actualize a world, in the third and final moment God possesses knowledge of all remaining propositions that are in fact true in the actual world, including future contingent propositions. Such knowledge is denominated 'free knowledge' by Molina because it is logically posterior to the decision of the divine will to actualize a world. The content of such knowledge is clearly not essential to God, since he could have decreed to actualize a different world. Had he done so, the content of his free knowledge would be different.

The doctrine of middle knowledge is a doctrine of remarkable theological fecundity. Molina's scheme would resolve in a single stroke most of the traditional difficulties concerning divine providence and human freedom. Molina defines providence as God's ordering of things to their ends, either directly or mediately through secondary agents. By his middle knowledge God knows an infinity of orders which he could instantiate because he knows how the creatures in them would in fact freely respond given the various circumstances. He then decides by the free act of his will how he would respond in these various circumstances and simultaneously wills to bring about one of these orders. He directly causes certain circumstances to come into being and others indirectly by causally determined secondary causes. Free creatures, however, he allows to act as he knew they would when placed in such circumstances, and he concurs with their decisions in producing in being the effects they desire. Some of these effects God desired unconditionally and so wills positively that they occur, but others he does not unconditionally desire, but nevertheless permits due to his overriding desire to allow creaturely freedom and knowing that even these sinful acts will fit into the overall scheme of things, so that God's ultimate ends in human history will be accomplished.[29] God has thus providentially arranged for everything that happens by either willing or permitting it, yet in such a way as to preserve freedom and contingency.

Molinism thus effects a dramatic reconciliation between divine sovereignty and human freedom. Before we embrace such a solution, however, we should ask what objections might be raised against a Molinist account. Surveying the literature, one discovers that the detractors of Molinism tend not so much to criticize the Molinist doctrine of providence as to attack the concept of middle knowledge upon which it is predicated. It is usually alleged that counterfactuals of freedom are not bivalent or are uniformly false or that God cannot know such counterfactual propositions. These objections have been repeatedly refuted by defenders of middle knowledge,[30] though opposition dies hard. But as Freddoso and Wierenga pointed out in an American Philosophical Association session devoted to a recent popularization of libertarian revisionism, until the opponents of middle knowledge answer the refutations of their objections – which they have yet to do – there is little new to be said in response to their criticisms. Let us consider, then, objections, not to middle knowledge *per se,* but to a Molinist account of providence.

Robert Adams has recently argued that divine middle knowledge of counterfactuals of creaturely freedom is actually incompatible with human freedom. Although inspired by an argument of William Hasker for the same conclusion, Adams's argument avoids any appeal to Hasker's dubious – and, I should say, clearly false – premise that on the Molinist view counterfactuals of freedom are more fundamental features of the world than are categorical facts.[31] Adams summarizes his argument 'very roughly' as follows:

> Suppose it is not only true that P would do A if placed in circumstances C; suppose that truth was settled, as Molinism implies, prior to God's deciding what, if anything, to create, and it would therefore have been a truth even if P had never been in C – indeed even if P had never existed. Then it is hard to see how it can be up to P to determine freely whether P does A in C.[32]

Granted that this summary is admittedly very rough, still it is frustratingly ambiguous. The argument seems to assume as a premise that there is a true counterfactual of creaturely freedom φ that *If P were in C, P would do A*, whose antecedent is true.

Is the objection then supposed to be aimed at the imagined claim that P *freely* brings about the truth of φ? Is Adams asserting that P cannot freely bring about the truth of φ because if, posterior to God's middle knowledge of φ, P were not in C or did not exist at all, φ would still be true, though P never does A in C, which is absurd? Is Adams saying that once the content of God's middle knowledge is fixed, P is no longer free with respect to A in C? If this is the argument, then it is just the old bogey of fatalism raising its fallacious head in a new guise, as Jonathan Kvanvig points out effectively in his critique of Adams's similar argument against the temporal pre-existence of 'thisnesses'.[33] Just as we have the power to act in such a way that were we to do so, future-tense propositions which were in fact true would not have been true, so things can happen differently than they will, in which case thisnesses and singular propositions which in fact exist(ed) would not have existed. Analogously, the Molinist could hold that it is within our power so to act that were we to do so, the truth of counterfactuals of creaturely freedom which is brought about by us would not have been brought about by us.

But perhaps this is not what Adams intends. Maybe the argument is that if φ is true logically prior to God's decree, then God still has the choice whether to instantiate worlds in which the antecedent of φ is true or not. If, then, God decrees to actualize a world in which P is not in C or does not exist at all, φ still remains true, being part of what Thomas Flint calls the 'world type' which confronts God prior to his decree.[34] But then how can P bring about the truth of φ, if P does not even exist? The Molinist answer to that question, however, is straightforward: P does not in that case bring about the truth of φ. The hypothetical Molinist against whom this objection is directed holds *ex hypothesi* 'that in the case of a true counterfactual of freedom with a true antecedent it is the agent of the free action described in the consequent who brings it about that the conditional is true'.[35] That claim is consistent – though I, like Adams, cannot imagine why any Molinist should want to maintain such a claim – with the further claim that in cases of true counterfactuals of creaturely freedom lacking true antecedents, their truth is not brought about by the agents described. In my opinion, it is better to say that in all cases of true counterfactuals of creaturely freedom, the truth of a counterfactual like φ is grounded in the obtaining in the actual world (logically prior to God's decree) of the counterfactual state of affairs that if P were in C, then he would do A, and that any further explanation of this fact implicitly denies libertarianism.[36] Just as a true, contingent, future-tense proposition of the form *It will be the case that P does A at t* cannot be explained in terms of the truth of a tenseless proposition of the form *P does A at t*, so it is futile to try to explain true counterfactuals of creaturely freedom of the form *If P were in C, P would do A* in terms of categorical, indicative propositions of a form like *P will do A in C*. Just as irreducibly tensed facts are needed in the former case, conditional subjunctive facts are needed in the latter. Be that as it may, however, Adams's intuitive reasoning provides no grounds for rejecting either the view that the truth of counterfactuals of creaturely freedom with true antecedents is brought about by the agents described or the view that the truth of counterfactuals of creaturely freedom of any kind is not brought about by the agents described.

Having summarized the intuitive basis of his argument, Adams develops the following more rigorous formulation:

1. According to Molinism, the truth of all true counterfactuals of freedom about us is explanatorily prior to God's decision to create us.
2. God's decision to create us is explanatorily prior to our existence.
3. Our existence is explanatorily prior to all of our choices and actions.
4. The relation of explanatory priority is transitive.
5. Therefore, it follows from Molinism (by 1–4) that the truth of all true counterfactuals of freedom about us is explanatorily prior to all of our choices and actions.
10. It follows also from Molinism that if I freely do action A in circumstances C, then there is a true counterfactual of freedom F*, which says that if I were in C, then I would (freely) do A.
11. Therefore, it follows from Molinism that if I freely do A in C, the truth of F* is explanatorily prior to my choosing and acting as I do in C.
12. If I freely do A in C, no truth that is strictly inconsistent with my refraining from A in C is explanatorily prior to my choosing and acting as I do in C.
13. The truth of F* (which says that if I were in C, then I would do A) is strictly inconsistent with my refraining from A in C.

14.   If Molinism is true, then if I freely do A in C, F* both is (by 11) and is not (by 12–13) explanatorily prior to my choosing and acting as I do in C.

15.   Therefore, (by 14) if Molinism is true, then I do not freely do A in C.

In his critique of Adams's earlier anti-Molinist argument, Alvin Plantinga charged that the argument is unsound because the dependency relation involved is not a transitive relation.[37] It seems to me that the present argument shares a similar failing. The notion of 'explanatory priority' as it plays a role in the argument seems to me equivocal, and if a univocal sense can be given it, there is no reason to expect it to be transitive.

Consider the explanatory priority in (2) and (3). Here a straightforward interpretation of this notion can be given in terms of the counterfactual dependence of consequent on condition:

2'.   If God had not created us, we should not exist.

3'.   If we were not to exist, we should not make any of our choices and actions.

Both (2') and (3') are metaphysically necessary truths. But this sense of explanatory priority is inapplicable to (1), for

1'.   According to Molinism, if all true counterfactuals of freedom about us were not true, God would not have decided to create us

is false. Molinism makes no such assertion, since God might still have created us even if the actually true counterfactuals of creaturely freedom were false or even, *per impossibile*, if no such counterfactuals at all were true. The sense of explanatory priority in (1) must therefore be different than it is in (2) and (3).

The root of the difficulty seems to be a conflation of reasons and causes on Adams's part. The priority in (2) and (3) is a sort of causal or ontic priority, but the priority in (1) is not causal or ontic, since the truth of all counterfactuals of creaturely freedom is neither a necessary nor a sufficient condition of God's decision to create us. At best, the truth of such counterfactuals is prior to his decision in providing a partial reason for that decision. Adams's mistake seems to be that he leaps from God's decision in the hierarchy of reasons to God's decision in the hierarchy of causes and by this equivocation tries to make counterfactuals of creaturely freedom explanatorily prior to our free choices.

Perhaps Adams can enunciate a univocal sense of 'explanatory priority' that is applicable to (1–3). But I suspect that any such notion would be so generic that we should have to deny its transitivity or so weak that it would not be inimical to human freedom. This suspicion is borne out by Hasker's very recent attempt to save Adams's argument by enunciating a very broad conception of explanatory priority which is univocal in (1–3) and yet transitive: for contingent states of affairs p and q,

EP: p is explanatorily prior to q iff p must be included in a complete explanation of why q obtains.

Hasker asserts: 'It should be apparent that explanatory priority as explicated by (EP) is transitive: if p is explanatorily prior to q, and q to r, then clearly p must be included in a complete explanation of why r obtains.'[38] But this is not at all clear. As Hasker observes, such a relation must also be irreflexive: 'a contingent state of affairs cannot constitute an explanation (in whole or in part) of itself'.[39] But if the relation described by (EP) is transitive, then it seems that the condition of irreflexivity is violated. My wife and I not infrequently find ourselves in the situation that I want to do something if she wants to do it, and she wants to do it if I want to do it. Suppose, then, that John is going to the party because Mary is going, and Mary is going to the party because John is going. It follows that if the (EP) relation is transitive, John is going to the party because John is going to the party, which conclusion is obviously wrong. Not only is such a conclusion explanatorily vacuous, but it also implies, in conjunction with (12), that John does not freely go to the party – the very conclusion Hasker wants to avoid.

Adams's *reductio* also fails because (12) is false. What is undeniably true is

12'. If I freely do A in C, no truth that is strictly inconsistent with my doing A in C is explanatorily prior to my choosing and acting as I do in C.

But why would we be tempted to think that no truth which is inconsistent with my *not* doing A in C is explanatorily prior to my freely doing A in C? Certainly

F**. If I were in C, then I would not do A.

cannot be explanatorily prior to my freely doing A in C; but why would F** not be explanatorily prior to my freely not doing A in C? Adams's intuition seems to be that if F* were explanatorily prior to my doing A in C, then I could not refrain from A, which is a necessary condition of my doing A freely.[40] But such an assumption seems doubly wrong. First, it represents once more the fallacious reasoning of fatalism. Though F* is (*ex concessionis*) in fact explanatorily prior to my freely doing A in C, it is within my power to refrain from doing A in C; only if I were to do so, F* would not then be explanatorily prior to my action nor a part of God's middle knowledge. Until Adams can show that the content of God's middle knowledge is a 'hard fact', his argument based on (12) is undercut. Second, my being able to refrain from doing A in C is not a necessary condition of my freely doing A in C. For perhaps I do A in C without any causal constraint, but it is also the case that God would not permit me to refrain from A in C. Perhaps it is true that

G. If I were to attempt to refrain from doing A in C, God would not permit me to refrain from doing A in C.

(G) is inconsistent with my refraining from doing A in C, and yet it may well be explanatorily prior to my freely doing A in C. Flint's essay on infallibility, which appears in the same volume as Adams's, provides a good illustration.[41] Suppose I am the Pope and A is promulgating *ex cathedra* only correct doctrine. God knew via his middle knowledge that if I were in C, I would freely do A. Therefore, his creative decree includes my being elected Pope. Given papal infallibility, (G) may also be true and part of God's middle knowledge, and so is explanatorily prior to my freely doing A in C. But (G) is inconsistent with my refraining from A in C. If such a scenario is coherent — and Flint seems to have refuted all objections to it — then (12) is false.

The sense of explanatory priority explicated in Hasker's (EP) is so weak that even if the Molinist simply concedes the truth of (5) in this sense, then (12) is all the more obviously false. For counterfactuals concerning our free actions may be explanatorily prior to those actions only in the sense that God's reason for creating us may have been in part that he knew we should freely do such things. But it is wholly mysterious how this sense of explanatory priority is incompatible with our performing such actions freely. In a footnote, Hasker claims that Adams's argument can be freed from reliance on (12), referring the reader to his own argument against middle knowledge.[42] But the duly attentive reader will find in that discussion nothing but a reiteration of Hasker's previous argument on this score with no refutation of the several objections lodged against it in the literature.[43]

Thus, it seems to me that both sides of Adams's *reductio* argument are unsound. His attempt to show that counterfactuals of creaturely freedom are explanatorily prior to our actions fails due to equivocation. And even if they were in some peculiar sense explanatorily prior to our actions because they are true and known by God logically prior to categorical contingent propositions, that would not be incompatible with the freedom of our actions. In short, neither Adams nor Hasker has been able to explicate a sense of explanatory priority with respect to the truth of counterfactuals of creaturely freedom which is both transitive and inimical to human freedom. Given that the objections against a Molinist doctrine of providence thus fail, the theological power of such an account ought to prompt us to avail ourselves of it.

Miracle

The biblical narrative of divine action in the world is clearly a narrative replete with miraculous events. God is conceived to bring about events which natural things, left to their own resources, would not bring about. Hence, miracles are able to function as signs of divine activity.[44] 'Why this is a marvel!' exclaims the man born blind, when confronted with the Pharisees' scepticism concerning Jesus's rectification of his sight. 'Never since the world began has it been heard that any one opened the eyes of a man born blind. If this man were not from God, he could do nothing' (John 9:30–33).

In order to differentiate between the customary way in which God acts and his special, miraculous action, theologians have traditionally distinguished within divine providence God's *providentia ordinaria* and his *providentia extraordinaria,* the latter being identified with miracles. But our exposition of divine providence based on God's middle knowledge suggests a category of non-miraculous, extraordinary providence, which it will be helpful to distinguish. One has in mind here events which are the product of natural causes but whose context is such as to suggest a special divine intention with regard to their occurrence. For example, just as the Israelites approach the Jordan river, a rockslide upstream temporarily blocks the water's flow, enabling them to cross into the Promised Land (Joshua 3:14–17); or again, as Paul and Silas lie bound in prison for preaching the gospel, an earthquake occurs, springing the prison doors and unfastening their fetters (Acts 16:25–26). By means of his middle knowledge, God can providentially order the world so that the natural causes of such events are, as it were, ready and waiting to produce such events at the propitious time, perhaps in answer to prayers which God knew would be offered. Of course, if such prayers were not to be offered or the contingent course of events were to go differently, then God would have known this and so not arranged the natural causes, including human free volitions, to produce the special providential event. Events wrought by special providence are no more outside the course and capacity of nature than are events produced by God's ordinary providence, but the context of such events, such as their timing, their coincidental nature, and so forth, is such as to point to a special divine intention to bring them about.

If, then, we distinguish miracles from both God's *providentia ordinaria* and *extraordinaria,* how should we characterize miracles? Since the dawning of modernity, miracles have been widely understood to be 'violations of the laws of nature'. In his *Dictionary* article on miracles, for example, Voltaire states that, according to accepted usage, 'A miracle is the violation of mathematical, divine, immutable, eternal laws' and is therefore a contradiction.[45] Voltaire is in fact quite right that such a definition is a contradiction, but this ought to have led him to conclude, not that miracles can thus be defined out of existence, but that the customary definition is defective. Indeed, an examination of the chief competing schools of thought concerning the notion of a natural law in fact reveals that on each theory the concept of a violation of a natural law is incoherent and that miracles need not be so defined. Broadly speaking, there are three main views of natural law today: the regularity theory, the nomic necessity theory, and the causal dispositions theory.[46]

According to the regularity theory, the 'laws' of nature are not really laws at all, but just generalized descriptions of the way things happen in the world. They describe the regularities which we observe in nature. Now since on such a theory a natural law is just a generalized description of *whatever* occurs in nature, it follows that no event which occurs can violate such a law. Instead, it just becomes part of the description. The law cannot be violated, because it describes in a certain generalized form everything that does happen in nature.

According to the nomic necessity theory, natural laws are not merely descriptive, but tell us what can and cannot happen in the natural world. They allow us to make certain counterfactual judgements, such as 'If the density of the universe were sufficiently high, it would have re-contracted long ago', which a purely descriptivist theory would not permit. Again, however, since natural laws are taken to be universal inductive generalizations, a violation of a natural law is no more possible on this theory than on the regularity theory. So long as natural laws are *universal* generalizations based on experience, they must take account of anything that happens and so would be revised should an event occur which the law does not encompass.

Of course, in practice proponents of such theories do not treat natural laws so rigidly. Rather, natural laws are assumed to have implicit in them certain *ceteris paribus* assumptions such that a law states what is the case under the assumption that no other natural factors are interfering. When a scientific anomaly occurs, it is usually assumed that some unknown natural factors are interfering, so that the law is neither violated nor revised. But suppose the law fails to describe or predict accurately because some *supernatural* factors are interfering? Clearly, the implicit assumption of such laws is that no supernatural factors as well as no natural factors are interfering. If the law proves inaccurate in a particular case because God is acting, the law is neither violated nor revised. If God brings about some event which a law of nature fails to predict or describe, such an event cannot be characterized as a violation of a law of nature, since the law is valid only on the assumption that no supernatural factors in addition to the natural factors come into play.

On such theories, then, miracles ought to be defined as naturally impossible events, that is to say, events which cannot be produced by the natural causes operative at a certain time and place. Whether an event is a miracle is thus relative to a time and place. Given the natural causes operative at a certain time and place, for example, rain may be naturally inevitable or necessary, but on another occasion, rain may be naturally impossible. Of course, some events, say, the resurrection, may be absolutely miraculous in that they are at every time and place beyond the productive capacity of natural causes.

According to the causal dispositions theory, things in the world have different natures or essences, which include their causal dispositions to affect other things in certain ways, and natural laws are metaphysically necessary truths about what causal dispositions are possessed by various natural kinds of things. For example, 'Salt has a disposition to dissolve in water' would state a natural law. If, due to God's action, some salt failed to dissolve in water, the natural law is not violated, because it is still true that salt has such a disposition. As a result of things' causal dispositions, certain deterministic natural propensities exist in nature, and when such a propensity is not impeded (by God or some other free agent), then we can speak of a natural necessity. On this theory, an event which is naturally necessary must and does actually occur, since the natural propensity will automatically issue forth in the event if it is not impeded. By the same token, a naturally impossible event cannot and does not actually occur. Hence, a miracle cannot be characterized on this theory as a naturally impossible event. Rather, a miracle is an event which results from causal interference with a natural propensity which is so strong that only a supernatural agent could impede it. The concept of miracle is essentially the same as under the previous two theories, but one just cannot call a miracle 'naturally impossible' as those terms are defined in this theory; perhaps we could adopt instead the nomenclature 'physically impossible' to characterize miracles under such a theory.

On none of these theories, then, should miracles be understood as violations of the laws of nature. Rather they are naturally (or physically) impossible events, events which at certain times and places cannot be produced by the relevant natural causes.

Now the question is, what could conceivably transform an event that is naturally impossible into a real historical event? Clearly, the answer is the personal God of theism. For if a transcendent, personal God exists, then he could cause events in the universe that could not be produced by causes within the universe. Given a God who created the universe, who conserves the world in being, and who is capable of acting freely, Christian theologians seem to be entirely justified in maintaining that miracles are possible. Indeed, if it is even (epistemically) possible that such a transcendent, personal God exists, then it is equally possible that he has acted miraculously in the universe. Only to the extent that one has good grounds for believing atheism to be true could one be rationally justified in denying the possibility of miracles. In this light arguments for the impossibility of miracles based upon defining them as violations of the laws of nature become fatuous.

The more interesting question is whether the identification of any event as a miracle is possible. On the one hand, it might be argued that a convincing demonstration that a purportedly miraculous event has occurred would only succeed in forcing us to revise natural law so as to accommodate the event in question. But as Swinburne has argued, a natural law is not abolished because of one exception; the counter-instance must occur repeatedly whenever the conditions for it are present.[47] If an event occurs which is, as Swinburne puts it, contrary to a law of nature and we have reasons to believe that this event would not occur again under similar circumstances, then the law in question will not be abandoned. One may regard an anomalous event as repeatable if another formulation of the natural law better accounts for the event in question, and if it is no more complex than the original law. If any doubt exists, the scientist may conduct experiments to determine which formulation of the law proves more successful in predicting future phenomena. In a similar way, one would have good reason to regard an event as a non-repeatable counter-instance to a law if the reformulated law were much more complicated than the original without yielding better new predictions or by predicting new phenomena unsuccessfully where the original formulation predicted successfully. If the original formulation remains successful in predicting all new phenomena as the data accumulate, while no reformulation does any better in predicting the phenomena and explaining the event in question, then the event should be regarded as a non-repeatable counter-instance to the law. Hence, a miraculous event would not serve to upset the natural law:

> We have to some extent good evidence about what are the laws of nature, and some of them are so well-established and account for so many data that any modifications to them which suggest to account for the odd counter-instance would be so clumsy and *ad hoc* as to upset the whole structure of science. In such cases the evidence is strong that if the purported counter-instance occurred it was a violation of the laws of nature.[48]

Swinburne unfortunately retains the violation concept of miracle, which would invalidate his argument; but if we conceive of a miracle as a naturally impossible event, he is on target in reasoning that the admission of such an event would not lead to the abandonment of a natural law.

On the other hand, it might be urged that if a purportedly miraculous event were demonstrated to have occurred, we should conclude that the event occurred in accordance with unknown natural causes and laws. The question is, what serves to distinguish a genuine miracle from a mere scientific anomaly? Here the religio-historical context of the event becomes crucial. A miracle without a context is inherently ambiguous. But if a purported miracle occurs in a significant religio-historical context, then the chances of its being a genuine miracle are increased. For example, if the miracles occur at a momentous time (say, a man's leprosy vanishing when Jesus speaks the words 'Be clean!') and do not recur regularly in history, and if the miracles are numerous and various, then the chances of their being the result of some unknown natural causes are reduced. In Jesus's case, moreover, his miracles and resurrection ostensibly took place in the context of and as the climax to his own unparalleled life and teachings and produced so profound an effect on his followers that they called him LORD. The central miracle of the New Testament, the resurrection of Jesus, was, if it occurred, doubtlessly a miracle. In the first place, the resurrection so exceeds what we know of natural causes that it can only be reasonably attributed to a supernatural cause. The more we learn about cell necrosis, the more evident it becomes that such an event is naturally impossible. If it were the effect of unknown natural causes, then its uniqueness in the history of mankind becomes inexplicable. Secondly, the supernatural explanation is given immediately in the religio-historical context in which the event occurred. Jesus's resurrection was not merely an anomalous event, occurring without context; it came as the climax to Jesus's own life and teachings. As Wolfhart Pannenberg explains,

> The resurrection of Jesus acquires such decisive meaning, not merely because someone or anyone has been raised from the dead, but because it is Jesus of Nazareth, whose execution was instigated by the Jews because he had blasphemed against God.
>
> Jesus' claim to authority, through which he put himself in God's place, was ... blasphemous for Jewish ears. Because of this Jesus was then also slandered before the Roman Governor as a rebel. If Jesus really has been raised, this claim has been visibly and unambiguously confirmed by the God of Israel, who was allegedly blasphemed by Jesus.[49]

We should therefore have good reasons to regard Jesus's resurrection, if it occurred, as truly miraculous. Thus, while it may, indeed, be difficult to know in some cases whether a genuine miracle has occurred, that does not imply pessimism with respect to all cases.

But perhaps the very natural impossibility of a genuine miracle precludes our ever identifying an event as a miracle. As Hume notoriously argued, perhaps it is always more rational to believe that some mistake or deception is at play than to believe that a genuine miracle has occurred.[50] This conclusion is based on Hume's principle that it is always more probable that the testimony to a miracle is false than that the miracle occurred. But Hume's principle incorrectly assumes that miracles are highly improbable. With respect to the resurrection of Jesus, for example, the hypothesis 'God raised Jesus from the dead' is not improbable, either relative to our background information or to the specific evidence. What is improbable relative to our background information is the hypothesis 'Jesus rose naturally from the dead'. Given what we know of cell necrosis, that hypothesis is fantastically, even unimaginably, improbable. Conspiracy theories, apparent-death theories, hallucination theories, twin brother theories – almost any hypothesis, however unlikely, seems more probable than the hypothesis that all the cells in Jesus's corpse spontaneously came back to life again. But such naturalistic hypotheses are not more probable than the hypothesis that God raised Jesus from the dead. The evidence for the laws of nature relevant in this case makes it probable that a resurrection from the dead is naturally impossible, which renders improbable the hypothesis that Jesus rose naturally from the grave. But such evidence is simply irrelevant to the probability of the hypothesis that God raised Jesus from the dead. That hypothesis needs to be weighed in light of the specific evidence concerning such facts as the post-mortem appearances of Jesus, the vacancy of the tomb where Jesus's corpse was laid, the origin of the original disciples' firm belief that God had, in fact, raised Jesus, and so forth, in the religio-historical context in which the events took place and assessed in terms of the customary criteria used in justifying historical hypotheses, such as explanatory power, explanatory scope, plausibility, and so forth. When this is done, there is no reason *a priori* to expect that it will be more probable that the testimony is false than that the hypothesis of miracle is true.

Given the God of creation and providence described in classical theism, miracles are possible and, when occurring under certain conditions, plausibly identifiable.

Notes

1 On Gen 1:1 as an independent clause which is not a mere chapter title, see Claus Westermann, *Genesis 1 – 11*, trans. John Scullion (Minneapolis, 1984), p. 97; John Sailhammer, *Genesis* (Expositor's Bible Commentary 2; Grand Rapids, 1990), p. 21.
2 See, e.g., Prov 8.27–29, cf. Ps 104:5–9; also Isa 44:24; 45:18, 24; Pss 33.9, 90:2; John 1:1–3; Rom 4:17; 11:36; 1 Cor 8:6; Col 1:16, 17; Heb 1:2–3; 11:3; Rev 4:11.

William Lane Craig

3 E.g., 2 Macc 7:28; 1QS 3.15; *Joseph and Aseneth* 12.1–3; *2 Enoch* 25.1ff.; 26.1; *Odes of Solomon* 16.18–19; *2 Baruch* 21.4. For discussion, see Paul Copan, 'Is *Creatio ex nihilo* a post-biblical invention?: an examination of Gerhard May's proposal', *Trinity Journal* 17 (1996), pp. 77–93.

4 *Creatio ex nihilo* is affirmed in the *Shepherd of Hermas* 1.6; 26.1 and the *Apostolic Constitutions* 8.12.6, 8; and by Tatian, *Oratio ad graecos* 5.3; cf. 4.1ff.; 12.1; Theophilus, *Ad Autolycum* 1.4; 2.4, 10, 13; and Irenaeus, *Adversus haereses* 3.10.3. For discussion, see Gerhard May, *Creatio ex nihilo: The Doctrine of 'Creation out of Nothing' in Early Christian Thought*, trans. A. S. Worrall (Edinburgh, 1994); cf. Copan's review article in note 3.

5 See Richard Sorabji, *Time, Creation and the Continuum* (Ithaca, NY, 1983), pp. 193–252; H. A. Wolfson, 'Patristic arguments against the eternity of the world', *Harvard Theological Review* 59 (1966), pp. 354–67; idem, *The Philosophy of the Kalam* (Cambridge, MA, 1976); H. A. Davidson, *Proofs for Eternity, Creation and the Existence of God in Medieval Islamic and Jewish Philosophy* (New York and Oxford, 1987); Richard C. Dales, *Medieval Discussions of the Eternity of the World* (Studies in Intellectual History 18; Leiden, 1990).

6 Thomas Aquinas, *Summa Theologiae* I, 2, 3; idem, *Summa contra gentiles* 2.16; 32–38; cf. idem, *Summa Theologiae* I, 46, 1; I, 46, 2. Though Aquinas discusses divine conservation, he does not differentiate it from creation (idem, *Summa contra gentiles* 3.65; *Summa Theologiae* I, 104, 1).

7 Philip L. Quinn, 'Divine conservation, continuous creation, and human action' in Alfred J. Freddoso (ed.) *The Existence and Nature of God* (Notre Dame, 1983), pp. 55–79. See also idem, 'Creation, conservation, and the Big Bang' in John Earman, Allen I. Janis, Gerald J. Massey and Nicholas Rescher (eds), *Philosophical Problems of the Internal and External Worlds* (Pittsburgh, 1993), pp. 589–612; idem, 'Divine conservation, secondary causes, and occasionalism' in Thomas V. Morris (ed.), *Divine and Human Action* (Ithaca, NY, 1988), pp. 50–73.

8 John Duns Scotus, *God and Creatures*, trans. E. Alluntis and A. Wolter (Princeton, 1975), p. 276.

9 As noted by Alfred J. Freddoso, 'Medieval Aristotelianism and the case against secondary causation in nature' in Morris, *Divine and Human Action*, p. 79. For the scholastics causation is a relation between substances (agents) who act upon other substances (patients) to bring about states of affairs (effects). *Creatio ex nihilo* is atypical because in that case no patient is acted upon.

10 To analyse God's conservation of *e*, along Quinn's lines, as God's re-creation of *e* anew at each instant of *e*'s existence is to run the risk of falling into the radical occasionalism of certain medieval Islamic theologians, who, out of their desire to make God not only the creator of the world, but also its ground of being, denied that the constituent atoms of things endure from one instant to another but maintained that they are rather created in new states of being by God at every successive instant. There are actually two forms of occasionalism threatening Quinn: (1) the occasionalism implied by a literal *creatio continuans* according to which similar, but numerically distinct, individuals are created at each successive instant, and (2) the occasionalism which affirms diachronic individual identity, but denies the reality of *transeunt* secondary causation.

11 On A- versus B-Theories of time, see Richard Gale, 'The static versus the dynamic temporal: introduction' in Richard M. Gale (ed.), *The Philosophy of Time* (New Jersey, 1968), pp. 65–85.

12 Wolfhart Pannenberg, 'Theological questions to scientists' in A. R. Peacocke

(ed.), *The Sciences and Theology in the Twentieth Century* (Oxford International Symposia; Stocksfield, 1981), p. 12.

13 According to Schleiermacher, the original expression of the relation of the world to God, that of absolute dependence, was divided by the Church into two propositions: that the world was created and that the world is sustained. But there is no reason, he asserts, to retain this distinction, since it is linked to the Mosaic account of creation, which is the product of a mythological age. The question of whether it is possible or necessary to conceive of God as existing apart from created things is a matter of indifference, since it has no bearing on the feeling of absolute dependence on God (F. D. E. Schleiermacher, *The Christian Faith*, 2nd edn, ed. H. R. MacIntosh and J. S. Stewart [Edinburgh, 1928], 36.1, 2; 41; pp. 142–3, 155).

14 Good examples of such timorousness include Langdon Gilkey, *Maker of Heaven and Earth* (Garden City, NY, 1959), pp. 310–15; Ian Barbour, *Issues in Science and Religion* (New York, 1966), pp. 383–5; Arthur Peacocke, *Creation and the World of Science* (Oxford, 1979), pp. 78–9.

15 Pannenberg, 'Questions', p. 12; Ted Peters, 'On creating the cosmos' in R. Russell, W. Stoeger and G. Coyne (eds), *Physics, Philosophy, and Theology: A Common Quest for Understanding* (Vatican City, 1988), p. 291; Robert J. Russell, 'Finite creation without a beginning: The doctrine of creation in relation to Big Bang and quantum cosmologies' in R. J. Russell, N. Murphy and C. J. Isham (eds), *Quantum Cosmology and the Laws of Nature* (Vatican City, 1993), pp. 303–10.

16 John D. Barrow and Frank J. Tipler, *The Anthropic Cosmological Principle* (Oxford, 1986), p. 442.

17 See William Lane Craig and Quentin Smith, *Theism, Atheism, and Big Bang Cosmology* (Oxford, 1993) for discussion.

18 In the case of quantum mechanics, for example, 'the state vector in the Schrödinger equation is not a physical magnitude, for it is an imaginary function and such functions do not represent real physical magnitudes' (C. Liu, 'The arrow of time in quantum gravity', *Philosophy of Science* 60 [1993], p. 622). Liu contends that in the mature theory of quantum gravity a fundamental arrow of time will obtain.

19 Hartle–Hawking's use of imaginary numbers for the time variable allows one to re-describe a universe with an initial cosmological singularity in such a way that that point appears as a non-singular point on a curved hyper-surface. Such a re-description suppresses and also literally spatializes time, which makes evident the purely instrumental character of the model. Such a model could be of great utility to science, but it would not, as Hawking boldly asserts (Stephen Hawking, *A Brief History of Time* [New York, 1988], pp. 140–1), eliminate the need for a creator.

20 See the interesting lecture by C. Rovelli, 'What does present day's [*sic*] physics tell us about time and space?' Lecture presented at the 1993–94 Annual Series of Lectures of the Center for Philosophy of Science of the University of Pittsburgh, 17 September 1993, p. 17, where he lists eight properties of time as characterized in natural language and compares the concepts of time found in thermodynamics, STR, GTR, and so forth; time as it is defined in quantum gravity has *none* of the properties usually associated with time.

21 See M. T. Liske, 'Kann Gott reale Beziehungen zu den Geschöpfen haben?', *Theologie und Philosophie* 68 (1993), p. 224.

22 The difficulty may be formulated as follows:

1. If God delays creating at t until t', he has good reason to do so.
2. If God existed from eternity past until creating at t', he delayed creating at t.
3. God can have no good reason to do so.
4. Therefore, God did not delay creating at t until t'.
5. Therefore, God has not existed from eternity past until creating at t'.

23 Such a view would not preclude the existence of time during hiatuses within the series of events, such as are envisioned by Sidney Shoemaker, 'Time without change', *The Journal of Philosophy* 66 (1969), pp. 363–81.

24 Thomas Aquinas, *De potentia Dei* 3.1, 2.

25 Keith Ward, *Rational Theology and the Creativity of God* (Oxford, 1982), p. 86.

26 D. A. Carson, *Divine Sovereignty and Human Responsibility: Biblical Perspectives in Tension* (Atlanta, 1981), pp. 24–35.

27 Carson, *Sovereignty and Responsibility,* pp. 18–22. One should mention also the striking passages which speak of God's repenting in reaction to a change in human behaviour (e.g., Gen 6:6; 1 Sam 15:11, 35).

28 See Luis Molina, *On Divine Foreknowledge: Part IV of the 'Concordia'*, trans. with intro. and notes by Alfred J. Freddoso (Ithaca, NY, 1988); also William Lane Craig, *The Problem of Divine Foreknowledge and Future Contingents from Aristotle to Suarez* (Studies in Intellectual History 7; Leiden, 1988), chs 7, 8.

29 Molina explains:

> . . . all *good* things, whether produced by causes acting from a necessity of nature or by free causes, depend upon divine predetermination . . . and providence in such a way that each is *specifically intended* by God through his predetermination and providence, whereas the *evil* acts of the created will are subject as well to divine predetermination and providence to the extent that the causes from which they emanate and the general concurrence on God's part required to elicit them are granted through divine predetermination and providence – though not in order that *these particular acts* should emanate from them, but rather in order that *other, far different, acts* might come to be, and in order that the innate freedom of the things endowed with a will might be preserved for their maximum benefit; in addition evil acts are subject to that same divine predetermination and providence to the extent that they cannot exist in particular unless God by his providence *permits them in particular* in the service of some greater good. It clearly follows from the above that all things without exception are *individually* subject to God's will and providence, which intend certain of them *as particulars* and permit the rest *as particulars*. Thus, the leaf hanging from the tree does not fall, nor does either of the two sparrows sold for a farthing fall to the ground, nor does anything else whatever happen without God's providence and will either *intending* it *as a particular* or *permitting* it *as a particular* (Molina, *On Divine Foreknowledge* 4. 53. 3. 17)

> On the way in which sins contribute to the eventual realization of God's purposes, see the powerful statement in *On Divine Foreknowledge* 4. 53. 2. 15.

30 Alvin Plantinga, 'Reply to Robert Adams' in James E. Tomberlin and Peter Van Inwagen (eds), *Alvin Plantinga* (Profiles 5; Dordrecht, 1985), pp. 371–82; Jonathan L. Kvanvig, *The Possibility of an All-Knowing God* (New York, 1986), pp. 121–48; Alfred J. Freddoso, 'Introduction' in *On Divine Foreknowledge*, pp. 68–78; Edward J. Wierenga, *The Nature of God: An Inquiry into Divine Attributes*

(Ithaca, 1989), pp. 150–60; William Lane Craig, *Divine Foreknowledge and Human Freedom,* pp. 247–69; Thomas Flint, 'Hasker's *God, Time, and Knowledge', Philosophical Studies* 60 (1990), pp. 103–15; William Lane Craig, 'Hasker on divine knowledge', *Philosophical Studies* 67 (1992), p. 30.

31 Hasker does attempt to re-defend his controversial premise in William Hasker, 'Middle knowledge: a refutation revisited', *Faith and Philosophy* 12 (1995), pp. 224–5; but his account fails to respond to any of the three objections advanced in Craig, 'Hasker on divine knowledge', pp. 106–7, and in the end he himself concedes that '... the complexity of the argument ... leaves a number of points at which doubts can arise and toward which critics can direct their fire' (Hasker, 'Refutation revisited', p. 226), so that he chooses to adopt Adams's alternative formulation.

32 Robert Merrihew Adams, 'An anti-Molinist argument' in James E. Tomberlin (ed.), *Philosophical Perspectives,* vol. V: *Philosophy of Religion* (Atascadero, CA, 1991), p. 356.

33 Adams had argued 'My thisness, and singular propositions about me, cannot have pre-existed me because if they had, it would have been possible for them to have existed even if I had never existed, and that is not possible' (Robert Merrihew Adams, 'Time and thisness', *Midwest Studies in Philosophy* 11 [1986], p. 317). This argument is parallel to the interpretation under discussion, counterfactuals of creaturely freedom and divine middle knowledge taking the place of thisnesses and singular propositions. As Kvanvig discerns, this reasoning is susceptible to the same response as is the argument for fatalism (Jonathan L. Kvanvig, 'Adams on actualism and presentism', *Philosophy and Phenomenological Research* 50 [1989], pp. 284–98).

34 Thomas P. Flint, 'The problem of divine freedom', *American Philosophical Quarterly* 20 (1983), pp. 255–64.

35 Adams, 'Anti-Molinist argument', p. 345.

36 See further my *Divine Foreknowledge and Human Freedom*, pp. 259–62.

37 Plantinga, 'Reply to Robert Adams', p. 376.

38 William Hasker, 'Explanatory priority: transitive and unequivocal, a reply to William Craig', *Philosophy and Phenomenological Research* 57 (1997), p. 3.

39 Ibid.

40 He writes: '... (12) expresses a ... distinctively incompatibilist intuition, that the explanatory antecedents of the totality of my choosing and doing, must leave the omission of the free action "open," at least in the sense of not being strictly inconsistent with the omission' (Adams, 'Anti-Molinist argument', p. 352).

41 Thomas P. Flint, 'Middle knowledge and the doctrine of infallibility' in Tomberlin, *Philosophy of Religion,* pp. 385–90.

42 Hasker, 'Explanatory priority', p. 1. The article referenced is Hasker, 'Refutation revisited', pp. 223–36.

43 Hasker revises the first part of his argument in deference to Adams's version, but the second part he leaves unchanged and undefended – indeed, in footnote 17 on p. 235 he actually commends Adams's (12) as an alternative to his argument for those 'who have qualms about some of the premises in my version of the argument'.

44 It is very often said by biblical scholars anxious not to be associated with a defunct evidential apologetic use of miracles that biblical miracles function as signs, not evidence. This, however, is a false dichotomy; it is precisely because of their evidential force that miracles serve effectively as signs (see William

Lane Craig, review article of *Miracles and the Critical Mind,* by Colin Brown, *Journal of the Evangelical Theological Society* 27 [1985], pp. 473–83).

45 Marie François Arouet de Voltaire, *Dictionnaire philosophique* (Paris, 1967), s.v. 'Miracles'.

46 For discussion see Stephen S. Bilinskyji, 'God, nature, and the concept of miracle' (PhD dissertation, University of Notre Dame, 1982); Alfred J. Freddoso, 'The necessity of Nature', *Midwest Studies in Philosophy* 11 (1986), pp. 215–42.

47 R. G. Swinburne, 'Miracles', *Philosophical Quarterly* 18 (1968), p. 321.

48 Ibid., p. 323.

49 Wolfhart Pannenberg, *Jesus – God and Man,* trans. L. L. Wilkins and D. A. Priebe (London, 1968), p. 67.

50 David Hume, *An Enquiry Concerning Human Understanding*, ed. L. A. Selby-Bigge, 3rd edn, rev. P. H. Nidditch (Oxford, 1975), ch. 10.

6

The problem of evil

Brian Davies OP

Introduction

Why is there physical pain? Why do people suffer from anxiety and psychological distress? Why are there people who act badly? These are the questions which have given rise to what contemporary philosophers call the 'problem of evil'. But what exactly is the problem supposed to be?

If Fred is dying of cancer, I might acknowledge a practical problem. I might ask 'What can I do to make Fred as comfortable as possible?' And I might take myself to have an equally practical problem on my hands should I have to deal with people who are morally wicked. I might wonder 'What can I do to get rid of them?' or (more charitably) 'What can I do to help them to become better human beings?'

But the general nastiness of much that occurs has led some to hold that there is what we might deem to be an 'intellectual problem of evil', one which is regularly presented as a problem for those who believe in God ('theists', as they are often called). The general idea here is that it is hard to see how pain, wickedness, and so on could ever have come to pass given that God is omnipotent, omniscient, and good (or 'wholly good' or 'perfect').

This 'intellectual problem of evil', however, could amount to different problems depending on who is raising it. For suppose one believes (or thinks that one knows) that there is, indeed, an omnipotent, omniscient, good God. In that case one's problem might be that of fathoming the place of evil in a world made by God. One might be trying to penetrate the mystery of the God in whom one believes, and one might feel that this is a very difficult job, something in which one might never succeed in this life.

But one might also take a different line. For, so one might say, there is a problem of evil which positively undermines belief in the existence of God. There cannot be a circle which is also square. But can there be a world made by God which contains evil? Taking it as obvious that the world

163

contains evil, one might conclude that God's non-existence is as certain as that of square circles. Alternatively, one might say that, though 'Evil exists' and 'God exists' are logically compatible, the evil that exists is positive or strong evidence that God does not exist. If one's house is dirty, that is evidence that it lacks a cleaner (even though it might have a bad one). By the same token, so one might argue, the evil in the world is evidence that the world is not created by God and that God, therefore, does not exist.

For the most part, when contemporary philosophers of religion speak of 'the problem of evil' they are concerned with evil as proof of God's non-existence or as evidence against God's existence. But how so?

Problems of evil

The charge of contradiction

The claim that evil is proof of God's non-existence is crisply stated by J. L. Mackie. As he puts it, in a famous and much-discussed paper called 'Evil and omnipotence':

> In its simplest form the problem is this: God is omnipotent; God is wholly good; and yet evil exists. There seems to be some contradiction between these three propositions, so that if any two of them were true the third would be false. But at the same time all three are essential parts of most theological positions: the theologian, it seems, at once *must* adhere and *cannot consistently adhere* to all three.[1]

But is it true that theists who acknowledge the reality of evil are somehow contradicting themselves? In the work from which I have quoted, Mackie defends the charge of contradiction in three ways.

(1)   First, he explains why we should think that God and evil cannot both exist.

(2)   Then he explains how they might both be thought to exist, though only in a way which rejects traditional views about God.

(3)   Finally, he considers a range of solutions to 'the problem of evil', solutions which, so he argues, are misguided.

(1) Why God and evil cannot both exist

Mackie concedes that 'God exists', 'God is omnipotent', 'God is wholly good', and 'Evil exists' do not, when affirmed together, obviously amount to the manifest self-contradiction of statements like 'One and the same assertion can be simultaneously both true and false' or 'This is green and red all over'. The contradiction, says Mackie, 'does not arise immediately; to show it we need some additional premises, or perhaps some quasi-logical rules connecting the terms "good", "evil", and "omnipotent"'.[2] Yet, so Mackie thinks, we can supply such premises or rules. As he puts it:

> These additional principles are that good is opposed to evil, in such a way that a good thing always eliminates evil as far as it can, and that there are no limits to what an omnipotent thing can do.

From these principles, says Mackie, 'it follows that a good omnipotent thing eliminates evil completely, and then the propositions that a good omnipotent thing exists, and that evil exists, are incompatible'.[3]

(2) Solving the problem of evil while giving up on theism

Mackie's second move is to acknowledge that the problem of evil can be set aside, but only at a cost. For, so he says, 'the problem will not arise if one gives up at least one of the propositions that constitute it'.[4] So the problem does not arise if one denies, for example, the assertion that God is omnipotent. Or again, it does not arise if one denies that evil is real. As Mackie implies, however, most theists would not want to deny the assertions now in question. So, as Mackie also implies, giving up 'at least one of the propositions that constitute' the problem of evil is not a serious option for theists.

(3) Misguided solutions

But some theists, without denying the reality of evil, have tried to explain how the existence of evil can be reconciled with the omnipotence and goodness of God. And, in seeking to clinch his case against theism, Mackie mentions four such explanations – to each of which he offers counter arguments.

According to the first, good cannot exist without evil.
According to the second, evil is necessary as a means to good.
According to the third, the universe is better with some evil in it than it would be with no evil.
According to the fourth, evil is due to human free will.

Mackie objects to the first claim by arguing that it effectively denies that God is omnipotent. For, so Mackie suggests, good can exist without evil. An omnipotent God, he says, 'might have made everything good'.[5] And, in response to the second claim, Mackie sees no reason why an omnipotent God has to put up with evil as a means to good. It may, he says, be true that causal laws in the universe necessitate certain evils if certain goods are to arise. But, so he adds, omnipotence can hardly be constrained by causal laws which obtain in the universe.

With respect to the third claim Mackie's main objection is that we are still left with a God who is prepared to allow for preventable evil. It has been argued that, even if good can exist without evil, there are lots of goods which could never have arisen without certain evils. Take, for example, the goodness displayed in the lives of people who consistently care for people in trouble. Such goodness, it would seem, depends for its very being on the fact that people get into trouble. But, says Mackie, in willing a world in which goodness such as this exists, God is willing evil – evil which need never have been.

In turning to the fourth claim Mackie is addressing what is, perhaps, the most popular move made by theists in the face of evil. Commonly referred to as the 'Free Will Defence', this maintains:

(1) Much evil is the result of what people freely choose to do.

(2) It is good that there should be a world with agents able to act freely, and a world containing such agents would be better than a world of puppets controlled by God.

(3) Even an omnipotent God cannot ensure that free people act well (for, if they are free and not puppets controlled by God, what they do is up to them).

(4) Therefore, much evil is explicable in terms of God allowing for the possible consequences of him willing a great good.

However, without denying the value of human freedom, Mackie finds fault with the Free Will Defence since he does not see why God could not have made a world in which people always freely act well. He writes:

> If God has made men such that in their free choices they sometimes prefer what is good and sometimes what is evil, why could he not have made men such that they always freely choose the good? If there is no logical impossibility in a man's freely choosing the good on one, or on several, occasions, there cannot be a logical impossibility in his freely choosing the good on every occasion. God was not, then, faced with a choice between making innocent automata and making beings who, in acting freely, would sometimes go wrong: there was open to him the obviously better possibility of making beings who would act freely but always go right. Clearly, his failure to avail himself of this possibility is inconsistent with his being both omnipotent and wholly good.[6]

The evidential problem

We shall be seeing more of the Free Will Defence later. For now, however, we may turn to the view that, though theists might not embrace contradictory beliefs in the way that Mackie thinks they do, the existence of evil is *evidence against* the existence of God.[7] Sometimes called the 'evidentialist' argument from evil, this line of thinking can be summarized by referring to William Rowe's much-discussed article 'The problem of evil and some varieties of atheism'.[8]

In general, Rowe allows that evil (e.g. intense human and animal suffering) might be justifiable if it leads to some greater good, a good not obtainable without the evil in question. With this allowance made, Rowe's basic argument is that there is unjustifiable evil which is evidence against God's existence. Or, in Rowe's own words:

1. There exist instances of intense suffering which an omnipotent being could have prevented without thereby losing some greater good or permitting some evil equally bad or worse.

2. An omniscient, wholly good being would prevent the occurrence of any intense suffering it could, unless it could not do so without thereby losing some greater good or permitting some evil equally bad or worse.

3. [Therefore] there does not exist an omnipotent, omniscient, wholly good being.[9]

Since Rowe takes this argument to be logically valid, his main concern is to argue for the truth of the first and second premises.

The second premise, says Rowe, 'seems to express a belief that accords with our basic moral principles, principles shared by both theists and non-theists'.[10] For Rowe, therefore, the really controversial premise is the first. And, so he admits, it might be false. Suppose we try to imagine an instance of pointless suffering. Though we may not be able to see that it serves a good which cannot be obtained without it, there might, so Rowe agrees, be such a good. And yet, so Rowe continues, we have *reason* to suppose that there are instances of pointless suffering even if we cannot definitively *prove* that there are such instances.

Take, for example, the case of a fawn dying in agony as a victim of a forest fire. 'Is it reasonable', asks Rowe, 'to believe that there is some greater good so intimately connected to that suffering that even an omnipotent, omniscient being could not have obtained that good without permitting that suffering or some evil at least as bad?' Rowe's answer is: 'It certainly does not appear reasonable to believe this. Nor does it seem reasonable to believe that there is some evil at least as bad as the fawn's suffering such that an omnipotent being simply could not have prevented it without permitting the fawn's suffering.'[11] For the sake of argument, Rowe concedes that perhaps he is wrong with respect to the example of the fawn. But what of the multitude of instances of 'seemingly pointless human and animal suffering that occur daily in our world'? Turning to this question, Rowe maintains that the only reasonable conclusion is one unfavourable to the theist.

In the light of our experience and knowledge of the variety and scale of human and animal suffering in our world, the idea that none of this suffering could have been prevented by an omnipotent being without thereby losing a greater good or permitting an evil at least as bad seems an extraordinarily absurd idea, quite beyond our belief.[12]

With this point made, Rowe holds that his first premise is a reasonable one and that, given also the reasonableness of his second premise, 'it does seem that we have *rational support* for atheism, that it is reasonable to believe that the theistic God does not exist'.[13]

Some theistic responses

Mackie and Rowe are clearly arguing for non-theistic conclusions.[14] But what have theists said in the face of evil? How have they responded to the charge that evil is proof of, or good evidence for, the non-existence of God? At the risk of simplifying somewhat, we may say that they have mostly done so by embracing one or more of the following lines of argument, some of which Mackie mentions.

The 'We know that God exists' argument

If I know that it often rains in England, I should rightly assume that something is wrong with any attempt to show either that frequent rain in England is impossible or that there is good evidence against its occurring. In a similar way, so it has been argued, we have grounds for supposing that God's existence is not impossible or subject to doubt even though evil exists. For, so it has been said, we can know, not only that evil exists, but also that God exists, from which it follows (a) that something is wrong with any attempt to show that God cannot exist, and (b) that something is wrong with any attempt to show that there is good evidence against God's existence. Defenders of this line of thought sometimes offer arguments for God's existence. Taking p to be equivalent to 'There is a good, omnipotent, omniscient God', their suggestion is that there are positive grounds for accepting p, grounds which entitle us to hold that the existence of God is logically compatible with the existence of evil, grounds which also entitle us to hold that there is no evidence based on evil which shows that God does not exist.[15]

The unreality-of-evil argument

This argument takes two forms. According to the first, evil is an illusion of some kind. This is the view of Christian Science, according to which, in the words of its founder, Mary Baker Eddy: 'Sin, disease, whatever seems real to material sense, is unreal ... All inharmony of mortal mind or body is illusion, possessing neither reality nor identity though seeming to be real and identical.'[16] According to the second form of the argument, evil is unreal since it is no positive thing or quality. Rather, it is an absence or privation of good (*privatio boni*).

What is this second view driving at? It can be found in the work of writers like St Augustine of Hippo (354–430) and St Thomas Aquinas (*c.* 1225–74), and the first thing to say about it (since this is often not appreciated) is that it is not siding with Mary Baker Eddy and it is not claiming that, for example, there is no pain, or that there are no wicked people or bad actions. Augustine and Aquinas would never have denied the reality of suffering or sin. They acknowledge that people and other animals suffer, and that people can be horribly vicious. Much of their theology depends on this recognition. On the other hand, however, they hold that what makes suffering or wickedness bad is the fact that it always amounts to a lack of some kind. On their account, 'evil' or 'badness' is not the name of some independently existing individual (like a particular human being, e.g. Mary) or of some positive quality or attribute (like being carnivorous). Rather, it is a word we use to signify a gap between what *is actually* there and what *could be* there (and *should be* there) but *is not*. There can be people, but there cannot, so Augustine and Aquinas think, be 'baddities' (things whose nature is captured simply by saying that they are bad).[17] There can be wooden boxes, just as there can be wooden chairs. But, so Augustine and Aquinas would have said, while 'wooden' signifies a positive property, shareable by different things (like boxes and chairs), 'evil' or 'bad' do not. 'Evil', says Aquinas, 'cannot signify a certain existing being, or a real shaping or positive kind of thing. Consequently, we are left to infer that it signifies a certain absence of a good.'[18] Just as to say 'There is nothing here' is not to say of *something* that *it* is here, so, in Aquinas's view, to say that *there is* evil is not to say that there is *any real individual or any positive quality*.[19] With respect to the topic of God and evil, Aquinas regards this conclusion as significant since he takes it to imply that God cannot be thought of as causing evil, considered as some kind of thing or positive quality. Aquinas holds that God, as Creator, causes the being of all that can properly be thought of as existing (i.e. actual individuals and all their actual, positive, properties). On his account, therefore, evil cannot be thought of as something caused (creatively) by God. It is, so he thinks, real enough (in the sense that it would be mad to say that nothing is bad or defective or

169

sinful). But it is not, so he thinks, something created; its 'reality' is always a case of something missing.

The Free Will Defence

As we have seen, Mackie refers to the Free Will Defence. And, as we have also seen, his verdict on it is negative. But according to many philosophers it is a good response to the charge that evil somehow shows that God cannot, or probably does not, exist. One such contemporary philosopher (famous for advocating the Free Will Defence) is Alvin Plantinga.

In 'Evil and omnipotence' Mackie rejects the Free Will Defence on the ground that an omnipotent God could have made a world in which people always behave well. According to Plantinga, however, we cannot know that this is so. He agrees that there is no contradiction involved in the notion of someone always behaving well. But, so he adds, whether someone freely behaves well in some actual situation cannot be determined by God. People must freely decide to act well. And they cannot do that if the fact that they act as they do is determined by God. 'Of course', says Plantinga, 'it is up to God whether to create free creatures at all; but if he aims to produce moral good, then he must create significantly free creatures upon whose co-operation he must depend. Thus is the power of an omnipotent God limited by the freedom he confers upon his creatures.'[20]

It might seem from this last quotation that Plantinga wishes to deny God's omnipotence. But that is not the way he sees it. Theists have regularly denied that divine omnipotence means that God can do what is logically impossible, and Plantinga's basic point is that it is logically impossible for God to create a creature whose actions are both free and determined by God. And he wants to say this since he thinks that a free action cannot be caused by anything other than the agent whose action it is. Or, in his words: 'If a person S is free with respect to a given action, then he is free to perform that action and free to refrain; no causal laws and antecedent conditions determine either that he will perform the action, or that he will not. It is within his power, at the time in question, to perform the action, and within his power to refrain.'[21]

The 'Means and End Approach'

You would probably think me bad if I cut off someone's leg just for the fun of it. But you would probably not think me bad if I were a doctor who amputated a leg as the only way known to me of saving someone with gangrene. Why not? You will probably say something like: 'Because it is not bad to aim for something regrettable, something we might truly deem to be bad, if one is working toward a good one ought to aim at (or is justified in aiming at) which cannot be achieved in any other way.' And this thought constitutes the basic thrust of what I am calling the 'Means and End Approach'. Here again we have a line of thought alluded to and rejected by Mackie. But it is one which has found many theistic supporters. According to them, the evil we encounter is a necessary means to a good. Considered as such, it cannot, so they think, be appealed to as part of a *proof* of God's non-existence. Nor is it *evidence* for God's non-existence.

One notable contemporary defence of the 'Means and End Approach' can be found in Richard Swinburne's book *The Existence of God*.[22] To begin with, Swinburne endorses a version of the Free Will Defence. It is good, he thinks, that people should be significantly free, but God can only allow them to be so by also allowing them to act badly. For this reason Swinburne deems human wrong-doing to be accountable in terms of means to an end (the end being a world of free creatures, the means being God's standing back and allowing them freedom). What, however, of pain and suffering not brought about by people? To this question Swinburne replies by suggesting that these can also be seen as necessary means to a good. For it is good, thinks Swinburne, that people have serious moral choice to harm or help each other. And, so he argues, choice like this can only arise against the background of naturally occurring pain and suffering. He writes:

> If men are to have knowledge of the evil which will result from their actions or negligence, laws of nature must operate regularly; and that means that there will be what I may call 'victims of the system' ... *if* men are to have the opportunity to bring about serious evils for themselves or others by actions or negligence, or to prevent their occurrence, and if all knowledge of the future is obtained by normal induction, that is by induction from patterns of similar events in the past – then there must be serious natural evils occurring to man or animals.[23]

One might say that there is *too much* naturally occurring evil. But Swinburne thinks it reasonable to conclude that this is not so. 'The fewer natural evils a God provides', he suggests, 'the less opportunity he provides for man to exercise responsibility.'[24] To say that there is 'too much' naturally occurring evil, says Swinburne, is effectively to suggest that 'a God should make a toy-world, a world where things matter, but not very much; where we can choose and our choices can make a small difference, but the real choices remain God's'.[25] Swinburne considers the possibility of God (or 'a God') giving us the knowledge to do great good and great evil by somehow informing us of the way things are and of what we can do in the light of this (e.g. by giving people verbal information). But, according to Swinburne, if God were to act in this way nobody could doubt his existence, and everyone would be forced to acknowledge him and to act as he wishes (this being a bad thing).[26] And none of us would be able to choose to acquire knowledge of the world for ourselves (this being a good thing). 'A world in which God gave to men verbal knowledge of the consequences of their actions', Swinburne concludes,

> would not be a world in which men had a significant choice of destiny, of what to make of themselves, and of the world. God would be far too close for them to be able to work things out for themselves. If God is to give man knowledge while at the same time allowing him a genuine choice of destiny, it must be normal inductive knowledge.[27]

A similar line of thinking to Swinburne's can be found in John Hick's *Evil and the God of Love* (a modern classic on the topic of God and evil).[28] Hick also employs the Free Will Defence: human freedom is a good which entails the risk of evil (the assumption being that a good God would be happy to take such a risk). Then he endorses a line of thought which he claims to find in the writings of St Irenaeus of Lyon (c. 140–c. 202). According to Hick, God cannot create a world in which people can morally mature and eventually enjoy a proper relationship with God (this being thought of as a good) unless he also creates a world in which there are obstacles to overcome. Hick understands evil in the light of God's desire not to coerce people into accepting him. He suggests that people are sin-prone creatures, created as such by God, but able, in a world containing naturally occurring evil, to rise to great heights precisely because they are given the opportunity to become mature in the face of evil. He writes:

> Let us suppose that the infinite personal God creates finite persons to share in the life which He imparts to them. If He creates them in his immediate presence, so that they cannot fail to be conscious from the first of the infinite divine being and glory, goodness and love, wisdom, power and knowledge in whose presence they are, they will have no creaturely independence in relation to their Maker. They will not be able to *choose* to worship God, or to turn to Him freely as valuing spirits responding to infinite Value. In order, then, to give them the freedom to come to Him, God . . . causes them to come into a situation in which He is not immediately and overwhelmingly evident to them. Accordingly they come to self-consciousness as parts of a universe which has its own autonomous structures and 'laws' . . . A world without problems, difficulties, perils, and hardships would be morally static. For moral and spiritual growth comes through response to challenges; and in a paradise there would be no challenges.[29]

'No pain, no gain', as the athletes say. And this is basically Hick's position when it comes to God and evil.

The 'We Can't See All the Picture' argument

Another theistic response to arguments such as those of Mackie and Rowe takes the form of suggesting that we just cannot be sure that the evil we know about disproves, or is evidence against, God's existence since our perspective is limited – since we lack, so to speak, a God's eye view of things. Shakespeare's Hamlet told Horatio that 'There are more things in heaven and earth than are dreamt of in your philosophy'. The 'We Can't See All the Picture' argument suggests that, though we might find it *hard* to see why there is evil in a world made by God, there *might* be a reason. More precisely, so defenders of the argument tend to hold, the evil we encounter might be something God allows or brings about while aiming at a good end which cannot be reached without it (an end which somehow justifies the evil) – though we might not be able to show this by argument (i.e. God has his reasons, even if we can't understand them).

A prominent contemporary writer who defends the 'We Can't See All the Picture' argument is William P. Alston. An opponent of theism (such as William Rowe) might suggest that there exist instances of intense suffering that God could have prevented without thereby losing some greater good (let us call this 'Thesis A'). According to Alston, however, 'the magnitude or complexity of the question is such that our powers, access to data, and so on are radically insufficient to provide sufficient warrant for accepting' Thesis A.[30] Hamlet's words to Horatio, says Alston, hit the nail on the head. 'They point to the fact that our cognitions of the world, obtained by filtering raw data through such conceptual screens as we have available for the nonce, acquaint us with only some indeterminable fraction of what there is to be known.'[31] Alston's thesis is that God knows what he is doing (or allowing, or whatever); and God might have reasons for doing what he does (or allows, or whatever); but we might not be able to understand what God is about as he lives his life.[32]

What kind of world can we expect from God?

Those who take evil to be a problem for theists tend to rely on assumptions about the kind of world which God (if God exists) would make. So we should therefore note that many theists have turned to the topic of evil and God by trying to call into question some of these assumptions.

Take, for example, the notion that relief from (or absence of) pain and suffering is an intrinsically good thing, something which God would always lay on for things like human beings. Many anti-theistic writers seem to embrace this notion, but many theists have not. As we have seen, some have held that pain and suffering can perfect human beings. They have held that austerity, sacrifice, poverty and pain can lead to desirable results. And some have held that what we may loosely call 'an absence of happiness' is not necessarily something which ought not to be brought about even though it could be prevented and even though we know nothing about desirable results. Suppose we have a child who is thoroughly retarded but who also seems perfectly content and happy. Suppose furthermore that we can render the child normal and healthy by means of an operation. Shall we leave the child as it is? Or shall we operate, and thereby release the child to the kind of life most people live – one which will certainly render it liable to varieties of pain and frustration? Many (perhaps most) people would vote for the operation, and drawing on the assumptions which seem to lie behind such a vote, many theists have argued that we have no reason to suppose that God would not create a world containing unhappiness.

Some critics of theism have said that God (if he exists) would create 'the best possible world'. Others have said that God (if he exists) would maximize happiness for his creatures. But theists have challenged these assumptions as well. They have said, for example, that talk of a 'best possible world' is as incoherent as talk of a 'greatest prime number'. According to C. J. F. Williams, for example: 'It is a consequence of God's infinite power, wisdom and goodness that, for any world we can conceive him creating, it is possible to conceive him creating a better world. More than that – for this has nothing to do with what we can or cannot conceive – for any world which God can create, there is another, better world which he could also have created.'[33] And, though one might be tempted to suppose that 'Maximize happiness' is an imperative which any decent-minded God could be expected to act on, some theists have challenged the idea that such an imperative is intelligible. Suppose we have a happy human being. This person could, presumably, be happier. Is there, then, a limit to happiness – some stage at which further increased happiness is impossible, some stage which God should have brought about for all from the start? Arguing somewhat along the lines of Williams, just cited, George N. Schlesinger has suggested that there is no such specifiable limit. We can, he suggests, always think of ways in which a person's happiness can be in some way increased, and it is no good objection to God's existence to say that God has made a world in which people are less happy than they could be.[34]

With an eye on the question 'What kind of world can God be expected to make?', we should also note that some theists have urged that we can have no reasonable expectations one way or the other. An example here is St Thomas Aquinas. Taking his lead from the Bible and his own philosophical reflections, Aquinas thinks of God as the source of the being (*esse*) of creatures. For Aquinas, God alone exists by essence or nature, and anything other than God exists because it is made to be by God. It is not, thinks Aquinas, characteristic of God that he should make things like *this* as opposed to things like *that* (though Aquinas is clear that God has made a world of varied things). Insofar as anything can be deemed to be a 'characteristic effect' of God, says Aquinas, it is being (*esse*) – the fact that there is something rather than nothing, the fact that there is any world at all. And this leads Aquinas away from suppositions as to what we can expect in a world created by God. We can, he thinks, expect that Vitamin C will have certain effects when taken by human beings. In general, so he thinks, we can have *lots* of expectations about what will be produced by what (such expectations are part of what Aquinas would have called a scientific understanding of the world).[35] For Aquinas, however, God is not an object of scientific enquiry, not a part of the world in which science can be developed. For him, God 'is to be thought of as existing outside the realm of existents, as a cause from which pours forth everything that exists in all its variant forms'.[36] If it is logically possible for something to be, then, thinks Aquinas, God can make it to be. But, so Aquinas also thinks, we have no means of determining what logically possible things God shall make to be. For Aquinas, we have to start by noting what God has, in fact, made to be. Reflections on the topic of God and evil must, so he thinks, start from that, and not from assumptions we might (on what basis?) have dreamed up concerning what God is or is not likely to create.[37] While defending Aquinas's account of what we can and cannot know of God by rational reflection, the contemporary philosopher Herbert McCabe writes: 'We do not appeal specifically to God to explain why the universe is this way rather than that, for this we need only appeal to explanations within the universe. For this reason there can, it seems to me, be no feature of the universe which indicates that it is God-made.'[38] Like Aquinas, McCabe is suggesting that, since God accounts for there being something rather than nothing, we have no basis as philosophers (i.e. apart from recourse to divine revelation) for expectations concerning the kind of world which God (if he chose to create) would make.

God suffers also

A survey of theistic responses to those who deny or call into question the existence of God because of the reality of evil would not be complete without a mention of a very contemporary angle on the topic of God and evil. According to this, evil is no more a ground for denying God's existence than it is for denying mine or yours. That is because, so it has been argued, God (like all human beings) is also a victim of evil, and he also suffers. Two authors who might be cited as defending this line of thought include the German theologian Jürgen Moltmann and the Latin American liberation theologian Jon Sobrino.

Classical Christian theists take it for granted that God is utterly changeless (immutable).[39] From this belief it follows that God cannot be acted on by anything. It also follows that God cannot undergo suffering (since to suffer is to be passive to the action of something which acts on one to bring about a change of a certain kind). Moltmann and Sobrino, however, deny that God is utterly changeless. According to them, if God is to be really acceptable to human beings he must be capable of suffering and, in this sense, must be affected by evil. According to Moltmann, the great thing about Christianity is that it offers us a suffering God revealed as such in the person of Christ. Traditional Christian teaching holds that Christ is God, but it also denies that this implies that we can say, without qualification, 'God suffers'. A distinction is made between what is true of Christ *as man*, and what is true of him *as God*. The conclusion then proposed is that, though Christ could suffer as man, he could not suffer as God. But Moltmann rejects this traditional way of talking. For him, the divinity of Christ means that divinity as such is capable of suffering. And in the light of this point we can, says Moltmann, offer some comfort to suffering human beings (the victims of evil). People in distress can be driven to say that because of their suffering they cannot believe in God. According to Moltmann, however, God and suffering are not to be thought of as irreconcilable with each other. For God suffers too. And that is what Sobrino also wants to say. As he puts it:

> For Saint John, God is love . . . Is that statement real? . . . We must insist that love has to be credible to human beings in an unredeemed world. That forces us to ask ourselves whether God can really describe himself as love if historical suffering does not affect him . . . We must say what Moltmann says: 'We find suffering that is not wished, suffering that is accepted, and the suffering of love. If God were incapable of suffering in all those ways, and hence in an absolute sense, then God would be incapable of loving.'[40]

As we have seen, in his discussion of the problem of evil J. L. Mackie accepts that (what he identifies as) the problem disappears if one gives up on the claim that God is omnipotent. Since they want to conceive of God as passive to the action of creatures and as himself suffering (a notion which seems at odds with traditional theistic accounts of omnipotence), Moltmann and Sobrino can fairly be taken as rejecting belief in God's omnipotence and as representing a response to the problem of evil which writers like Mackie would presumably deem to dissolve the problem as conceived by them.

God and the problem of evil

It should now be clear to the reader that the topic of God and evil raises numerous questions to which philosophers have responded in a variety of ways. I cannot here comment on all the lines of thinking noted above, but it would be wrong to conclude this chapter on a purely expository note. At this point, therefore, and with an eye on what I have reported, I shall offer some reflections of my own with respect to the question 'Does evil disprove God's existence or render it unlikely?' I shall start by calling into question what seems to be a basic assumption of most contemporary treatments of the problem of evil. This is the assumption that the goodness of God is moral goodness (or, to put it another way, that God, if he exists, is a moral agent, or someone well behaved). Secondly, I shall say something about the Free Will Defence. Thirdly, I shall offer the reader comments on some questions which might be raised about what I argue concerning the goodness of God and the Free Will Defence. I shall then say something about evil and the mystery of God.

The problem of evil and the goodness of God

The problem of evil, for many contemporary philosophical detractors of theism, is clearly a problem concerning God's moral integrity. Consider, for example, what we have seen argued by J. L. Mackie and William Rowe. Both of these authors (like many other writers opposed to theism because of the problem of evil) take it for granted that God's goodness is moral goodness. Mackie's talk about what 'a good thing' will do makes no sense unless construed as talk about *a morally good thing* (presumably conceived of as something like a good human being). The same goes for Rowe's talk of justification for evils, and for his allusion to what accords with our basic moral principles. Rowe thinks that God does not exist since, if he did, he would be morally culpable (and therefore does not exist).

What of contemporary philosophical defenders of theism? Taking their lead from arguments to be found in the work of people such as Mackie and Rowe, many of these are also clearly presuming that God's goodness is moral goodness. Alvin Plantinga, Richard Swinburne, William Alston and John Hick (like many other defenders of theism not mentioned above) are all evidently assuming that the proper theistic line on the topic of God and evil is one which defends God's moral integrity. Their positions on the topic of God and evil make no sense unless construed as starting from this assumption.

But should we begin by supposing that the goodness of God is moral goodness, or that God is a moral agent? I ask the question not in order to

Brian Davies OP

suggest that God is immoral or sub-moral, but in order to suggest that it is wholly inappropriate to think of God as something able to be either moral (well behaved) or immoral (badly behaved). I ask the question in order to suggest that both foes and friends of theism might do well to fight shy of statements like 'God is a moral agent' or 'God is morally good' (both of which I take to be equivalent to 'God is well behaved').

To start with, note that goodness is not always moral goodness, and that 'God is good' should not, therefore, automatically be deemed to be equivalent to 'God is morally good'. We speak, for example, of good doctors, good dinners, good singers, good houses, good exam results, good holidays . . . good *all sorts* of things. And we do so without suggesting that we are talking in moral terms (a good doctor or tenor, for instance, can be a morally bad person; a good house or a good holiday is neither morally good nor morally bad).[41] As P. T. Geach puts it, 'good' is an 'attributive' adjective, not a 'predicative' one.

Let us say that 'in a phrase "an AB" ("A" being an adjective and "B" being a noun) "A" is a (logically) predicative adjective if the predication "is an AB" splits up into a pair of predications "is a B" and "is A"'. Let us also say that, if such is not the case, 'A' is a (logically) attributive adjective.[42] On this account, 'big' and 'small' are attributive adjectives and 'red' is predicative. As Geach says:

> 'X is a big flea' does not split up into 'X is a flea' and 'X is big', nor 'X is a small elephant' into 'X is an elephant' and 'X is small'; for if these analyses were legitimate, a simple argument would show that a big flea is a big animal and a small elephant a small animal . . . On the other hand, in the phrase 'a red book', 'red' is a predicative adjective . . . for 'is a red book' logically splits up into 'is a book' and 'is red'.[43]

By the same token, 'good' is logically attributive. It does not signify a common property shared by everything which has it. Its use on a given occasion cannot be understood unless one knows to what it is being applied. In this sense, goodness is relative: 'good' works like 'big' and 'small', and differs from 'red'. To appreciate what is meant when told that something is good, one needs to know what is being talked about.

So what are we talking about when we talk about God? There is a long-standing Christian tradition (which exists in Islamic and Jewish thinking also) which says that we do not know what we are talking about since God is incomprehensible.[44] For present purposes, however, I take it that God is the creator.[45] And I take it that to call God 'creator' is to say that he is the source of the being of everything, the reason why there is something rather than nothing, the cause of the existence of the universe (whether or not the universe had a beginning). I take 'something' to be a word we use to allude to an individual of some kind, a member of the world, something we can distinguish from other things because of its own special characteristics (its own special way of being and acting), as a distinct thing recognizable as such because it exists in the context of a world in which there are many other such individuals and many other things with which they may be contrasted as they exist alongside each other as possible objects of scientific enquiry. I take it that if you can single something out as an intelligible individual (something you can get your mind around, something there alongside you in the real world (no matter how far away and no matter how inaccessible to contemporary or future science), something with its own nature as part of a world), then it is being made *to be what* it is and *to be as* it is by God. And I take it that to call God 'creator' is to say all this since the Bible (as I read it), and the mainstream Christian tradition (as I understand it), think along such lines.[46]

If that is so, however, theists (and their opponents) have very good reason for denying that God is or could be 'well behaved' (a moral agent, morally good). It is people (limited, finite creatures) who can be well behaved as they live their creaturely lives in the order established by God.[47] It is people who are moral agents, or morally good or bad things. It is people who are well or badly behaved.

Theists (Jews, Muslims, Christians) will not, of course, find it amiss to speak of God as just. But they cannot (and, traditionally, do not) mean by this that God gives others what he owes them (commutative justice). For the notion of God being indebted to creatures makes no sense. If God is the source of everything creaturely, he cannot receive and gain by what is creaturely, and then return it to those to whom he is indebted. If we are entitled to call God just it can only be because he can be said to act in accordance with his own decrees (as revealed), or because he gives to his creatures what is good for them given their natures as made by him (this not implying that he gives the same to every creature). Such, in fact, is the view of God's justice found in the Old Testament. There, the justice (or righteousness) of God lies in him acting in accordance with his declared will for Israel (to whom he gives laws as one not bound by them). In Old Testament terms, the justice of God lies in his keeping of the law in accordance with the terms of the covenant as laid down by him. As one commentator puts it:

> The essence of the original biblical concept of God's righteousness lies neither in the ethical postulate of a moral world-order nor in an ideal of impartial retribution imposed by some inner necessity nor in the personification of the ethical by God. Instead it exalts over all abstract ethical ideas a *loyalty manifested in the concrete relationships of community*.[48]

It might be said that some creatures are such that God ought to give them certain things, e.g. that he ought to reward virtuous people with happiness.[49] At this point, however, we come to the issue of God's duties or obligations, and the point to make here is that we have good reason for resisting the suggestion that God can intelligibly be thought of as having duties or obligations.

Could he, for instance, have duties or obligations to himself? Should he, for example, strive to keep himself healthy? Should he try not to let his talents or abilities go to seed? Anyone seriously raising such questions would simply show a failure to grasp what the notion of God as creator amounts to.

One might say that God has obligations to creatures – that he is, for example, obliged to reward good people with happiness. But this suggestion also makes no sense. What can oblige God in relation to his creatures? Could it be that there is a law which says that God has obligations to them? But what law? And where does it come from? Is it something set up by someone independently of God? But how can anyone set up a law independently of God? Is God not the Maker of everything apart from himself?

Someone might say that there are duties and obligations binding on God, and that this just has to be accepted. But why should we believe that? What, indeed, are we to suppose ourselves to believe when believing that? Perhaps we should be thinking that there are moral laws (implying duties) with which God is presented just as he is presented with logical laws. And perhaps we should say that, just as God has to accept that there cannot be any square triangles (logical law), so he must accept that there are certain courses of action which he must either refrain from or adopt (moral law). But the cases cited here are not parallel. God must 'accept' that there cannot be any square triangles. We can speak of him as 'bound' by the truth that there cannot be any such things. But, since it cannot be known that there is any square triangle, that only means that God cannot know what cannot be known (that omniscience does not extend to knowing what is not an object of knowledge). It does not mean that God is bound by any command to do what can be done (e.g. by a human being). And it does not mean that he has a duty or obligation to do anything we care to mention. One has duties and obligations as part of a definite, describable context. A nurse, for example, has certain duties in the light of things such as hospitals, drugs, sickness, doctors, death and patients. The duties and obligations of nurses arise because of their role as nurses (something which makes no sense apart from the context in which nurses operate). A parent has obligations as someone living with families, children, money, schools, social services, and the like. The duties and obligations of parents arise because of their role as parents (something which makes no sense apart from the context in which parents operate). In that case, however, it seems fair to deny that God has duties and obligations. In the light of what context can he be said to have them? Given the notion of God as creator, there would seem to be no context at all (God is the cause of all contexts), and the notion of him having duties and obligations would therefore seem to be empty. If anything, it would seem better to say that God must be the source of all duties and obligations. For, if God is the creator, he must be the cause of there being situations in which people have duties and obligations.

Someone might reply that God does have obligations since he has obligations to his creatures as parents have obligations to their children. Before you produce a child, someone might argue, you have no obligations to it (because it is not there); but, having produced the child, you do have obligations. And, so the argument might continue, this is how it must be with God. Having fathered me, he is bound to act towards me in certain ways.

But this argument would simply miss the point I am now trying to make. Passing over the fact that God is not a human father living in the created world, let us suppose that God does have obligations towards his creatures. And let us ask how he is supposed to fulfil them. Being God, he can only do so by bringing it about that certain events come to pass. But he can only do that by bringing about the existence of things creatively (not by acting within a world over and against him, but by making the world to be). And how can he be obliged to do that? God, the creator, cannot be a labourer working on things existing over and against him before he sets to work on them. He makes the difference between things being there and things not being there. He is the creator *ex nihilo* (i.e. he makes the difference between there being something rather than nothing). God is also the sustainer *ex nihilo*, not in the sense that he sustains things which do not exist (a contradictory notion), but in the sense that what is sustained (made to continue to be) by him would not be there to be what it is over time (would be nothing, so to speak) if God were not making it to be what it is.

As Rowan Williams has recently put it (writing on the topic of God and evil): 'God is never going to be an element, a square centimetre, in any picture, not because God's agency is incalculably greater but because it simply cannot be fitted into the same space.'[50] Williams's point (to which he acknowledges a debt to Aquinas) is that to conceive of God as morally responsible is to commit a mistake of the kind which we would be making if we took 'salt' or 'beef' to be the names of things we might buy two of in a shop.[51] Rather, to use Aquinas's words, we should think of God as 'existing outside the realm of existents, as a cause from which pours forth everything that exists in all its variant forms'.[52] Aquinas certainly holds that God is good.[53] But it never seems to cross his mind that God's goodness consists in him doing his duty or being virtuous (being well behaved). For Aquinas, God is the source of the world in which people with duties exist (in this sense, Aquinas takes God to be the source of human moral obligations). And he would have thought it quite blasphemous to suggest that God displays virtues. For Aquinas (like Aristotle), virtues are what people need in order to be happy as human beings. But God, on his account, is not a human being and needs no human ways of being happy. To suggest the contrary, Aquinas thinks, would be to think of God in a deeply erroneous way: it would amount to confusing the creature with the creator. It would amount to idolatry. The same conclusion can, I think, be found (directly stated, or stated by implication) in the writings of the major patristic authors, including Augustine, and in the writings of major post-patristic Christian authors from the time of Augustine to the time of the Reformation and beyond. I also take it to be expressed (directly or by implication) in the Bible and in the teachings of the Church Councils up to and including Vatican II.

So, to be blunt, I suggest that many contemporary philosophers writing on the problem of evil (both theists and non-theists) have largely been wasting their time. It has been said that error in philosophy often consists in exploring the details of a road one should never have turned into in the first place. I am suggesting that philosophers who argue for or against God's existence by concentrating on God's supposed moral goodness are well down such a road. They are like people attacking or defending tennis players because they fail to run a mile in under four minutes. Tennis players are not in the business of running four-minute miles. Similarly, God is not something with respect to which moral evaluation (whether positive or negative) is appropriate.[54]

The Free Will Defence

Those who embrace the Free Will Defence take the topic of God and evil essentially to require an essay on God's morality. For the Defence suggests that God is allowing something (the evil committed by free agents) in order that there may come to pass a good (the existence of free agents) – and that God might therefore be defended as being morally good in spite of certain evils we encounter. But, forgetting about objections we may have to the project of defending God's moral integrity, there is another difficulty with the Free Will Defence which ought to be highlighted since it is commonly not alluded to by contemporary philosophers (not surprisingly, in my view, since contemporary philosophers frequently tend to conceive of God as if he were an item in the universe).

We can approach the difficulty in question by referring once again to something said by J. L. Mackie. As we have seen, he thinks it possible for God to have made a world in which people always freely act well. As we have also seen, however, Mackie's view has been contested (e.g. by Alvin Plantinga). But is it really obvious that Mackie is wrong?

Those (like Plantinga) who reject Mackie's view do so because they have in mind a certain picture of human freedom. On their account, there cannot be any such thing as a free human choice which is also caused by God. Why not? Because a choice caused by God would not be a choice at all. It would be something determined, or unfree. But why so?

Most philosophers (though there are some exceptions) would agree that if what I do is the result of something acting on me to make me behave as I do, then my freedom is infringed.[55] And this is a conclusion which seems right. If my arm hits the table because you are gripping my wrist and forcing my arm to the table, then I am not freely hitting the table. If I lunge to left and right because a drug is acting in me, then I do not freely move from left to right. But is it so obvious that if God causes me to do something I am also unfree in what I do?

If we think of God as something existing alongside us (as you are alongside me), and as something acting on us from outside to make us do as we do (like a drug), then it would seem that there cannot be any human freedom if what we do is caused by God. And that, I presume, is why authors such as Plantinga wish to reject Mackie's suggestion that God could have made a world in which people always act well. As we have seen, Plantinga holds that human actions can only be free if 'no causal laws and antecedent conditions determine' that they occur or do not occur. I take 'causal laws' to refer to codifiable ways in which unfree bits of the world behave of necessity. And I take 'antecedent conditions' to mean 'the state of the world prior to a human choice'. And on that reading of Plantinga's words, I take him to be right.[56]

But Plantinga is wrong to speak as though divine causality is something subject to causal laws or as something exemplifying them somehow. And he is wrong to think of it as an antecedent condition of anything that happens. If we are thinking of God as the cause of the whole universe, if God is what makes things to be (whenever they are), then God (to use Rowan Williams's language) 'cannot be fitted into the same space' as causal laws and antecedent conditions. He is not 'an element' in 'any picture' – including that of determining causes having their inevitable way with things with which they connect.

Here, once again, Aquinas proves illuminating. Just as he insists that God is good (though not morally good, like people), Aquinas also insists that we are able to choose freely. The view that all human action is determined is something he regards as 'anarchic' and as undermining all sensible moral thinking. 'Human beings', he says, 'are masters of their own actions, able to act or not to act. But this can only be so if they can freely choose. So human beings can freely choose their actions.'[57] Unlike fans of the Free Will Defence, however, Aquinas finds it unthinkable that any created event, including whatever we take to be there when human choosing occurs, should come to pass without God making it to be. Why? Because he takes seriously the claim that creatures really do owe their entire being to God. Or, in his words:

> God exists in everything; not indeed as part of their substance or as an accident, but as an agent is present to that in which its action is taking place ... Since it is God's nature to exist, he it must be who properly causes existence in creatures, just as it is fire itself that sets other things on fire. And God is causing this effect in things not just when they begin to exist, but all the time they are maintained in existence ... Now existence is more intimately and profoundly interior to things than anything else, for everything as we said is potential when compared to existence. So God must exist and exist intimately in everything.[58]

Does God's existence in things extend to his existence in human choices? Aquinas answers 'Yes'.

> Physical things are acted on in the sense that they are directed to an end by another; they do not act like self-determining agents who shape themselves to a purpose, in the manner of rational creatures who deliberate and choose by free judgement ... Yet because the very act of freewill goes back to God as its cause, we strictly infer that whatever people freely do on their own falls under God's Providence ... The divine power must needs be present to every acting thing ... God is the cause of everything's action inasmuch as he gives everything the power to act, and preserves it in being and applies it to action, and inasmuch as by his power every other power acts.[59]

With these points in mind, Aquinas argues that human freedom is not something to be thought of as threatened by God's causality. On the contrary. For Aquinas, I am free not *in spite of* God but *because of* God. My free choices are as much a part of creation as the rock of Mount Everest. And, so Aquinas reasons, if all that is real in Everest is made to be by God, the same is true of all that is real in me.

Aquinas has reason on his side in proposing this conclusion. Unless they are prepared to deny that the being of creatures is God's work, theists cannot view human free choices as not caused to be by God. In that case, however, the Free Will Defence is of no avail to them. It is useless as a way of defending God's moral integrity – even supposing that God has any moral integrity to defend. That is because it denies that humans acting freely are caused to act as they do by God. It conceives of human free actions as events which God must somehow stand back from and learn about as an observer. Effectively, it conceives of them as uncreated. But, as Herbert

McCabe has nicely put it (assuming that God really is the cause of the entire being of creatures), 'to be free means not to be under the influence of some other *creature*, it is to be independent of other *bits of the universe*; it is not and could not mean to be independent of God'.[60]

The goodness of God and the freedom of people

I can imagine all sorts of objections being raised against what I have said about the goodness of God and about God's relation to human free choices. Since I cannot deal with all of them, I shall focus on what I would expect to be the first most likely to occur to the reader. They may be put in the form of two questions:

(1)   If God is not morally good, what can it mean to call God good?
(2)   How can one avoid holding that human choices are determined (or unfree) if one also takes them to be caused by God?

(1) If God is not morally good, what can it mean to call God good?

This question is forcefully pressed by the contemporary Christian philosopher Paul Helm. In *The Providence of God* Helm notes how some have resisted the suggestion that the goodness of God is moral goodness. But he finds their position puzzling. 'What sort of goodness might God have that is not *moral* goodness?', he asks. 'What is the concept of non-moral goodness?'[61] 'The goodness of God', says Helm, 'must bear some positive relation to the sorts of human actions we regard as good. Otherwise, why ascribe *goodness* to God?'[62] Helm's questions are perfectly fair ones. So let me try to answer them. I shall do so by suggesting (a) that God is good since God is perfect, and (b) that we have reason to call God good since we know him as the maker of all creaturely goodness, which must therefore reflect him somehow.

(a) God as perfect

I take it that to call something perfect is to imply that it is good (though not *vice versa*). If we have reason to call God 'perfect', therefore, we have reason for calling him good. And it seems to me that we have reason to call God perfect. Furthermore, we have reason for calling God perfect in a way which does not imply moral excellence on his part.

I said above that we shall not understand 'it's good' unless we know what 'it' is. And the same is true when it comes to 'it's perfect'. What perfection amounts to in something of one kind (e.g. a perfect wife) may be descriptively very different from what it amounts to in something of another kind (e.g. a perfect horse). But it does not follow from this that we are wholly at sea when trying to give some general account of what

185

perfection is. For, though perfect things may not all share the same attributes or properties, they are all alike in one respect. For they are all succeeding in some respect. Or, rather, they are all as good as it is possible to be considering the sort of thing they are. A perfect X is an X which cannot be improved upon as an X. A perfect X is a wholly successful X which, as an X, cannot have anything added to it to make it better.

Now this notion of 'not being improvable' is one we can employ when talking about God. For if God is the source of the being of everything, then God is no inhabitant of the world. And if God is no inhabitant of the world, then God is not something changing or changeable, for he is no inhabitant of space and time.[63] From this it follows that there can be no gap between what God is and what God might become, from which it follows, in turn, that the notion of God improving (or, for that matter, getting worse) can have no place in thinking about divinity. If God exists, then God is unchangeably all that it takes to be God. And from this I conclude that God can be said to be perfect and, therefore, good.

Here I agree with what Aquinas says when he turns to the topic of God's perfection. Aquinas thinks that perfection is the opposite of imperfection. He also thinks that imperfection is present when something which is potentially perfect (i.e. able to be perfect, though not actually perfect) is actually imperfect. For Aquinas, something imperfect fails because it is not what it could and needs (or ought) to be, because, in Aquinas's language, it lacks a certain sort of actuality.[64] And, since he takes God to be wholly actual, Aquinas therefore concludes that God can be thought of as perfect.

> The first origin of all activity will be the most actual, and therefore the most perfect, of all things. For things are called perfect when they have achieved actuality, the perfect thing being that in which nothing required by the thing's particular mode of perfection fails to exist ... Because things that are made are called perfect when the potentiality of them has been actualized, we extend the word to refer to anything that is not lacking in actuality, whether made or not.[65]

Aquinas is saying that God must be perfect since he is in no way potential – since there is nothing which he could be but is not. Since God, for Aquinas, has no potentiality, he cannot be modified and cannot, therefore, be either improved or made worse. There is with him no 'could be thus and so but is not'. For God to be, therefore, is for God to be as divine as it takes divinity to be. It is for God to be fully God and, therefore, perfectly God. Since I find Aquinas's reasoning sound at this point, I suggest that God is perfect and therefore good. The suggestion, please note, makes no claim to understand what the perfection of God amounts to. It belongs to what is sometimes called 'negative theology' (theology which reminds us of what

God cannot be). All the same, it is enough to give sense to the claim that God is good. And it does so without asserting that God is morally good like good, human, moral agents.

(b) God as the maker of creaturely goodness

In suggesting that we have reason to call God good since we know him as the maker of all creaturely goodness, which must therefore reflect him somehow, I am again indebted to Aquinas. To be precise, I am in sympathy with what he says when he writes:

> Goodness should be associated above all with God. For goodness is consequent upon desirability. Now things desire their perfection; and an effect's perfection and form consists in resembling its cause, since what a thing does reflects what it is. So the cause itself is desirable and can be called 'good', what is desired from it being a share in resembling it. Clearly, then, since God is the primary operative cause of everything, goodness and desirability fittingly belong to him. And so Dionysius (*The Divine Names*, 4, 4) ascribes goodness to God as to the primary operative cause, saying that God is called good as the source of all subsistence.[66]

This is a difficult passage, however, so let me try to unpack it a little.

In saying that 'goodness is consequent upon desirability' Aquinas, echoing Aristotle, means that 'good' can be thought of as equivalent to 'attractive'. In the *Nicomachean Ethics*, Aristotle says that goodness is 'that at which all things aim'.[67] According to Aristotle, goodness is what attracts or is desired. Aristotle, of course, is perfectly aware that people might be drawn to what is bad for them and for others. So he does not assume that what I actually desire on a given occasion is actually good for me or for others. But, so he thinks, we can make nothing of the suggestion that something is good without introducing the notions of attractiveness or desirability. And that is what Aquinas thinks. He thinks, for example, that a *good* bicycle is one you would be *attracted* by if you wanted one for *cycling* (as distinct from, say, an object to photograph or help you over a wall). And, with this thought in mind, Aquinas wants to say that God is good since God is attractive.

But how is God attractive? In the above quotation from Aquinas, his answer lies in the words: 'Now things desire their perfection; and an effect's perfection and form consists in resembling its cause, since what a thing does reflects what it is. So the cause itself is desirable and can be called "good", what is desired from it being a share in resembling it. Clearly, then, since God is the primary operative cause of everything, goodness and desirability fittingly belong to him.' Here Aquinas's idea seems to be (1) that all things seek their good (that which attracts), (2) that all things seeking their good are effects of God (things made to be by God), (3) that effects are somehow like their causes, and (4) that the goodness which creatures are drawn to is therefore like God, who can therefore be thought of as attractive (or good) like the goodness to which creatures are attracted. But, here again, we have some puzzling notions which need explanation. The most puzzling, perhaps, is the suggestion that effects are like their causes, which seems evidently false. A stew, for example, does not look at all like a human cook. A car crash does not look like the factors that brought it about.

In trying to understand Aquinas at this point, however, it is important to recognize that he is not asserting that effects always *look* like their causes (though he thinks that they sometimes do since, for example, children often look like their parents). Rather, his thesis is that causes (in the sense of agents in the world which bring about changes in the world) explain their effects and do so precisely because of what they are. For him, we have an explanation of some development in the world when we reach the point of saying 'Oh, I see. Of course that explains it.' And we have this, he thinks, when we see how a cause is expressing its nature in its effect.

Suppose that Fred is staggering around. We ask 'How come?' Then we learn that he has drunk a lot of whisky, and we say 'Oh, I see. Of course that explains it.' But what do we 'see'? One might be tempted to say something like 'We see that it is not surprising that Fred should be staggering since people who drink whisky often do that'. One might say that what 'seeing' means here is that we note that what is now occurring has happened a large number of times before. But if one occurrence is puzzling (if, for example, Fred's staggering is puzzling), why should a thousand such occurrences be less puzzling? That drinking whisky is followed (or regularly followed) by staggering does not *explain* what has happened. It simply reports what we have become used to experiencing. Someone offering only such a report would be in the position of what Aristotle calls the man of 'experience' as distinct from the 'wise' men who do *see why* the drinking is connected with the staggering.[68]

Until quite recent times, nobody did see the connection. To see it you need a chemical account of alcohol and an account of the effect of this substance on the brain (molecular biology is relevant here), and of the effect of these events in the brain on the movements of the legs. Only when you have developed this kind of understanding to give an account of what is happening with the staggering drunk can you be said to *see why* he is staggering. And what you would at last see is why it has to be the case that the drunk is staggering. To see, in this sense, is to have what Aquinas would have called *scientia*. And when he says that causes are *like their effects* he simply means that seeing why the effects spring from their causes is seeing how the nature of the cause explains the effect and renders its effect necessary, and therefore unsurprising. He means that though, when drunk,

I cannot be described as looking like alcohol, I am, when drunk, certainly showing forth what alcohol is. And in this sense, so he thinks, I resemble it. For him, the drunken man is, when properly understood, alcohol in action, alcohol expressing its nature in something – something which is, therefore, 'like' alcohol.

Hence, so Aquinas argues, creatures which aim at their good can be thought of as expressing what God is in himself. We cannot, so he thinks, have a *scientia* which allows us to say something like 'Now we can see why God has produced these particular effects'. Aquinas does not suppose that God is something with respect to which we can develop a science which explains why God has the effects which he has. For him, any such thing would be a creature. But, trying to say something about the source of the being of all things, Aquinas finds it natural or appropriate (or, at least, not inappropriate) to suggest that since effects in nature show forth the nature of their causes, we can think of God as being shown forth in his effects. And since the goodness which creatures seek is something created by God, it can, thinks Aquinas, be thought of as being like what God is. Aquinas does not mean that God's goodness depends on his having created. Nor does he mean that we have any picture or image of God's goodness. But, so he thinks, we have grounds for calling God good since, whether or not God created, he would still be whatever he is as shown forth by the created world. And, since Aquinas thinks that the created world gives us grounds for calling God good as being 'like' that to which all creatures are attracted (i.e. goodness), he thinks we have grounds for calling God 'good'.

And Aquinas, I think, is right. In the sense implied by him, effects do 'resemble' their causes. If you pour exactly one mole of sulphuric acid on one mole of zinc metal, the zinc will always fizz, and disappear, and give off an inflammable gas, and the sulphuric acid will lose its corrosive power.[69] But why? Because:

$$Zn(s) + H_2SO_4(aq) \rightarrow ZnSO_4(aq) + H_2(g)$$

Here you see (in a literal sense) that what is on the right side of the $\rightarrow$ is the same as the elements on the left side. In this sense, the products of the reaction resemble the reactants. So you can now say 'Yes, I see, of course'. Effects really do reflect what their causes are. What Aquinas calls the likeness of an effect to its cause is precisely what we are seeking as we look for scientific explanations. And since all effects are ultimately God's effects, and since these include creatures who are attracted to what is good, God can be called 'good' as the source of all that is attractive. He can be called this even on the (traditional Christian) assumption that the created world is in no way necessary to God (that there might never have been a world created by God). For, so we may say, in calling God good with an eye on his creation, we are alluding to what God is in himself, whether or not he

189

creates — that the reality of the created order gives us a reason to say what God essentially is. Mary and John might decide never to have children. But the children they actually produce reflect what they are whether or not they choose to procreate. By the same token, so we may argue, the actual world reflects what God is apart from creation. You cannot give what you have not got, and God, so we may say, is what the goodness aimed at (and often achieved) by creatures is. He is attractive and, therefore, good (since 'good' can be equated with 'attractive' or 'desired'). This is not, of course, to say that we have any understanding of what God's goodness amounts to. But it is to say, as I argued above with respect to 'God is perfect', that we have a reason for calling God good — a reason which does not amount to the suggestion that God is a morally good individual, like a morally good human being. But, as should be obvious, it does not warrant the conclusion that God is good as a human moral agent is good. The argument I am now employing entails that human moral goodness reflects God and shows us something of what God is. So I have no problem in agreeing that human moral goodness reflects what God is. But that is not the same as saying that the goodness of God is moral goodness (a matter of being well behaved).

(2) How can one avoid holding that human choices are determined (or unfree) if one also takes them to be caused by God?

I have rejected the Free Will Defence since it rests on the assumption that human free choices are not caused by God. But how can my choices be caused by God without me being the puppet of God — something really lacking anything we can mean by 'freedom'? Should we not equate 'is caused' with 'is determined' (the assumption being that if X is 'determined' it cannot be 'free')? And should we not therefore conclude that if human choices are caused by God they simply cannot be free?

I think that the answer to these questions is 'No' since I see no reason to think of God as the sort of cause which can render what it causes unfree. Quite the contrary. For our knowledge of human free choices, and our knowledge of causes which determine their effects (i.e. render them necessary rather than free), depends on God as causing the existence of the world as a whole (including those things which act freely and those things which do not).

Consider, to begin with, what we mean when saying that a person chooses freely. The topic of human freedom has been hotly debated by philosophers over the centuries, but, when all the philosophical dust has settled, we surely have to say that human beings choose freely if nothing else alongside them acts on them from outside to make (force) them behave as they do.[70] By the same token, someone behaves unfreely if the proper explanation of their behaviour lies in an understanding of the nature and

190

action of something else, or of the purposes and action of someone else. Thus, my falling because of the poison I have taken is unfree and explicable in terms of the nature of the poison I have taken. So we say, for example: 'He swallowed arsenic; that, of course, is why he fell to the ground.' Or we say: 'Jones hit him on the head; that, of course, was why he fell to the ground.' But God, so I argue, is not something alongside human beings with a nature displayed by certain particular typical effects and not others (like arsenic or another human being). God accounts for there being a world in which some explanations of human behaviour rightly refer to the intentions of humans to act as they do (explanations in terms of free choices) and some explanations of human behaviour rightly refer to the action on us of other things with the power to make us behave in ways which cannot be thought of as chosen by us.

With these thoughts in mind, I again refer the reader to Aquinas, who seems to me to talk more sense than most on the topic of God and human freedom. We have seen him arguing that God exists 'intimately in everything'. Bearing in mind the question 'How can we be free in a world made by God?', he argues that what we can understand as existing free and determined things must, as distinct or distinguishable existing things, all be caused to be by God, who must therefore be the condition of human freedom, not something which abolishes it.[71] Or, in Aquinas's words:

God's will is to be thought of as existing outside the realm of existents, as a cause from which pours forth everything that exists in all its variant forms. Now *what can be* and *what must be* are variants of being, so that it is from God's will itself that things derive whether they must be or may or may not be and the distinction of the two according to the nature of their immediate causes. For he prepares causes that must cause for those effects that he wills must be, and causes that might cause but might fail to cause for those effects that he wills might or might not be. And it is because of the nature of their causes that some effects are said to be effects that must be and others effects that need not be, although all depend on God's will as primary cause, a cause which transcends this distinction between *must* and *might not*. But the same cannot be said of human will or of any other cause, since every other cause exists within the realm of *must* and *might not*. So of every other cause it must be said either that it can fail to cause, or that its effect must be and cannot not be; God's will, however, cannot fail, and yet not all his effects must be, but some can be or not be.[72]

What Aquinas is driving at here has, I think, been nicely captured by James F. Ross. As he puts it:

The being of the cosmos is like *a song on the breath of a singer*. It has endless internal universal laws, and structures nested within structures, properties that are of *the song* and *not* of the singer or the voice or the singer's thought, though produced by them and attributively predicated of them ... The universe is continuously depending, like a song or a light show ... ; its being is its own, yet it is from a cause, everywhere, and at no *including* time ... God produces, for each individual being, the one that does such and such (whatever it does) throughout its whole time in being ... God does not make the person act; he makes the so acting person *be* ... The whole physical universe, all of it, is actively caused to be. Still, to say that freedom or human agency is thereby impeded is absurd. Nothing can be or come about unless caused to be by the creator. So the fact that God's causing is necessary for whatever happens cannot impede liberty; it is a condition for it. Similarly, in no way is our liberty impeded by the fact that God's causing is sufficient for the being of the very things that do the very things that we do. Nothing possible can be impeded by its necessary conditions ... God did not make Adam to be the first man to defy God; God made Adam, who was the first man to defy God, to be. God made Adam, who undertook to sin ... God makes all the free things that do *as* they do, instead of doing otherwise as is in their power, by their *own* undertaking. So God does not make Adam sin. But God makes the sinning Adam, the person who, *able* not to sin, does sin. It follows logically that if Adam had not sinned, God would have made a person who, though able to sin, did not. And, surely, God *might* have made a person who, though able to sin, did not ... It is the whole being, doing as it does, whether a free being or not, that is entirely produced and sustained for its time by God.[73]

What Aquinas and Ross have to say seems to me correct. So I therefore suggest that my grounds for rejecting the Free Will Defence allow me to believe in the reality of human freedom as well as in the reality of God, the source of the being of creatures.

Evil and the mystery of God

I have now rejected the idea that God has some moral case to answer. And I have also denied that human choices should be thought of as uncaused by God. But I do not want to suggest that there is nothing more to be said on the topic of God and evil. On the contrary, I want to suggest that there is, indeed, a serious problem of evil. In my view, it is one which philosophy cannot solve. But I also think that it does nothing to suggest that God does not exist. Rather, it serves to highlight the mystery that God is to us as people trying to think about God in a philosophical way.

'Evil suffered' and 'evil done'

To start with, we need to note that there are two kinds of evil. There is, as Herbert McCabe nicely puts it, 'evil suffered' and 'evil done'.[74]

'Evil suffered' is anything which can be seriously thought of as diminishing or thwarting something. People who are ill are victims of evil suffered. So too are animals who are attacked (and maybe killed) by other animals (including us), or animals who endure pain for some other reason. Among victims of evil suffered we may even include plants, whose lives are ended by people who pluck them and eat them.

'Evil done' is what we have in mind when we say that someone acts badly (i.e. morally badly), for 'evil done' is something which renders the badly acting agent bad in his or her self. We often think of moral evil chiefly with an eye on the victims of morally bad people. In thinking of people as morally bad we are often concentrating on, for example, the unhappiness they cause. And, if asked why they are bad, we may simply refer to this. But someone can act in a morally bad way without anything else suffering (the bomb I planted might not have gone off). And the same result as can be caused by a morally bad person can also come about simply in the course of nature (a human being murdered by someone using the branch of a tree might, to forensic experts, look just the same as someone struck by a branch falling from a tree in a storm). So we need to remember that people acting morally badly are *themselves* bad, regardless of their effects. Agents of 'evil done' are first of all victims of themselves.

God and the badness of evil suffered and evil done

But what is the badness of evil suffered and evil done? With this question in mind, it seems to me that the *privatio boni* theory, noted above, is one which has to be taken very seriously. Evil is not an individual with a life or character of its own. Nor is it a positive quality, like being square or being plastic. Victims of evil suffered, and those who are morally bad, are all perfectly or entirely real. They are individuals there to be described. But what renders them bad is the gap between what they are and what they should be but are not. Human sickness would not worry us if it did not amount to there being people deprived of some thriving, prospering or flourishing. Acting people would not strike us as morally bad unless we recognized that, in acting as they do, they fail to do what they ought or need to do (or they fail to be what they ought or need to be). Such failure cannot, of course, occur without something positive being there. I cannot, for instance, murder someone if my body does not behave in certain ways. Evil done may exemplify skills and excellences which we might, without reference to context, desire and applaud. Successful practitioners of genocide tend to be people who exhibit unusual abilities in planning and organization (a good thing). They are normally rather intelligent or quick-witted (good again). And, given their goals, they employ their intellect to good effect (i.e. they succeed in their dreadful aims). But they are evil. And that is because of what they are not. While succeeding in what it takes to commit genocide, they are failing in some way. While perfectly real, they also lack something (e.g. justice, charity, proper concern for others).

With these thoughts in mind, an important point worth making with respect to God and evil is that evil cannot intelligibly be thought of as made to be by God (assuming that we take God to make the difference between something being and not being). So, at this point, I agree with what Aquinas says when he suggests (see above) that, though evil is no illusion, it cannot be thought of as a substance or quality the existence of which is caused by God.

There are holes in walls, but holes have no independent existence. There are holes in walls only because there are walls with something missing. There are blind people. But blindness has no independent existence. There are blind people only because there are people who cannot see. In a similar way, evil has no independent existence. It 'is there' only in the sense that something 'is missing'. But what is *not there* cannot be thought of as made to be by the source of the being of things. It cannot be thought to be made to be by God. Following Aristotle, Aquinas distinguishes between the use of 'is' in sentences like 'John is blind' and 'John is' (i.e. exists). He takes the first use to signify that a predicate (i.e. '_____ is blind') can be attached to the name 'John' so as to result in a true statement. He takes the second use to signify that 'John' is a genuine name (i.e. a word which labels something in the real world, something which has what Aquinas calls *esse*, or actual existence). In the light of these considerations, Aquinas maintains that, since God is the source of there being what has *esse*, God cannot be thought of as causing evil to be. For evil is not anything actual (whether a substance or a property). It is what we may talk of things as 'being' only in the sense that we may speak of people as 'being blind'. It is the unreality we acknowledge when we call things bad, sick, maimed, defective, thwarted, and so on. And here, so I suggest, Aquinas is right. Evil cannot intelligibly be thought of as something which God has made to be.

On the other hand, however, there is evil suffered (e.g. there are ill human beings), and there is evil done (e.g. there are people who act unjustly). So what is going on when these come to pass?

Notice that, confronted by evil suffered, we naturally look for a natural explanation. If Mary is sick we try to discover what (in the world) accounts for her state. If we come across the corpse of a zebra, we assume that something (in the world) was responsible for the zebra's death. In other words, we never assume that evil suffered is *naturally inexplicable*. We assume, in fact, that there is something (even if we do not, as yet, know what exactly that is) which, by being *good in its way*, is causing something else to be *bad in its way*. We assume, in effect, that nothing ever suffers evil except at the hands of some other being which is gaining some good (even though, in the case of a free creature, it may be, in a deeper sense, damaging itself by practising evil done).[75]

What does this tell us about God and evil suffered? It tells us, I suggest, that evil suffered is a necessary concomitant of certain goods, and that God can only be said to have brought it about in the sense that he brought about those goods. As we have seen, it has been suggested that there is *too much* evil suffered in God's world (the implication being that God is either bad or non-existent). But, if evil means 'evil suffered', there is no more evil than there need be. Any evil suffered that is *more than there need be* would be *lacking a natural cause*. It would be scientifically inexplicable. The evil suffered in the world is neither *more* nor *less* than what we can expect in a material world in which scientific explanations can be given for what happens. As we have seen, William Rowe thinks that there are multitudes of instances of 'seemingly pointless human and animal suffering that occur daily in our world'. But no human or animal suffering is pointless if 'pointless' means 'lacking a natural explanation' and if the suffering in question is what I am calling 'evil suffered'. For a natural explanation is exactly what we are looking for when seeking to account for evil suffered. One might, perhaps, say that evil suffered could always be prevented by a constant series of miracles and that it is, for this reason, pointless (sometimes or always). But a world governed by a constant series of miracles would not be a material world. It would not be an object of scientific enquiry. It could, perhaps, have been created by God, but the fact of the matter is that it has not been.[76] What God has created is a material world in which there is evil suffered. And in making this world to be, God is making what is good. Indeed, he is making nothing but what is good.

What about 'evil done', however? Unlike evil suffered, this can hardly be thought of as *benefiting* something. People who wrong others harm their victims. And, in doing so, they are bad in themselves. With evil done, unlike evil suffered, there is no concomitant good. There is nothing but failure. Evil done often involves success, of course. To return to my previous example, the perpetrator of genocide may be succeeding in all sorts of ways – as a killer, a strategist, and so on. But agents of evil done are fundamentally failing to be good and nothing is benefiting from this (except accidentally). The evil in their actions is nothing but such failure.

In that case, however, it can hardly be thought to be made by God. The evil in a morally evil act is not something which God can make to be since it is not something existing. It is no kind of individual or positive quality. It can no more be made to be by God than can square circles. And, in that case, we have to say that evil done represents no action of God. Evil suffered does, and the same goes for the positive realities which are there in those who are morally wicked. But the evil in evil done is nothing but failure. Considered as such, it is not something produced by those who are morally evil. Nor can it be thought of as something produced by God.

What God might have produced and the problem of evil

If we think of God as the source of the being of things, then God can make to be whatever can be thought of as possibly existing. As Aquinas writes:

> Since every agent enacts its like, every active power has a possible objective corresponding to the nature of that activity which the active power is for ... The divine being, on which the notion of divine power is founded, is infinite existence, not limited to any kind of being, but holding within itself and anticipating the perfection of the whole of existence. Whatever can have the nature of being falls within the range of things that are absolutely possible, and it is with respect to these that God is called all-powerful.[77]

Aquinas means that created causes have a determinate range of effects depending on their natures, while God has no such range. And that seems to me to be true. There is no definite limited range of possibilities in what God can bring about. Things belonging to a distinct genus and species are limited in what they can bring about, for they can only produce effects which are characteristic of things in that genus and species. But God is not limited in this way. A man and a woman can bring it about that something is a human being. Two dogs can bring it about that something is a dog. But God can bring it about that something is, *period*. So if it *could be*, then God can bring it about, and his power is relative to the bringing about of what can be.

As far as I can see, it is this thought that gives us anything we might fairly call 'the philosophical problem of evil'. As I have suggested, the 'problem' of God's moral integrity is a pseudo-problem. It is analogous to the problem expressed in the question 'Why don't tennis players run a mile in under four minutes?' I have also suggested (a) that there can be no question of human free choices not being caused to be by God, and (b) that evil suffered could be abolished by a series of miracles. Since I take morally good behaviour to be something which can be, I take (a) to imply that God could have made a world in which there was no moral evil. And I take (b) to imply that, absolutely speaking, there might have been no evil suffered. So why has God not made a world in which there is no moral evil? And why has he not made a world in which there is no evil suffered?

Along with many thinkers, we might try to answer these questions by alluding to the good which often comes out of evil suffered and evil done. And it is true that good always comes out of evil in the case of evil suffered (in the sense that there is no evil suffered without concomitant good). It is also true that good sometimes (as a side-effect) comes out of evil done (in the sense that evil done is sometimes followed by consequences which can be thought of as good). But these truths do nothing to explain why there is any evil done or any evil suffered. Those who try to argue that God is well behaved think that they have such an explanation. It lies in God's morally good intentions. But if the notion that God is well behaved is suspect from the start, it can do nothing to explain why there is any evil done or any evil suffered. And if the Free Will Defence is brought in as a defence of God's moral integrity, it fails on two counts. It fails because its intention is to defend the morality of God. And it fails since it erroneously supposes that human free choices are not made to be by God. As far as I can see, God could have made a world in which people, angels, or any other creatures who might sensibly be thought of as moral agents (subject to duties, obligations and the like) always act well. So why has God not done so? And does his not having done so mean that he is bad?

To take the second question first, my suggestion is that we have no grounds for thinking of God as bad. I have been arguing that God is not good as a morally good human being is good. And I have given reasons for saying that God is good. One might suppose that God is bad since he has made the kind of world we inhabit (one which lacks various imaginable goods) even though he could have made a world with more good things in it (given that more good things than there are in the world are things able to be and, therefore, things which God can make or have made to be). But this supposition only makes sense on the assumption that God has a duty or obligation of some kind to make a world which is different from the real one. And, so I have argued, such an assumption is misguided.

To take the first question second, I invite the reader to consider what people can mean by questions of the sort 'Why has God ... ?' Are they asking for an account of reasons which God has? Perhaps they are. If so, however, they are surely as off-beam as those who ask questions like 'Why don't tennis players run a mile in under four minutes?' We know what it is to act with a reason since we know of human beings who, being language-users existing in time, sometimes act because they can conceive of something they want to come to pass in the future. But if God is the cause of the being of everything, he cannot be seriously thought of as a language-user existing in time acting because he wants something to come to pass in the future. The notion of God literally having 'reasons for acting' seems highly dubious (if the literal sense of 'reasons for acting' signifies what people have when they have reasons for acting). The notion of God literally having reasons for acting seems to imply that God is all too human. I am not denying that God has knowledge and will. Nor am I denying that what God has brought about can be talked of as intended. I am, however, suggesting that we cannot think of God as acting with reasons as human beings do. We can come to understand why Fred sold his house. We cannot, so it seems to me, come to any similar understanding of why God has made things to be the way they are and not otherwise.

And it is here, so it seems to me, that the real problem of evil lies. God could have created a world in which no evil suffered comes to pass (though I do not know what such a world would look like). And he could have created a world full of moral agents who always act well. But God has evidently not done that. Why not? I have no idea. And that is why I think that there is a problem of evil. But it is not a problem which casts doubt on what we say if we assert that divinity is not something fictional. It is not a problem which suggests that there is no God. Rather, it is something which invites us to reflect on the mystery of divinity, something which serves to remind us that God is nothing less than the beginning and end of all things, the source from which everything we can understand derives its existence.

Notes

1 J. L. Mackie, 'Evil and omnipotence' in Marilyn McCord Adams and Robert Merrihew Adams (eds), *The Problem of Evil* (Oxford, 1990).
2 Adams and Adams, op. cit., p. 26.
3 Ibid.
4 Ibid.
5 Adams and Adams, op. cit., p. 30.
6 Adams and Adams, op. cit., p. 33.
7 It should be noted that in *The Miracle of Theism* (Oxford, 1982), Mackie softens his charge of contradiction and argues, instead, that evil renders God's existence unlikely.
8 William Rowe, 'The problem of evil and some varieties of atheism', reprinted in Adams and Adams, op. cit.
9 Adams and Adams, op. cit., pp. 127f.
10 Adams and Adams, op. cit., p. 129.
11 Adams and Adams, op. cit., p. 131.
12 Ibid.
13 Adams and Adams, op. cit., p. 132.
14 The reader should recognize that I focus on Mackie and Rowe since they present in a clear form arguments offered by a variety of non-theistic critics of theism writing with respect to the topic of God and evil.
15 To my knowledge, there is no contemporary author who presses the 'We know that God exists' argument while discussing the topic of God and evil. But the argument is implicit in a great deal of Christian philosophical thinking. I take it to be evident, for instance, in the writings of St Anselm and St Thomas Aquinas.

16 Mary Baker Eddy, *Science and Health with Key to the Scriptures* (Boston, 1971), p. 257. Eddy's account of evil clearly takes 'evil' as equivalent to something like 'pain' or 'human sickness'. As such, it makes no contribution to discussions of evil which have a broader focus.

17 That is why Aquinas holds that even Satan cannot be nothing but bad. If Satan were that, thinks Aquinas, then Satan would not exist.

18 *Summa Theologiae* I, 48, 1.

19 For Augustine expressing the same line of thought, see *Enchiridion*, ch. XI and *Confessions*, III, vii, 12. For contemporary defences of the evil as *privatio boni* notion, see Paul Helm, *The Providence of God* (Leicester, 1993), pp. 168ff. and Herbert McCabe, *God Matters* (London, 1987), pp. 27ff.

20 'God, evil, and the metaphysics of freedom', reprinted in Adams and Adams, op. cit., p. 106. Plantinga's position is echoed by many contemporary philosophers of religion. Cf., for example, William Alston, according to whom 'It is logically impossible for God to create free beings with genuine freedom of choice and also guarantee that they will always choose the right' ('The inductive argument from evil' in Daniel Howard-Snyder [ed.], *The Evidential Argument from Evil* [Bloomington and Indianapolis, 1996], p. 112).

21 Adams and Adams, op. cit., pp. 84f.

22 Richard Swinburne, *The Existence of God* (Oxford, 1979).

23 *The Existence of God* (rev. edn, 1991), pp. 210f.

24 *The Existence of God*, p. 219.

25 *The Existence of God*, p. 220.

26 Swinburne seems to think that a clear recognition of God would abolish human freedom.

27 *The Existence of God*, pp. 210ff. For development of this position by Swinburne see also 'Knowledge from experience, and the problem of evil' in William J. Abraham and Steven W. Holtzer (eds), *The Rationality of Religious Belief* (Oxford, 1987).

28 John Hicks, *Evil and the God of Love* (2nd edn; London, 1977).

29 *Evil and the God of Love*, pp. 372ff.

30 William P. Alston, *The Evidential Argument from Evil*, p. 98.

31 *The Evidential Argument from Evil*, p. 109.

32 Alston's line of reasoning may be compared with that of Peter van Inwagen's 'The problems of evil, air, and silence' in *The Evidential Argument from Evil*, pp. 151ff.

33 C. J. F. Williams, 'Knowing good and evil', *Philosophy* 66 (1991), p. 238.

34 George N. Schlesinger, *New Perspectives on Old-Time Religion* (Oxford, 1988), ch. 2.

35 See below.

36 Thomas Aquinas, *Commentary on Aristotle's 'De Interpretatione'*, I.14.

37 Some contemporary theists have offered arguments based on the idea that God can be expected to bring about certain specifiable things. Notions of what God can be expected to do play a prominent part in, for example, the writings of Richard Swinburne. My reading of Aquinas and Swinburne leaves me convinced that Aquinas, though sharing Swinburne's Christian faith, is far removed from him when it comes to expectations concerning God.

38 Herbert McCabe, 'God: 1 – Creation', *New Blackfriars* 61 (1980), p. 412. This article is reprinted in Herbert McCabe, *God Matters* (London, 1987).

39 Examples of such theists would be St Augustine, St Anselm, Boethius, and Aquinas. The teaching that God is immutable is *de fide* for Roman Catholics.

Cf. Vatican I's *Dogmatic Constitution Concerning the Catholic Faith*, chapter 1.

40 Jon Sobrino, *Christology at the Crossroads* (London, 1978). For Moltmann, see his *The Crucified God* (New York, 1974) and *The Trinity and the Kingdom of God* (London, 1981), ch. 2.

41 For this reason, 'good' can be taken to be the general word we use when approving or admiring things.

42 P. T. Geach, 'Good and evil', reprinted in Philippa Foot (ed.), *Theories of Ethics* (Oxford, 1967), p. 64.

43 Ibid.

44 Cf. David Burrell, *Knowing the Unknowable God* (Notre Dame, 1986).

45 Christians traditionally deny that God has to create. So we may say that God is not essentially creator. But all discussions of God and evil start from the fact that God has created and that what should be said of God should be based on that. Note that, as countless theists have insisted, to say that God is Creator is not to deny that God is incomprehensible. For the most part, indeed, the claim that God is incomprehensible has sprung from reflection on the notion of God as Creator (coupled with reflection on the Old and New Testaments).

46 Throughout the Jewish and Christian Scriptures (the Old and New Testaments), God is the transcendent source of all things. He makes the world to begin, he keeps it in being, and he does with it what he wills. He is not a 'god' – i.e. some material or spiritual individual conceived of (or conceivable as) as something alongside other things. He is the reality which lies beyond the world and makes it to be as it is.

47 We might include creatures such as angels, since the Christian tradition speaks of good and bad angels.

48 Walter Eichrodt, *Theology of the Old Testament*, vol. I (London, 1961), p. 249.

49 In the book of Job, a good man is afflicted by God. He is eventually recompensed to some extent, but it is never suggested that this is because God owes this to him.

50 Rowan Williams, 'Reply: redeeming sorrows' in D. Z. Phillips (ed.), *Religion and Morality* (New York, 1996), p. 135. That is why the use of 'he' (or 'she') when talking about God is always a constant reminder of the limits of our language. Since theists want to say that God is real (not a fiction), they have to talk of God as if he were a thing in the world, for we naturally make assertions by singling out a subject (something nameable, something which might be a man or a woman or a material object) and by saying what properties it has. But God is not a nameable object in the world and our way of speaking of him as such needs to be understood accordingly.

51 You can buy two *boxes of* salt and two *portions of* beef. But you cannot buy two 'salt' or two 'beef'.

52 Commentary on Aristotle's *De Interpretatione* or *Perihermeneias*, Book 1, chapter 9, 18b26–19a22: lectio 14.

53 Cf. *Summa Theologiae* I, 5.

54 I develop this point in 'How is God love?' in Luke Gormally (ed.), *Moral Truth and Moral Tradition: Essays in Honour of Peter Geach and Elizabeth Anscombe* (Dublin and Portland, OR, 1994). For an interesting development of the point see also D. Z. Phillips, *The Concept of Prayer* (London, 1965), ch. 5. See also Herbert McCabe, *God Matters*.

55 A good defence of this thesis can be found in Peter van Inwagen, *An Essay on Free Will* (Oxford, 1983).

56 Perhaps Plantinga would not accept this reading of his words. Perhaps he

thinks that God's making-to-be of creatures is governed by causal laws and that God is something existing at times before particular human choices occur. If that is so, then all I can say is that Plantinga seems to think that God is a creature of some sort.

57 *Quaestio Disputata de malo* 6.

58 *Summa Theologiae* I, 8, 1.

59 *Summa Theologiae* I, 22, 2, *ad* 4; *De Potentia*, 3, 7.

60 *God Matters*, p. 14. Cf. Paul Helm, *The Providence of God* (Leicester, 1993). Helm refers to the notion that God does not cause, but somehow observes and waits upon, human free choices (which he may just have to put up with) as a denial of a 'no risk' view of divine providence. As biblical texts supporting a 'no risk' view of God, Helm (quite reasonably) cites 1 Thess 1:5; Rom 1:6; 9:11; 1 Cor 1:9; Eph 4:4; 2 Tim 2:25; and Eph 2:8. Alluding to John 8:36, Helm, rightly to my mind, observes that 'The New Testament appears to find no incoherence in the idea of being made to be free' (p. 55).

61 Helm, op. cit., p. 167.

62 Helm, op. cit., p. 167. Cf. also p. 201.

63 On these grounds I would reject the teaching of Moltmann and Sobrino noted above.

64 Cf. *Compendium of Theology*, ch. 20: 'Imperfection occurs in a thing for the reason that matter is found in a state of privation. On the other hand, perfection comes exclusively from form.'

65 *Summa Theologiae* I, 4, 1.

66 *Summa Theologiae* I, 6, 1.

67 I, 1, 1094a3.

68 Cf. Aristotle, *Metaphysics*, I, 1.

69 This is the language of Aristotle's man of 'experience'.

70 I know of no contemporary secular determinists who argue their case on theological grounds.

71 For an analysis of Aquinas on this topic, see Harm J. M. J. Goris, *Free Creatures of an Eternal God: Thomas Aquinas on God's Infallible Foreknowledge and Irresistible Will* (Leuven, 1996).

72 Commentary on Aristotle's *De Interpretatione* or *Perihermeneias*, Book 1, chapter 9, lectio 14.

73 James F. Ross, 'Creation II' in Alfred J. Freddoso (ed.), *The Existence and Nature of God* (Notre Dame and London, 1983), pp. 128–34.

74 Cf. *God Matters*, ch. 3. Medieval authors distinguish between *malum poenae* (evil of penalty) and *malum culpae* (evil of fault) – a distinction presupposing various theological beliefs about what results in what. Later writers distinguish between 'natural evil' (or 'metaphysical evil') and 'moral evil' (a distinction presupposing various philosophical beliefs about what results in what). McCabe's distinction between 'evil suffered' and 'evil done' nicely avoids theological and philosophical theories about what results in what while clearly drawing attention to the kinds of evil which we encounter.

75 *God Matters* (London, 1987), pp. 31–2.

76 Actually, I have no idea what I would be agreeing to if I agreed that God could have made a world continually governed by miracles.

77 *Summa Theologiae* I, 25, 3.

7

Faith and revelation

John Jenkins CSC

Faith is the human response to God's revelation in history. Theologians have much of importance to say about the nature and content of God's revelation and about the response of faith. Philosophers can contribute to this discussion in a number of ways, but traditionally they have been primarily concerned with the question of whether and how faith is reasonable or rational.[1] This question of the rationality of faith will be the theme of this chapter's discussion.

I will focus on two very important thinkers in the history of philosophy, John Locke and St Thomas Aquinas. Although Locke wrote over 300 years ago, and Aquinas wrote over 700 years ago, I will argue that understanding the thought of each is important for us today as we ask whether and why faith is rational, for they give us two very important options for thinking about this question. I will suggest that we can best move forward in our reflection on this question if we take a careful look backward to the history of philosophical thought.

Faith and reason: the philosophical problem

Before we can say whether faith is rational, we must say something about what faith is and what rationality is. These questions will bring us to the heart of the philosophical problem.

The English word 'faith' is often used to signify simply a belief that God exists. Since our topic is faith *and revelation*, our concern is more specifically with belief in divine revelation and not simply with the belief that God exists. Again, 'faith' is often used to signify commonly the attitudes of adherents to any of several religions, such as Judaism, Buddhism, Islam, Hinduism or Christianity. Such a use of the word, however, can blind us to important differences among the respective religious attitudes demanded by these various traditions, and thereby distort our understanding of them.

As I will use the word in this chapter it will signify specifically Christian faith. I limit myself in this way not because of any Christian chauvinism, but for the sake of clarity. Much of what I will say can perhaps be applied to other religious traditions, but I will not attempt to apply it here.

In both the Hebrew Bible and the Christian New Testament Abraham is held up as the model or exemplar of faith. (See Sir 44:19–21; Rom 4:1–12.) For when God promised Abraham, while he and Sarah his wife were aged and childless, that his descendants would be as numerous as the stars, Abraham 'believed the Lord; and the Lord reckoned it to him as righteousness' (Gen 15:6). The Hebrew word that is translated 'believed' in this passage is *he' emin*, and its meaning is not entirely clear. The best paraphrase seems to be 'to gain stability, to rely on someone, to give credence to a message or consider it true, to trust someone'.[2] This attitude of confidence or reliance, which the Bible discourages toward humans but commends when its object is God, was more than detached intellectual assent. It was an attitude grounded in a relationship with God; it involved a hope in God's promises even when all appearances were to the contrary (Gen 17:15–27); and it required of Abraham obedience to God's commands (Gen 22:1–19).

In the Christian New Testament 'faith' and 'to believe' or 'to have faith' translate the Greek words *pistis* and *pisteuein*. In Paul's letters *pistis* or faith signifies obedient acceptance of and trust in the proclamation of God's salvation in Christ. Paul insists that it is by this faith, and not by works of the Law, that the Christian attains righteousness and salvation. The Synoptic Gospels (of Matthew, Mark and Luke) speak of faith as trust and confidence in the coming Kingdom of God which Jesus proclaims, and how such faith requires a conversion, a *metanoia*, on the part of the believer (Mark 1:14–15). It seems to be deep trust and confidence which is at issue when Jesus rebukes the disciples for their fear and lack of faith in the middle of a stormy sea (Mark 4:40; Matt 8:23–27), and he commends the centurion at Capernaum for his faith (Matt 8:5–13). John's Gospel emphasizes faith particularly in the person of Jesus, who is sent by the Father (5:24), is in the Father and the Father is in him (17:21), and is the Christ, the Son of God (11:27). Throughout the New Testament this *pistis* or faith in God's revelation in Christ and the conversion this requires are portrayed as central to the definition of a Christian life.

Biblical faith, it seems, is more than simply intellectual assent to certain propositions. Full faith requires conversion, is grounded in a deep trust in and even love of God, requires obedient acceptance of God's will and leads to a firm hope in the fulfilment of God's promises. But although all these may be features of faith, it nevertheless seems clear that one essential component of faith is the holding of certain beliefs. In human relationships, I may have a deep trust or confidence in, for example, my doctor and a firm hope in her ability to heal me. Although this attitude may involve more than merely belief, it nevertheless involves some beliefs, such as the belief that she is a responsible, skilled and dedicated physician. Similarly in the biblical accounts, although the notion of faith is a rich one, it involves at least belief that certain propositions are true.

This aspect of faith as belief in or assent to the truth of particular propositions became more clearly articulated in the first five hundred years of Christianity when, after centuries of doctrinal conflict and controversy, the Church agreed to formulations of certain truths essential to Christianity. The propositions were expressed in creeds, such as the Nicene Creed. Christians shared a common faith, it was thought, and that commonality consisted at least in the fact that they all assented to the propositions of a common creed.[3] When the Latin-speaking writers of this period spoke of this faith, they used the Latin word *fides*, and it is is from this word that the English word 'faith' is derived.

Whatever else faith may be, then, it seems to be a believing that certain propositions are true. This belief is based on a trust in God who revealed certain truths. We can perhaps put this succinctly by saying that faith is believing God that certain propositions are true. Although one may want to add more conditions to arrive at a full account of Christian faith, we can say that faith is at least this.[4] Because generally philosophers are interested primarily in beliefs, this is the aspect of faith on which we will focus.

We turn now to reason or rationality, which has traditionally been the particular concern of philosophy and philosophers. Socrates, the man who coined the term 'philosophy', seemed to embody the philosophical dedication to reason (at least as he is portrayed in Plato's dialogues). In discussions about virtue, happiness, politics, knowledge, truth and so forth, many of Socrates' interlocutors were swayed by their desire to appear clever, or by their craving for power, or for pleasure. Socrates in contrast shows an unflappable dedication to follow the reasoning of an argument wherever it leads. In *Phaedo*, for instance, Socrates, facing his imminent death, engages his friends and disciples in a discussion of whether the soul survives the death of the body. When a strong objection is brought against Socrates' thesis that the soul is immortal, all except Socrates are downhearted and discouraged. Though it was Socrates who was soon to die, Phaedo comments on 'the pleasant, kind and admiring way [Socrates] received the young men's argument, and how he was aware of the effect the discussion had on us, and then how well he healed our distress and, as it were, recalled us from our flight and defeat and turned us around to join him in the examination of the argument' (*Phaedo*, 89a).[5] He then admonishes those present that 'there is no greater evil than to hate reasonable discourse' (89d).

Philosophers, then, generally hold up for us all the ideal of being reasonable, of judging and behaving rationally. It is a disputed matter among them, however, just what it is to be rational. At a very abstract level of description, being rational consists in following correct standards of reason. The standards of reason would specify what sorts of propositions it would be rational for someone to believe in what circumstances and at what degree of belief or conviction.[6] They would also specify what propositions could be inferred from other propositions, either inductively or deductively, and at what degree of belief. At this abstract level of description, then, we can say that a person's belief that a proposition, P, is true is rational if and only if he adhered to correct standards of reason in arriving at this belief. We can for the moment leave it an open question just what set standards of rationality are correct, and whether there is only one correct set of standards.[7]

The central philosophical question about faith and reason is: can one who holds the beliefs which faith involves do so while adhering to correct standards of reason? In short, can the person of faith be reasonable or rational in believing? Of course, just how we answer this question depends upon what we take the correct standards of reason to be. To gain perspective on this latter question, I will argue, we must turn to the history of philosophy.

Philosophy and the history of philosophy

Analytic philosophy – the predominant form of philosophy in the English-speaking world in the twentieth century – has been characterized by an ahistorical approach to enquiry and debate. The writings of Bertrand Russell, W. V. O. Quine or Donald Davidson consist of careful and brilliant analysis of concepts and development of arguments, but considerations of the historical development of philosophical debate of the question at hand play no role in the argument. Historical figures may be mentioned, but it is simply to present an alternative view; they are treated almost as contemporary philosophers offering an alternative account. Unsurprisingly, then, when analytic philosophers turn to questions of faith and reason, we find a presentation of the nature of rationality which seems most defensible to the author, a review of the evidence for or against belief, and arguments for or against the rationality of belief. Historical figures may be mentioned, but a consideration of the historical development of thought is not intrinsic to the argument.[8]

Recently, however, several philosophers within the analytic tradition have argued that philosophical debate and enquiry cannot be successfully conducted without attention to the history of philosophical debate. Charles Taylor is one who contends that philosophy is 'inherently historical', and he argues that this fact about philosophy 'is a manifestation of a more general truth about human life and society, from which ... certain things follow about validity and argument in philosophy'.[9]

Taylor characterizes philosophy as the activity of giving descriptions of 'what we are doing, thinking, believing, assuming, in such a way that we bring our reasons to light more perspicuously, or else make the alternatives more apparent, or in some way or other are better enabled to take a justified stand to our action, thought, belief, assumption' ('Philosophy and its history', p. 18). His point seems to be that we find ourselves with and engaged in religious, or moral or political beliefs and practices. Philosophy is the activity of seeking a more reflective, deeper description of our reasons for these beliefs and practices. In light of the reasons which emerge from this philosophical description, we may continue, modify or even reject some or all of these beliefs and practices. Although we might want to elaborate or add to Taylor's characterization of philosophy, it does seem to capture at least one of philosophy's primary tasks. And if this is so, Taylor contends, then philosophy requires 'a great deal of articulation of what is initially inarticulated' (p. 18); it requires that we bring to perspicuous expression the deeper reasons for some of our most important beliefs and practices.

The importance of the history of philosophy for philosophy follows, Taylor believes, from a general truth about the way certain social practices influence our understanding of ourselves and our world. Social practices as Taylor uses this term are roughly 'the ways that we regularly behave to/ before each other, which a) embody some understanding between us, and which b) allow discrimination of right/wrong, appropriate/inappropriate' (p. 22). Although such practices involve common understandings and norms of judgement, these need not be and generally are not articulated. For the most part one acquires a sense of the common understanding and norms by either acting or observing others act in concrete situations, and having others correct or approve behaviour.

As an example, consider the various ways it is appropriate for young people to address, behave in the presence of and generally deal with their parents and elders. Various cultures differ greatly on what is considered appropriate behaviour, but all discriminate appropriate and inappropriate behaviours. Thus members of the culture are aware of norms or rules for discrimination, even though these are generally not fully articulated. People inducted into the society learn these norms by being corrected or applauded for certain behaviours in certain situations. In this way, members of a society acquire an implicit understanding of the norms for appropriate behaviour regarding parents and elders, even though these may never be made explicit.

Social practices are shaped by many factors, but often a particular philosophical outlook becomes dominant in a culture and influences its practices. A broad philosophical account can, while allowing for disagreements on more specific issues, become the dominant model for understanding a particular area of reality, and can then become 'the organizing principle for a wide range of practices in which we think and act and deal with the world' (p. 20). When this occurs, those inducted into the practices of the society can thereby acquire the outlook and background assumptions, even though the model, its assumptions and the arguments for it are never explicitly articulated for them. To those so inducted in a society, once the model is articulated and presented to them, it tends to appear simply obvious, a matter of common sense; it can seem a truism which does not even stand in need of supporting arguments and justification.

Taylor offers as an example the philosophical understanding of individuals within a political society as rights-bearers, and of the role of government as protecting those rights. We who have grown up in modern liberal democracies have learned to think of and speak of ourselves as having rights against the government, other institutions and other individuals simply by learning how to live and deal with others in such a political society. We learn to respect others' rights, and to demand our own when we think they are being violated. Thus when we think about political philosophy, it can seem obvious and beyond question that this is at least part of the correct understanding of political life. What has happened in this case and others, though, is that we have forgotten that our understanding of our political life arose at a particular point in our philosophical past, that it was one position among others and that arguments were needed and were given for it.[10]

When a philosophical model becomes embedded in our social practices in this way, it can constrict our philosophical horizons. It can seem that the model gives us the *only* plausible way to think about a particular area. But this appearance is due to what Taylor calls 'philosophical forgetting'; we have forgotten that the dominant model was one alternative among others, that reasons for embracing it rather than an alternative were needed and were given. The power of philosophical outlooks in our cultural history is manifest in their ability to influence our social practices and, in turn, to shape profoundly our self-understanding; but ironically this very power can lead and has led to the impoverishment and narrowing of subsequent philosophical reflection.

Sometimes a philosophical model becomes dominant because it is the most adequate understanding in a particular area. At times, however, a model may become dominant, and organize social practices, and yet in the course of subsequent debate and enquiry its limitations may be revealed and it may begin to show signs of strain. It is precisely here that serious attention to the history of philosophy is needed, to the genesis and development of the dominant model. As Taylor writes, 'to understand ourselves today, we are pushed into the past for paradigm statements of our formative articulations. We are forced back to the last full disclosure of what we have been about, or what our practice has been woven about' (p. 26). We can then begin to understand the reasons behind our dominant model. Moreover, it is helpful to discover what alternatives there were to the dominant model in our philosophical past, and what reasons recommended those alternatives. Our self-understanding and our awareness of philosophical alternatives are thereby enriched.

Thus in the philosophical enterprise of describing the deeper reasons for our beliefs, actions and assumptions, a serious consideration of our philosophical history is essential. And this historical consideration is especially important when the dominant model is showing signs of strain. In coming pages I will suggest that the dominant model for our understanding of the relationship between faith and reason is derived from John Locke. This model, I suggest, has been embedded in the social practices of modern liberal democracies, but it is now showing signs of strain. I will summarize Locke's approach, and some of the objections to it. I will then go on to consider an alternative account which was prior to Locke's, that of St Thomas Aquinas.

John Locke and the epistemological project

John Locke (1632–1704) was educated at Oxford University, and upon graduation briefly lectured there in Latin and Greek. He eventually became interested in the new empirical science of his time, took up the study of medicine, and intermittently practised medicine. He was the physician, friend and adviser of Lord Ashley (later the first Earl of Shaftesbury), a dominant political figure in England at the time. Locke wrote several extremely influential works in political philosophy. He fled to Holland when Shaftesbury fell from favour with King James II, but returned when William of Orange deposed James, and held several influential positions during William's reign. His greatest philosophical work – and perhaps his greatest contribution – was *An Essay Concerning Human Understanding*.

Locke lived and wrote at the dawn of the Enlightenment and helped shape its philosophical agenda.[11] Perhaps his most momentous contribution to subsequent centuries was to set forth clearly and cogently a certain strategy for the rational resolution of religious questions and controversies. We can call Locke's strategy the *epistemological project*. It begins with the attempt to find universal norms and principles of correct human reasoning. Once these are found, they could, it was thought, help us to resolve religious disputes and divisions of the sort which were prevalent in Locke's day. For if we let these norms and principles guide our enquiries and debates we can make progress toward the rational resolution of some disagreements or, at least, show that the evidence on a particular question is not decisive and that alternative positions on the issue ought to be tolerated. Locke set forth this epistemological project in his *An Essay Concerning Human Understanding*. Subsequent thinkers would differ sharply with Locke on aspects of his epistemology or metaphysics, but the philosophical mainstream embraced the strategy of beginning by formulating the principles of a universalist epistemology, and then considering, in accord with these epistemological principles, arguments and evidence for and against the beliefs of faith.[12]

Although Locke did not complete *An Essay Concerning Human Understanding* until the later 1680s (its initial publication was in December of 1689), he began writing it in 1671 after a discussion with several friends about the principles of morality and revealed religion.[13] The discussion had reached an impasse and, in spite of their best efforts, the participants could make no further progress. It then occurred to Locke that 'before we set ourselves upon enquiries of that nature it was necessary to examine our own abilities, and see what objects our understandings were or were not fitted to deal with'.[14] The *Essay* is Locke's systematic examination of human understanding. In this work he attempts to identify the norms and principles of human understanding which are then applied in Book IV to resolve questions and disputes about revealed religion.

Locke's insight during this conversation was hugely influential, for he and many of his readers saw it as much more than a strategy for resolving polite debates among learned friends. From 1517, when Martin Luther nailed his 95 theses to the church door at Wittenberg, until Locke's own day, religious conflicts, wars and persecutions had racked Europe. The degree of social, political and economic disruption was immense, and the amount of bloodletting horrific.[15] If all could agree to recognize certain universal principles of reason, it was thought, these could guide public debate and discussion. And if debate would be so conducted, then either the differences could be resolved or the disputing parties would accept that decisive arguments were lacking for their respective positions, and they would therefore tolerate various positions and practices. Such was the hope which inspired many in Europe and America at the time. Reason, not wars, persecutions and purges, could resolve religious disputes.

What then were the principles of Locke's epistemology and what were the consequences for religious faith? In his *Essay* Locke drew a critical distinction between what he called knowledge and judgement. *Knowledge*, the highest form of human apprehension, is the certain perception of the agreement or disagreement of ideas. *Intuitive knowledge* is the immediate perception of a relationship between ideas; e.g. one immediately sees that *the whole is greater than the part*, or that *two bodies cannot be in the same place*. In the case of *rational* or *demonstrative knowledge*, however, one reasons discursively to a conclusion through a series of intermediate ideas whose connection one perceives intuitively; e.g. one reasons to the conclusion that *the interior angles of a triangle are equal to two right angles* through a series of perceptions of the relationships between pairs of intermediate ideas in a geometrical demonstration.

   Although philosophical discussions of Locke have generally focused on knowledge, Locke was clear that in most human affairs judgement is most important. For though knowledge is most certain, its scope is extremely limited, and in most matters of significance to us we must be content with judgement, a determination of the mind on merely probable grounds. Locke writes:

> As Demonstration is the shewing the Agreement, or Disagreement of two *Ideas*, by the intervention of one or more Proofs, which have a constant, immutable, and visible connexion one with another; so *Probability* is nothing but the appearance of such an Agreement, or Disagreement, by the intervention of Proofs, whose connexion is not constant and immutable, or at least is not perceived to be so, but is, or appears for the most part to be so, and is enough to induce the Mind to *judge* the Proposition to be true, or false, rather than the contrary. (IV, 15, 1, p. 654)

Locke's ultimate aim in the *Essay* was to aid people in correctly forming judgements regarding matters of greatest importance for humans – those of religion, morality and our ultimate happiness. Since rational enquiry and deliberation require large expenditures of time and energy, ordinary people cannot be expected to meet the full demands of reason regarding every assent. But Locke thought they can and should make an effort to do so regarding questions which concern their eternal happiness.[16] For Locke held that we have a moral duty or obligation to make judgements on issues of morality and religion according to the principles of reason. God created us with cognitive faculties, Locke reasoned, and out of obedience to our creator we have a duty to do our best to use these faculties correctly. Although human reason is fallible even when we are doing our best to discover the truth, nevertheless if we fulfil our epistemic duty we can expect to receive an eternal reward in the next life. As Locke writes:

> This at least is certain, that [a person] must be accountable for whatever Mistakes he runs into: whereas he that makes use of the Light and Faculties GOD has given him, and seeks sincerely to discover Truth, by those Helps and Abilities he has, may have this satisfaction in doing his

Duty as a rational Creature, that though he should miss Truth, he will not miss the Reward of it. (IV, 17, 24, p. 688)

Although the norms of correct reasoning are complex, in one place Locke summarizes the central principles:

Probability wanting that intuitive Evidence, which infallibly determines the Understanding, and produces certain Knowledge, *the Mind if it will proceed rationally, ought to examine all the grounds of Probability*, and see how they make more or less, *for or against* any probable Proposition, before it assents to or dissents from it, and upon a due balancing the whole, reject, or receive it, with a more or less firm assent, proportionably to the preponderancy of the greater grounds of Probability on one side or the other. (IV, 15, 5, p. 656)

There seem to be three main principles implicit in Locke's account of the rational formation of judgements. First, before rendering a judgement on a matter of great importance or 'concernment' (as Locke says) to oneself, one must endeavour to gather the evidence relevant to the proposition in question. Secondly, one must examine the evidence to determine the probability of the proposition on that evidence. Finally, when one arrives at a judgement on one side or the other of the question, one must proportion the firmness of one's assent to the degree of probability of the proposition on that evidence.[17]

Near the end of the *Essay* Locke briefly discusses how the principles of correct reasoning which he identified in the course of this work ought to be applied to the assent of faith in a revealed religion. In chapter 18 of Book IV he included a discussion of Faith and Reason and, in the fourth edition, he added chapter 19, entitled 'Of Enthusiasm', which was an attack on Protestant extremists of his day (whom Locke called 'enthusiasts') who claimed to have private revelations from God.

Faith, Locke writes, is assent to some proposition not on the basis of 'the Deduction of reason; but on the Credit of the Proposer, as coming from GOD' (IV, 18, 2, p. 689). Reason is 'the discovery of the Certainty or Probability of such Propositions or Truths, which the Mind arrives at by Deductions made from such *Ideas*, which it has got by the use of its natural Faculties, *viz.*, by Sensation or Reflection' (ibid.). Although reason and faith are distinct, reason nevertheless plays a role in the assent of faith because it is by reason that we determine whether what has putatively been divinely revealed is in fact a genuine revelation. In other words, if we are to assent in faith to a proposition, P, then, although reason does not establish that P is true, nevertheless reason must establish that *God revealed that P is true*. As Locke writes, in any normal case, 'the believing, or not believing that Proposition, or Book, to be of Divine Authority, can never be Matter of *Faith*, but Matter of Reason' (IV, 18, 6, p. 693).

Locke thought that there are sufficient grounds for reason to determine that the central truths of Christianity ought to be believed as divinely revealed. Indeed in some places he speaks as if the assent of faith is virtually certain. Faith, he writes, can 'challenge the highest Degree of our Assent upon bare Testimony, whether the thing proposed, agree or disagree with common Experience, and the ordinary course of Things, or no' (IV, 16, 14, p. 667). When we assent on the basis of ordinary human testimony, we must take into account both the credibility of the one who testifies and the conformity of what he proposes to the rest of our knowledge, observation and experience (IV, 15, 4, p. 656). However, in the case of divine revelation, the credibility of God is beyond question; and because God's knowledge is so superior to ours, we may accept something as divinely revealed of which we can have little knowledge or experience. In the case of faith 'the Testimony is of such an one, as cannot deceive, nor be deceived, and that is of God himself. This carries with it Assurance beyond Doubt, Evidence beyond Exception' (IV, 16, 14, p. 667).

When Locke assures us of the virtual certainty of the assent of faith, however, he seems to be saying simply that if we can be sure that something has been revealed by God and that we have understood it correctly, we can have what approaches the very highest degree of confidence in our assent. But these statements about the exalted certainty of faith are significantly qualified when Locke adds that we must employ discursive, probable reasoning to decide whether some *alleged* revelation is in fact *genuine*, and to understand what it means. Such reasoning is fallible, and 'in those Cases, our Assent can be rationally no higher than the Evidence of its being a Revelation, and that this is the meaning of the Expressions it is delivered in. If the Evidence of its being a Revelation, or that this its true Sense be only on probable Proofs, our Assent can reach no higher than an Assurance or Diffidence, arising from the more, or less apparent Probability of the Proofs' (IV, 16, 14, p. 668).

Locke provides only a few, general remarks on how assent to particular propositions as divinely revealed is to be rationally justified. What he does say, however, indicates what he thinks the broad structure of such a justification must be. First, one must prove that God exists. Locke believed that the existence of God is 'the most obvious truth that reason discovers', that 'its Evidence be (if I mistake not) equal to mathematical Certainty' (IV, 10, 1, p. 619). He presented a version of the cosmological argument which begins from 'a clear Perception of [one's] own Being' (IV, 10, 2, p. 619) to establish the existence of a creator that is eternal, immaterial, knowledgeable and possessing the other perfections of all His creatures in a higher degree. In the second stage of the rational justification of faith one must consider those who have delivered what they claim is a revelation from God. This amounts to examining the miracles which such people were said to have performed. As Locke writes, the holy men who received revelations from God 'have a Power given them to justify the Truth of their Commission from Heaven; and by visible Signs to assent to the divine Authority of the Message they were sent with' (IV, 19, 15, p. 705). Locke believed that if we examine the evidence for the miracles of Jesus, we have sufficient reason to conclude that what he claimed to be God's revelation was in fact such.

Such, then, is Locke's account of the rationality of Christian faith. It is difficult to exaggerate its importance for subsequent reflection on religious questions in Western thought. As Nicholas Wolterstorff has recently written:

> John Locke's philosophy of religion is one of the great creative achievements in the history of philosophy of religion in the West. It has also proved powerfully influential; at least until recently, probably most modern Western intellectuals have thought about the interconnections among reason, responsibility, and religious conviction along Lockean lines.[18]

Indeed, I want to suggest that in its general strategy for dealing with questions of faith and reason, Locke's approach became the dominant model. It was the model in which philosophers were trained. And, perhaps more importantly, it shaped the way non-philosophers spoke about, thought about and practised debate and enquiry regarding religious matters. There were important dissenters from Locke's approach in subsequent centuries, but it became embedded in training and practice so that both philosophers and non-philosophers came to have difficulty imagining an alternative.

Recently, however, some philosophers have raised objections to key claims or presuppositions of the Lockean approach. Alvin Plantinga has challenged what he calls *evidentialism*, a position which Locke espoused. Plantinga's views are summarized by John Greco in Chapter 1 above, in the section 'Foundationalism and philosophy of religion'. The evidentialist holds, first, that some beliefs are rational because they are foundational or (to use Plantinga's term) basic. A belief is basic if it is believed, but is not inferred from other beliefs which serve as evidence for that belief. A belief is *properly basic* if it can be rationally believed as basic. On a foundationalist picture non-basic beliefs are rational because they are inferred from other beliefs. The second key claim of evidentialism is that beliefs that God exists cannot be properly basic. Therefore, if belief in God is to be rational, it must be inferred from other beliefs which constitute one's evidence for the belief that God exists.

Plantinga and others raise the question of why belief in God cannot be properly basic for a believer. Plantinga argues against foundationalist accounts of rationality which attempt to exclude belief in God from the foundations. Moreover, he offers his own account according to which belief in God can be properly basic.

A second sort of objection to a Lockean approach arises from the claim that some have a direct experience or awareness of God. William P. Alston has examined such claims, and summarizes the arguments for and against their veracity in Chapter 2 above, in 'God and religious experience'.

Reports among religious believers that they have had some direct experience of God are quite common. Alston calls these experiences *mystical perceptions*, and asks whether any of them can rationally be taken as genuine or veridical. In the case of ordinary sensory perceptions, when we perceive the existence of people, birds and trees we take these as veridical unless we find compelling reasons to doubt them. By analogous reasoning, it seems we ought to take mystical perceptions as veridical, unless we have compelling reasons to doubt. At this point philosophers offer arguments and counter-arguments for and against the claim that compelling reasons exist for a general doubt about the veridicality of mystical perceptions, but not for a corresponding doubt about ordinary sensory perceptions.

Plantinga and Alston in their discussions tend to focus on the belief that God exists. The central belief of Christian faith, as we have seen, is not the belief that God exists; it is a believing God that certain propositions (i.e. alleged revelations) are true. It would not be difficult, however, to adapt Plantinga's and Alston's arguments to the latter sort of belief. Indeed, as we will see in the next section, Aquinas's account of the rationality of Christian faith understands it as a sort of mystical perception that God has revealed certain specified truths.

We have seen, then, that Plantinga and Alston, as well as others, have raised objections to key aspects of a Lockean approach. Others have responded to these objections, and the debate continues and undoubtedly will continue. It is not the case that either side has marshalled a 'knock-down' argument for or against the rationality of the beliefs of faith.

The point to be emphasized, however, is that the very existence of the controversy attests the failure of Locke's epistemological project. Recall that Locke, finding himself in an age beset by religious and political disputes, felt that progress could be made by focusing on epistemology, on the nature and principles of correct human reasoning. Once such principles were clarified and agreed upon, they could guide subsequent debate and enquiry to a resolution, or to the recognition that certain questions were in doubt. But such a project can only bear fruit if the principles of reasoning are sufficiently clear and obvious that disputing parties can agree on these principles prior to addressing what is at issue among them. But the objections of Plantinga, Alston and others have called into question the possibility of arriving at a non-controversial or neutral set of epistemological principles. For a religious believer may favour a set of principles which reflects what he claims to know or believe, which includes, among other things, that God exists or has revealed certain truths. In other words, disagreements on religious questions can be and are reflected in disagreements about the principles of correct reasoning or rational belief.

It is important to see that what is at issue here is not religious belief itself: Locke was a religious believer, as are Plantinga and Alston. What is at issue is Locke's epistemological project: the hope that a 'neutral' epistemology can provide common principles for the resolution of disputes. This hope has, it seems, evaporated. But this is not to say that an epistemology of religious faith, an account of its rationality, is unimportant. The religious believer, as any other sort of believer, would do well to give an account of how he knows (or rationally believes) what he claims to know (or rationally believe), an account which will reflect, no doubt, the various things he claims to know – and among these are religious beliefs. In order to begin to formulate such an account, I will turn to the thought of St Thomas Aquinas.

St Thomas Aquinas

St Thomas Aquinas (1224/25–1274) was a priest and a member of a religious order called the Order of Preachers which, because it was founded by St Dominic, is more commonly referred to as the *Dominicans*. After extensive studies in philosophy and theology, Aquinas[19] was appointed a professor (or, in Latin, a *magister*) of Christian theology at the University of Paris, which was in the thirteenth century one of the greatest centres of Christian theology which has ever existed. Aquinas was greatly influenced by the philosophy of Aristotle, but as a Christian theologian he strove to bring Aristotelian philosophy into harmony with Christian faith. He was therefore very interested in the question of the reasonableness or rationality of Christian faith.[20]

Although Aquinas lived and wrote four centuries before Locke, many have understood Aquinas's view of the rationality of Christian faith to be very similar to Locke's. According to this interpretation, the Christian believer is first convinced by metaphysical arguments of natural or philosophical theology that God exists. Subsequently he believes on the basis of testimony and other evidence that there were miracles and signs in biblical times and in the history of the Church. From these beliefs he is led to the conclusion that God has made revelations in history, and the essence of these revelations is contained in the Christian Creed as this is defined by the

Church. Thus the individual assents to the propositions of the Creed – which Aquinas calls the *articles of faith* – because he accepts, first, proofs of philosophical theology which purport to show that God exists and, second, arguments from testimony of miracles and signs from Scripture and the history of the Church that what the Church claims to have been God's revelation is in fact such, and hence to be believed.[21]

Despite its wide acceptance, there are profound problems with this interpretation. First, as has been said, Locke thought that in a normal case whether or not one assented to a proposition as divinely revealed is a matter of reason, where reason is understood to involve only a person's natural cognitive faculties.[22] But Aquinas explicitly states that Christian faith requires something more than natural principles:

> But as far as . . . the assent of a human person to those things which belong to faith, two causes can be considered. One is that which leads externally: as a miracle which is witnessed, or the persuasion of another human leading [one] to faith. Neither one of these is a sufficient cause, for of those who witness one and the same miracle, or hear the same speech, some believe and some do not. And therefore we must posit a further interior cause, which moves a human being internally to assent to what belongs to faith . . . . For because a human being who assents to what belongs to faith is elevated above his nature, it must be that this occurs in him from a supernatural principle moving internally, which is God. And therefore faith, as regards the assent of faith (which is the principal act [of the theological virtue] of faith), is due to God moving internally through grace.[23]

Thus, for Aquinas believing the articles of faith is due to something more than reason, at least as Locke understood this term.

Secondly, Locke recognized that on his account the assent of faith is much less certain than that of knowledge. This must be so for there are only probable grounds for believing that some particular proposition has in fact been divinely revealed and that one has understood it correctly. But in his *Commentary on the Sentences of Peter Lombard*, a very early work, Aquinas writes:

> And to the objection that one is not most certain in this doctrine, we say this is false: for one assents more faithfully and firmly to what belongs to faith than [one does] even to the first principles of reason.[24]

And in his work *On Truth*, regarding the firmness of the conviction of the assent of faith, he says 'faith is more certain than all understanding and knowledge . . .'.[25] The first principle of theoretical reason is the principle of non-contradiction, the principle that no proposition can be simultaneously true and false. Therefore these passages from Aquinas imply that the faithful hold the articles of faith with even greater certainty than the principle of non-contradiction. In his more mature works, Aquinas does not make such a strong claim for the certainty of the assent of faith. Nevertheless, he does write in the *Summa Theologiae*:

> With respect to matters having to do with divinity human reason is most deficient: a sign of this is that philosophers, who through investigations of natural reason study human affairs, have fallen into many errors and have contradicted one another. Therefore, so that there would be indubitable and certain cognition about God among humans, it was necessary that divine matters were passed on to them in the manner of faith, as something said by God, who cannot lie.[26]

This passage clearly implies that the beliefs of faith are held with greater certainty than the conclusions of arguments of philosophy and natural theology. But on a Lockean view, philosophical and natural theological arguments are the *grounds* of faith, and so the assent of faith cannot be more certain than these arguments.

Thirdly, Aquinas seems to deny explicitly that a person can come to make the assent of faith simply on the basis of discursive arguments of (what Locke calls) reason. The first question of the First Part of the *Summa Theologiae*, article 8 is headed 'Whether sacred doctrine is argumentative'. Sacred doctrine is the science of revealed Christian theology whose first principles are the articles of faith. Aquinas writes: 'this doctrine does not argue to prove its principles, which are the articles of faith; but from these one proceeds to establish something else ...'.[27] He goes on to say that argument about the articles of faith is possible only when the opponent admits something which is had through revelation. From this premise, some sort of argument can be presented for other truths of faith. 'But if the adversary believes none of the things which have been divinely revealed', he writes, 'there remains no other way to prove the articles of faith through arguments; it is only possible to refute arguments, if any are brought forward against faith.'[28] It seems, then, that arguments which appeal to reason alone cannot of themselves bring a person to faith.

Those who interpret Aquinas along Lockean lines, I conclude, misinterpret him. Such misinterpretation is perhaps not surprising, for one way in which a philosophical model becomes dominant is that its proponents succeed in interpreting philosophers of previous generations in the model's own terms. They interpret past proponents of rival views as saying the same thing they are, for they have become convinced that theirs is the *only* plausible view. But despite the wide acceptance of the Lockean interpretation, Aquinas cannot be plausibly read as a proto-Lockean. His account of the rationality of faith is, however, complex, and a full description and analysis of it cannot be given in this chapter. In what

217

follows I will give a brief summary of what I think is a more accurate interpretation of Aquinas, and one which lets us see Aquinas's view as an alternative to Locke's.[29]

Faith is among what Aquinas calls the *theological virtues*. In order to understand what Aquinas means by this and what the nature of faith is, we must first briefly consider virtue and the good to which virtues are directed.

Aquinas, quoting Aristotle, wrote '"a virtue is what makes the one possessing it good, and renders its work good": hence "the virtue of a human being", about which we are speaking, is "that which makes a human being good, and renders his work good" '.[30] Such a human virtue, as Aquinas understands it, is a steady disposition to act well in some respect or other. The most obvious examples of virtues are moral virtues, which we will call – for reasons which will be explained below – *merely human virtues*. For example, the virtue of courage is the steady disposition to act well (i.e. neither rashly nor with cowardice) when one is faced with a dangerous or difficult situation; whereas the virtue of temperance is a steady disposition to act well (i.e. neither indulgently nor insensitively) when faced with something pleasant. These merely human virtues are directed to what we can call the *merely human good*, which consists in acting in accord with reason. As Aquinas writes, 'it belongs to human virtue to make it that the human being and his work is according to reason'.[31] Courage, for example, is the virtue whereby fear and the desire to flee are subordinated to considerations of reason.

Aquinas, following Aristotle, believed that all humans have a natural aptitude to acquire the merely human virtues, which are virtues proportionate to our nature: 'there exists in us', he writes, 'a natural aptitude to acquire [merely human virtues] – that is, insofar as there is in us by nature an aptitude to obey reason'.[32] This aptitude is not sufficiently strong and steady to be called a habit; it is merely an inclination which Aquinas calls an 'inchoate habit'[33] and a 'seed of virtue'.[34] We will, for the sake of a convenient label, refer to this aptitude as a *rudimentary inclination to virtue*. It is only through training and practice that this mere aptitude, this inclination, becomes the settled and steady disposition which is the virtue of courage. Acquiring the merely human moral virtues is a matter of undergoing this training and practice.

So far we have spoken of the merely human virtues and the merely human good, which consists in activity in accord with reason. Aquinas also believed that through Jesus Christ there is possible for humans a good beyond the merely human good, a *supernatural good*. This good is perfect beatitude or blessedness, which consists in the full vision of God in heaven, and it is the good which humans are called to through Christ. Since this good is supernatural and hence beyond the powers of unaided human reason to attain, its attainment requires the supernatural virtues of faith, hope and charity. These are what Aquinas calls the theological virtues.

In contrast to the merely human virtues, then, the theological virtues direct us to an end which is beyond our nature. Because the end is beyond our nature, there does not naturally exist in us a rudimentary inclination to acquire these virtues. New principles, new inclinations must be instilled in us to attain a supernatural end, and these infused principles are what Aquinas calls the theological virtues:

> In place of natural principles God confers on us theological virtues, by which we are directed to a supernatural end . . . Hence it must be that to these theological virtues there correspond divine habits caused in us, which are related to the theological virtues as the moral and intellectual virtues are related to the natural principles of the virtues.[35]

Aquinas suggests here that what he calls the theological virtues do *not* correspond to the merely human virtues, such as courage or temperance, but *to the rudimentary inclinations we naturally have to these virtues*. Because the theological virtues direct us to something beyond our nature, these principles of action are imperfectly possessed and are not by themselves sufficient to steadily dispose us to act well with regard to our supernatural good. 'That which imperfectly possesses some nature or form, or power', writes Aquinas, 'cannot act through itself, unless it is moved by another.'[36] In addition to the infused theological virtues, then, the person must be moved by another, and the further moving principle is the indwelling Holy Spirit: 'in reason's order to the ultimate, supernatural end, to which it moves insofar as it is in some way and imperfectly formed by the theological virtues, the movement of reason itself is not sufficient, unless there is also added the promptings and movement of the Holy Spirit'.[37] But in order to be moved by the Holy Spirit certain further graces are needed which dispose a person to be readily moved by the Spirit, and these are called *gifts of the Holy Spirit* (*dona Spiritus Sancti*): 'the gifts of the Holy Spirit are certain habits by which a human person is perfected to obey readily the Holy Spirit'.[38] Thus for the 'divine habit' of faith we must consider not only the infused virtue, but also the promptings of the indwelling Holy Spirit and the gifts which enable one to respond readily to these promptings.

What, then, brings a person to the steady and firm assent which is Christian faith? The acquisition of Christian faith must begin, of course, with hearing the Gospel proclaimed. As Aquinas writes:

> Faith is 'from hearing', as is said in Romans 10:17. Hence it must be that some things proposed to a human person for belief are not [proposed] as seen, but as heard, to which he assents through faith.[39]

The mere hearing of the Gospel proclamation is not by itself sufficient to bring a person to faith. For this one must receive an infused intellectual principle, the light of faith, which enables him to understand the Gospel message in a way which will lead to genuine Christian faith:

> As a human person through the natural light of the intellect assents to principles, so the virtuous person through the virtuous habit has correct judgement about the things which concern that virtue. And in this way through the light of faith divinely infused a person also assents to these things which belong to faith, but not to their contraries. And therefore there is 'no' danger nor 'condemnation in those who are in Christ Jesus' (Romans 8:1), by whom we have been illumined through faith.[40]

But just what sort of understanding is attained through the infused light of faith? To answer this we must consider the two gifts associated with faith. They are the Gift of Understanding (*donum intellectus*) and the Gift of Knowledge (*donum scientiae*).

As understanding precedes judgement, so the Gift of Understanding proceeds that of Knowledge, which concerns judgement. Faith, as was said, begins with hearing the Gospel proclaimed. In the normal case, once an utterance is heard, understanding it would consist in understanding the meanings of the words uttered – or, as Aquinas would say, in grasping the forms or essences of things signified by the words heard. One might initially think that the role of the intellect strengthened by the infused light of faith and the Gift of Understanding is to grasp the forms or essences of those things signified by the words in the proclamation of faith. Some of what Aquinas says might be taken to suggest this.[41] But it is clear from a consideration of Aquinas's texts that even a believer whose cognition is strengthened by the grace of faith cannot in this life grasp the divine essence, which is spoken of in the articles of faith. Such a grasp of God's essence would be to enjoy the state of beatitude, a state in which one does not have faith.[42] In this life growth in understanding consists in the negative understanding that God surpasses whatever we might imagine him to be.[43]

The Gift of Understanding, rather, enables the person to understand the propositions of faith *as divinely revealed*. Aquinas writes: 'although not all having faith fully understand the things which are proposed to be believed, they nevertheless understand that these things are to be believed and that one ought not deviate from them for any reason'.[44] The Gift of Understanding, which the faithful enjoy, does not give any positive understanding of God's essence or of other things or events mentioned in the Creed. Rather, the faithful understand that these propositions were divinely revealed and so they are to be believed and for no reason is one to deviate from adherence to them. To return to the phrase of William Alston employed above in our discussion of Locke, Aquinas seems to be speaking of a sort of 'mystical perception' that these propositions have been revealed by God.

Having grasped that the propositions of faith are to be believed, the prospective believer subsequently judges them to be true. Since the prospective believer lacks the understanding which comes with perfect knowledge, Aquinas believes, the assent requires a deliberate act of will; and this act of will in turn requires a distinct gift or grace from God. This is the 'Gift of Knowledge':

> And therefore two things are required for the human intellect to assent perfectly to the truth of faith. The first of these is that one soundly grasps the things which are proposed; and this pertains to the Gift of Understanding, as has been said. But the other is that one has certain and correct judgement about these matters, distinguishing what is to be believed from what is not to be believed; and for this the Gift of Knowledge is necessary.[45]

In summary, then, faith must begin with a hearing of the Gospel, the essentials of which are contained in the Creed, which is proclaimed as divinely revealed. This requires no infused light. Subsequently, by virtue of the infused light of faith and with the theological virtue along with the Gift of Understanding, the prospective believer, by a non-discursive intuition, understands the articles of faith as propositions to be believed on divine authority and to which he should adhere in spite of considerations to the contrary. Finally, through a second operation of the infused light and with the theological virtue along with the Gift of Knowledge, one immediately (i.e. not as the result of discursive reasoning) assents to the articles as divinely revealed. Unlike assent to principles naturally known, Aquinas believes this assent requires a deliberate act of the will co-operating with grace, and so it is voluntary and meritorious.

We must add to this interpretation something about the evidence from miracles recorded in Scripture and in histories of the Church, for Aquinas clearly implies that this plays a role in bringing one to faith.[46] Although Aquinas does not discuss this issue at any length, in his *Commentary on the Sentences of Peter Lombard*, he suggests that such evidence disposes the will to command assent:

> An argument which is adduced in accord with faith does not make seen what is believed; and hence the difficulty of the work, as it is in itself, is not diminished. But with respect to [the work] in itself, [the argument] makes the will more prompt to believe.[47]

And in the *Summa Theologiae* Aquinas meets the objection that the argument from the evidence of miracles and the intuitive certainty due to grace cannot *both* play a role in bringing one to faith, when he writes:

221

> Through knowledge (*scientia*) faith also is nourished in the manner of external persuasion (*modum exterioris persuasionis*), which comes to be from a certain sort of knowledge. But the principle and proper cause of faith is that which moves internally to assent.[48]

That which moves internally is the infused, theological virtue and the promptings of the Holy Spirit moving someone with the gifts; this is, Aquinas says, the principle and proper cause of faith. But what role does the evidence from miracles have, moving 'through the manner of external persuasion'? Aquinas's point seems to be that such evidence serves to dispose one's will to prompt assent to the articles of faith in light of the interior cause of faith. Although the interior cause is primary in bringing one to assent, it does not compel it; a person who is resistant, although he may hear the Gospel proclaimed, may believe only reluctantly, or even refuse assent. The evidence from miracles disposes a person to be moved by the primary, interior cause of faith.

Perhaps the role of the argument from the evidence of miracles can be made clear by the following analogy. Consider two undergraduate students, Frank and Mary, who are good friends. Frank is very impressed by the evidence for extra-sensory perception, and he is trying to convince his sceptical friend Mary that she should take these phenomena seriously. A speaker is coming to deliver a lecture on such phenomena, and though Frank urges Mary to go, Mary does not think the topic is serious enough that she should take the time to attend a lecture on it. Frank, however, tells Mary about the speaker's renown as a serious scientist and of his substantial accomplishments in research. Mary is sufficiently impressed, and agrees to attend the lecture. Because of her newly acquired respect for the speaker, Mary listens carefully, considers the evidence adduced judiciously, and by the end is convinced that such phenomena are important and should be taken seriously.

The evidence from miracles with regard to faith, I would suggest, plays a role similar to Frank's presentation in the story above of the speaker's scientific reputation and accomplishments. They do not convince Mary that what the speaker says should be believed; rather, they dispose her to take the speaker's lecture seriously and consider the arguments and evidence he presents carefully. When Mary is convinced of the speaker's claims, it is his *arguments and evidence* which convince her, not Frank's claims about the speaker's reputation and past accomplishments. However, Frank's arguments are important for convincing Mary to go to the lecture, and disposing her to consider seriously the arguments and evidence which eventually convince her. Similarly, the argument from the evidence of miracles is important in bringing one to attend to and take seriously what is put forward for belief in the proclamation of the Gospel. However, it is the interior movement of grace and the Holy Spirit which is primary in bringing one to see that these truths have been divinely revealed and are to be believed.

Despite a superficial similarity between Locke and Aquinas regarding the grounds for faith, I contend that the differences are profound. For Locke the natural philosophical arguments for God's existence and the evidence of miracles, as unaided reason discovers and evaluates these considerations, provide the sole grounds for the assent of faith. Moreover the firmness of this assent ought to be proportioned to the perceived weight of this evidence. This view implies that, if the assent of faith is to be firm, one must formulate a relatively rigorous metaphysical argument that God exists; and one must give compelling considerations that miracles occurred; one must also present arguments, as Locke does, that an individual ought to undertake serious study and careful evaluation of the evidence regarding religious claims. Aquinas does speak about the evidence from miracles, but for him this plays a different role in the assent of faith. It is not the sole *ground* for the assent of faith, but only a consideration which disposes a person's will to an assent whose primary cause is the infused virtue and the promptings of the indwelling Spirit, which enable him to see that certain propositions have been revealed and hence are to be believed. For Aquinas, then, rigorous metaphysical and historical arguments are not necessary prior to faith. One need not construct a metaphysical system and rigorously examine historical evidence before assenting to the claims of Christian faith.

The most fundamental reason for the differences between Locke and Aquinas is that they were engaged in very different efforts. Locke, with his epistemological project, first sought to establish universal, neutral principles of reason which all parties to debates would accept. To discover these, he had to set aside any religious beliefs or experiences, for these might be in dispute among people. He then asked whether, on the basis of these principles, it was rational to assent to the claims of Christian faith. Aquinas, on the other hand, was not engaged in Locke's epistemological project, was not seeking neutral principles of reason. He was trying to formulate an account of the rationality of Christian beliefs given all he thought he knew – which included the propositions of Christian faith. His account of reason was therefore shaped by many of his theological convictions as well as other beliefs.

John Jenkins CSC

Faith and philosophy

Undoubtedly objections can be raised to Aquinas's account of the rationality of Christian faith, just as they were to Locke's. I have not attempted to establish here that Aquinas's account is superior to any alternative. I have simply tried to present it as an alternative – to enable us to see it as an alternative.

People often come to philosophy seeking definitive answers to the important questions of human life. They quickly learn, however, that in most cases one can only hope through the study of philosophy to attain a clearer, more elaborate and better-justified stance on these questions. If one is honest, one recognizes that there are other plausible positions, that there are objections to one's own, and that debate and enquiry must continue. Philosophy does not seem to provide answers so definitive as to preclude further questions, objections or alternative perspectives. But it is perhaps just this fact about philosophical enquiry which leads some to seek answers to life's deepest questions in a teaching beyond the merely human teaching of any philosophical doctrine. It is just this which leads some to believe that the most profound teaching is one whose truth cannot be manifest to our human intellects, but is one which nevertheless demands of us a response of faith.

Notes

1 In this chapter I will use the words 'reasonable' and 'rational' and their cognates as synonyms.
2 C. Johannes Botterweck and Helmer Rugen (eds), *Theological Dictionary of the Old Testament*, vol. I, trans. John T. Wills (Grand Rapids, 1974), p. 308.
3 For an account of the development of these doctrines, see J. N. D. Kelly, *Early Christian Doctrines* (San Francisco, 1978).
4 Extremely important in the history of Christianity is the Reformation dispute about the nature of faith. For St Thomas Aquinas, the foremost theologian in the Roman Catholic tradition, the faith which is merely believing God that certain propositions are true is genuine faith, but it is what he calls 'unformed' or 'lifeless' faith (*Summa Theologiae* II-II, 4, 4; 6, 2). Formed faith was a faith perfected or completed by the theological virtues of hope and love. Formed faith leads to salvation, but unformed faith does not.

  Martin Luther attacked this distinction. For him unformed faith is a 'counterfeit faith' in which one 'hears about God, Christ, and all the mysteries of the incarnation and redemption, one that also grasps and hears and can speak beautifully about it; and yet only a mere opinion and vain hearing remain, the hollow sound about the Gospel . . . ' (*Luther's Works*, ed. Helmut T. Lehmann, vol. xxvi: *Lectures on Galatians* [Philadelphia, 1966], p. 269). Thus, for Luther, it seems that mere opinion that the Gospel proclamation is true is not genuine faith. True faith, Luther believes, is not a faith formed by love, but is, on one hand, a despair that one's own works and merits can save oneself, and on the other hand, a clinging to Christ with complete confidence that one is saved by and through him alone. 'Eternal life is granted to us', writes Luther, 'not for our own merits and works but for our faith, by which we take hold of Christ. Therefore we, too, acknowledge a quality and a formal righteousness in the heart; but we do not mean love, as the sophists do, but faith, because the heart must behold and grasp nothing but Christ the Savior' (p. 133).

5 This translation is from *Plato: Five Dialogues,* trans. G. M. A. Grube (Indianapolis, 1981).

6 One's degree of belief in a proposition is the level of one's certainty about the truth of that belief. We might get a rough idea of what this is by asking a person how much he is willing to bet that the proposition believed is true.

7 It is important that we are asking whether the person of faith *can* be rational, not whether all are in fact rational. It may be that there are perfectly good reasons for believing some proposition, P, and indeed it may be that most who believe P do so with good reasons, yet that some believe P for bad reasons. For example, I may believe that the stock market will fall next year because I have consulted many financial experts and they all agree that there will be a downturn. My friend George, however, believes the market will fall solely because his astrologer told him so. Though we hold the same belief, my belief is rational and George's is not.

8 Richard Swinburne's significant contributions to the philosophy of religion, which have been admirable in their clarity and care of their reasoning, provide a good example of this ahistorical approach. (See, for example, his *Faith and Reason* [Oxford, 1981].)

9 Charles Taylor, 'Philosophy and its history' in *Philosophy in History: Essays on the Historiography of Philosophy*, ed. Richard Rorty, J. B. Schneewind and Quentin Skinner (New York, 1984), p. 17. Another very important author who argues for the importance of the history of philosophy for philosophy is Alasdair MacIntyre. See 'The relationship of philosophy to its past', ibid., pp. 31–48; and *Whose Justice? Which Rationality?* (Notre Dame, 1988), esp. ch. 18.

10 The emergence and eventual ascendency of this model can be traced through Hugo Grotius (1585–1645), a Dutch jurist, statesman and legal and political philosopher; Samuel von Pufendorf (1632–94), a German statesman and legal and political philosopher; John Locke (1632–1704), an English philosopher who is discussed on pp. 208–15 above; and Jean-Jacques Rousseau (1712–78), a French philosopher.

11 'The Enlightenment' is a commonly used label for a collection of ideas and movements which arose and held sway in seventeenth- and eighteenth-century Europe and America. Although the thinkers and doctrines identified with the Enlightenment are diverse, the term does pick out a broad intellectual movement which has greatly influenced Western thought generally, and in particular views on the relationship between faith and reason. Central to the Enlightenment was the extolling of reason over (what was portrayed as) superstition or blind obedience to authority or convention.

12 René Descartes (1590–1650) is often portrayed as the originator of what I am calling the epistemological project. However, Nicholas Wolterstorff has argued persuasively that those who read Descartes in this way misread him. Wolterstorff contends that on the issue of what Wolterstorff calls 'a general ethic of belief' (which is closely related to what I am calling the epistemological project), Descartes's writings reflect a medieval understanding rather

than a modern one, and that Locke was 'the first great modern'. ('What is cartesian doubt?', *American Catholic Philosophical Quarterly* 67 [Autumn 1993], p. 468.)

13 In the 'Epistle to the Reader' at the beginning of the *Essay* Locke tells us that the work arose from a discussion among 'five or six Friends meeting at my Chamber', but does not mention the subject under discussion. However, James Tyrrell was one of these friends, and in a manuscript note in his copy of the *Essay* Tyrrell wrote that the discussion in which Locke 'first raised the issue of human understanding' was 'about the principles of morality and religion'. (See Maurice Cranston, *John Locke: A Biography* [New York, 1957], pp. 140–1.)

14 John Locke, 'Epistle to the Reader' in *An Essay Concerning Human Understanding*, ed. Peter H. Nidditch (Oxford, 1975), p. 7. Hereafter all references to Locke's essay will be to this edition. References will give in order the book, chapter, chapter section and page number.

15 For a good history of this period, see Justo L. González, *The Story of Christianity*, vol. II: *The Reformation to the Present Day* (San Francisco, 1985), parts I and II.

16 Locke thought that 'GOD has furnished Men with Faculties sufficient to direct them in the Way they should take, if they will but seriously employ them that Way, when their ordinary Vocations allow them the Leisure. No Man is so wholly taken up with the Attendance on the Means of Living, as to have no spare Time at all to think of his Soul, and inform himself in Matters of Religion. Were Men as intent upon this, as they are on Things of lower Concernment, there are none so enslaved to the Necessities of Life, who might not find many Vacancies, that might be husbanded to this Advantage of their Knowledge' (IV, 20, 3, p. 708).

17 These principles are summarized and discussed in Nicholas Wolterstorff, *John Locke and the Ethics of Belief* (Cambridge Studies in Religion and Critical Thought; Cambridge, 1996), ch. 1, section d, 'Belief and its governance'. My summary of Locke's views is greatly indebted to Wolterstorff's work.

18 Nicholas Wolterstorff, 'Locke's philosophy of religion' in *The Cambridge Companion to Locke*, ed. Vere Chappell (Cambridge, 1994), p. 172.

19 Thomas Aquinas was known in his own day as Thomas d'Aquino – Thomas of Aquino, since he and his family were from what was then the county of Aquino, which was between Rome and Naples. Later writers have taken to referring to Thomas as simply Aquinas, and I will follow this convention (even though Thomas's contemporaries would not have referred to him in this way).

20 For a good, recent biography of Aquinas see Jean-Pierre Torrell's *Saint Thomas Aquinas*, vol. I: *The Person and His Work*, trans. Robert Royal (Washington, DC, 1996).

21 This reading is embraced by John Hick in *Faith and Knowledge* (Ithaca, NY, 1966), pp. 20–1; by Terence Penelhum in 'The analysis of faith in St Thomas Aquinas', *Religious Studies* 3 (1977), p. 145; by Alvin Plantinga in 'Reason and belief in God' in *Faith and Rationality: Reason and Belief in God*, ed. A. Plantinga and N. Wolterstorff (Notre Dame, 1983), pp. 40–7; and by Louis P. Pojman in *Religious Belief and the Will* (New York, 1986), pp. 32–40.

22 Locke acknowledged the possibility that God might reveal that certain propositions were divinely revealed (IV, xviii, 6, p. 693). But he obviously thought that this was highly unusual, and he does not seriously entertain the possibility when, for example, he discusses the claims of Enthusiasm.

23 *Summa Theologiae* II-II, 6, 1. This translation and all translations of Aquinas's

works in the chapter are mine. When citing Aquinas's *Summa Theologiae*, I follow the convention of giving the part, question, article, and part of the article. If there is no reference to a part of the article, the reference is to the corpus.

24 *Commentary on the Sentences of Peter Lombard* I, *prologus* quest. 1, art. 3, sol. 3.
25 *On Truth* quest. 14, art. 1, resp. 7.
26 *Summa Theologiae* II-II, 2, 4; see also *Summa Theologiae* I, 1, 1.
27 *Summa Theologiae* I, 1, 8.
28 Ibid.
29 A fuller account of Aquinas's views can be found in ch. 6 of my book *Knowledge and Faith in Thomas Aquinas* (Cambridge, 1997).
30 *Summa Theologiae* II-II, 123, 1; the quotation from Aristotle is from *Nicomachean Ethics*, Book II, ch. 6, 1106a 15–23.
31 Ibid.
32 *Commentary on Aristotle's Nicomachean Ethics*, Book II, lect. 1, para. 249.
33 *Summa Theologiae* I-II, 50, 1.
34 Ibid.; *Summa Theologiae* I-II, 83, 1.
35 *Summa Theologiae* I-II, 63, 3.
36 Ibid.
37 Ibid.
38 *Summa Theologiae* I-II, 68, 3.
39 *Summa Theologiae* II-II, 8, 6. See also II-II, 6, 1. In both these passages, Aquinas is speaking of the normal route to faith, and not that of those who saw the risen Christ, such as the Apostles.
40 *Summa Theologiae* II-II, 2, 3, *ad* 2.
41 E.g. *Summa Theologiae* II-II, 8, 1.
42 *Summa Theologiae* I, 12, 1.
43 *Summa Theologiae* II-II, 8, 8.
44 *Summa Theologiae* II-II, 8, 4, *ad* 2.
45 *Summa Theologiae* II-II, 9, 1.
46 *Summa Theologiae* II-II, 2, 1, *ad* 1; II-II, 2, 9, *ad* 3; II-II, 6, 1.
47 *Commentary on the Sentences of Peter Lombard* III, dist. 24, quest. 1, art. 3, sol. 3.
48 Ibid.

8

Philosophy and Christianity

Hugo Meynell

The best brief formula to describe the relation between the faith of Christians and their philosophy seems to me that due to Anselm: 'faith seeking understanding'. The understanding of Christianity roughly divides into two parts – seeing how self-consistent or inconsistent it is, and providing other reasons for believing or disbelieving it. A student once asked me, in some exasperation, 'How *many* Christian doctrines are there?' This suggested that she felt that they were just a collection of claims, without rhyme or reason; one would expect a Christian philosophy to show how they all tend to reflect and enhance one another, their 'form' as Hans Urs von Balthasar would have said; while an anti-Christian philosophy might delight in trying to bring out their pointlessness or arbitrariness.

The claim is still sometimes made that there is something basically incoherent about Christianity as such; that fully to 'understand' it is to see that it is at bottom unintelligible, or that it depends on some latent contradiction.[1] But this claim seems generally to be based on barely repressed logical positivist assumptions which would almost universally be repudiated now when made explicit. Even the late J. L. Mackie, who was certainly no friend to Christianity or any kind of theism, pointed out that it certainly cannot be refuted on the basis of logical positivism, which itself is demonstrably incoherent[2] since the 'verification principle' which is diagnostic of logical positivism, when consistently applied, shows that it itself is nonsense – being neither true by definition, nor such that it can even in principle be verified or falsified by sense-experience.

It is tempting simply to reject the verification principle root and branch. But it is more useful, I think, to take it as masking an important insight. A statement which is not merely formal surely does not amount to much, unless its being the case could in principle make a difference to the course of someone's experience. That Christian believers make claims with massive implications of this kind, but (when intellectually sophisticated) are apt to withdraw the implications in the face of modern science and scholarship and the facts of evil and suffering, has been argued in a short paper by Antony Flew which amounts to a minor classic.[3] However, while the faith of some educated 'Christians' *may* have died Flew's 'death of the thousand qualifications', there is no good reason why it *must* do so. In reply to Flew, Ian Crombie pointed out that there are three kinds of claim made by traditional Christianity that have a bearing on actual or conceivable experience, which are a matter respectively of future expectation, past history, and the course of the present life. Christians expect some kind of life after death where injustices will be corrected;[4] they believe that the historical Jesus spoke and acted at least roughly in the manner depicted by the four Gospels; and they may think that other people, even if not yet themselves, have some experience of divine help and guidance through the perplexities and difficulties of living here and now.

Christianity obviously presupposes theism;[5] it also, in its classical form at least,[6] is committed to the doctrines of the Trinity, the Incarnation and the Atonement. How are these to be understood? And if we can gain some understanding of them, can we provide any reason for believing that they are true, or false for that matter?

In the face of actual or possible embarrassments arising from developments in New Testament scholarship, it has become quite fashionable for some sophisticated 'believers' to reject an assumption which has been made almost universally by believers and unbelievers alike – that Christianity, at least in its traditional sense, presupposes the overall historical veracity of the Gospel narratives. To forestall an objection which might be made at this point – obviously there is *more to* Christianity being true than for the Gospel narratives to be at least roughly veracious. But that does not imply that Christianity could somehow be true all the same, if they were not. As philosophers would put it, their general veracity is not a *sufficient* condition of the truth of Christianity, but it does appear to be a *necessary* condition of it. One should not need to spell out this point; yet it does seem to be rather frequently overlooked. To deny it seems to be rather like maintaining that a scientific theory could be correct while none of the observational and experimental reports on which it was supposed to depend were true.[7]

Michael Dummett has written that many New Testament scholars, including some who would call themselves Christians, operate on two assumptions: that Jesus did not have sources of knowledge that are not shared by other human beings; and that Christianity as traditionally believed and formulated is founded not on what he said and thought about himself, but on what was proclaimed about him by his immediate followers after his death. But Dummett says that these assumptions are clearly incompatible with the historical presuppositions of the Christian faith. He adds, however, that they also imply in the disciples a degree of mendacity or mental instability which do not consort at all well with what we know that they achieved.[8]

If God must exist for Christianity to be true, and if there are also historical truth-conditions of Christianity, it may well be inferred that there are at least two kinds of investigation which are relevant to the defence or refutation of Christianity. Metaphysical arguments may confirm or impugn belief that there is a God; historical arguments the claim that Jesus acted and spoke in the kind of way that Christian faith presupposes that he did. But it may be protested that the whole business of arguing that a metaphysical 'God' must exist to account for the world or some feature of it, or that the historical Jesus must have acted and spoken in one kind of way rather than another, is totally irrelevant to the reality of religion. Religious faith as it actually exists, and always has existed, has nothing to fear from the failure of such arguments; but neither would it gain anything from their success. The God of the Bible, at least, is the object of worship, and that which is addressed in prayer – in fact, that with which one has to do in the religious form of life; not a subject for philosophical or quasi-scientific speculation, at the mercy of arguments based on principles supposed to be acceptable to believers and unbelievers alike. One should in fact rather say that the believer and the atheist see different worlds[9] than that there is one world, such that they may profitably dispute whether or not there is a 'God' in some kind of relation to it. The most distinguished and prolific defender of this view is D. Z. Phillips,[10] who has used for this purpose some thoughts of the later Wittgenstein. Religious faith, argues Phillips, is not a hypothesis which might depend on evidence, or be shown to be so or not so as a result of the kind of argument employed in science or traditional philosophy. For the believer in the God of the Bible, God's reality is inescapable; this is illustrated by Psalm 139, where the writer exclaims that he would remain in God's presence even if he journeyed into the heights of heaven or the depths of hell.[11] Outside the specifically religious contexts of prayer and worship, the term 'God' exemplifies what Wittgenstein called 'language gone on holiday'. And the moral may be applied to all attempts to 'prove' or 'disprove' the existence of that abstraction that some people call 'God' but which has nothing to do with what is worshipped and prayed to by the genuine religious believer.

Those who are less than happy with Phillips's conception of the relation between religion and philosophy may argue somewhat as follows. It would usually be conceded to Phillips that faith is in an important sense not a hypothesis or a collection of hypotheses. But there are a number of ways in which a claim, or what may be taken to be a claim, can fail to be a hypothesis: (1) one can take it for granted; (2) one may hold it confidently rather than tentatively or provisionally; (3) one may be sure that relevant evidence, if it did turn up, would tend to confirm it; or (4) it may not really amount to a 'claim' in the ordinary sense at all, but rather (say) an expression of feeling or self-commitment to a moral stance. The faith of a religious person might be non-hypothetical in any of the first three senses, without being so in the fourth; and it may be argued that this is and has been so in the case of the great majority of believers. Paul's insistence, in the First Epistle to the Corinthians, that the Christian faith stands or falls with the resurrection of Jesus, and that the occurrence of this event could be established in his own time by appeal to witnesses,[12] shows as clearly as could well be that the Apostle's Christian faith, while being non-hypothetical in the second and third senses that I distinguished, is not so in the fourth. As to the Psalmist, it may reasonably be supposed that his faith was much like that of other Jews in pre-Christian times – in a God who had performed particular actions in the past on behalf of his people, like rescuing them from bondage in Egypt by a series of mighty deeds, and would so act in the future. But such faith, however confident and free from doubt, is in a sense hypothetical; since it is surely a theoretical possibility that no such events had happened in the past as were construed as the saving acts of God, or would happen in time to come. I infer, in contradiction to Phillips, that the most natural reading of the Psalm in question is that it is a sense of the presence of a God who has acted and would act in these ways that the Psalmist finds inescapable.

An unsympathetic critic might suggest that Phillips's 'God', so far from being that on which the whole universe depends for its existence, is rather dependent on human religious practices and on the experiences that people enjoy when they engage in them. Now we assume as a matter of course, if we are sane, that our sense-experience puts us in touch with a world of objects which exist prior to and independently of us and our experience. This is not because philosophers have ever propounded a generally acceptable theory of how and why we have a right to do so, which notoriously they have not. Why, it might be asked, should not the same apply to religious experience? May we not properly be said to perceive an independently existing God through our religious or mystical experience, much as we perceive physical objects through our sense-experience? This line of thought has been elaborated at length and with great skill by William P. Alston.[13]

As Alston sees it, sense-perception is properly to be described as perceiving an actual or supposed object as dark blue, jagged, harshly noisy, or whatever. Similarly, mystics have 'perceived' their actual or supposed God as merciful, forgiving, all-knowing, and so on.[14] It is not as easy as the sceptic might suppose to impugn the suggested parallel between sense experience as alleged grounds for knowledge of objects assumed to be independently real on the one hand, and a real God as similarly given to religious experience on the other. It might be urged, for example, that sense-experience is publicly verifiable as putting us in touch with a real world in a way that religious experience is not. But believers often find that, when they join together in prayer and worship, they have experience together as of a God who is all-knowing, merciful and so on. Could not the person who fails in these circumstances to have such an experience be analogous to one who is tone-deaf or lacking in a sense of smell? As Alston says, the fact that some people have such experiences, while others do not, explains the fact that many people of high intelligence are unbelievers, but many are believers; in a substantial proportion of cases at least, the believers will have had the relevant experiences, the unbelievers not.[15]

I would agree with Alston that, if God exists, it is not unreasonable to say that 'perceptions of God' (or perhaps one had better say, to avoid begging any questions, ' "perceptions" *as of* God') can properly be described as really perceptions of God. But I would emphasize, more strongly than I think he would,[16] that the main weight of the question whether there is good reason to think that God exists must lie on other types of argument. If there are no other sound arguments for God's existence, it seems to me that one ought to conclude that 'perceptions' as of God are not really perceptions of God. One might believe in the existence of an aunt in Australia on the evidence of letters supposed to be written by her; and even come to have what might subjectively seem to be a relationship of great intimacy with this individual. Presumably those who have had relatively intense 'experiences' as of God, but have later ceased to believe that there is a God, are in a state of mind rather like that of such a person after convincing evidence had been shown to them that the letters had been faked.

It might be naively suggested that one is justified in being a Christian so far as there is good evidence for the truth of Christianity; not if there is not so. But it has been objected to this that it presupposes an epistemological 'evidentialism' which is at best dubious; one may instead be a 'reliabilist', that is to say, a person who maintains that beliefs are acceptable so far as they have been arrived at by a 'reliable belief-producing mechanism'.[17] But it seems to me that we have here a distinction without a difference. Either the reason why one's 'belief-producing mechanism' is 'reliable' can in principle be shown, or it cannot. If it cannot, the claim that it is reliable is merely arbitrary; and what is asserted arbitrarily may just as well be denied. But if it can be shown, one seems to be back with some kind of 'evidentialism'; since it is difficult to see what other kind of justification could be given for the judgement that one's belief-producing mechanism is reliable other than that it is a matter of maintaining or rejecting beliefs in accordance with the relevant evidence. Beliefs held on authority do not really constitute an exception; I have good evidence that what the British Astronomer Royal has to say about globular clusters is more likely to be correct than the opinions on the subject of my five-year-old grandson.

The recently fashionable tendency to treat 'evidentialist'[18] as a term of abuse seems due to the supposed fact that there are fatal objections to the view that human knowledge has or ought to have foundations. It is often argued that all foundationalist claims are vitiated by infinite regress. Whenever any candidate for the foundations of knowledge is proposed, the objector can ask 'What is the justification of this being taken as foundational?' When some answer is given, the question can be repeated; and so on for ever. In any case, the most obvious candidates for foundations of knowledge, logic and sense-experience, are by themselves hopelessly inadequate for the purpose; one gets nowhere without hypothesis-formation, which has never been reduced to rule. Also, the view that the sole foundations of knowledge are logic and experience seems to lead to logical positivism, which is demonstrably untenable for the reasons that we have already sketched. And, after all, the view itself, that the sole foundations of knowledge are logic and experience, can hardly be founded on either logic or experience.

It is interesting that the logical positivists did not by and large, in spite of the collapse of the foundations which they had proposed, become sceptics or relativists; they merely affirmed the basic beliefs constitutive of the scientific world-view. But if they can affirm such basic beliefs, which may be maintained without appeal to other beliefs, but from which these others can properly be derived, why cannot the theist claim that the same applies to belief that there is a God?[19] This position has been adopted by such 'Reformed epistemologists' as Alvin Plantinga and Nicholas Wolterstorff. Alston has put it that for the foundationalist, our epistemic practices are guilty until proved innocent; whereas for the 'Reformed' epistemologist, they are innocent until proved guilty.[20] Phillips objects to both positions, that the very notion of an external justification is a confused one in the religious context.[21] This I find rather surprising. Some sorts of talk seem irrational, at least in the light of what we know now; others immoral. Thus talk about the world in terms of phlogiston is irrational in the light of evidence now available to scientists; it would lead one to expect, for example, that a metal would be heavier than (what we now call) its oxide, when in fact it is lighter. Again, it is said that in South Africa, until very recently at least, if one used the noun 'kaffir' as the subject of a sentence, it amounted to a sort of grammatical error to employ a polite predicate. Kaffir-talk, in fact, was not only misleading as to what was the case – it made one assume that no South African of black race was to be admired as very intelligent, cultured or morally virtuous – but evinced a corrupt moral attitude as well. How could it *not even make sense* to claim, as so many have in fact done, that the same applies to God-talk? What is so absurd about the claim that it not only distorts the facts, but involves a dishonest evasion of obvious experience, to believe that human life is directed by a benign Providence, in the light of the crying horror and misery which confront us in this world?

The obvious trouble with the 'Reformed' position is quite simply that, if the theist pleads that the existence of God may be a 'properly basic belief', it is difficult to see why any bizarre tenet whatever cannot be defended on the same grounds. Why should not belief that Adolf Hitler was assumed bodily into heaven, or that Down's syndrome is caused by witchcraft, be also properly basic at this rate? The point can be generalized into an objection to anti-foundationalism which may seem to be as decisive as it is obvious. If one takes literally the view that knowledge has no foundations, it seems to follow that no judgement is any better founded than its contradictory; and total scepticism or relativism inevitably ensues.

Of course Plantinga is too thorough a philosopher not to have considered this objection. Can one claim that belief in God is properly basic, he asks, without implicitly allowing the same privilege for any absurd belief whatever, like belief in the Great Pumpkin which returns regularly at Halloween? Certainly one can, he says. It is true that the Reformed epistemologist rejects the criteria for proper basicality proposed by classical foundationalists. But these all seem to be self-destructive, for the reasons pointed out in connection with logical positivism; or subject to the problem of infinite regress. Is the objection, then, that Reformed epistemologists not only reject the criteria just mentioned, but seem unable or unwilling to produce any of their own? But surely, says Plantinga, one has a right at least to reject some propositions as not properly basic, without meeting any such condition. I might properly, for example, reject as properly basic the denial of something that seemed self-evident to me, like that there are trees, or that I see a tree here and now, without being able to produce on demand reasons for some beliefs being properly basic. It is not to be denied, Plantinga admits, that 'some propositions seem self-evident when in fact they are not'; but this concession, he insists, in no way impugns his argument.[22]

Yet devotees of the Great Pumpkin may just as well say that the belief of the theist is absurd; much as one influential modern atheist philosopher has suggested that no cultured and intelligent modern individual can believe in God except by a miracle.[23] Unless some criterion for proper basicality is offered, believers in the Great Pumpkin can be put in the wrong only by mere assertion. Belief that there is a God happens to be still quite respectable in some intellectual circles; but then, so at one time was belief that the earth was at the centre of the cosmos. A thousand years ago, to maintain that the earth went round the sun would presumably have seemed almost as absurd to most people as to maintain that the Great Pumpkin returns every Halloween does now. By what right do we insist that the latter proposition is intrinsically more absurd than the former, unless we can offer some kind of a reason why it is so?

In spite of the ingenuity of Plantinga's arguments to the contrary, it looks as though criteria were needed for absurdity, non-absurdity and propriety in basic beliefs, other than the mere assertion of influential persons or groups. Plantinga rightly says that some proposed criteria for proper basicality suffer from self-referential incoherence. But do they all do so? I would argue that they do not. One is inclined to say, as a first approximation, that a belief is worthy of assent so far as there is more evidence for it than against it. There is now abundant evidence that the earth goes round the sun, and not *vice versa*; some informed persons, like the philosopher Richard Swinburne and the physicist John Polkinghorne, would claim that there is substantial evidence for the existence of God,[24] and even for the truth of Christianity.[25] As to the objections to foundationalism, I believe that they are to be met by appeal to what may be called basic method, which includes logic and sense-experience (thus far the logical positivists were on the right track) but goes beyond them.[26] It is from basic method that the principle which I mentioned above, that a belief is worthy of credence so far as there is adequate evidence for it, is to be derived.

Fully to justify this position would evidently take us far beyond the scope of this discussion; but something must be said, in the face of contemporary fashions, by way of its exposition and defence. Basic method is properly foundational in that the contradictories of its constitutive principles are self-destructive – I cannot truly judge that I never judge truly, or rationally judge that I never make a judgement rationally. Furthermore, true judgements are nothing other than what we tend to make in so far as we are as rational as possible in making them. One is rational to the extent that one is attentive, intelligent and reasonable;[27] that is, so far as one attends to the relevant experience in any case; envisages the possible explanations; and judges that possibility to be (probably or certainly) so which is best corroborated by the experience. Deductive logic greatly facilitates the application of intelligence and reasonableness to experience, but is no replacement for it. One has to propound the hypotheses from which deductions are to be made; and one has to match the deductions with items of experience – and neither procedure is reducible to logic in the strict sense. (It might be objected that these things are a matter of 'inductive' as opposed to 'deductive' logic; but it appears to me that 'inductive logic' is no more than a misleading term for all the principles of basic method which are reducible neither to sense-experience nor to deductive logic.) Reality, or the actual world, is nothing other than what true judgements are about, and rational judgements tend to be about; metaphysics, or the most general theory of reality, is related to epistemology as the overall articulation of the nature of what is to be known is related to that of the process by which it is to be known. The natural and human sciences apply basic method to particular ranges of data.[28] This brings us back to the claim that Christianity stands or falls with the truth of certain historical propositions, which I have argued to be true, and to the view of very many thoughtful people — that the application of 'basic method' to the relevant data indicates that these propositions are very probably false.

It has often been argued that people cannot at once be believing Christians and critical modern historians who grasp the full implications of what they are doing. The case for this position has been well made in Van Harvey's book *The Historian and the Believer*. It may be insisted, on behalf of views like Harvey's, that historians have an obligation to be as scientific as possible in their work. But such a demand is crucially ambiguous. It may be accepted wholeheartedly that the historian is obliged to be as rational as possible in the sense that I have outlined; and such rationality is indeed magnificently exemplified by the physical sciences. But the demand is often understood in a narrower sense, as implying that all acceptable explanation must in principle be reducible to that of the kind represented by physics and chemistry. Such an account, however, is not merely questionable, but can be conclusively refuted. If all mentalistic explanations are ultimately replaceable by physicalistic ones, then it is not really the case that scientists ever really say what they do because there is good reason for them to do so. But if this is so, there is no good reason to believe what they say; why should anything that people say be believed, unless it is assumed that they really say what they say because they have good reason to do so? Certainly the events narrated by the Gospels are not credible according to a kind of explanation which is 'scientific' in this narrow sense; but the same seems to apply to all reports of human agents and their actions which involve people doing things because they have reasons for doing them.

Still, it does not of course immediately follow that it is rational, in the broader sense that I have been at pains to outline, to believe in the overall historical veracity of narratives like the Gospels, where supernatural agency is freely invoked, and persons are alleged to exercise powers far beyond those usually possessed by human beings. At the root of most historically sceptical accounts of the Gospels, including Harvey's, there are a number of beliefs and assumptions about the reports of 'miracles' which are so conspicuous a feature of them. First, such events, being exceptions to the laws operating in nature, are impossible. Second, even if they were apparently to occur, explanations of them in terms that were not miraculous would always be rationally preferable in the very nature of the case. Third, there is no non-arbitrary way in which we could assess the evidence for the occurrence of a miracle.

In the famous section on miracles in Hume's *Inquiry Concerning Human Understanding*, a miracle is defined as a violation of the laws of nature.[29] Now it seems to me that the notion of laws of nature and exceptions to them could be misleading as applied to the events reported by the writers of the Gospels. Someone might conceivably say: 'I dare say that events like those recorded by the Evangelists actually happened. But why need this involve any exceptions to laws of nature? Might it not be that, in the presence of the remarkable kind of being that Jesus unquestionably was (whatever one's theological beliefs), the odd events in question should have been expected to happen, given "laws of nature" which we do not as yet understand?' In the light of such considerations as these, I prefer Augustine's definition of miracle to that of Hume. As Augustine sees it, when God carries on in the usual kind of way, we call it nature; when God acts in an exceptional manner, for our instruction and admonition, we call it a miracle.[30] I submit that, whether one believes that 'miracles' occur or not, Augustine's definition is more satisfactory than Hume's, if the 'miraculous' acts attributed to Jesus in the Gospels are what is in question.

It should be noted that there are two aspects to miracles as conceived in accordance with Augustine's definition. A phrase in the Gospel of John has been translated as 'signs and wonders' (*sēmeia kai terata*).[31] One might say that the two aspects of a miracle, that of the 'sign' and that of the 'wonder', are respectively that by reason of which it is a divine means to human instruction, and that in virtue of which it is an exception to the normal course of events.[32]

It may seem surprising that the issue of miracles should be of so much importance for Christians. Are they not irrelevant, it may be asked, to the true mission and message of Jesus? As Matthew Arnold remarked, whatever the majority of people may assume, one does not really make what one says or writes truer or more convincing by being able to change one's pen into a pen-wiper.[33] The turning of a pen into a pen-wiper is a convenient example of a 'wonder' which is not a 'sign'. Of course, the miracles ascribed to Jesus in the Gospels are not *mere* wonders – to go no further than the Fourth Gospel, Jesus shows by miracles that the water of traditional precept and ritual is turned into the wine of his presence, that he is the answer to the hunger of humankind, that he is the life that is ultimately victorious over death, and so on.[34] The converse does not apply; there are plenty of 'signs' in the Gospels which are not 'wonders', of which the outstanding example is the crucifixion. (Unfortunately, there was nothing very unusual, at that time and place, about political pretenders and social deviants being tortured to death on crosses.)

There is one obvious difficulty about the kind of Christianity that dispenses with miracles. As I have said already, there is a good case for saying that the approximate historical accuracy of the Gospels is a necessary condition for the truth of Christianity. But the miracle stories are hardly detachable excrescences on the body of the Gospels; the person who described Mark's Gospel as just a string of miracle stories rounded off with a passion narrative was perhaps exaggerating a little, but not much. If one believes that the miracle stories are fictions, how much reliance can one place on the rest of the Gospel material? On the other hand, a traditional Christian may perhaps take comfort from the brevity of the time-span between when Jesus lived and when the Gospels were written or reached their final form. This could be held to make somewhat implausible the view that enough deceit or misapprehension was involved to generate the narratives, as we have them, from a real course of events which was very different from the one that they describe.[35]

In the case of what are often labelled 'paranormal phenomena' – a useful term for 'wonders' of which the status, if any, as 'signs' is not in question (for example alleged instances of telepathy, precognition, poltergeist activity, and physical mediumship) – it is surely conceivable in principle, even if it were never actually the case, that the concurrence of testimony, or the generally reliable character of some witnesses, might make it rational to believe that some event of this sort had occurred, especially if it were of a kind which substantial evidence suggested to have happened on other occasions.[36] Such considerations may be only dubiously applicable to the reports of miracles in the Gospels; but there are other considerations to be taken into account. The traditional Christian claim is that God has acted at a definite point in history in a certain way for certain purposes; and that this action includes the performance of miracles. Questions immediately suggest themselves to the enquiring mind. Are there grounds for believing that there is a God? If there are, would it be appropriate for God to have acted in history in the manner and for the purposes alleged? If so, is it plausible to suppose that that part of history might have been marked by acts like those attributed to Jesus in the Gospels? It could be asked, if principles of historical investigation like those expounded by Van Harvey are unsound, how one is to approach the Gospels with a proper degree of historical rationality at all. I suggest that the answer to this question may be summarized as follows. *If* there is good reason for supposing that there is a God, and that it would be appropriate for God to have acted in history in a manner that incidentally involved exceptions to the normal course of events; and *if* a particular section of history recommends itself as the locus of such special divine action; *then* it might not be unreasonable to conclude that, on the balance of the evidence, such exceptions to the normal course of events had actually taken place. *With these provisos in mind*, one may say that the historical investigation of the Gospels should be carried out in exactly the same manner as that of any set of documents whatever. A similar point has been made by Richard Swinburne, who has suggested that one cannot make properly informed judgements about biblical texts without taking account of the questions of whether there is a God, and, if there is, whether God would be liable to make a special intervention in history for purposes such as revelation and atonement.[37]

In defending the Christian's dependence on the Gospels as history, Peter van Inwagen has pointed out the astonishing degree of difference of opinion among well-reputed scholars as to the reliability of the Gospels as reports of what Jesus actually said and did. A Christian may properly believe, he suggests, that providence has preserved the words and deeds of Jesus with sufficient accuracy for Christian purposes. This would be compatible with, for example, some of the sayings attributed to Jesus being examples of *the kind of thing* he used to say rather than of what he actually did say; and with the real occasions of some of his acts and sayings being different from what is reported by the evangelists.[38]

Rivers of ink have of course flowed over the issue of the rationality of belief in God; which in any case goes beyond the scope of this chapter. More germane to it is the question of how or why a human life such as that attributed to Jesus should or could play a part in a divine plan for the salvation of humanity. When C. S. Lewis came to hold that there were compelling reasons for belief in God, he could not at first bring himself to embrace Christianity. The reason for this was as follows. He could see that the whole human race might be lost in sin, rather in the same sort of way that particular human individuals may be so enslaved by (say) alcohol that one would say that only a miracle could save them. What he could not make sense of was the notion that the life and death of one human being, however good, could remedy the situation.[39]

A survey of traditional theories of the atonement may do little to dispel this kind of disquiet. Apparently, the doctrine amounts to the claim that while other human beings have done grievous wrong, one who is completely innocent has taken their punishment upon himself, thus appeasing the divine wrath. However inspiring this conception of the matter may be to the Christian imagination, when one looks at it rationally it may appear at first sight at best to make little sense, and at worst to cast a lurid light on the character of God. Suppose I have two acquaintances, Smith and Jones; and one day Smith savagely kicks me in the shin. I feel extremely angry about this; but I cease to do so when I have given Jones a right hook to the jaw. That I regard my action against Jones as in any way a means of redressing the wrong done to me by Smith plainly indicates that I am either very irrational or very immoral. Matters are not improved, indeed they are made considerably worse, if one attributes this kind of travesty of retributive justice to God.

These considerations strongly impressed Peter Abelard (1079–1142). 'How cruel and wicked it seems', he wrote, 'that anyone should demand the blood of an innocent person as the price for anything; or that it should in any way please him that an innocent man should be slain – still less that God should consider the death of his Son so agreeable that by it he should be reconciled to the whole world!'[40] Abelard accordingly proposed that the doctrine should be understood in the following way: '[I]n that [God's] Son has taken upon himself our nature and persevered therein in teaching us by word and example even unto death – he has more fully bound us to himself by love; with the result that our hearts should be enkindled by such a gift of divine grace, and true charity should not now shrink from enduring anything for him ... Our redemption through Christ is that deeper affection in us which not only frees us from slavery to sin, but also wins for us the true liberty of sons of God, so that we do all things out of love rather than fear – love to him who has shown us such grace that no greater can be found.'[41] In fact, the Atonement consists in the love of God which is inspired in us by Christ's example, and which gives us the heart to repent of our sins and come to do God's will. Abelard's view of the matter was revived by liberal Protestants in the nineteenth century, and given extended expression in Hastings Rashdall's work early in the twentieth.[42] However, this 'exemplarist' account of the Atonement has usually been felt by Christians to do insufficient justice to our helplessness in the grip of sin short of divine grace, as known in ordinary Christian experience, and as conveyed by the New Testament and the most representative authorities within the Christian tradition. So one may well wonder whether any acceptable explication of this absolutely central Christian doctrine is available at all.[43]

As is rather well known, Lewis did finally become a Christian. Crucial in the process of his conversion was a suggestion made to him by his fellow Oxford dons J. R. R. Tolkien and Hugo Dyson. Lewis was acutely aware of the power exerted on the human imagination by the great myths; indeed, at about this time he had remarked, regarding a performance of *The Winter's Tale*, that he was moved more and more by literary works which had overtones reminiscent of the great myths.[44] What Tolkien and Dyson put to him was this. Lewis seemed to be sensitive to the power exerted by myth-like stories everywhere but in the context of Christianity. Could he not think of God as doing for human beings, by means of an actual history, what they had tried to do for themselves from time immemorial by the profound but literally false stories which are the great myths? A few weeks after his conversation with Tolkien and Dyson, Lewis became a Christian.[45] The story of the dying and rising God is a well-known mythological motif; in this case it seemed that it had actually happened – as Lewis later expressed the matter, here myth became fact.[46]

C. G. Jung has outlined the typical features of the world-wide hero myth – mysterious origin, hazardous birth and rescue in the nick of time, precocious development, miraculous deeds, tragic and early end, symbolical manner of death,[47] and post-mortem phenomena.[48] Again, R. C. Zaehner has remarked on the hunger for an incarnate God that expresses itself in the numerous non-historical incarnate gods of Hinduism (and, one might add, the effectively divinized political leaders of modern times like Che Guevara, Stalin and Mao); and which seems to force itself into religious traditions, like those of Islam and Buddhism, to which it is essentially alien.[49] F. N. Davey said of the sixth chapter of John's Gospel – where Jesus proclaims himself as the Bread of Life after the multiplication of the loaves[50] – that it displays Jesus as the answer to the hunger of humankind.[51]

To approach the matter from a somewhat different angle, Konrad Lorenz has remarked that, if one wants either to release or to control the terrifying force of human aggression towards other members of our own species, four things above all are required: a cause, a group, an enemy, and a leader.[52] If God wished to direct our affection and harness our aggression,[53] without abrogating our intellects and the freedom of our wills, would it not be very appropriate to provide a group to cut other group loyalties down to size, for the cause of truth and goodness, with the enemy as falsity and evil as such rather than the human beings who are their slaves and dupes, and its leader the only human being who could not let us down, the one who is also divine? All these considerations bring out what the older scholastic theologians would have called the *convenientia* of the Incarnation,[54] and how the Atonement may best be understood. God lives a human life which has the form of the universal hero myth, and is offered to us as the leader of the ultimate community where we partake of the divine life through the means, which go back into the depths of human prehistory, of recitation of the hero's deeds and partaking of a sacred meal. So, little by little, the evils within ourselves and our society may be purged away.

In his magisterial work on the philosophy of Christian doctrine, Richard Swinburne follows the consensus of Catholic theologians (against what was apparently Anselm's opinion) in maintaining that there was a 'generous propriety',[55] rather than a strict necessity, about God saving humankind by means of an incarnation. He suggests that the message of salvation, and about what human beings are to do in response to it, carries greater conviction as coming from the divine self rather than merely from an inspired prophet. Also, we are set an example of how to live a human life, as well as being taught the dignity of human nature and the extent of the divine love for us. Furthermore, it is fitting that God should undergo along with creatures the suffering to which they have been subjected for their own greater good.[56]

People have often wondered whether it would not have been better for all concerned if the Fathers of the Church had avoided complicated metaphysical questions about the status of Jesus and contented themselves from the first with what became fashionable in the nineteenth century as the 'liberal Protestant' position – that there is a God, and that Jesus proclaimed with incomparable lucidity and force the sisterhood and brotherhood of all human beings under divine rule. But it seems clear, on any objective assessment of the evidence, and whether one likes it or not, that Jesus did arrogate a special status to himself, the implications of which were naturally and inevitably a matter for speculation among his followers. It appears that from very early times Christians were worshipping Jesus, and treating as authoritative a collection of documents pretty close to that which constitutes our New Testament. Now it is clear enough that Jesus is described in the New Testment as a man; but at the same time, it is implied that he is to all intents and purposes a divine being. The preparation of the 'day of the Lord' announced by the prophets is the preparation for Jesus's coming;[57] Jesus feeds his people 'in a desert place' as God fed their fathers in the wilderness; he rules the sea as God rules it according to the Psalmist;[58] he is the equal of God, and was with God at the creation of the world.[59] In a very few texts (which should *not* be taken as the sole basis for the doctrine of Christ's divinity) he is actually stated to be God.[60]

A number of early attempts were made to state precisely what was implied by this about the nature and status of Jesus, most of which were rejected by the Christian community as inadequate. The Ebionites said that Jesus was just a man with a unique mission and message (rather like Muhammad in the eyes of orthodox Muslims); the Docetists that he was really divine and only seemed to be human; the Patripassians that he was identical in all respects with God the Father; the Arians that he was the greatest and first created of all creatures, and so not really divine. At the Council of Nicaea, it was solemnly declared, by use of the formula 'consubstantial (*homoousios*) with the Father', that Christ is strictly speaking divine. (The term *homoousios*, in the current usage of the time, meant 'of the same sort of stuff', as two desks may be made out of the same kind of wood; it did not have currency in philosophy then, but was used by the Council in a technical sense.[61]) For the Son to be 'consubstantial with the Father' is for him to be fully divine, as the Father is; just as for me to be consubstantial with a goat called Billy would be for me to be really a goat, and as much so as Billy.[62] After this had been determined for the Son, the same question inevitably arose for the third being, who is said in the New Testament to have been sent by the Father and the Son,[63] is reported as coming down upon the apostles at Pentecost,[64] and is mentioned together with the Father and the Son in a number of texts.[65] The divinity of this 'Holy Spirit' was affirmed at the First Council of Constantinople.

Christians never thought of themselves as other than monotheists; yet they believed in three Beings distinct from one another who were all God.

To affirm both of these things together is to believe in the doctrine of the Trinity. But is this not a direct contradiction?[66] Nothing can be real which is logically inconsistent; it is merely ignorant or evasive to appeal in this connection to the intricacies of the historical evolution of dogma, or the deep significance of Trinitarian talk in salvation history. Surely, if every divine Person is God, there cannot be fewer Gods than divine Persons; any more than, if every university administrator is a rogue, there can be fewer rogues than university administrators.[67] One of the main reasons why the philosopher Franz Brentano left the Church was that he could not see, for all the formidable logical ingenuity that he applied to the problem, how the doctrine of the Trinity could be anything other than a contradiction. Some claim that the best one can say is that, although the doctrine has never been proved conclusively to be self-contradictory, it has never been proved not to be so either.[68] A. P. Martinich, following a suggestion of Peter Geach, claims that 'nothing is identical with something absolutely, but only in a certain respect'; thus the Persons of the Trinity might be identical with one another as God, but not as Persons.[69] One is scarcely reassured, however, by Peter van Inwagen's remark that, '[a]s far as I can tell, relative-identity logic has no utility outside Christian theology'.[70]

As early as the Arian controversy in the fourth century, someone suggested that the difficulty might be resolved if the Persons differed only in their relations to one another. (We know this because Arius himself rejected the suggestion.[71]) Eight centuries later, Anselm made what was in effect the same proposal – that in God all is one where the mutual opposition of relations is not involved;[72] and this was confirmed by the Council of Florence. We human persons largely are and are what we are through our relations with other persons; we may understand that the divine Persons are entirely so. It is their being so that enables it to be said without contradiction, that there are three distinct divine Persons without there being more than one God.[73]

That God is to be conceived on the analogy of our spiritual[74] rather than our corporeal nature has generally been taken for granted by thoughtful Christians; and the analogy has been applied in detail to the doctrine of the Trinity by Augustine, Aquinas and (in the twentieth century) Bernard Lonergan.[75] As Lonergan sees it, while God as creator is to be conceived on the analogy of our practical consciousness, God as Trinity is to be conceived on the analogy of our existential consciousness. As to the former, God the creator makes the things to exist and the states of affairs to occur which constitute the contingent universe, rather as we human beings will to bring about our own actions and products. As to the latter, we can form a more or less accurate or distorted conception of ourselves, and love ourselves more or less accordingly. Evil in human affairs is largely the result of false conception and disordered evaluation of ourselves and others; we misrepresent our enemies because we hate them, and the misrepresentation forms a pretext for still deeper hatred. The divine consciousness is not subject to this sort of limitation or distortion. God's conception of the divine self is no less than the divine self, and divine love is evinced according to this conception. As understanding forming conception through which love is evinced, God is Father; as conception formed by understanding through which love is evinced, God is Son; as love evinced by understanding through conception, God is Holy Spirit. Such is the psychological analogy for understanding the Trinity developed by Aquinas[76] and transposed into terms of modern thought by Lonergan.[77] No one takes the psychological analogy to be a matter of defined dogma; it is merely a hypothesis through which, as Aquinas and Lonergan propose, the mystery of mysteries may be made remotely amenable to human comprehension, as well as being shown not to be a sheer contradiction. The Incarnation will thus be God's conception of the divine self expressed through the medium of a human life; united in love with God thus incarnate, we are heartened to apply ourselves to the Herculean labour of fighting evil and its effects in ourselves and in the world.

According to Swinburne, the nature of God as love entails that God not only may but must be triune, with the persons individuated by their relations one with another. To love is to give and to receive, and to combine together in doing good to a third party. It is of the nature of love both to share, and to co-operate in sharing.[78]

As the Arian heresy was the occasion for the definition of the strict divinity of Christ, so was the Nestorian heresy for that of the unity of his person. It is often said that Nestorius was not a Nestorian; what is undoubtedly true, however, is that his refusal to accept the formula of Cyril of Alexandria, that Mary is the mother of God, logically implies what the Church has rejected as Nestorianism – that the eternal Word of God and the man Jesus are strictly speaking two individuals. Cyril was such an unpleasant man that it is easy not to give him credit for the importance of the point that he was making: if Mary is the mother of Jesus, and Jesus is God, then Mary is the mother of God.[79] (Later orthodox theologians admitted that she was his mother with respect to his humanity, and not with respect to his divinity; but that is a different matter.)

The crucial question is whether it is *one and the same* being – the phrase stressed so strongly by Cyril – who is at once both really human and really divine. Nestorians ancient and modern may have been at pains to stress how intimately 'the historical Jesus' and 'the theological Christ' are related; but that is not the point. An analogy may serve to make the matter clearer. It is by no means the same thing to say that the favourite child of the chief of police is intimately associated with the blonde in the bikini, and to say that these personages are one and the same. The point is no trivial one, no mere matter of logic-chopping by people who were looking for a pretext to quarrel. The special magic of Christianity, whether it is true or false – that which gives it a large amount of the power which it indisputably has had, for better or for worse, in human life – is to a considerable extent due to its claim that a particular man was divine; that the eternal Divine Word, born of the Father before all ages, was also born in a manger in the reign of Augustus Caesar. The Council of Chalcedon, in its talk of Christ as one 'Person' in two 'natures', does no more than assert unequivocally that it is really one and the same who is both really human and really divine.[80] To deny what is essentially asserted by the Council is to take away what it is in Christianity that satisfies the hunger for a human God, or a divine human being, which I mentioned earlier:

Lo! Within a manger lies
He who built the starry skies.

Enough for him whom cherubim
Worship night and day,
A breast full of milk,
And a manger full of hay.

How is one to understand the statement that someone is truly both human and divine? However appealing it may be to the feelings and the imagination, it will not do to affirm it if it is logically incoherent.[81] It has been stated roundly, for example by John Hick, that it is simply contradictory, like the claim that a circle is square.[82] To this claim Brian Hebblethwaite has objected that Christians should derive their ideas of what God and the human are from the revelation vouchsafed to them in Jesus Christ, and not take their stand on abstract definitions which may foreclose real possibilities.[83] However, it is difficult to feel that Hick has not something of a *prima facie* case, even on fairly minimal definitions of divinity and humanity; how could one and the same being be at once creator and creature, eternal and coming into existence in time, and infinite in knowledge and power and limited in respect of both? And if the concepts of 'God' and 'human being' are indefinitely vague, it is hard to see what sense there is in speaking of God's incarnation as a human being at all.

One obvious answer that might be suggested to the problem, of how a single individual might be human and divine, is to say that that individual would be conscious of self as both; and it is not obvious that any other kind of answer is possible. To say that it is so 'ontologically', without being so 'psychologically', makes at best questionable sense; what is expressed ontologically in the ecclesiastical formula seems naturally to demand a psychological explication. (That the New Testament authors were not interested in Christ's consciousness would not be relevant, even if one granted, as I do not, that it is true; what they said might have implications for his consciousness that they themselves did not draw out.) Now the Council of Chalcedon states that the two natures of Christ are united not only 'inseparably' (*adiairetōs*) but also 'unconfusedly' (*asunchutōs*). A number of modern authorities have hit on an account of Jesus's consciousness which seems to take a lead from this. Aquinas anticipated them by distinguishing the 'acquired' knowledge obtained by Jesus through the ordinary human means[84] from the kind of human knowledge which he had always and from the first by reason of his direct apprehension of divinity.[85] For the rest of us, the overall movement of our conscious life is (if all goes well) an advance towards God; for Jesus, it will have been towards more complete expression in human terms of the knowledge of God which he always had.

The mystery of Christ's human consciousness, and its relation to his divine consciousness, may perhaps be rendered less obscure than it might otherwise be by analogies more directly available to us. Two in particular suggest themselves: the consciousness characteristic of some mystics, and the *a priori* components (if indeed there are such) in the knowledge of ordinary human beings. The Advaita school of Hindu philosophers envisages conscious human subjects as really identical with the one *ens realissimum* or most real being; and experience as though this was so seems typical of a certain kind of mystic.[86] Christians might say that only Jesus Christ among members of the human race could properly so identify himself. As to the *a priori* components in human knowledge, human beings assume from the first, whether or not they ever clearly spell it out to themselves, that our sensations are clues to the nature of things in a real external world, that these things are on the whole when and where they appear to us to be, that there are centres of consciousness other than ourselves, that the things and events that we perceive are intelligibly connected with one another, that there are reasons why things happen as they do, and so on. As David Hume and Immanuel Kant notoriously showed, such assumptions are not derivable in any straightforward way from experience. Rather similarly, we may suppose, Christ as human, in his human consciousness, had in addition, always and from the very first, a direct apprehension of God and of all things in relation to God. Rather than approaching apprehension of God, as other human beings may do by the expansion of their intellects and the appropriate exercise of their wills, Christ throughout his life would have striven to express, through deeds and through words, in terms appropriate to the social and cultural situation in which he and his initial witnesses lived, the nature of God, the divine will for human beings, and the means necessary for human salvation.

How far does the much greater magnitude of the universe as known to modern human beings, as opposed to those in ancient and medieval times, militate against the rational acceptability of the doctrine of the Incarnation? Many have thought that it was a decisive objection; during the eighteenth and nineteenth centuries, it was a major factor in the rejection of Christianity by intellectuals, including Horace Walpole and Ralph Waldo Emerson. (They did not necessarily infer that theism as such was impugned.) Certainly Christianity, in common with the other great religions, came into existence at a time when the universe was assumed to be immeasurably smaller than it is now known to be. And the earth was almost universally assumed to be the centre of the cosmos, rather than a tiny body travelling round a moderately sized star which is one among billions in a galaxy, that is itself one of billions. On the other hand, human beings do seem in a sense to be in a special position in relation to the rest of the cosmos, just by virtue of the fact that they are able to get to know about it. For all the confinement of each human being, and even of humanity at large, to an exiguous pocket of space and time, we can obtain knowledge of what is enormously removed from us in respect of both. By virtue of our potential knowledge of the universe, we are remarkably privileged among its constituents; the feeling that this privilege of ours is less significant than the illusions of comparative size and physical centrality which we have lost would seem to be based on a somewhat vulgar scheme of values.

But suppose that there have evolved rational beings in the universe other than ourselves, as many informed persons would now reckon to be vastly probable. Would it not then be absurd to suppose that the creator has become incarnate only in human form, and on this planet? Certainly, if there are other rational beings in the universe, one would confidently expect the creator to act in their regard in a manner that is appropriate to their needs. Would this necessarily involve a divine incarnation, even if the beings in question had sinned? Most representative Christian theologians have maintained that, in the case of human beings themselves, God could have saved them otherwise than through an incarnation; one can argue no more than that the means is an appropriate one – as I myself tried to do earlier. But in any case, I am not sure why it should be necessarily ruled out by Christian belief that God could have assumed the nature of some of the other sorts of rational creature that may inhabit the universe.[87]

Notes

1 Cf. Kai Nielsen, *Philosophy and Atheism* (Buffalo, 1985).
2 J. L. Mackie, *The Miracle of Theism* (Oxford, 1982).
3 'Theology and falsification' in A. G. N. Flew and A. C. MacIntyre (eds), *New Essays in Philosophical Theology* (London, 1955).
4 'Eschatological verification' as making sense of Christian claims has been especially stressed by John Hick. Cf. his 'Theology and verification', originally

published in 1960, and reprinted in B. G. Mitchell (ed.), *The Philosophy of Religion* (Oxford, 1971). Indeed, Hick does not now think of religions as differing from one another in central cognitive claims, but only as opposed collectively to naturalism in that they expect some form of life after death. See his 'On religious experience' in J. J. MacIntosh and H. A. Meynell (eds), *Faith, Scepticism and Personal Identity* (Calgary, 1994).

5 Unless one counts some lunatic versions that were fashionable in the 1960s. For an overview of some of these, see Thomas W. Ogletree, *The 'Death of God' Controversy* (London, 1966).

6 It is convenient to label as 'classical Christianity' what is held in common, at least officially, by Eastern Orthodox, Roman Catholic, traditional Protestant (i.e. Lutheran and Reformed) and Anglican Christians – what C. S. Lewis called 'mere Christianity'.

7 N. T. Wright is a good example of a historian who combines the utmost knowledge and sophistication with a belief in a degree of historical veracity in the Gospel narratives which is certainly compatible with orthodox Christianity. See his *The New Testament and the People of God* (Minneapolis, 1992); and *Who Was Jesus?* (Grand Rapids, 1993).

8 See Michael Dummett, 'The impact of Scriptural studies on the content of Catholic belief'; also John Collins, 'The impact of dogmatism on rational discourse: comments on the paper of Michael Dummett'; and Dummett's 'Response to Collins' in Eleonore Stump and Thomas P. Flint (eds), *Hermes and Athena: Biblical Exegesis and Philosophical Theology* (Notre Dame, 1993).

9 D. Z. Phillips, 'Religion and epistemology: some contemporary confusions', *Australasian Journal of Philosophy* (1966), p. 322. I owe this citation to P. J. Sherry.

10 D. Z. Phillips, *Faith After Foundationalism* (London and New York, 1988).

11 Phillips, *Faith After Foundationalism*, pp. 9–10.

12 See 1 Cor 15:1–20.

13 See William P. Alston, *Perceiving God* (Ithaca and London, 1991).

14 Ibid., pp. 38–9.

15 Ibid., p. 5.

16 Alston admits that other types of argument for God, based for example on revelation, tradition, or natural theology, may together with this one conspire to make theistic belief rationally acceptable (*Perceiving God*, pp. 286, 289).

17 See C. Stephen Evans, 'Critical historical judgment and biblical faith', *Faith and Philosophy* (April 1994), p. 187. In my discussion of Harvey's position, I am greatly indebted to this article.

18 For a useful discussion of 'evidentialism', see Patrick Lee, 'Evidentialism, Plantinga, and faith and reason' in L. Zagzebski (ed.), *Rational Faith: Catholic Responses to Reformed Epistemology* (Notre Dame, 1993).

19 It is called 'Reformed epistemology' because its principal proponents are 'Reformed' or Calvinist Protestants. See N. Wolterstorff, *Reason Within the Bounds of Religion* (Grand Rapids, 1984), and A. Plantinga, 'Rationality and religious belief' in Steven M. Cahn and David Shatz (eds), *Contemporary Philosophy of Religion* (New York, 1982). The position is closely related to that of Karl Barth, with his polemic against 'natural theology', and his view that the existence of God and the fact of divine revelation in Jesus Christ must always be the premise, but never the conclusion, of an argument.

20 William P. Alston, 'Christian experience and Christian belief' in A. Plantinga and N. Wolterstorff (eds), *Faith and Rationality* (Notre Dame, 1983), p. 119.

21 Phillips, *Faith After Foundationalism*, p. 25.
22 See Plantinga, 'Rationality and religious belief', pp. 274–7.
23 Cf. note 1 above.
24 See R. Swinburne, *The Existence of God* (Oxford, 1979) and Hugo Meynell, *The Intelligible Universe: A Cosmological Argument* (London, 1982).
25 See Richard Swinburne, *Faith and Reason* (Oxford, 1981); *The Christian God* (Oxford, 1994). Also Hugo Meynell, *Is Christianity True?* (London, 1994).
26 See especially Bernard Lonergan, *Insight: A Study of Human Understanding* (Toronto, 1992), ch. 11; *Method in Theology* (London, 1971), ch. 1.
27 The terminology is Lonergan's; see *Method in Theology*, p. 20.
28 See Lonergan, *Insight*, especially chs 11–17; *Method in Theology*, ch. 1.
29 David Hume, *An Inquiry Concerning Human Understanding*, Section X, Part I.
30 *De Trinitate* III, 5.
31 John 4:48.
32 The 'sign' aspect is especially emphasized in John's Gospel, but is always at least implicit in the miracle stories of the Synoptic Gospels.
33 Matthew Arnold, *Literature and Dogma* (London, 1876), p. 132.
34 John 2:1–11; 6:1–13, 30–35, 40–58; 11:1–44.
35 The very late dates argued for the Gospels by some authorities in the middle of the nineteenth century, e.g. those of the Tübingen School, have now been universally abandoned. The usual dates given are about 65 CE for Mark, 85 for Matthew and Luke, and 90–100 for John. But recently some powerful arguments have been advanced for much earlier dates. See John Wenham, *Redating Matthew, Mark and Luke* (London, 1991).
36 For the astounding intellectual immorality of some so-called 'sceptics' in relation to such alleged phenomena, see the 'Introduction' to Stephen Braude, *The Limits of Influence: Psychokinesis and the Philosophy of Science* (London and New York, 1987).
37 R. Swinburne, 'Comments on the paper of Harold W. Attridge' in E. Stump and T. Flint (eds), *Hermes and Athena: Biblical Exegesis and Philosophical Theology* (Notre Dame, 1993), p. 226.
38 Peter van Inwagen, 'Critical studies of the New Testament and the user of the New Testament' in Stump and Flint, op. cit., pp. 159–90.
39 See R. L. Green and W. Hooper, *C. S. Lewis: A Biography* (London, 1988), p. 117.
40 Peter Abelard, *Exposition of the Epistle to the Romans* in Eugene R. Fairweather (ed.), *A Scholastic Miscellany: Anselm to Ockham*, Library of Christian Classics, vol. X (Philadelphia, 1956), p. 283.
41 Ibid., pp. 283–4.
42 Hastings Rashdall, *The Idea of Atonement in Christian Theology* (London, 1925).
43 The incoherence of many standard accounts of the Atonement is well argued in Michael Martin's instructive and powerful book *The Case Against Christianity* (Philadelphia, 1991).
44 Lewis wrote in a letter 'I must confess that more and more the value of plays and novels becomes for me dependent on the moments when, by whatever artifice, they succeed in expressing the great *myths*'. See Green and Hooper, op. cit., p. 115.
45 Ibid., pp. 117–18.
46 C. S. Lewis, *Undeceptions: Essays on Theology and Ethics* (London, 1971), p. 39. It is tempting to interpret the passage in Revelation about the Lamb breaking the

seals (5:1–5) in this sense. If Lewis's account of the matter is right, as I believe that it is, then Karl Rahner's judgement that 'the Christian dogma ... has nothing to do with the divine man myths of antiquity' (*Foundations of Christian Faith* [London, 1978], p. 291) is seriously wrong.

47 Odin and Attis hung on trees, and the early European visitors to America found crosses with victims on them.

48 C. G. Jung, *Psychology and Religion*, Collected Works, vol. XI (London, 1958), pp. 154–5.

49 R. C. Zaehner, *Concordant Discord: The Interdependence of Faiths* (Oxford, 1970), pp. 428–43.

50 John 6:51.

51 See E. C. Hoskyns and F. N. Davey, *The Fourth Gospel* (London, 1947), p. 76.

52 K. Lorenz, *On Aggression* (London, 1966), pp. 234ff.

53 Cf. Lonergan, *Insight*, p. 745.

54 Richard Swinburne makes the charming suggestion that for God to become incarnate has the same sort of appropriateness as for a man to wear a coat that he has designed himself (*The Christian God* [Oxford, 1994], p. 218). His analogy is to some extent anticipated by a scriptural metaphor; the Spirit of God is said to 'clothe herself' in someone or other (cf. 2 Chronicles 24:20).

55 Swinburne, *The Christian God*, p. 218.

56 Ibid., pp. 216–20.

57 Joel 3:4; Mal 3:1; Mark 1:2; Acts 2:20; 1 Cor 1:8; 2 Cor 1:14; 2 Thess 2:1–2.

58 Exod 16:35; Ps 24:3; Mark 4:35–41; 6:35–4.

59 John 5:16–30; John 1:1. For more material to this effect, see Hugo Meynell, *The Theology of Bernard Lonergan* (Atlanta, 1986), pp. 60–5.

60 John 20:28; Titus 2:13; Heb 1:9; 2 Pet 1:1; 1 John 5:20.

61 Cf. G. L. Prestige, *God in Patristic Thought* (London, 1936), pp. 197, 209. One might compare the use of the term 'particle' by twentieth-century physicists.

62 See Bernard Lonergan, *The Way to Nicaea*, trans. Conn O'Donovan (London, 1976).

63 John 14:16–17; 15:26.

64 Acts 2:1–4.

65 E.g. John 16:13–15; Gal 4:4–6; Rom 15:16; Eph 2:18.

66 For the rest of this paragraph, see John Macnamara, Marie La Palme Reyes and Gonzalo E. Reyes, 'Logic and the Trinity', *Faith and Philosophy* (January 1994).

67 The substance of this point is due to Richard Cartwright, 'On the logical problem of the Trinity' in *Philosophical Essays* (Bradford, MA, 1987), pp. 187–200.

68 Thus S. T. Davis, *Logic and the Nature of God* (Grand Rapids, 1983), p. 140.

69 A. P. Martinich, 'Identity and Trinity', *Journal of Religion* (1978), pp. 169–81.

70 Peter van Inwagen, 'And yet they are not three Gods but one God' in Thomas V. Morris (ed.), *Philosophy and the Christian Faith* (Notre Dame, 1988), p. 259. Macnamara *et al.* insist that there are 'commonplace examples where each A is a B and yet there are fewer Bs than As' ('Logic', p. 7). For example, if Smith travels by one airline on several occasions, she is quite properly regarded by the company as several passengers; and the same might apply to 'patients admitted to a hospital, diners in a restaurant, or customers in a shop'. But these examples

can all be explicated as applying to the same individuals at different times and places; which would not do for infinite and omnipresent divine Persons.

71 In a letter to Alexander, Bishop of Alexandria. See Bernard Lonergan, *De Deo Trino* I: *Pars Dogmatica* (Rome, 1964), p. 200.

72 Anselm, *De processione Spiritus sancti*, 2. Lonergan, *De Deo*, p. 224.

73 Cf. Aquinas, *Summa Theologiae*, I, 28; I, 31, 2 *ad resp.*: ' . . . we must shun the use of the terms *diversity* and *difference* in God, lest we take away the unity of essence; we may, however, use the term *distinction* on account of the relative opposition'.

74 I.e. our nature as intellectually conscious, as capable of understanding and exercising our wills accordingly, rather than merely undergoing sensations and feelings in the manner of most types of animal.

75 See Bernard Lonergan, *De Deo Trino* and *Verbum: Word and Idea in Aquinas* (London, 1968), ch. 5.

76 *Summa Theologiae* I, 27, 1 and 3.

77 For a wonderful contemporary exposition of the same view, see C. J. F. Williams, 'Neither confounding the persons nor dividing the substance' in A. G. Padgett (ed.), *Reason and the Christian Religion: Essays in Honour of Richard Swinburne* (Oxford, 1994).

78 Swinburne, *The Christian God*, p. 178.

79 See Bernard Lonergan, 'The origins of Christian realism' in *A Second Collection* (London, 1974), pp. 253–60.

80 The terms 'person' (*hupostasis*) and 'nature' (*phusis*) did have currency in the philosophy of the time, in Stoicism and Aristotelianism respectively; but the Church Fathers were using the terms in their own way and for their own purposes.

81 That it is paradoxical, and gains much of its force from the fact that it is so, is not to be denied. Paradoxes are what they are because they are *prima facie* contradictions; but no rational person ought to assent to actual contradictions. Theologians who talk too readily of 'paradox' should bear in mind Charles Hartshorne's caustic suggestion, that '[a] theological paradox, it appears, is what a contradiction becomes when it is about God rather than something else, or indulged in by a theologian or a church rather than an unbeliever or a heretic' (*The Divine Relativity* [New Haven and London], 1948).

82 'Jesus and the world religions' in J. Hick (ed.), *The Myth of God Incarnate* (London, 1977), p. 178; cited Thomas V. Morris, *The Logic of God Incarnate* (Ithaca and London, 1986), p. 21.

83 Brian Hebblethwaite, 'Incarnation: the essence of Christian theology?', *Theology* 80 (1977), p. 86; Morris, *The Logic of God Incarnate*, p. 73.

84 There is surely good evidence not only that his acquired knowledge was limited, but that his beliefs were sometimes erroneous. Abiathar was not high priest when David and his men ate the showbread (cf. Mark 2:26 with Matt 12:4; Luke 6:4). The Zechariah who was victim in the last murder recorded in the Jewish scriptures (2 Chron 24:21) was not the son of Berechiah; there seems a confusion here with Isaiah 8:2 (cf. Matt 23:35 with Luke 11:51). On the 'prefer the more difficult reading' principle, it is surely more likely that the slips of memory were dominical, and were preserved because they were so, and later corrected, than that they were introduced by the evangelists. Presumably, the kind of error that is ruled out by the hypostatic union would be those that are due to moral fault (for example when someone, due to prejudice about race or gender, fails to take account of the evidence that non-Caucasians might be

first-rate scientists or that women might be great writers); cf. Heb 4:15.

85 *Summa Theologiae* III, 9, 4.

86 For the great Indian philosopher Shankara, who taught early in the eighth century, and is the supreme representative of the strict non-dualist school of Hindu thought, there is only one ultimately real being, and to be free of illusion is to realize one's identity with it. For Ramanuja, the eleventh-to-twelfth-century thinker who is the great exponent of what is called 'modified non-dualism', even when we are finally rid of the faults and illusions of the present, we will know ourselves as still in some sense distinct from the only supremely real being. One might say that according to Christians, only for Jesus is an account like Shankara's correct; for the rest of us, Ramanuja's doctrine applies. For useful summaries and discussions of the philosophies of Shankara and Ramanuja, see C. Sharma, *A Critical Survey of Indian Philosophy* (London, 1960), chs 15 and 18.

87 For a much fuller treatment of these issues, see Morris, *The Logic of God Incarnate*, pp. 169–80.

9
Morality and religion
H. O. Mounce

The category of the moral is a comparatively recent one. By this I do not mean that people have only recently distinguished between good and evil. The distinction has no discernible origin; it appears in all societies. But the moral as a distinct or autonomous category is of comparatively recent origin. In earlier cultures, there was no sharp distinction between the moral and the religious. The Ten Commandments of the ancient Hebrews will serve as an example. The first four concern our duties to God; the remaining six, our duties to our neighbour. Nowadays, it may be said that the last six are moral, the first four religious. But to the ancient Hebrews there was no such distinction. Throughout, the commands instruct us in our duties to God. Thus the last six do not instruct us in how to serve our neighbour as distinct from serving God. Rather they instruct us in how God wishes us to serve him in our dealings with our neighbour.

The moral, as an autonomous category, emerges only with the secularization, first of learning, then of society more generally. The secularization of learning we attribute to the development of modern science. Many attribute the secularization of society to the same cause. But that is not the view most commonly held by historians and sociologists. The majority of them hold that the causes of secularization are social not intellectual. They lie in particular in the process of industrialization. In all societies people have been occupied for much of their time in providing the materials for their existence. But in earlier societies, material activities are interwoven with religious ceremonies which link them to a reality that transcends the immediate life of the society. For example, there are prayers for a good harvest and thanksgiving when the harvest is brought in. In the course of industrialization, when people were transferred from the countryside to the towns, they lost the traditional ceremonies and found none to replace them. The moral remained; but it was now autonomous, for it was no longer interwoven with a religious view of the world.[1]

To some philosophers, this process simply made apparent what had always been true. For them, the connection between morality and religion had always been accidental. During the nineteenth century, the point was emphasized especially by the scientific rationalists and positivists. It was axiomatic amongst them that morality and religion are independent, so that the passing of religion would have no effect on morality. Some indeed believed that this was *necessarily* so. Their argument was that since the belief in God is illusory, it could never have served as a real foundation for morality. Consequently, morality cannot be affected by its removal. Unfortunately, that is fallacious. If God is illusory, he could never have served as a foundation for morality. But it is not illusory that people did indeed *believe* in him. Consequently, it has still to be shown that morality must be unaffected by the removal of that *belief*.

Moreover when we consider earlier societies, the connection within them between morality and religion does not appear accidental. Rather it seems organic. The moral is so connected with the religious as to derive from it something of its point or meaning. It is true that in considering such a society we may extract from it those elements we term moral. But a certain violence is involved; connections are broken and what we have in our hands is not quite what was there before.

Now it is a real question whether a similar point does not apply to that very category which appears in secularized societies as the moral. The scientific rationalists and positivists believed that the morality which they held in their hands was the real article, freed from superfluous decoration. But there is another possibility. Perhaps what they had in their hands was the survival from a wider system, lacking its connections with that system and lacking therefore, also, something of its point or meaning.[2]

In considering this issue, it will be natural to look for evidence in ethics or moral philosophy. We shall begin with moral philosophy as it appears in the classical period, which runs, roughly, from the time of the ancient Greeks to the sixteenth or seventeenth century. We shall then consider the modern period, in which the secularization of learning has flourished. In this way, we shall have before us a survey of the views which have been held in Western culture on the relation between morality and religion. But before embarking on this survey, let us bring morality into sharper focus. There are many forms of value. How is the moral to be distinguished from the others, such as the aesthetic or the instrumental?

In answering that question, we may follow Wittgenstein's procedure in his *Lecture on Ethics*.[3] He there makes a distinction between absolute and relative value. Words such as 'right' or 'good' may be used in different ways. We may speak, for example, of the right road or a good fire-extinguisher. A fire-extinguisher is good because it enables you to extinguish fires; a road is right because it takes you where you want to go. Here what is right or good is relative. It depends on what you want or need.

For example, the road which is right for you may be wrong for someone else. Wittgenstein contrasts this use with an absolute one. He gives an example to illustrate his point. Suppose you watch a person play tennis and then later tell him that he is playing badly. He replies 'I know; but I'm not interested in playing better'. You would say 'Oh! That's all right then'. But suppose he is behaving badly. He is untruthful, perhaps, or unkind. You tell him this and he replies 'I know, but I don't want to behave any better'. You would now reply 'Well, you *ought* to want to'. Many will feel that Wittgenstein has here isolated a feature which is distinctive of the moral. Unlike other values, it is not relative to what you happen to want or need. It is absolute not relative. It is like a road you must go along, whether you want to or not. But *why* must you? That is not easy to explain. Wittgenstein says in his lecture that it is impossible to do so, if you confine yourself to the language of science or to a purely naturalistic view of the world. Within that language or that view, you may explain readily enough the relative forms of value. For example, if I tell you that this is the right road, I merely inform you that it will take you where you want to go. In short, I merely state a fact, like any other. But I do not inform you of what you want, when I tell you that you ought to behave better. For even if you do not want to behave better, still you *ought* to. Wittgenstein, in short, believed that what is distinctive in morality cannot be explained by a secular or purely naturalistic view. But, then, he might have been mistaken. Let us therefore consider what light may be thrown on this matter by a more general survey of moral philosophy.

* * *

The classical period covers more than two thousand years. It may seem impossible, in limited space, to survey the moral philosophy of so long a period. In fact that task is not as difficult as it seems. For the period has a certain unity, being dominated by the two great Greek philosophers, Plato and Aristotle. Plato lived from 427 to 347 BC; Aristotle from 384 to 322 BC. Together they represent the culmination of Greek philosophy. Moreover their influence extended to subsequent ages. On the revival of learning during the Middle Ages, for example, Aristotle was treated as a supreme authority, being referred to as the Philosopher.

To understand their thought, it will be useful to consider for a moment its background in earlier Greek philosophy. Taken as a whole, Greek philosophy is a search for measure or order. The world as it appears in its multitudinous detail is not self-explanatory. The earliest Greek philosophers, the so-called Ionians, looked for unity in some underlying substance. Thales (*c.* 625–*c.* 545 BC), for example, who is usually treated as the first of the Greek philosophers, argued that the fundamental substance is water, the other substances, such as earth, fire and air, being transformations of water into different states, having different qualities. But then the question arose of how one was to explain the qualities of water itself. If it is fundamental, there is no further substance to explain it; but then its qualities are inexplicable. It is obvious that the same difficulty arises if one substitutes for water one of the other substances, such as air or earth. It was perhaps in response to this difficulty that Anaxagoras (c. 500–428 BC) referred to the fundamental substance as the boundless. In other words, the explanation for the different substances, with their different qualities, must lie in something which does not possess those qualities, which is itself undifferentiated. This, however, is to exchange one difficulty for another. For if the fundamental substance is undifferentiated, there are no differences within it. But how then can it give rise to differences? It may be noted that this line of explanation has now reached an impasse. The differing qualities can be explained only as transformations of some underlying substance. But if this substance itself possesses qualities, it needs itself to be explained. Consequently it must be undifferentiated. But if it is undifferentiated, it cannot give rise to differing qualities.

It is here that we encounter the ideas of the Pythagoreans, which are amongst the most original in Western philosophy.[4] These ideas probably arose through the study of geometry. Geometry is the study of shape, which proceeds independently of matter. I may illustrate a theorem by drawing a circle in chalk on a blackboard. But it is irrelevant that the substance of the circle is chalk. I might have used ink on paper. The same shape can be embodied in different matter. The same matter can embody different shapes. Thus geometry proceeds to study qualitative differences, which exist in nature, but which depend not on matter but on structure or form. The Pythagoreans extended this idea in the study of acoustics. They discovered that the sound given forth by a vibrating string depended not on its matter but on the rate of its vibration. This enabled them to explain, also, how sounds differ in their aesthetic qualities. Thus two vibrating strings give forth sounds which are concordant or discordant depending on the ratio between their rates of vibrations. Within the ratios 1:2, 2:3, 3:4, the intervals are concordant; beyond that they become progressively discordant. The Pythagoreans here illustrate the process known as quantification, on which the whole of modern science depends. Quantification is the application of mathematics to nature or the study of nature in its mathematical structure.

The Ionians reached an impasse because they treated matter or substance as a luminous notion and attempted to explain the world in terms of it. The Pythagoreans advanced because they treated matter as obscure and subordinate and sought to explain the world in terms of form or structure. It is likely that a similar advance was made independently by Heraclitus (flourished c. 500 BC). I say 'likely' rather than 'certain' because his writings survive only in a fragmentary and obscure form. He identified the world with fire and, at first sight, he seems to be following the Ionians in explaining the world by means of a fundamental substance. It is likely, however, that he was using fire as a symbol or model. A single flame is a striking instance of unity in diversity. Its identity lies not in its substance, which is in continuous change, but in the structure it preserves through those changes. Its unity lies in the *relations* between its elements, not in the elements themselves. Herein, also, lies the unity of the world. One finds it not in its substance, which is in continuous change, but in the *relation* between one change and another, in the *structure* it preserves through its changing elements. There is an even more striking instance of Heraclitus's point in the human body, which is in continuous exchange of matter, so that the matter of a body at a certain time may be entirely different from what it was at an earlier one. Nevertheless it preserves its form and functions.

The priority of forms or function over matter is one of the greatest discoveries of human thought. In modern times there has been a revival of materialism, this being taken as in the line of scientific progress. In fact it is a reversion to the most primitive stage of scientific enquiry. Modern science has made progress precisely where it has ignored the substance of the world and has concentrated on its mathematical structure. The point is especially evident in contemporary physics, where the fundamental elements of physical theory can no longer be represented in material form, except in a shifting and approximate way. For example, the electron is sometimes a particle and sometimes a wave. Its reality is revealed through mathematical formulae, whose application is verified not by observation of the electron but through the consequences they have at the phenomenal level. In short, the only precise form of representation is mathematics.

Now Plato's philosophy is a development of Pythagorean ideas.[5] The great discovery which he contributed to this development is that form is *transcendent*. It is the manifestation *in* the world of what *transcends* the world. It is this view which he expresses in his famous doctrine of the Forms. The doctrine may be illustrated by reference to a simple concept such as red. It is a striking feature of such a concept that it is incommensurable with its instances. Thus a child is taught the use of the word by reference to a finite number of red objects. But so far as he applies the word simply to those instances he has not acquired its use. He is treating the word as though it were a name for just those objects. He has acquired its use only when he *goes beyond* the objects we have shown him and applies it to objects we have not shown him at all. Thus what he has learned − the concept or form of redness − is not identical with the particulars we have used in teaching him. But neither is it identical with the particulars to which he goes on to apply it. For if he has really acquired its use, he can go beyond those particulars also. Indeed he can go on indefinitely. What he has acquired transcends any set of particulars.

It is essential to note, however, that it is *through* the particulars that he acquires the concept of red. It is through his immersion in the particulars that he acquires what transcends them, so that the concept he acquires — with regard to those particulars — is both immanent and transcendent. He does not, for example, acquire the concept by inspecting some entity over and above the particulars. The point is important because a view of that kind has often been attributed to Plato himself. Thus the positivists of the nineteenth century attributed to him a radical dichotomy between the empirical world, which is the object of the senses, and the world of the Forms, which is the object of mind. According to them, he held that the object of knowledge is not at all the empirical world, which is illusory, but only the transcendent world of the Forms. They completed their analysis by claiming that his whole view rested on a confusion of language or, as they termed it, the hypostasization of concepts. By this they meant that Plato had taken abstract nouns, such as red, beauty and good, and had treated them as real entities.

Now there would be some excuse for the above interpretation were we confined to Plato's earlier dialogues, for he there uses language which on a hasty reading would suggest it. But the interpretation is impossible to sustain on any serious reading of the later work. In the *Parmenides*, for example, he explicitly raises and criticizes a view comparable to the one that the positivists attributed to him.[6] His argument, roughly put, is that if in order to gain the concept red, we needed to compare particular red objects with an entity redness, we should need another entity to judge that we had made the comparison correctly, and then a further entity to ascertain we had made *that* judgement correctly, and so on *ad infinitum*. The question therefore arises of whether a form is entirely separate from its particulars or whether it is wholly *in* those particulars. Plato rejected both those alternatives. Form is a manifestation *in* particulars of what *transcends* them. It is therefore both immanent and transcendent. That is not a contradiction. One thing transcends another when it *goes beyond* the other, *not* when it is wholly distinct from it. It is true that Plato tended to emphasize the transcendent aspect of form. But that was because it was this aspect which he thought had been neglected. The immanence of form he did not deny but took for granted.

Difficulties in understanding Plato's conception arise from considering the relation between a form and its particulars in physical terms. For example, take a number of small red discs and place them in a line on a table. Now take a large red disc. You can place it above the line of the small ones, or you can place it on the same line. You cannot put it in both places at once. The large red is either on the same line as the small ones (immanent) or above them (transcendent). But that is because you are dealing with physical objects. For Plato, form is *not* physical. In technical terms, it is *intentional* not extensional. In short, it is akin to mind. Plato's point is precisely that the mind can make sense of the world only because it has a structure or order of which the mind partakes. For that reason, it is absurd to suppose that he denied the intelligibility of the empirical world. The empirical world would be unintelligible if it consisted simply of indefinite change, or mere flux. The proof that change has order and is not a mere flux is that in some measure we can make sense of it. Moreover in this we prove the reality of order itself. The point is evident in what we have said about the Pythagoreans. The proof of their ideas is that they were enabled to make discoveries in the empirical world, for example in the field of acoustics, which could not have been made by their predecessors.

Plato's view of morality or justice follows from the ideas we have just considered. The form of justice, like that of red, is grasped through its particulars but cannot be identified with them. Plato was no doubt influenced in this view by his great teacher Socrates, who was himself influenced by Pythagorean ideas.[7] In the Platonic dialogues, Socrates continually seeks for a measure of justice and rejects any attempt to identify it with this or that example. In the dialogues, Plato attributes to Socrates the view that justice is transcendent. It is likely, however, that this was the effect of modesty on Plato's part and that he was attributing to Socrates what was implicit in his views but which was first emphasized by Plato himself. At any rate, it is clear in the dialogues that justice transcends its particulars. This means that the particulars stand to the form not as *instances* but as *approximations*. For Plato, there can be no instance in this world of perfect justice. There is in the world an implicit order of justice which if it is assimilated to the soul can lead a person towards the perfect form. But that itself cannot be embodied in the world, for it is transcendent. That also is why in order to grasp the form it is both impossible and unnecessary to inspect perfect justice. It is impossible, because perfect justice is transcendent. It is unnecessary, because the order of justice in the world is already informed by perfect justice, to which the soul is in some measure attuned. Being thus attuned, it can attain an implicit grasp of the form simply through an immersion in its particulars. In reading Plato, one must continually remind oneself that for him the relation between the transcendent and the immanent is not an external one. The immanent is, as it were, an image of the transcendent which is therefore implicit within it.

The above points are essential to bear in mind in considering *The Republic*, which contains Plato's most extended discussion of justice.[8] In that work, he treats justice as an order in the soul, which he illuminates by comparing it with that of a perfect city state. Many commentators have treated this work as though it advanced a political programme, the political arrangement which Plato considered ideal and hoped to apply in concrete circumstances.[9] That, however, is a radical misunderstanding of the work. As we have said, for Plato there can be no instance on earth of perfect justice and therefore no instance of a perfect city state. He expresses the point in *The Republic* by saying that were the perfect city to exist, it would immediately be subject to change and thereby would cease to be perfect. The sketch of the perfect city should be likened to the use of a diagram in a geometrical proof. The diagram represents the perfect line or circle. The aim of the geometer is not to embody the perfect line or circle, but to develop a measure which may be used the better to understand lines and circles in their imperfect forms. Plato's procedure is analogous. Thus immediately after completing his sketch of the perfect city, he uses it as a measure to understand city states in their imperfect forms. The method he employs is to imagine how the perfect city would decline into increasingly less perfect ones. Again, the method is not empirical but conceptual or geometrical. In other words, Plato is providing a measure, or set of concepts, by which disorder in the city can be understood and in some degree mastered.

Plato's point, then, is that the justice which is immanent in this world is always imperfect but it is the manifestation of a transcendent justice and it is only those who have been turned or led towards justice in its transcendent form who can fully understand it in its imperfection. The point is expressed in *The Republic* by means of a wonderful image or parable.[10] Plato imagines a set of people who are imprisoned within a cave. These people are chained and are unable to move, being able to direct their gaze only towards one of the walls of the cave. Behind them there is a great fire. Between them and the fire there is a raised path along which their warders pass, casting shadows on the wall in front of the prisoners. The prisoners themselves, being unable to move, take the shadows for real figures. They study how they come and go, make predictions about when they will reappear, and so on. Plato then imagines a turning around of the body, a sort of conversion, by which one of the prisoners sees behind him the fire. At first he is dazzled by the fire and cannot find his bearings. But if he persists he will become accustomed to his condition. He will then acquire a knowledge different in kind from what he had before, for it is not acquired by calculating the shadows on the wall of the cave. Rather it is a knowledge which enables him to understand what he was doing when he studied those shadows, what it was that formerly passed with him as knowledge. But he must not linger in this position. For he has a path before him, an ascent to make. He has to make the ascent from the cave into the daylight, into the full flood of the sun. Here the experience with the fire is repeated, though with incomparably greater intensity. But at last he will know the sun, the symbol of all joy, the only object of lasting satisfaction.

It is only someone who has undergone these experiences who will fully understand the nature of good and evil and who will appreciate the misery of those who live in the cave, who are in love with its darkness and cannot find deliverance.

It is likely that this parable is symbolic at a number of levels, representing at its most fundamental a set of actual experiences. It is clear, however, that the sun represents divine goodness, a goodness which transcends this world, and that the cave represents the empirical world or world of ordinary sense-experience. It is important to note that the cave is not illusory. Indeed it represents what is only too real. It is the inhabitants who are in a state of illusion, but that is because they identify the *whole* of reality with the cave. They cannot grasp its connection with the world which transcends it and is the very source of its reality. Similarly, sense-experience is not in itself illusory. Rather it is relative. The contact with reality which the senses afford, though genuine, is partial. For in sense-experience the world appears only in modes that are relative to the subject. Reality is in a manner veiled by the mode that reveals it. The senses become illusory when they absorb us into the world as they reveal it, so that we take as absolute what is merely relative.

Deliverance from the cave occurs in two stages. The first, represented by the fire, consists in grasping that sense-experience is inadequate to explain even the natural world. In *The Republic*, Plato shows how this can be achieved by a rigorous training in the sciences and especially in mathematics. Study of the natural world will reveal that it can be understood only by grasping the order amongst its elements and that this can neither be grasped nor explained by sense-experience alone. That corresponds to the discovery of the Pythagoreans. The second stage, represented by the sun, consists in seeing that just as the natural world stands to that of sense-experience so reality stands to the natural world. In other words, the natural world is itself a manifestation of what transcends it. This corresponds to Plato's own discovery that there is a transcendent element in all order or form.

It is essential to note, however, that the process of deliverance involves a transformation not simply of the intellect but also of the soul. Indeed, for Plato, the intellect can be transformed only when it works within a soul which is ordered by a love of the good. The reason for this is given in the parable of the cave. The reality of the cave can be revealed only to those who have transcended it. Indeed even those who have transcended it will seem for a while to be in a worse condition than those they have left behind, for they will be dazzled by the fire. They will adjust to their condition if they persist but they will persist only through desire and will, not through the intellect. It is impossible, simply through reasoning, to persuade the people in the cave that there is a reality transcending their own, because they will accept no reasoning as valid unless it is a calculation of the shadows on their wall. But that process of calculation already excludes the idea that there is a reality transcending their cave. Similarly it is impossible to persuade many people that the world which appears to them in sense experience is relative not absolute. For to them it is not relative, and therefore they will judge the truth of what you say according to whether it corresponds to the world as it appears in sense-experience. The source of truth lies not in the individual but in his relation to the objective order of the world. If a soul is disordered, he will judge the truth of what you say on the basis of his disorder. Consequently there can be no deliverance unless there is a transformation of the will as well as the intellect and unless there is an objective order of value by which the individual can be drawn towards the good.

In the parable of the cave, Plato portrays, in figurative form, various stages in the transformation of the will. But he says little about what, in the earlier stages, arouses the will and serves to inspire it. For example, what makes the prisoner turn around and, in spite of his suffering, persist in his journey. Plato says more about this in his other works, where he speaks of how the particular loves, and especially the love of beauty, may serve as a source of inspiration. He speaks, for example, of how the love of particular beautiful things may lead to a love of the beauty inherent in the order of the world, and that, in its turn, to a love of the source of that order and of all beauty. In recent times, especially, he has been criticized for this view, on the ground that it denigrates the particular loves by treating them as devices for obtaining higher experience. But that is to misunderstand what he means. The man who decided to fall in love in order to obtain higher experiences would fall short not simply of the higher experiences but also of love. And then he could hardly be inspired. Plato's point is that even in the particular loves, the will is already transformed through having been drawn into relations not of its own choosing. And the will once transformed may be transformed further, but only if there are still further relations, not of its own choosing, into which it can be drawn. Once again, transformation is possible only because there is an order of value, implicit in the world, which has its source in the transcendent good.

Plato was not only a great philosopher but also a great artist. His dialogues may be read simply for their portrayal of the intellectual life of his time. One of the most striking features of this portrayal is how often the Greeks of this time anticipated doctrines which have flourished in our own. It will be useful to illustrate the point, for we shall have occasion later to consider some of these doctrines ourselves. In an early dialogue, *Euthyphro*, Socrates raises the problem of whether holiness is loved by the gods because it is holy or whether it is holy because it is loved by the gods.[11] As we shall see, philosophers in modern times have raised a similar problem in order to establish that morality is autonomous and especially that it is independent of religion. Their argument is that God wills honesty because it is good; it is not good because God wills it, for then it would be an arbitrary matter that it is morally good at all. In other words, if honesty is morally good, it is inherently so. Consequently morality is autonomous and does not require the support of religion.

It is amongst the Sophists, however, that we find the most striking anticipations of modern doctrines. The term 'Sophist' means lover of wisdom, but amongst the Greeks of Plato's time it had a more restricted usage, being applied to certain teachers of rhetoric. The Greeks were great lovers of skill in oratory and disputation and the leading Sophists earned considerable sums of money as teachers of that skill. What is more to our purpose, however, is that there was a philosophy associated with the Sophists which strikingly anticipates modern forms of relativism. The philosophy arose through noting variations amongst different peoples in their moral and legal codes. Fire burns both in Greece and in Persia, but the laws of the Persians differ from those of the Greeks. This leads to a distinction between nature and convention. That fire burns is a law of *nature*. That one should bury rather than burn one's dead is a matter of *convention*. Value is relative; fact is objective. This distinction, however, is highly unstable. Those who are sufficiently reflective, having denied the objectivity of value, will soon find themselves denying the objectivity of fact. At first sight, it is not obvious why this should be so. Judgements of value can be settled only by reference to human standards, but judgements of fact can be settled by reference to the objective world itself. It will be obvious on reflection, however, that whether one is referring to the objective world may itself be a matter of dispute. One man says one thing; another contradicts him. Which is correct? The objective world will not step in and settle the matter for us. At some point, we have to make an *evaluation*. We have to fall back on some human standard of what constitutes objective fact. But in that case, judgements of fact, no less than judgements of value, are being settled by reference to human standards. All is relative.

The classic expression for this relativism is that man is the measure of all things. The expression is attributed to the famous Sophist Protagoras,[12] and in the dialogues Plato represents him as arguing that each man is the measure of what is true for himself. In short, that there is no objective truth. But though there is no objective truth, there is still persuasion. If you persuade a man to accept your opinion, you have made it true for him as well as for yourself. In other words, you have made it, in the only coherent sense, true. This philosophy was congenial to the Sophists, who were skilled in the art of persuasion. So far as they could make their opinions prevail, they could make them true, for the only measure of whether an opinion is true is that it prevails.

This philosophy is in conflict at every point with Plato's own. For him, truth is distinct from persuasion. Whether you succeed in persuading a person of the truth will depend not simply on your relation to him, but on the relation in which you both stand to an objective order. If it is only you who stand in the right relation to that order, you are not likely to succeed in persuading him. Nevertheless, it is your view, not his, which will be true.

This means that man is *not* the measure of all things. There can be no objective truth unless there is already in the world an intelligible order, of which the mind can partake. But to speak of intelligibility and order is to speak of value. The objectivity of value is therefore presupposed in the objectivity of truth, so that to deny the one is inevitably to deny the other. In this the Sophists testify, though unwittingly, to the truth.

Plato's philosophy is inescapably religious. The point is made explicit in his last work, *The Laws*.[13] In the tenth Book of that work, he explains his theology, which includes a sustained critique of atheism. The atheism with which he deals is the one that was prevalent amongst certain philosophers in his own day. It depends on a reversion to the Ionian conception of the world. Thus it argues that order has evolved out of chance distributions of matter, thereby presupposing that matter is prior to order. Plato rejects this view as incoherent, defends the view that order is prior to matter, and argues that in order the transcendent is already implicit. For Plato it is God not man who is the measure of all things.

We must now turn to Aristotle, the philosopher who, apart from Plato himself, exerted the greatest influence on the classical tradition. It is usual to emphasize the differences between the two. Aristotle himself emphasized those differences. But here we come upon a problem of some delicacy. Aristotle spent about twenty years in the academy which Plato founded; he knew him personally and must have been thoroughly familiar with his views. He expresses for Plato the greatest admiration. Nevertheless in expounding his views he frequently misrepresents him. We may take an instance, noted by Eric Voegelin,[14] which, though small in itself, is representative. In *The Laws*, Plato states that the population of the city state should stand at 5,040. Aristotle misrepresents this number as 5,000, takes it as literal, and criticizes it on that basis. Voegelin points out (what should in any case be evident) that Plato's number is symbolic. It is part of a complicated system of numbers, divisible by twelve, which is intended by Plato to symbolize the relation between the order of the city state and the order of the cosmos. As Voegelin says, Aristotle's admiration for Plato was undoubtedly genuine but one suspects that it contained a certain admixture of resentment.

In estimating the differences between the two, it will be useful to begin with the most obvious one. Aristotle denied that Forms exist separately from the objects of the world. Rather, they are immanent in these objects. This is supposed to mark a striking contrast with the views of Plato. But Aristotle must have known that Plato did not deny the immanence of form. Moreover it is obvious from his works that he himself did not deny its transcendence. We may illustrate the point by means of a passage in the *Metaphysics*.

> In what way does the nature of the world contain what is good and what is best – as something separate and independent, or as its own orderliness? Rather, in both ways, as an army does. For the excellence of an army resides both in its orderliness and in its general, and especially in the latter. For he does not depend on the orderliness but it depends on him. And all things – fish and birds and plants – are ordered in a way, yet not in the same way; and it is not the case that there is no connection between one thing and another – there is a connection.[15]

Here Aristotle, like Plato, identifies order and goodness and argues, again like Plato, that it is both immanent and transcendent. Thus the orderliness amongst the foot-soldiers is something they really possess but it has its source in the general who is above them. Again, in Book VIII of the *Physics*, he follows Plato in arguing that the order of the world is not self-explanatory. Thus the changes of the world must have their source in what transcends them, being itself changeless. This unmoved mover is therefore outside the universe.

> Must there be something unchanging and at rest outside what is changing and no part of it, or not? And must this be true of the universe too? It would presumably seem absurd if the principle of change were *inside* it.[16]

The more one studies Aristotle, the more obvious it becomes that he is working within a basic set of ideas that he has inherited from Plato. His analysis of perception will illustrate the point. According to Aristotle, one perceives through sensory experience, which produces a reproduction in the body of the object experienced. In sight, for example, one has in one's body a copy of the object seen. At this point, Aristotle seems to be advancing a representative view of perception. One knows an object by perceiving its copy. But that is not at all Aristotle's view. What the mind apprehends is the *form* which is *common* to the copy and its object. This form is *not* material. The copy and its object are materially distinct but their common form is one and the same. Thus the mind in perception takes on the form of its object and does not reproduce but literally becomes one with it. We may take a further illustration from hearing. The sounding object produces vibrations. These affect the body which reproduces them. The vibrations in the body are materially distinct from those in the sounding object. But the *rate* or *order* of vibration is identical in the two cases. It is this which the mind apprehends. Aristotle's account becomes immediately clear once one realizes that he is following Plato's view, according to which what is known in perceiving an object is not its matter but its form or order.[17] Aristotle has produced an account which is essentially similar. Thus, for him, the mind perceives an object by apprehending its form, leaving, as it were, its matter behind. This account is entirely obscured by modern commentators who treat Aristotle as though he reduced the body to pure matter and the soul to its material functions. But that is a radical misunderstanding. For Aristotle the body is *not* purely material. Indeed *nothing* is purely material. Pure matter is mere potentiality. It is actual only as the embodiment of form. Thus the human body is both material and immaterial. It is embodied form or soul. Moreover the embodied soul exists in different modes. In the highest mode, the intellectual, it can apprehend pure or disembodied form. The thoughts of God, for example, are thus disembodied. So far as the soul can apprehend any of these thoughts it becomes identical with the thought of God; it becomes in a manner divine. For that reason, as Aristotle acknowledges, the soul in its intellectual mode may exist quite independently of the material body.

It may be illuminating at this point to compare Aristotle's view of the relation between soul and body with that of Descartes (1596–1650). It has long been fashionable to attribute many of the difficulties in modern philosophy to Descartes's malign influence. It has often been said, for example, that he gave rise to these difficulties by making too radical a distinction between soul and body; and in this respect he has been compared unfavourably with Aristotle. Now with regard to the relation between soul and body, the differences between the two have been greatly exaggerated. Descartes knew very well that there is a certain unity between soul and body. He denied, for example, that the relation could be understood on the model of a pilot in his vessel. When we feel pain, we may know our body is damaged without having to observe it. But it is only by observing his vessel that a pilot can know whether it is damaged.[18] Moreover, Aristotle knew very well that the soul cannot be reduced to its material base. As we have said, he saw no contradiction in supposing that the soul might exist quite independently of the body. Where the two really differ is in what they say not about the relation between soul and body in the knowing subject but about the relation between the knowing subject and the rest of the world. For Descartes, the objects of the physical world are purely material, being wholly explicable as matter in motion. It follows that there is an unbridgeable gulf between the knowing subject and its object, the latter being purely material, the former immaterial. Of course, one can bridge this gulf by treating the knowing subject and its object as alike material. But then it is impossible to explain how the one can know the other. For Aristotle, these difficulties did not exist, because for him the essence of the world is not matter but intelligible order. This order is all-pervasive. Consequently the knowing subject and its object are alike both material and immaterial. For that reason, there can be no gulf between them.

It will be important to dwell for a moment on the non-material side of natural objects. An acorn grows into an oak. Let us consider the acorn itself. It has a certain stuff or matter and it has a history, having arisen from its parent tree. But it also has a future. It will grow into an oak. Is this future development connected only accidentally with the acorn which is before us here and now? No one believes that this is so. In some sense, it belongs to the nature of the acorn to develop in that way. But if you consider the acorn as material stuff you will nowhere discern that development. That is because its development is controlled not by its material base alone but by a real though non-material teleology. It is the same with the growth of the human body. At a certain point, the proliferating cells shape themselves into an arm and then into a hand. It is commonly supposed that all this can be explained by the DNA structure of the gene. But you can study the chemical structure of the gene for as long as you wish and nowhere will you find the organization of the body, which develops over time and cannot be located in a material particle. It will be obvious on reflection that no process of growth can be sufficiently explained by its material base. For the process of growth consists of successive stages, each of which has properties which are not contained in the earlier ones. That is what it is for a thing to grow. But then it follows that the earlier stages cannot be sufficient to explain the later ones. Consequently we must assume either that in the process of development each stage emerges purely by chance from an earlier one – which is fantastic – or that the process has a unity and is controlled throughout by a real teleology. The latter view is Aristotle's. There is in nature a real teleology which is not the mere projection of human purpose. Indeed it seems evident that human purpose is itself the outgrowth of a natural teleology. For it would be absurd to suppose that human beings have invented purpose. Invention is itself a purposive process. Nor is the child *taught* to behave purposively. Its behaviour is inescapably so; otherwise, it could not be taught at all.

We may note that the prevalence of Darwinism, especially in its vulgar form, has served to obscure the truth in Aristotle's view. It is still widely believed, for example, that the process of evolution can be wholly explained by reference to chance and the struggle for existence. But this is a delusion. It has long been known that the development of biological form is independent of the environment. The inheritance of acquired characteristics, for example, which Darwin came to think essential to his theory, has been dismissed by most biologists as impossible. The struggle for existence may serve as a selective mechanism but it cannot conceivably explain biological form, since without biological forms there would be nothing to select. Moreover it was known in the nineteenth century, through the work of Mendel and De Vries, that one species cannot evolve into another through random variations. The change from one species to another involves a change in *form*, which requires a series of *co-ordinated* changes, not an accumulation of small changes occurring at random. In short, the forms are fixed, so that the change from one to another can occur only through a mutation or jump. The followers of Darwin attempt to reconcile his theory with these facts by claiming that all mutations themselves occur purely by chance. But this is in conflict with the principles of rigorous thought. The striking feature of the evolutionary process is that it involves the development of increasingly more complex forms of organization. The operation of chance is detected by the randomness of its effects and by the increasing randomness of those effects the longer it operates. In short, the evolutionary process exhibits precisely those features which are not produced by the operation of chance.[19]

Now in considering Aristotle's view of ethics or morality, it is essential to take it in relation to his teleological view of the world. Unfortunately there is a tendency amongst modern commentators to take it separately. Thus there is a movement in modern moral philosophy – sometimes called Neo-Aristotelian – which seeks to remove as outdated his general view of the world whilst retaining what he says, for example, about the virtues. But this is an impossible task since his view of the virtues is inextricably involved with his general view of the world. We must consider the matter in some detail.

For Aristotle, it is through the exercise of virtue that a person fulfils his nature and becomes happy or blessed.[20] But none of this can be understood unless we consider what constitutes a person's nature. It is determined not by the peculiarities of his character but by what he has in common with other human beings. But what human beings have in common is not something they all happen in fact to possess. They have in common what they are *meant* to be. In short, human nature is teleological. Each of us instantiates in various degrees of imperfection a common form which, through us, is striving to fulfil itself. Consequently our nature is to be determined not by assessing, statistically, how we are, but by considering what we are intended to be. For that reason happiness or blessedness (the Greek is *eudaimonia*) is not to be confused with personal satisfaction. We achieve *eudaimonia* by achieving what we are intended to be, *not* by achieving what we *happen* to intend. In other words, the purpose we are here to fulfil is not our own.

Now if one removes the teleological structure of Aristotle's ethics, one may still retain some semblance of an Aristotelian view. For example, one may define *eudaimonia* as personal satisfaction and one may argue – some might think implausibly – that this is achieved by being virtuous. But one will have replaced an objective with a subjective ethics. The difference is not minimal; it evidently goes to the root. One may, it is true, attempt to preserve some element of objectivity by taking satisfaction in the collective not the individual sense. One may take as one's end the sum of human satisfactions. But that is only to take as good what at a given time, or in the long run, happens to satisfy the majority of people. The difference from Aristotle's view is as great as it was before. For Aristotle *eudaimonia* is an activity of the soul in accordance with that excellence which is intended for us by nature, and which has been infused into nature by God. It is not likely that this will be achieved, at any given time, by more than a few. The idea that what is good is what satisfies the majority would have seemed to Aristotle not simply erroneous but pernicious. For its effect is to divert people from what is essential in their nature to what is contingent. It bids them be satisfied with what they are as distinct from striving towards what they ought to become.

We can clarify the above points if we turn for a moment to Aristotle's view of the relation between form and chance. For Aristotle, the element of chance in life is real, and it is intimately related to the existence of matter. For matter, though it embodies form, is in some manner recalcitrant to that embodiment. Thus the embodiment of form is imperfect. There is an obvious relation to Plato's view that perfect justice is transcendent and that in this world justice is always an approximation. Common to both is the view that there is a striving throughout this world towards a perfection which can be only imperfectly realized. A biological analogy will illuminate the point. The form of a leaf is evident in the pattern of its veins. But if you examine the pattern closely, you will find that it becomes obscure in its ultimate ramifications, breaking up into minor lines, which are never exactly the same in any two leaves. Here we have a beautiful image of the relation between form and chance. The common form or pattern of the leaf is always affected in its embodiment by chance or contingent circumstances, so that two leaves having the same form are never exactly the same. Now human beings have reason. Their divergences from the pattern of their nature may be apprehended, however dimly, and will then appear as imperfection. They will be aware of the difference between what through contingent circumstances they have become and what they are intended to be. So far as they have acquired virtue they will be enabled in some measure to control the effects of chance, to approach what they are intended to be, and in this to achieve *eudaimonia*.

The basic philosophy of Plato and Aristotle may be described as classical or transcendental realism. For both, value is not a projection of human feeling but an objective order, and this order is not self-explanatory but has its source in what is transcendent and divine. The elements in this philosophy are locked together into a whole. If you remove the divine source, you undermine the order of nature; if you undermine the order of nature, you destroy all value. As we have noted, this philosophy had its critics, even in ancient Greece; nevertheless it was the predominant philosophy and continued as such until the close of the Middle Ages. To illustrate this continuity, we may look, if only briefly, at the moral philosophy of Aquinas, the greatest of the medieval philosophers.

In moral philosophy, Aquinas is best known for his view that morality is based on natural law.[21] It is important, however, to be clear about what he meant by that view. Some have taken him to mean that moral principles can be verified as one might verify the law of gravity, by appealing to facts that can be appreciated even by people who otherwise have no sense of good and evil. But that is not what he meant. His view, rather, is that moral reasoning depends on principles which do not themselves depend on reasoning but are given us by nature. Anyone can appreciate his point by reflecting on what reason he has for some moral principle he considers fundamental. For example, why do I think that murder is wrong? I can think of a number of reasons. But if I reflect further, I find that none is more certain than my belief that murder is wrong. Thus, suppose someone says that murder is wrong because it leads to the degeneration of society. In that case, it would not be wrong where it did not have those consequences. One can easily conceive of circumstances where it is only by committing murder that one can *prevent* the degeneration of society. In those circumstances, there would be nothing wrong with committing murder. Some have held that view, but not many have agreed with them. We almost all feel, at the very least, that in those circumstances we should be confronted by a terrible dilemma. But there could be no dilemma unless we felt that there is something wrong not simply with the degeneration of society but also, quite independently, with murder. Our feeling towards murder is thus an example of what Aquinas means when he says that there are moral principles which are not based on reasoning but are given us by nature.

It is important to note, however, that such principles are not *incompatible* with reasoning. Quite the contrary, Aquinas holds that moral reasoning is cogent only so far as it is informed by such principles. I can reason in the given case about what is good or evil only because I know the difference between the two. I know the difference between the two not because I have discovered it but because it has been given to me. It has been given to me as a natural habit or disposition, a natural way of reacting to good and evil when they appear. The alternative is to suppose that for every moral belief I need another belief to justify it. But then I should never arrive at a moral belief. For every reason I should need another, and so on *ad infinitum*. Aquinas here follows the views of Aristotle or, as he calls him, the

Philosopher. Together they hold that all reasoning, whether theoretical or practical, depends ultimately on natural principle.

> The human act of reasoning, since it is a certain movement, proceeds from the understanding of certain things – namely, those which are naturally known without any investigation on the part of reason, as from an immovable principle – and ends also at understanding, inasmuch as, by means of those principles naturally known of themselves, we judge of those things we have discovered by reasoning. Now, it is clear that, as the speculative reason argues about speculative things, so practical reason argues about practical things. Therefore, it is fitting that we have bestowed on us by nature not only speculative principles but also practical things. Now, the first speculative principles bestowed on us by nature do not belong to a special power but to a special habit, which is called 'the understanding of principles', as the Philosopher explains. Wherefore, the first practical principles bestowed on us by nature do not belong to a special power but to a special natural habit, which we call *synderesis*.[22] Thus synderesis is said to incite to good and to murmur at evil, inasmuch as we proceed from first principles to discover and judge of what we have discovered.[23]

Given that by nature we are incited to attain the good and to murmur at evil we have in us a natural law which, if we follow it through, will enable us in particular cases to reason with some purpose. Otherwise, we reason in a void; in short, we do not genuinely reason at all. Note that there is something given to us and something we do ourselves. It is we who have to reason in particular cases; nature will not do it for us. Moreover in morals, as distinct from some of the sciences, we deal so often not with what is permanent and necessary but with what is particular and contingent. In consequence we cannot expect to find in moral reasoning the degree of precision which may be found in other forms. The point is important because it is sometimes assumed that natural law, on Aquinas's view, will enable us to arrive at clear-cut solutions to every moral problem. In fact he held the opposite view.

> The practical reason is concerned with practical matters, which are singular and contingent, but not with necessary things, with which the speculative reason is concerned. Wherefore human laws cannot have that inerrancy that belongs to the demonstrated conclusions of sciences. Nor is it necessary for every measure to be altogether unerring and certain but according as it is possible in its own particular genus.[24]

In moral reasoning, we cannot always expect clear-cut answers to our problems; often we must shift for ourselves, making do with the best we can. Nevertheless we are very far from being delivered over to pure arbitrariness. For the natural law, which is in us, is itself the reflection in nature of divine wisdom. Here as in Plato and Aristotle we have the same interlocking of elements into a whole. Moral value is real because it reflects objective order which itself reflects its transcendent source.

> As on the part of the speculative reason, by a natural participation of divine wisdom, there is in us the knowledge of certain general principles but not the proper knowledge of each single truth, such as that contained in the divine wisdom, so too on the part of the practical reason, man has a natural participation of the eternal law according to certain general principles but not as regards the particular determinations of individual cases, which are, however, contained in the eternal law.[25]

* * *

We see therefore that throughout the classical period there was an intimate connection between morality and the idea of a transcendent reality. But, as we have said, this connection has frequently been denied in the modern period. The secularization of learning has proceeded apace since the sixteenth century and during this time there have been many attempts to give an account of morality in purely secular or naturalistic terms. We must consider whether any has succeeded in giving an account which is wholly coherent. The modern period lacks the unity of the classical, and we are confronted in moral philosophy with a number of different and conflicting systems. To bring them into order, we shall sort them into three categories: the utilitarian, the deontological and the relativist. We shall take them in that order, explaining what each involves, as we proceed.

Utilitarianism was first developed by Jeremy Bentham (1748–1832).[26] He was aware that morality has its basis as much in feeling as in reason, that feelings differ and that where people disagree in morals, there often seems no way to settle that disagreement. We have noted this point in dealing with classical philosophers. Aquinas, for example, held that there is in moral reasoning an element of uncertainty or imprecision, which arises from the gap between the imperfection of this world and the reality it reflects. For that reason, he took the feature to be inevitable and he warned that in dealing with morality, one should not attempt to force on it a greater degree of precision than it will bear. For Bentham, however, the feature was not inevitable. He took it to reveal a confusion which could be removed by the application of scientific method. The aspect of scientific method which figures prominently in Bentham is that of quantification. We have already implied, in dealing with the Pythagoreans, that the natural sciences owe much of their success to their transforming qualitative distinctions into quantitative ones. The difference between a 12 lb and an 8 lb bag of coal is a quantitative one. The one bag contains *more* of what is contained in the other. By contrast the difference between red and blue is qualitative. One cannot say that the one colour is different from the other through containing more of what they have in common. The colours are just different. But scientists have succeeded in transforming the qualitative difference into a quantitative one, by translating it into a neutral vocabulary. Thus we speak of light waves rather than of colours. And now the difference between red and blue can be expressed through different frequencies in the common medium, the light wave. Once nature is quantified in this way, it can be handled mathematically and this enormously increases our ability to predict and control it.

Now Bentham applied a similar procedure to morality, taking as his neutral term pleasure or happiness. He held that we are all bound to pursue happiness and that we differ only in our ways of obtaining it. Consequently pleasure or happiness provides him with the neutral term by which he can transform the qualitative difference between good and evil into a quantitative one. Now where we differ in morals we do not have to argue about it. Instead, we can calculate. To determine whether one act is better than another, we have only to calculate which produces the greater amount of pleasure or happiness. Here we have Bentham's famous principle of utility or of the greatest happiness. By means of it, he not only provides a criterion for settling moral disagreement but also elucidates the point or meaning of morality. For morality is now integrated with the rest of our lives. The principles of morality merely indicate how in the rest of our lives we can best obtain our happiness. Here we have an account which makes sense of morality in purely scientific or naturalistic terms.

Unfortunately, there are difficulties. As J. S. Mill,[27] Bentham's own follower, pointed out, we distinguish between qualities of pleasure and happiness itself. For example, the pleasure which the sadist finds in his cruelty does not mitigate the evil of his act. Rather, it makes it worse. In short, some pleasures are themselves bad. But if pleasure is sometimes bad, it cannot be the ultimate criterion of good. It cannot be the ultimate criterion of evaluation, since it can itself be evaluated. The point is sound. Moreover it takes us to the weakness which is at the centre of Bentham's system. This lies in his idea of pleasure. For Bentham it is essential that pleasure be the primary end which gives value to all our activities. Otherwise, it would be impossible to hold that we all have a single end in common and therefore that there is a single measure for all our values. For example, suppose one person gets pleasure from music and another from football. They can be said to pursue a common end only if what they value is not the music or the football but simply the pleasure it gives them. In fact, however, pleasure is not the primary but a secondary end. Pleasure can be an end only to someone who already values other things. For otherwise there would be nothing to give him pleasure and then it could not figure for him as an end at all. For example, it cannot be that the person who gets pleasure from music values the pleasure as distinct from the music. If he did not value music, he would not get pleasure from it. Indeed it will be evident on reflection that the pleasure which music gives a person is merely the sign of how much he values *music*. Similarly the pleasure which football gives a person is the sign of how much he values *football*. But now it is evident that these two do not value the same thing at all; they value *different* things.

At this point, Bentham's whole position begins to crumble. If people take pleasure in different things, this is not a sign that beneath apparent differences there is ultimate unity. Rather it is precisely the sign of how much people differ in what they value. There now approaches a still darker shadow. If there is a common end which people are bound to follow and which can be achieved only by acting morally, then people are bound to act morally. Here we have a plausible explanation in naturalistic terms for that absolute element in morality which we noticed when we were discussing Wittgenstein's *Lecture on Ethics*. But if there is no such end, the plausibility vanishes. Suppose, for example, that there is a person who is prepared to put the happiness of others before his own. Such a person has a reason to act morally, to be generous, just, and so on. But suppose I prefer my own happiness to that of others. It can no longer be said that I value the same thing as the other person. But in that case what reason do I have to be moral? Why is the claim of morality absolute not simply in his case but also in my own? The absolute element, it seems, has still to be explained.

We may note, however, that there are views which are akin to the utilitarian but which are not based in the same way on pleasure or happiness. An example is the so-called Neo-Aristotelian view, which we mentioned earlier. It will be useful to consider it in more detail. According to this view, the central element in morality are the virtues. These have an absolute claim on us, because they are what anyone needs in order to flourish or fare well in this life. The notion of flourishing or faring well differs from the utilitarian end in that it allows of variety. One may flourish in various ways. But the claim is that however one aims to flourish, one will need such virtues as courage, justice and prudence. A view of this kind was very clearly stated in the 1950s by Philippa Foot.[28] Her argument was that a virtue such as justice cannot be binding on everyone unless everyone has a reason to pursue it. But it cannot be that everyone has a reason to pursue it, unless everyone needs it in order to flourish or fare well in this life. She then claimed that this is precisely what is true of justice.

The difficulty with the Neo-Aristotelian view is that many virtuous people seem not to flourish and many who flourish seem not to be virtuous. What is in the interest of justice, for example, seems not to be identical with what is in the interest of the just person, and many in being just have sacrificed their own interest. The reply is that the harm which befalls the just person is in a manner accidental. It does not effect the *point* of virtue, which is that *in general* it is what one needs in order to flourish. There are two difficulties in this reply. The first is that those who suffer harm in being virtuous serve us as examples of supreme virtue. We may cite, for instance, Socrates or Thomas More. If the point of virtue is to flourish, it is hard to see why we express the greatest admiration for its exercise precisely where it fails to achieve its point. The second difficulty is even graver. The harm which befalls those of great virtue seems to occur too often for it to be entirely accidental. In this world, there are few circumstances where one is ill-served by a lively sense of one's own interest. It is therefore not surprising that those who are blind to their own interest and wholly committed to justice should so often fall into harm. Here we have the difficulty which haunts every attempt to make sense of morality in purely naturalistic terms. In the nature of the case, a naturalistic account will deny the existence of a transcendent reality and seek to make sense of morality by showing how it fits the conditions of this world alone. The difficulty is that the conditions of this world seem rarely to fit virtue. Or rather, they fit it only so far as it is confined to a certain level of mediocrity. Beyond that level, what is striking is the incompatibility between the requirements of virtue and the conditions for flourishing in this world.

But we must not move too quickly. We have still to consider two further categories. We may find that the incompatibility disappears. In our second category, we have the deontological view. On this view, morality is strictly autonomous, the only motive for duty being duty itself. We may consider this view as it was developed by two so-called intuitionists, G. E. Moore (1873–1958) and H. A. Prichard (1871–1947).[29] They are called intuitionists because they hold that morality is immediately apprehended. Moore, it is true, distinguishes in this respect between right and good.[30] Good is immediately apprehended; right is calculated. But this, for our purpose, is a minor complication, since it is good which Moore takes as fundamental. The calculation of what is right depends on the more fundamental intuition of what is good. Moore describes good as a non-natural property and he calls any attempt to define it in other terms the naturalistic fallacy. For this reason, he has been looked at askance by many philosophers wedded to the naturalistic view. They have taken him to hold that good is a property which transcends the natural world. But in this they have misunderstood him. The reason why it is a fallacy to define good in other terms is simply that there are no other terms in which to define it. In other words, Moore calls good a non-natural property not because it is transcendent but because it is *sui generis*. It is what it is. For Moore, it is just a brute fact about the world that some things are binding on us independently of our own interest. Consequently, for him, there is no problem in explaining why a person should sacrifice his own interest in pursuing the good. The good is precisely that which, when it is immediately apprehended, compels us to pursue it independently of our own interest.

A similar view was defended by H. A. Prichard. In a celebrated paper, he noted that moral philosophy often consisted in the attempt to provide a reason for being moral.[31] He then produced an ingenious *reductio ad absurdum* argument against any such attempt. He argued, in effect, that were such an attempt to succeed, it would thereby fail. Thus, suppose it succeeds. For example we induce a person to be moral by showing it will make him happy. But if he acts morally for that reason, he is really pursuing his own interest and not acting morally at all. We have failed. We cannot give anyone a reason for being moral, for one acts morally just so far as one pursues morality for its own sake and not for any reason. In this way, it can be demonstrated that morality is *sui generis*.

Here we have the philosophy which gives definitive expression to the modern view that morality is autonomous. Indeed, the view that morality is independent of religion is often supported by arguments of Prichard's type. For example, in Christianity morality is connected with the hope of immortal life. We are told to find our treasure not in this world but in heaven. Against this it is argued that a person who acts morally for the sake of heaven is not genuinely moral. He treats morality as a means to some further end and therefore implies that it has no value in itself.

It is therefore important to see that Prichard's argument is fallacious. What is true is that *some* reasons are incompatible with morality. It is plausible, for example, that if a person acts morally *simply* in order to serve his own interest, he is not genuinely moral. It plainly does not follow that *any* reason is incompatible with morality. Prichard's argument, in fact, involves a confusion about the relation between means and end which is common in philosophy. Thus it is commonly assumed that a means derives its value entirely from its end and therefore has no value in itself. That is why it is assumed that if a person has any end in view when he acts morally, his moral action in itself cannot have genuine value for him. But the assumption is plainly false. There are many ends which can be achieved only where the means also has genuine value. For example, if a person takes pleasure in music, that surely gives him a reason or motive to pursue it. But, as we have seen, he cannot take pleasure in music unless he genuinely values not simply the pleasure but also the music. Again, the study of literature can teach one much about life. But this requires that one has a genuine interest not simply in life but also in literature. We may take a further case. If a man loves a woman, he wants the happiness of their being together. It is obvious that this adds point or motive to his love. But it would surely be absurd to infer that since he wants this happiness, he does not really love her. Plainly it is because he loves her that he wants and anticipates this happiness. There is an evident parallel in the case of the Christian. His hope of immortal life adds point or motive to his love for God. It would be no less absurd to infer that since he wants this happiness, he does not really love God. It is precisely because he loves God that he wants and anticipates the happiness.

We may note that Moore's views are equally fallacious. The point can be illustrated by means of an example that he used himself. He likened good to a colour such as yellow, in order to emphasize that good is similarly unanalysable and immediately apprehended. In fact the differences between a value and a colour term are more striking than the resemblances. For example, one can imagine two objects which are exactly alike except that one is yellow and the other is not. Think, for instance, of a yellow and a red snooker ball. The colour of each is independent of its other qualities. But can one imagine two faces which are exactly alike, in shape of feature, colouring, etc., except that one is beautiful and the other is ugly? If one is beautiful and the other ugly, there must be some difference between them in shape of feature, colouring, etc. In short, the beauty of a face is not independent of its other qualities. The same point applies to moral qualities. For example, two characters cannot be identical in every respect except that one is base and the other noble. This means that morality is not autonomous; it presupposes other things.

David Hume (1711–76) in his *Treatise of Human Nature* had already made this point in arguing that good and duty are *secondary* ends. We do not value a thing because it is good; in calling it good we already express that we value it. Hume gave the example of a parent who does not love his children but cares for them out of duty. This is a possible case, as he acknowledges, but it presupposes that there are parents who care for their children because they do love them. We do not value the care of children because it is a duty; in calling it a duty, we already express that we value it. Where it is called a duty, it may appear as an end in itself. But as an end it is then secondary. For example, most people would say that a parent who cares for his children simply out of duty is not better but worse than one who cares for his children without thinking of his duty at all. In short, good and duty have a use only where there is *already* some object of love or desire.

Now for the religious person the primary object of love or desire is God. A religious morality, therefore, cannot focus on morality itself, for its every duty is expressive of that love or desire. The belief in God may be false. But a religious morality cannot be incoherent in focusing on God rather than on morality itself. As we have seen, morality is a secondary end. *Every* morality focuses on something other than morality itself. If its object is not God, it is family, class, nation, humanity or whatever. A religious morality differs from others in that its object is absolute. For the religious believer God is the source of all other loves or desires. It is because the object of a religious morality is absolute that its duties are themselves absolute. They derive their absoluteness from their object. Now it is not surprising that when God is removed, there should be a difficulty in explaining the absolute element in morality. As we have seen, this absolute element comes not from morality itself but from the object to which it is directed. But without God there is no such object. Morality may still be felt as absolute but there is no object adequate to explain that feeling. It is this which explains the confusion in the writings of Moore and Prichard. In their writings, the sense of morality as absolute is retained. What has disappeared is the object which makes it absolute. Consequently morality is turned into an object absolute in itself.

It will be useful at this point to return to that famous argument in *Euthyphro* which we mentioned earlier. As we said, it has often been used by modern writers to establish the autonomy of morality. The argument, roughly, is that the goodness of honesty cannot depend on God's will, for then it would be an arbitrary matter that it is good at all. Consequently God must will honesty because it is good. But then its goodness is independent of God's will. Therefore morality is autonomous. If we reflect we shall find that this argument presents us with two alternatives both of which are incoherent. The first supposes that God is arbitrary in what he wills, so that for all we know, or he knows himself, he might will honesty today and dishonesty tomorrow. The supposition, however, makes no kind of sense. God is being treated as though he were an exceptionally unstable human being. But God *is* reality or truth. To suppose that he could as easily will dishonesty as honesty is to suppose he is in conflict with himself. The other alternative supposes that God wills honesty *because* it is good. But, as we have seen, good is a secondary end. God cannot hold anything good unless he *already* values it. But then his valuing it cannot *depend* on its being good.

We must now turn to our third and final category. The views in this category differ radically from those in the other two. Both the utilitarian and the deontological views attempt in naturalistic terms to explain morality by treating it as absolute or objective. The views in our third category hold that it is not necessary to treat morality as absolute or objective in order to explain it. We are turning, in short, to the various forms of *relativism*.[32] On this view, both the utilitarian and the deontological views are imperfectly naturalistic. They attempt, on the one hand, to explain morality in naturalistic terms whilst, on the other, retaining elements of the absolute or objective which presuppose a religious background. The remedy is to make sure the background is entirely removed and to adopt a thorough-going naturalism. When religion is removed there remains a feeling for morality or sense of good and evil. This can be adequately explained in relativist terms. The question we have to consider is whether an explanation in those terms is really adequate to that sense or feeling.

But before considering relativism we must pay some attention to the term itself, for 'relativism' can be used in different senses. Thus any coherent view of morality is likely to attribute to it some element of relativity. For example, Plato's view is often taken as the paradigm case of objectivism. Yet, as we have seen, he clearly allowed for a certain relativity in moral views. Together with the other philosopher in the classical tradition, he held that human systems of morality reflect a perfect goodness which is at the centre of reality but that they do so only imperfectly or approximately. Between one or other of these systems, at least at certain points, there may be little or nothing to choose, so that which is the better may be an unanswerable question. Indeed there seems to be a relativity in all human knowledge. That is because the conditions for our knowledge of an object are different from the conditions for its existence. For example, you cannot see an object unless it reflects light. But it exists whether or not it reflects light. Consequently the object itself must transcend what you can know of it under those conditions. It will be noted, however, that what is relative here is our knowledge, not its object. Indeed it is precisely because the object exists independently of ourselves that our knowledge of it is relative. Similarly, for Plato our knowledge of good is relative precisely because it transcends us, precisely because it exists independently of ourselves.

Now the relativism we have to consider holds that the *existence* of good is relative to ourselves. Precisely what good cannot do is transcend us. For outside ourselves it cannot exist. Let us note that the plausibility of this view does not depend on its immediate fidelity to our *sense* of good and evil. Quite the contrary, the sense of good and evil shows itself most vividly in the feeling that goodness transcends us. For example, it shows itself in the feeling of guilt. Guilt is precisely the feeling of a discrepancy between what one is and what one ought to be. Judged by moral *experience* the view we are to consider, so far from being plausible, appears as a paradox. But it is not on moral experience that the view depends for its plausibility. It depends, rather, on the naturalistic view of the world. Science has made progress by removing from the natural world those categories which it employed in its earlier forms. The earlier forms explained nature by means of such categories as purpose, meaning and value. These have been revealed as anthropomorphic. They are the projection on the world of categories specifically human. In all its workings nature is in fact governed simply by chance and blind causation. It follows that there can be no foundation for value other than the human will. To call an object valuable is to value it. In valuing an object, I am moved of course by its objective features. Those objective features, however, have value not in themselves but only in relation to my valuing them. But what about valuing itself, how is that to be explained? It may be explained by various causes, sociological and biological. But these causes are blind, having in themselves neither purpose nor value. Consequently the only source of value is the human will.

Given, however, that value is relative to the will, what precisely is the relation between the two? Here relativism takes different forms, according to whether it emphasizes the social or the individual. Let us begin with the social form. Here morality has a certain objectivity, for it is relative to social practice. Thus the individual may be right or wrong depending on whether his judgement conforms to the standards of his society. But what is right or wrong, it may be noted, is relative to those standards. It follows that the standards themselves cannot be right or wrong. Indeed if in this account the standards were answerable to something independent of themselves, we should no longer be dealing with relativism. Consequently, where societies differ in their standards, each has its own idea of right or wrong and there can be no question which is right or wrong in itself. The logic here is similar to that of games. For example, what is right or wrong in association football is different from what is right or wrong in rugby. In rugby one can pick up the ball and run with it; in association football one cannot. But the games simply have different standards. In rugby, for example, one is not attempting and failing to play association football. Consequently it would be absurd to ask whether rugby is right or wrong in allowing a player to pick up the ball and run with it. For the relativist, a similar point applies to morality. There are various moralities, each with its own standards. One may, of course, persuade a person to leave one morality and to adopt another, as one may persuade a person to stop playing association football and to start playing rugby. But this is mere persuasion; it would be incoherent to suppose that there is any truth in the matter.

Now it is certain that this account is in conflict with moral experience. An example will illustrate the point. Relativism is often said to encourage tolerance, and many relativists espouse the values of Western liberalism. Let us contrast such values with those of a Nazi. It is evident that the Western liberal differs from the Nazi not simply in particular judgements but also in his standards. A Nazi, for example, is not attempting and failing to be a Western liberal. But in that case it would be incoherent for the liberal to condemn him. His condemnation must be confined to those amongst his fellow liberals who fail to meet their common standards. The Nazi cannot be condemned, for he is not attempting to conform to those standards. But that is evidently in conflict with moral experience. When it comes to what is fundamental in his morality, every person speaks in absolute terms. He expresses himself as though he were speaking not simply for his fellows but for the whole of humanity. In this, the liberal is no different from anyone else. Thus his condemnation of intolerance is not confined to those who in principle already acknowledge tolerance as a value.

Some relativists, it is true, claim that the Nazi is an exceptional case. Some indeed deny that he has moral standards at all. It is not likely that the Nazi himself would agree. But the move in any case is idle. For suppose that he does agree. His standards are not those of morality. But if he is outside morality, then, again, he cannot be condemned in its terms.

But relativism in its social form has a still graver weakness. It is inherently unstable. On reflection, it collapses into a relativism of the individual form. In short, a morality which is relative to the *general* will soon reduce itself to a morality which is relative to *my* will. For if I am at all reflective, I shall soon find myself wondering why, if there is a conflict between the two, I should follow the general will rather than my own. That cannot be settled by referring to the authority of the general will, for it is precisely that authority which is in question. Moreover there is no further authority which can adjudicate between my own and the general will. Consequently, even if I decide to conform to the general will, I evidently do so through the exercise of my *own* will. Even more evidently do I exercise my own will if I decide not to conform. A *fortiori*, therefore, it is my own will which is the source of all my values.

Here then is the ultimate consequence of a purely naturalistic philosophy of morals. *I* am the source of my moral values.[33] The trouble is that moral value disintegrates on just that supposition. It is important to realize that morality is a phenomenon of the will. For example, when I bemoan the evil I have done, that is not because I failed to achieve what I want; it is because I did achieve it. In short, the evil was in me. It was my will which was bad. But if my will was bad, how can it be the source of my values? Perhaps it will be said that my earlier will is judged by my later and better will. But if there is no measure outside my will, how can the later will be better or worse than the earlier? The earlier will is mine no less than is the later.

We may rephrase the point. As we have said, the sense of good and evil shows itself most strikingly in the feeling that one is not as one ought to be. Now that is not a distinction between what I occasionally will and what I really want. Quite the contrary, it is when I realize that I am wrong in what I really want that I recognize I am not what I ought to be. For example, when it comes to a choice between my own interest and that of another, I am disposed to favour my own. I am self-centred. I have to admit and bemoan the fact. But what I bemoan is not what I occasionally will; it is what I really want. It is the very bent of my nature. For if I favour my interest over yours, that is not because I am prevented by some obstacle from doing what I really want. What I really want is to favour my own interest. But where is the sense in this if the source of my values is in my own willing? Where is my willing, if not in the bent of my nature? But that is what I bemoan.

We have now completed our survey of the attempts to account for morality in purely naturalistic or non-religious terms. Our conclusion is that these attempts have not been successful. It is true that we have been forced to confine ourselves to samples of those attempts. But the samples are representative. Moreover we have reason to doubt whether we shall profit from dealing with further variations on the views we have considered. That is because the faults in those views arise not so much from their details as from the naturalistic assumption on which they are based. One cannot account for the sense of good and evil on the assumption that the world is wholly the product of chance and blind causation. If one is faithful to the sense of good and evil, one will be in conflict at certain points with that assumption; if one is faithful to that assumption, one will be in conflict at certain points with the sense of good and evil. We have reason to suppose, therefore, that faults similar to those we have considered will reappear in any other account based on the same assumption. The naturalistic view itself is of course very prevalent in contemporary philosophy. It has about it the appearance of rigorous thought. But one may doubt whether it is rigorous thought which accounts for its prevalence. One may suspect rather that it is an intellectual fashion, which is acquired like any other. It is beyond our theme to go into this in detail, but it will be useful to consider some of the central difficulties in the view and some of its further consequences.

The essence of the naturalistic view is that the fundamental features of reality have already been revealed through the activities of the physical sciences. This in its turn presupposes that the physical sciences have achieved an account of the world which is at least approximately *complete*. This idea arose in the eighteenth and nineteenth centuries through the prestige of the Newtonian system. Even during this time, it was evident that this system gives rise to acute difficulties when it is taken as a complete account of the world. But the system seemed unassailable. Every feature of reality – or so it seemed – could be explained within the categories which applied to the motions of inert matter. The appearance of Darwin's theory served to confirm this view (see pp. 267–8 above). The prevalence of the naturalistic view at that time is therefore understandable.

We must emphasize, however, that what is understandable is the prevalence of the naturalistic view *at that time*. For it has long been apparent that people were mistaken in their estimate of the Newtonian system. It is fruitful in dealing with matter only in its grosser forms. In dealing with matter at a more fundamental level it has been abandoned. Moreover what has been abandoned is not simply the Newtonian system but the very idea of completeness which it represented. It is now apparent that physical science, so far from giving a complete account of the world, does not even give a complete account of the world in its purely physical aspects. No scientific account is in that way complete; each is tentative and is always liable to be replaced. The naturalistic view works on the opposite assumption. As we have said, it presupposes that science has given an account of the world which is already at least approximately complete. In short, it is based on a view of science which has been abandoned by science itself.

The inadequacy of the naturalistic view may be revealed as readily by considering its consequences. We may illustrate the point by returning to the Newtonian system. As we have said, it has long been apparent that this system gives rise to acute difficulties when taken as a complete account of the world. For when it is so taken, it reveals the world as having evolved solely out of the accidental distributions of inert matter and as being governed fundamentally by chance and blind causation. Meaning and purpose, therefore, have no objective base. It follows that value is subjective. But it follows almost as immediately that scientific reasoning is also subjective. For reasoning, whether in science or elsewhere, is itself a species of value. To call one belief more reasonable than another is to evaluate those beliefs; it is to indicate which belief one *ought* to hold. Some principle of value is necessary in all reasoning. But if all such principles are accidental products of blind nature then principles of values in reasoning are as subjective as any principle of morals. If this consequence has not been immediately apparent, that is largely because the philosophy of science has been dominated by empiricism. On the empiricist view, sense-experience automatically reflects an objective world and thereby serves as a measure for distinguishing a true theory from a false one. But the view is mistaken. Hume and Kant, for example, showed that science is underdetermined by sense-experience not simply in its particular theories but even its basic procedures. Thus causal inference is underdetermined by sense-experience. In short, sense-experience itself needs to be evaluated. But there can be no objective evaluation if the naturalistic view is correct. The consequences of the naturalistic view, therefore, are as ruinous for science as they are for morals.

In a society which has a purely naturalistic or secular view of the world, moral value will be in some measure anomalous. It may nevertheless survive. For the sense of good and evil is not acquired through intellectual considerations; it is acquired rather, as Aquinas pointed out, under the aspect of desire and aversion. But intelligence is also a value. Anyone in such a society who is reflective will be likely to feel a tension between his moral feelings and his view of the world. It will strike him that he cannot fully account for the point or meaning of what he feels.

Notes

1 For an account of secularization by a sociologist see Peter L. Berger, *The Sacred Canopy* (Garden City, NY, 1969).
2 For views similar to that one, see G. E. M. Anscombe, 'Modern moral philosophy', *Philosophy* (1958), and Alasdair MacIntyre, *After Virtue* (Notre Dame, 1981).
3 See *Philosophical Review* (1965), pp. 3–12.
4 Pythagoras himself, to whom is attributed the famous theorem, is a shadowy figure who lived some time during the sixth century BC.
5 For a more detailed discussion of the relation between Plato and the Pythagoreans see R. G. Collingwood, *The Idea of Nature* (Oxford, 1960), pp. 49–72.
6 Plato, *Parmenides*, trans. Mary Louise Gill and Paul Ryan (Indianapolis, 1996). See esp. 132a–133b.
7 Socrates, who was born in 470 BC and died in 399, left no writings. His personality and his views are alive for us through Plato's remarkable portrayal in the dialogues.
8 For a useful translation, see A. Bloom, *The Republic of Plato* (New York, 1968). This contains also a lively, though somewhat controversial, interpretive commentary.
9 For an example of this approach, see Karl Popper, *The Open Society and Its Enemies* (London, 1995).
10 *Republic*, 514a–517b.
11 See *Socratic Dialogues*, trans. W. D. Woodhead (Edinburgh, 1953), p. 16.
12 Protagoras flourished during the second half of the fifth century BC.
13 See Plato, *The Laws*, trans. Trevor J. Saunders (Harmondsworth, 1970).
14 E. Voegelin, *Order and History*, vol. III: *Plato and Aristotle* (Baton Rouge, 1957), pp. 120–1.
15 *Metaphysics*, Book XII, Sect. 10. I have used a translation of this passage by Jonathan Barnes. See *Aristotle* (Oxford, 1982), p. 65.
16 Again, see *Aristotle*, p. 64.
17 It is worth noting, incidentally, that the modern Gestalt psychologists produced an account of perception which is strikingly similar to the Platonic.
18 See *Meditations* in *A Discourse on Method, Meditations and Principles*, trans. John Veitch (London, 1989), p. 135.
19 Note that this does not prevent one's acknowledging that chance has *some* part to play in the process. It is, indeed, one of the tactics of vulgar Darwinism to emphasize the chance elements in the process whilst ignoring all the rest. The other tactic is to give the impression that the only alternative to Darwin's theory is an extreme form of biblical creationism.
20 Aristotle's main work in ethics is the *Nicomachean Ethics*. See the translation by Terence Irwin (Indianapolis, 1985).
21 Aquinas's views in moral philosophy have been conveniently brought together by William P. Baumgarth and Richard J. Regan SJ in *Saint Thomas Aquinas: On Law and Morality and Politics* (Indianapolis/Cambridge, 1988).
22 This means much the same as conscience. Synderesis is the natural habit or disposition which issues in conscience as an act. Conscience is synderesis in action.
23 Baumgarth and Regan, *Aquinas*, p. 2.

24 Ibid., p. 22.

25 Ibid.

26 Bentham was born in 1748 and died in 1832. See his *Introduction to the Principles of Morals and Legislation* (1789; Oxford, 1907).

27 J. S. Mill was born in 1806 and died in 1873. See his *Utilitarianism* (1861; Glasgow, 1962).

28 See Philippa Foot, 'Moral arguments', *Mind* (1958). See also P. Geach, *The Virtues* (Cambridge, 1977).

29 The deontological view is also associated with Immanuel Kant, perhaps the greatest of modern philosophers, who was born in 1724 and died in 1804. In some of his writings, however, Kant plainly holds that morality requires the existence of God and the immortality of the soul. Moreover, where his writings support the deontological view, they involve the same difficulties I consider in dealing with Moore and Prichard, as well as others peculiar to themselves. See *Groundwork of the Metaphysics of Morals*, trans. H. J. Paton (New York, 1964).

30 See *Principia Ethica* (Cambridge, 1903).

31 See 'Does moral philosophy rest on a mistake?', *Mind* (1912).

32 The reader will recall that we are dealing with views already familiar to the Greeks. Thus Protagoras gave vivid expression to views of this kind. For a modern version see G. Harman, *The Nature of Morality* (New York, 1977).

33 Friedrich Nietzsche (1844–1900) is an example of an influential modern writer who held that value depends on the individual will. See *Beyond Good and Evil*, trans. R. J. Hollingdale (Harmondsworth, 1973).

10
People and life after death
Hugo Meynell

There are three sorts of life after death in which religious people have characteristically believed: (1) the survival of the 'soul', or that aspect of the human person which is supposed somehow to be able to exist, whether naturally or by special divine dispensation, after the dissolution of the human organism; (2) the 'resurrection of the body' or reconstitution of the person, by which she or he is brought into existence again in some embodied form at the end of time as we know it; (3) reincarnation, which is a matter of the 'soul' or its equivalent[1] being re-embodied in an organism, human or otherwise, at some later point or points in time. These beliefs are not mutually exclusive; in fact the principal hope of Christians from the earliest times has been in the resurrection of the body, though they have generally also expected an interim state of survival as disembodied souls. But they have not generally believed in reincarnation. Hindus and Buddhists, as well as believing in reincarnation, have also expected some sort of subjective existence between incarnations, and a state of ultimate release or fulfilment at the end of the whole process.[2]

Expectations of post-mortem existence nearly always seem to have attached to them some element of reward or punishment for one's behaviour and attitudes in the present life. Now it is presumably among the most certain of contingent propositions, that when the present life only is taken into account, happiness is not always apportioned to virtue, or misery to vice. (Someone who doubts this may compare the state of successful but unscrupulous business-persons in the West with children starving to death in the Third World; or consider whether people were usually better off for harbouring Jews under the Nazi regime, or campaigning for justice in Soviet Russia.) So promises of reward and threats of punishment hereafter have played an important part in much religion, and continue to do so. There are the promise of heaven and the threat of hell in Judaism, Christianity and Islam; and we are told by one of the Upanishads that a person who has led a beastly life may expect to enter the beastly womb of a dog, a pig, or a member of the 'untouchable' caste. The moral point of such doctrines appears particularly clearly, perhaps, in the religious philosophy of Immanuel Kant. He clearly insists, of course, that rational beings should act dutifully for the sake of duty. On the other hand they ought to hope for something which cannot be proved or disproved by theoretical reason, that a *summum bonum* will come about in which rational beings achieve complete virtue, and their happiness is proportionate to this. This ideal can only be realized if the soul is immortal, and if there is an almighty and just being to ensure that its fate is in accordance with its deserts.[3] One sympathetic with Eastern religions might well maintain that belief in an impersonal *karma*, which operates in an inexorable and quasi-scientific manner to reward virtue and punish vice over a series of lives, does the job as well as or better than a personal God.

It could be argued that the main reason why religion has clung to society for so long, and continues to do so in spite of the inroads of rational enlightenment, is just that many or most people cannot bear to renounce selfishness to the degree that is necessary for social stability and co-operation, without the expectation that things will be better for them in the long run if they do. But the fact, if it be admitted, that such an expectation in a substantial number of people makes for social cohesion does not begin to provide grounds for believing that it is actually *true*. The view has been attributed to Leo Strauss and his disciples, that at least some rudimentary form of religious belief has to be held by most ordinary people, if the fabric of society is to hold together; the wise must bear the burden of knowing it to be false, while living virtuously all the same, and keeping their knowledge to themselves.[4] The secularist may also appeal to the spectacular advances of science, especially the science of medicine, as tending to show how consciousness is ineluctably dependent on the functioning of our brains. If consciousness is now, or is at least liable to be at some time in future, fully explicable in terms of brain function, it may well be concluded that every kind of expectation of life after death is at worst senseless, at best wildly improbable.

What kinds of reasons have been adduced for the conviction that we have to hope for or fear some sort of life after death? It seems to me that such reasons tend to fall under three heads: (1) religious, (2) philosophical and *a priori*, (3) empirical and quasi-scientific. I shall spend little time on the first. A person may believe, for reasons good or bad, in a religious revelation of some kind, of which the prospect of life after death for some or all human beings is an essential component. For example, a person could well believe that there were good grounds for maintaining that there is a God; and that this God has issued an authoritative revelation of the divine nature and purposes; and that these purposes include a destiny for humankind which is beyond the present span between cradle and grave.

The *a priori* and philosophical grounds, both for and against expectations of an afterlife, derive from reflection on human nature. According to an influential modern view, human beings are essentially physical organisms with certain peculiar characteristics. At this rate, 'survival of death' is a mere contradiction; as Antony Flew has remarked, death is not lived through.[5] And even if, in the case of human organism A, another human organism B, in all respects similar and with what seem to be memories of being A, should be brought into existence some time after the death and dissolution of A, it could not literally be one and the same individual as A, which would presumably be a necessary condition of A's resurrection or reincarnation. Two other accounts are more compatible with traditional religious notions. One involves a radical dualism of body and soul, and is associated especially with the philosophies of Plato and Descartes. The other stresses rather, with Aristotle, the unity of the person of which body and soul are both aspects. The dualist view obviously makes it an easy matter to believe in the survival of bodily death by the soul, which merely divests itself of a temporary garment or dwelling-place. Such an account fits in very well with most forms of Hinduism, which envisage the aim of human life as the deliverance of the soul from imprisonment by the body with its senses and passions; and seems at least at first sight to consort well with the more ascetic tendencies in Christian piety. However, it does not sit very easily with the doctrine of the resurrection of the body, which, as I have already mentioned, has been the primary focus of the hope of most Christians. To consign the redeemed soul for ever to a body would at that rate seem to be rather a scurvy trick on the part of the deity, when the whole aim of life had been to free it from such a gaol.

Aristotle's teaching, with its conception of the soul playing 'form' to the body's 'matter', would seem to have just the opposite advantages and disadvantages. A 'disembodied soul' is at best incomplete at this rate, at worst inconceivable; a fully realized existence, such as one would suppose to be inaugurated by the resurrection of the body, could at that rate hardly be anything but embodied. And, whatever Aristotle's own views on the matter (which are disputed), it is easy to infer from his general account of the relation of soul to body as form to matter, that it is no more possible for a soul to continue in existence after the dissolution of its body than for a dish to do so after the china of which it consists has been shattered. The Averroist and Alexandrist schools of Aristotelianism, in the Middle Ages and the Renaissance, both inferred from Aristotle's teaching that the individual human soul did not outlast its body. The view of Thomas Aquinas, who tried to combine the belief that the human soul could be shown on philosophical grounds to be immortal, with the Aristotelian conception that the relation of soul to body was that of form to matter, was held by these thinkers to be inconsistent.[6]

As a result of the well-known 'linguistic turn' characteristic of twentieth-century philosophy, much of what former philosophers might have argued to be true or possible, or false or impossible, as a matter of fact, has been claimed to be self-contradictory or nonsensical; thus to maintain that the 'soul' survives the death of the body is now concluded by many to be not so much a factual error as an abuse of language. As David Stove caustically remarks, everyone knows that they will die; but religious persons contrive to believe at the same time what is in flat contradiction to this, that somehow they will not die.[7] In *Language, Truth and Logic*,[8] A. J. Ayer argued that the expectation of the soul's survival of death, like belief in the existence of God, made no sense; that of the 'resurrection of the body', however, was distinguished among religious doctrines as being meaningful, but unfortunately as improbable as could well be as a matter of fact. Others have been less charitable; Antony Flew and Jack MacIntosh have declared that expectation of the 'resurrection of the body' or reconstitution of the person is really incoherent too. The most that could be said, for example, of the putative Hugo A. Meynell who reappeared in the twenty-ninth century would be that he looked and behaved very like his distinguished predecessor. It might be protested, that if he had memories of having been that person – or perhaps, if some still later individual remembered having been both the man in the twentieth and the man in the twenty-ninth centuries – this would surely amount to evidence that he really *was* the same person. But MacIntosh plausibly argues that memory *presupposes* personal identity, and so cannot be used to *establish* it; and that personal identity is a matter of bodily continuity. However vivid the memory-like impressions possessed by the twenty-ninth-century figure as though of having been his twentieth-century predecessor, and however well they checked out historically, they would not be actual memories short of bodily identity and continuity between the two. Of course, the same considerations that would rule out resurrection would also rule out reincarnation.

Such sceptical views have been encouraged by the kinds of psychological theory that have prevailed during the twentieth century. In 1913, J. B. Watson maintained that a properly scientific psychology could only be a study of human behaviour. Behaviourism was comprehensively developed in the work of B. F. Skinner. As he saw it, a properly scientific account of behaviour would eschew vague talk of what a situation 'means' to a human or other organism, or of the 'experience' or 'intentions' of that organism. It would confine itself to relating the dependent variables which are the behaviour of the organism to the independent variables which are the external conditions impinging on it.[9] An event of a particular kind is said to be *reinforcing* to an organism when its occurrence or non occurrence causes a response of that organism to alter in frequency. Either the addition of something to the environment, like food or sexual stimulation, or the removal of something, like an electric shock or a loud noise, may be reinforcing; the former class of events are labelled *positive*, the latter *negative reinforcers*. When a response becomes less and less frequent, this is called the *extinction* of that response. The aim of a science of behaviour 'is simply to account for probability of response, in terms of a history of reinforcement and extinction'.[10]

What amounted to a philosophically sophisticated type of behaviourism was expounded by Gilbert Ryle in *The Concept of Mind*, which first appeared in 1949. Ryle set out to attack the conception of the mind and its relation to the body that is typified by the philosophy of Descartes, which he calls that of 'the ghost in the machine'. When we say that people are intelligent, or that they are at present angry about something, we are implying that they will speak and behave in certain ways in the appropriate circumstances; we are not speaking of some inner being, who will on suitable occasions bring this behaviour about in a manner which has always been inscrutable. Similarly, when we say that someone knows how to load a bren-gun, we are not talking about some state that obtains in a kind of inner theatre that he has; we are saying that in suitable circumstances – when someone of superior military rank tells him to do so, or when he is in danger from the enemy and needs to defend himself – he will load the weapon. An act that is willed, again, is not one that is preceded by some inner 'volition'; we can distinguish voluntary and involuntary actions (was he coerced? was his lateness due to his dallying on the way, or to the fact that the bus broke down?) without resort to any such weird hypothesis. The same principles apply to our talk of emotions. When I say of someone that 'he boasted out of vanity', I am not saying that he had a private vanity-itch just before he boasted, but rather that it was his habit to try to provoke others to admiration or envy by his actions and utterances. 'Those human actions and reactions, those ... utterances, those tones of voice, facial expressions, and gestures, which have always been the data of all the other students of men, have, after all, been the right and only manifestations to study. They and they alone have merited, but fortunately not received, the grandiose title "mental phenomena".'[11]

A Rylean analysis in terms of dispositions to behaviour has been applied by U. T. Place to some mental properties, as when it is said of someone that she knows or desires something. In the case of others, like those concerned with sensation or feeling, this kind of analysis seemed unsatisfactory to him. If I claim that someone understands Pythagoras' Theorem, or wants to eat a piece of bread and jam, I am implying nothing more or less than that they have a disposition (a favourite Rylean term) to behave in certain ways in appropriate circumstances. But surely, when I say that someone feels an itch in her foot, or seems to hear a sound like that of an oboe playing A, I am saying more than that she is disposed to act in appropriate ways. Place proposed that to experience sensations or feelings is identical with being in certain bodily states, typically of the brain or central nervous system. There is an obvious objection to be made at this point, that the psychological and the physical state simply cannot be identical with one another, since, even if it is always in fact the case that someone in psychological state A is in physical state B, it is never self-contradictory to claim that in a particular instance someone is in the one state but not in the other. Place answers that the kind of identity in question is that between the same phenomenon as observed on the one hand, and as scientifically explained on the other. It is perfectly correct to state that an observed flash of lightning is identical with an electrical discharge, even though it is not actually contradictory to say that the flash of lightning was observed, while denying the fact of the discharge. It is in this manner that, according to Place, a sensation or feeling may be identical with a bodily state. D. M. Armstrong went further than Place; he identified all psychological states with states of the brain or central nervous system that caused dispositions to behaviour, rather than with the dispositions to behaviour themselves. It is plain enough, I think, that such accounts of the human mind, in terms of behaviour or physical states of the organism, do not sit well with expectations of life after death, and are flatly incompatible with belief in the survival of disembodied souls.

Paul Churchland is among the most distinguished of those authors who argue that the ultimate secrets of our inner nature would be revealed by a completed neuroscience. As he sees it, behaviourism has proved inadequate, and has consequently been succeeded by what he calls 'functionalism'. Behaviourism attempted to identify mental states exclusively by their causal relation with the effects of the environment on the body on the one hand, and bodily behaviour on the other. Functionalism acknowledges that their causal relation with other mental states has also to be taken into account; and it is probably, according to Churchland, the most widely held theory of mind among contemporary philosophers, psychologists and researchers into artificial intelligence. Evidently functionalism combines very well with the 'identity' theory, the view that mental events are identical with physical events in the brain in the sense I described in connection with Place. An increasingly broad consensus of scientists and philosophers maintain, accordingly, that 'conscious intelligence is an activity of suitably organized matter'.[12]

It is commonly believed that there are two discontinuous gaps in evolution, that between the living and non-living, and that between what is conscious and what is not. But nature contains no such discontinuities; there are plenty of examples of what is intermediate between these classes (for example viruses, and all the gradations of intelligence among the animals up to humanity). Churchland suggests that a living being is 'any semiclosed physical system that exploits the order it already possesses, and the energy flux through it, in such a way as to maintain and/or increase its internal order'. A thing is intelligent so far as it 'exploits the *information* it already contains, and the energy flux through it (this includes the energy flux through its sense organs), in such a way as to *increase* the information it contains'. A thing of this kind 'can learn, and that seems to be the central element of intelligence'. It will be seen that these definitions are closely analogous to one another, so that one may say that the operations of intelligence are 'just a high-grade version of the operations characteristic of life, save that they are even more intricately coupled to the environment'. At this rate, life and intelligence are explicable as natural products of evolution, given sufficient time and the necessary raw materials.[13]

It appears to me that one may usefully distinguish two aspects of mental properties, for which it will be convenient to use understanding as an example. First, there is the conscious aspect – whatever it is that is inaugurated by the so-called 'aha' experience, which puts an end to the feeling of puzzlement, failing to get the point, and so on. Second, we have the behavioural aspect – the ability to write out the proof of Pythagoras's theorem, to show by a sympathetic comment that one knows what another person is going through, and the rest of it. It seems natural to say that the behavioural aspect is caused by, or is expressive of, the conscious aspect; and that we attribute the latter to other persons because we observe the former. (There is thus an instructive parallel, which I shall discuss at a little greater length later, between our knowledge of other minds on the one hand, and our knowledge of the theoretical entities of physics, and the things and events of the past, on the other; in all these cases, we have knowledge of what we *cannot* perceive, as the best explanation of what we can perceive.) Now computers have been deliberately designed to reproduce parts at least of the behavioural aspect of understanding, and there is no good reason to doubt that in time they will be able to reproduce more of them. Is it reasonable, then, to attribute to them the conscious aspect? It seems to me that it is not. And the reason is, that there is a perfectly good alternative explanation of their output: the intention and the technological know-how of their designers and programmers. The hypothesis that they themselves are characterized by the conscious aspect of understanding is thus superfluous. It may be remarked in passing that the well-established use of the term 'information' in connection with computers could be a trap for the unwary; since the obtaining, storing and using of information can either be a conscious process expressible in behaviour, or amount simply to the disposition to such behaviour – in which case, of course, computers are undoubtedly capable of it.

What applies to understanding applies equally to feeling and emotion. I have no doubt that it will be possible, in the not too far distant future, to manufacture and programme a computer to sigh and gurgle as though with pleasure when exposed to a performance or recording of one of Handel's great operatic *sicilianos*, and similarly to provide a passable simulation of indignation and revulsion at the strains of Heavy Metal. But I would not admit that such a computer appreciated music; the necessary conscious component of appreciation would not be needed to explain its output, when the motives and skill of the manufacturer and programmer did the job perfectly well.

An unsympathetic critic of Churchland's philosophy of mind might wonder whether, though giving an impressive account of the behavioural aspect of intelligence and other mental attributes, he had not rather side-stepped the question of the conscious component. The title of Daniel Dennett's *Consciousness Explained* might well lead its reader to expect that the author would meet this problem head-on. Dennett discusses at length a well-known argument due to John Searle which is supposed to disprove the possibiity of 'strong AI',[14] or the view that 'the appropriately pro-grammed digital with the right inputs and outputs would thereby have a mind in exactly the sense that human beings have minds'.[15] Searle invites the reader to imagine him in a room, playing the part of a component in a vast computer which appears to understand Chinese. He himself does not understand Chinese; nor, clearly, do the other components. The program foils every human attempt 'to distinguish it from a genuine understander of Chinese'. Searle insists, however, that '[i]t does not follow ... from this merely behavioral indistinguishability that there is any genuine under-standing of Chinese, or any Chinese consciousness, in the Chinese Room'.[16]

Why is it, Dennett wonders, that this conclusion seems not only correct, but obviously so, to so many people? He suggests that they do not imagine the case in enough detail. Any computer that could understand, or effectively simulate understanding of, a language to the degree stipulated 'would have to be an extraordinarily supple, sophisticated, and multi-layered system, brimming with "world-knowledge" and meta-knowledge and meta-metaknowledge about its own responses, the likely responses of its interlocutors, and much, much more'. It is not that Searle actually denies that computers can have such a vastly elaborate structure; he merely tries to stop us from paying attention to the fact. 'Searle's thought-experiment depends, illicitly, on your imagining too simple a case, and drawing the "obvious" conclusion from it.'[17]

Plainly it is true that any understanding of Chinese that there is in the Chinese Room does not pertain to Searle; or to any bit of programming there that would be small and simple enough to be easily imaginable. Then comes the suppressed premise. Surely *more of the same*, no matter how much more, would never add up to genuine understanding. But why should anyone think this was true?' Of course dualists of the school of Descartes would assume that an immaterial soul is needed to achieve the miracle that is understanding. But materialists will be confident that our brains can do the job without such assistance. The argument which starts with the premise that the activity of *this* little part of the brain does not constitute understanding, neither does that of *that* somewhat larger part, leads to the unacceptable conclusion that the activity of the brain as a whole is not enough to account for understanding. It may be hard to imagine how understanding could be found in the activity of the brain as a whole, when it is found in that of none of its parts; but since as materialists we have excellent reason to think that it does, we should just try harder.

Thus far Dennett. It is far from obvious, however, at least to me, why greater elaboration of structure should ever account for what I have distinguished as the conscious aspect of intelligence, though plainly it is helpful in elucidating the behavioural aspect. I must admit some sympathy with the reviewer of Dennett's book who entitled his review 'Consciousness ignored'.[18] Dennett, as a card-carrying materialist, is bound to be convinced that 'more of the same', in the way of structural complication, must ultimately do the trick of producing consciousness. His way of arguing reminds me of the manner in which Smith purported to repay a considerable sum of money that he owed to Jones. On the day on which he had agreed to discharge the debt, Smith turned up carrying the equivalent of the sum in the pretence-money used in the game of Monopoly; which, strangely enough, Jones refused to accept. The next day he offered Jones a hundred times as much Monopoly money; which when Jones again refused to accept, Smith demanded, in an aggrieved tone, 'How much *more* would you need to satisfy you?' When Jones patiently tried to explain that, *however* much 'more of the same' Smith offered, it would not amount to the repayment of an actual debt, Smith asked him why he was so sure of this; and added angrily that Jones's attitude was redolent of old-fashioned prejudice.

Dennett does not commend his case, at least to those not already prejudiced in his favour, by calling his readers names if they venture to disagree with him – they can only do so if they are 'Cartesian dualists' and believe in 'miracles'. Whether one believes in miracles or not, conscious agency is no miracle, but part of the normal course of things; the question between Dennett and his opponents is how far and in what way complicated physical systems are useful in elucidating its nature. That they are to a considerable extent thus useful, I would by no means deny; it seems that an entity cannot at once be a conscious agent and a material object, as we human beings undoubtedly are at least during the course of the present life, without being a material object of a rather complicated sort. Exploring the likeness between our brains and computers seems to be one of the best means available of finding out the nature of this complication and the reasons for it.

It is often regarded as a necessary consequence of the scientific world-view that the laws of physics and chemistry must provide the real explanation for all those motions of our bodies which naive reflection would interpret as due to conscious purpose, like my taking a pill in order to avoid depression, or writing an article in order to clarify problems in the philosophy of religion and meet a deadline. But this view gives rise to difficulties which are no less fatal for being frequently brushed aside. It seems to follow from it either that talk in terms of agents and their purposes is based on an illusion; or else that it is merely a simple way of talking about sequences of events whose description and explanation at the level of small detail is totally different in kind. On the former account, it would seem to be the singular consequence of physical science that no one ever really accepts a scientific theory because there is good reason for them to do so. But why should we accept any judgement offered to us, including those made by scientists, except because we have good reason to do so? We believe scientists, and quite properly so, because we assume that they make the claims that they do because they have good reason for doing so.

The second way out seems no more satisfactory; if really we are predetermined in all the motions of our bodies, including those of our brains, by the laws of physics and chemistry, the belief that we sometimes act because there are good reasons for us to do so seems fit rather to be eliminated, than to be kept on as a convenient way of talking, in the manner that we can still say that the sun is going down, when we know perfectly well that its appearance of doing so is due to the rotation of the earth. I conclude that what is often thought to be a consequence of the scientific world-view is in fact incompatible with the very existence of science. For science to be possible, our beliefs and reasons as such must be causally efficacious, in the sense that we as agents can act really because of them; and not merely by way of the physical state of the brain with which they happen to be concomitant.

Another difficulty in principle about explaining the thoughts and actions of conscious agents exhaustively in physical terms derives from the nature of what is called 'intentionality'. It is characteristic of our thoughts and expressions that they can be *about* things and states of affairs, whether real or unreal; thus I can think, speak or write about the periodic table of the elements, King Henry VIII of England, Mr Micawber, or the highest prime number. Material objects and aggregates *as such* (the qualification is important) do not seem to be able to be *about* things in the manner of the expressions of conscious agents. It will be objected that maps and computers are examples of material objects which can refer – as a map may refer to the streets of a city, or the output of a computer to the accounts of clients at a bank. But the marks on the map refer, and the output of the computer refers, by virtue of the fact that they have been designed to do so by some conscious agent or agents. One could perhaps rescue a materialistic doctrine of the human person, in face of the problem of reference, by arguing that the rather complex material objects which are human beings could refer by means of their thoughts, words and gestures on the ground that they had been programmed to do so by their creator; but I doubt whether most materialists would thank me much for this way out of the difficulty.[19]

It is often urged that the gradual formation of human beings through evolution by mutation and natural selection can and does equip them to refer to things in the world, with Mother Nature in the role of quasi-programmer. But surely it is one thing to be equipped to leave descendants and survive in an environment; another to have the capacity to refer to objects in the world which may have no bearing on one's survival or capacity to leave descendants. Supposing the existence of a world to be known by the mental creation of hypotheses, and their testing in experience, I am willing to concede, for the purposes of argument, that in time creatures might arise who were able to understand it, since such understanding would no doubt be useful to them as a means of survival. But I do not see how the existence of this kind of a world could in general be compatible with reductive or eliminative materialism. Much the same applies to the notion that psychic states are mere 'epiphenomena' of physical states, without causal significance in their own right and of their own kind. It seems to follow from this that agents cannot really act because of the reasons that they have for doing so; but only because of the electro-chemical events in the brain which occur each time someone thinks that they are really acting for a reason.

Searle proposes a solution which appeals to the distinction between the submicroscopic and the larger-scale properties of material things. Evidently water is wet; but the hydrogen and oxygen atoms of which water consists are not themselves wet. Similarly, says Searle, the fact that the individual neurons, dendrites and so on of which the brain consists are not themselves conscious, does not imply that the brain as a whole cannot be conscious either. Mental events and acts, Searle proposes, at once are, and are caused by or realized in, the brain as a physical system. The one complex of events, or, if one prefers to put it in this way, the two sets of complexes of events one of which is 'caused by' or 'realized in' the other, causes or cause other series or double sets of events in a way that is intrinsically unproblematic, however complicated in detail. Our thoughts are not really other than our brain-states; we may consider the same brain-state on the one hand as a physical state of affairs, and on the other hand as a state of mind. The problem of meaning or intentionality should be approached along the same lines. The fact that a neuron cannot individually mean, be about or refer to what is other than itself, does not entail that a complex structure of neurons and other such things may not do so. Thirst is at once a specific state of an organism, and a longing for water or some other suitable liquid – that is, it has a certain rather simple kind of intentional relation to it; and a more complicated version of the same story goes for other sorts of intentional relation.[20] But in the supposedly parallel cases adduced by Searle, what happens at one level is ultimately explained by what happens at the other. The feeling of wetness that we have when we dip our hands into a basin of water is explained by the structure of the water molecule. I do not see how this applies to the relation of mental phenomena with their underlying physical manifold. Sometimes structured aggregates have properties that their individual components do not; but I do not see any reason why the point should apply in this case. It is presumably true that matter has to be at a certain level of complexity to be a vehicle for the expression of mind, such that it can use it to get to know the rest of the world in the manner that our own minds clearly use our bodies; but this is a slightly different matter.

If neither materialism, nor the identity theory, nor epiphenomenalism are compatible in the last analysis with acting for reasons, it looks as though we are left with some form of interactionism.[21] As is well known, twentieth-century physics is indeterministic and, at least as usually interpreted, reveals a state of things which there is no good reason to suppose will turn out to be deterministic at a more basic theoretical level. At this rate, I do not see why conscious agency should not have the effect of closing options which are genuinely left open by the operation of physical laws. Also, perhaps, one might hazard the suggestion that it is perhaps just that aspect of human beings by virtue of which they are conscious agents, which might continue to exist after the destruction of that aspect of them in virtue of which they are subject to physical laws – their bodies.

The young Bertrand Russell, when he first caught the philosophical itch, used to be irritated by well-meaning relatives who would say to him: 'What is mind? No matter. What is matter? Never mind.' We have seen that, in spite of the efforts of so many philosophers, psychologists, and *aficionados* of what is called 'artificial intelligence', there are persistent difficulties about reducing the mental to an organization of the physical, or to a mere function of a physical system so organized. Such organization is presumably a necessary condition of a physical being having mental properties; but that is another matter. As I have said, one of the main problems on which any attempt to reduce the mental to the physical seems to founder is that of intentionality.[22] What are the prospects for resolving the issue from the opposite direction – for setting out the nature of matter somehow in terms

297

of mind? Confronted with this question, many philosophers will take fright at the bogey of idealism; but perhaps, if one is really interested in finding a solution to the problem before us, rather than merely corroborating philosophical prejudices that happen to be fashionable at the present time, the bogey is worth facing. Suppose that the real world, including all its material objects, is nothing other than what is to be known by enquiring minds proceeding in a manner which is in very general terms scientific, that is to say by attending to experience, by envisaging possibilities, and judging to be so the possibilities best confirmed by the experience.[23] Actual scientific investigation, in this respect confirming both common sense and the philosophy of Aristotle, reveals a reality consisting of things at various levels of organization, each level obeying laws peculiar to itself as well as those of all the levels below – thus organisms follow laws of growth peculiar to themselves, while also obeying the laws of chemistry and physics. The things at each level, together with the explanatory laws constitutive of them, are nothing other, it must be remembered, than what are to be known by the threefold mental process mentioned earlier in this paragraph. Judgement has characteristically to be provisional, since there is always more experience to be attended to, and more possibilities to be envisaged; so it is that scientists come to reject the notion that there is a luminiferous aether, and Newton's cosmology is succeeded by Einstein's.

Within the real world thus to be known, there are important divisions, notable among which is that between beings that are themselves capable of knowing, and beings not so capable. Here it may be said that there is an element of dualism – or worse, since the contrast in question is only one among the several distinctions and divisions which have already been mentioned – within the world that is to be known. I have already argued that there need be no insuperable difficulty about the existence of beings, for example ourselves, which are to be known both as physical objects and systems, and as knowing agents. The question of life after death is the question whether such knowing agents could conceivably, or actually do, continue to exist while no longer being embodied, at least in the ordinary manner in which they are so far as our normal knowledge goes (survival of the soul);[24] or whether they could or will be in some manner reconstituted as embodied agents after an interval (reincarnation or resurrection). Later, I shall draw attention to the kind of evidence which may be adduced to show that such possibilities are realized in fact.

If the view that I have outlined in the last few paragraphs is correct, in what sense, if any, might mental events and acts be thought to occur in some kind of 'private theatre'; and why, if at all, should this be deemed objectionable, from a scientific or any other point of view? It is obvious at first sight that our thoughts and feelings are private, in the sense that while (characteristically at least[25]) you and I are directly aware of them, they are not directly observable by anyone else. On the other hand, there is a clear sense in which they may be known to others, as providing satisfactory explanations of our observable speech and behaviour. They share this feature with two other classes of entity which can, at least in the usual sense, be known without being able to be perceived – that is, the entities postulated by nuclear physicists, and the things and events of the past. The 'problem of other minds' disappears, along with the 'problem' of our knowledge of these other types of things and events, if we abandon the superstition that everything knowable is perceivable, and realize that our knowledge is often of what is to be hypothesized and judged as the *best explanation* of what is perceivable. The best explanation of your observable behaviour, and the truth about what you are thinking and feeling, may be that you believe I have cheated you, feel angry with me, and very much want me to leave the house; just as the best explanation of certain other phenomena may be unusually large quantities of carbon monoxide or radioactivity in the environment, or that the mammoths perished in a catastrophe caused by a large extra-terrestrial object, or that Mr Tony Blair did or did not brush his teeth on the morning of the day that he became Prime Minister of Great Britain. It follows from all this that one of the standing temptations to behaviourism – that if our thoughts and feelings were in any sense private to ourselves, other people could not get to know about them – is based on a mistake. (The same applies to 'operationism' in physics – the view that protons, electrons and so on do not really exist, but are useful practical fictions.)

Whether the epistemological and metaphysical position which I have just sketched is 'idealist' is moot. It is certainly not materialist; and it is idealist so far as every attempt to conceive the world as what is to be known by minds is so by definition. It is not idealist, if this implies that the world to be known does not exist, or is not already largely what it is progressively found out to be, prior to and independently of the beliefs of any human individual, group or society; to be *potentially knowable*, at least in principle, is one thing, while to be *actually known* is quite another. It is perfectly compatible with, indeed it implies, the common-sense assumption that there was oxygen before it was discovered in the late eighteenth century, and quasars before scientists first claimed that there were such objects in the 1960s. Perhaps it is best to label this view as a form of realism which takes into account what has always been stressed by idealists, but tends to be neglected by naive realists and materialists: that the real world is to be apprehended only through the medium of creative acts of intelligence (in conceiving possibilities which may then be confirmed or disconfirmed by experience). For better or for worse, it is an account strongly suggestive of theism; it seems not implausible to maintain, after all, that a universe which is so ineluctably *for* mind is best to be explained in the last analysis as due to the will *of* a mind. A degree of dualism is involved, as I have said; what is to be known consists largely of objects which are not knowers, but partly of beings who are. However, one usual objection to dualism, that mind cannot know anything about the material world, except by special divine dispensation, does not remain to trouble us on this view; 'matter' is simply an aspect of the universe that is to be known. Another objection, that matter and mind as conceived by the dualist cannot interact with one another, has already been answered; in an indeterministic universe, conscious agency may determine what is undetermined by physical law acting on given conditions.

As Searle sees it, there are four crucial problems to be dealt with in our understanding of the mind and its relation to the material world. How is consciousness to be explained as arising from non-conscious matter? How is intentionality, that strange capacity of our thoughts and feelings to be about what is other than themselves, to be accounted for? How is the *sub*jectivity of mental states, the fact that I can feel my pains but you cannot, to be accommodated within the scientific world-view with its ideal of total *ob*jectivity? Lastly, how does mind interact with matter, as when our intention to raise our hand causes it to rise, or when a cloud passing over the sun causes us to think of rain?[26]

How might these problems be met on the basis of the position that I have outlined? The question of how consciousness arises from matter seems left in as much obscurity as ever; but perhaps a more fruitful question to ask is, at what level of complexity a physical system becomes such that a conscious subject can use it as a medium for knowledge and action in the manner that we obviously use our bodies. Intentionality is taken care of by the fact that the real world, including what is material, is nothing other than what we as conscious subjects could in principle come to know if we directed our consciousness rightly. I have already shown how one might conceive the action of a free conscious subject on a physical system that was not totally determined by its initial conditions and the laws operating on it. The 'subjective' is to be known in the same basic way as the 'objective'; I may conceive possibilities as to what you are thinking or feeling, and judge them to be more or less correct by testing them against your observed speech and other behaviour. The notion of 'objectivity' is in fact misleadingly ambiguous. For investigators to be 'objective' may be taken to imply that they reject all talk of thoughts and feelings as primitive and 'unscientific', redolent perhaps of 'folk-psychology'; but 'objectivity' may rather involve merely the scrupulous use of evidence in determining what is the case, including within the 'subjective' realm of what persons think and feel.

Classical philosophical accounts of the human 'soul' which imply that it survives bodily death are to be found in Plato's *Phaedo* and Descartes's *Meditations*. One of the arguments advanced in *Phaedo* is based on the nature of human knowledge, especially in mathematics and ethics.[27] We never encounter in the world of our experience a line which is perfectly straight or circular, or a wine or university administrator that is perfectly good. Nor do we ever find a perfectly beautiful person, symphony or statue. How then do we come by the notions of perfect straightness, goodness, and beauty against which we measure the examples that we encounter in the world, to find that they all fall short? In Ian Fleming's *Goldfinger*, Pussy Galore says that she had never met a real man until she beheld James Bond. From whence, then, did she get her idea of a real man, assuming it was not by hearsay? Plato's Socrates maintains that such difficulties are to be resolved by the fact that the particular things which we experience remind us of our previous existence as disembodied souls, in which we apprehended directly the 'forms' of straightness, goodness and other universals; it is here that Pussy Galore will have encountered genuine manhood. (In another Platonic dialogue, *Meno*, a slave-boy is represented as shown to have innate geometrical knowledge, this being elicited from him simply by questioning.[28]) Ethically, this view tends to lead to a pronounced austerity; to fit ourselves to return to the real world of the 'forms', it may be argued, we should strive vehemently for detachment from the senses and the passions which bind us to the lower world of appearances. The moral attitude apt to ensue from Aristotle's conception is not so ascetic; the cultivation of sense-pleasure is allowed, even encouraged, within the limits of rational self-mastery.

One of Socrates' interlocutors suggests that the soul may be related to the body as its tuning is to a musical instrument; in that case, it could hardly survive the death of the body. Socrates objects that, if this were the case, it would not be so independent of the body as to be able to set rational and abstract goals for a person to follow, and to enable her to implement them.[29] Yet there seems no doubt that one can envisage what it would be like to live more virtuously, or set oneself to find out the truth in some area of enquiry, and act accordingly.

The dualism for which René Descartes is notorious is closely connected to his method of universal doubt. At the beginning of the *Meditations*,[30] Descartes asks himself how much of the supposed 'knowledge' he has gained for himself, or been taught by others, is really true and well-founded. In order to answer this question, he sets himself to doubt whatever can coherently be doubted. The existence of the material world and other people, he thinks, might conceivably be a dream, or even a deception practised upon him by an almighty deceiver. But even in order to be deceived, he must exist, and moreover be the kind of being who is capable of being deceived, that is, a thinking being or a soul. So he can be certain at least of his own existence, and of his existence as a mind or soul, a being capable of thinking. But he can by no means be so sure of the existence of any material body, including his own. He can only conclude to the existence of bodies by arguing that God, as a perfect being, must not only exist, but be of such good character as not to permit Descartes to be deceived on a matter so fundamental, unless he had given him a means of seeing through the deception.

One can be sure, then, according to Descartes, of the existence of bodies, including one's own, only at the end of quite a long chain of argument. At this rate, there is a clear sense in which my soul is my inalienable self, in a way that my body is not. The survival by the soul of bodily death is only too easy to conceive on this view; the wonder is that two such heterogeneous entities as a soul or spiritual substance on the one hand, and a body or material substance on the other, were ever associated in the first place. And there is the notorious problem of how they could ever interact, for all that it seems obvious that they do. When my hand is cut or burned, my soul is affected in such a way that I want to withdraw my hand from the source of pain; when I wish to write a sentence in this paper, the hand holding the pen, or the fingers tapping the keyboard of the computer, duly oblige. Descartes thought that body and soul affected one another through the pineal gland;[31] but this rather makeshift solution to the problem was soon rejected by his 'Occasionalist' successors. These held the remarkable 'two clocks' view – to the effect that God had set things up from eternity in such a way that, when I wanted to write this sentence, the laws of matter operating on the universe from its initial conditions onwards would co-operate in such a way that my hand would write; there would be no real influence of my will and intention on the motion of my fingers.

It is easy to laugh at the Occasionalists; but at least they are to be commended for taking the measure of the problem. While we ourselves do not usually conceive the matter in terms of the interaction, or apparent interaction, of two totally heterogeneous 'substances', it would be premature indeed to say that the difficulty had been resolved, or was in any immediate prospect of being so.[32] The fact is that we humans are beings who seem to operate according to two different and apparently incompatible sets of laws – as conscious and more or less rational and responsible agents on the one hand; and as material objects or systems subject to the laws of physics and chemistry on the other.

I mentioned before the speculation that it might be the active part of our minds, which hypothesizes, judges and decides in accordance with the experience provided us by our senses and feelings, that could be a candidate for whatever it is in human beings that is supposed to survive bodily death. Something like this view seems to have been held by Thomas Aquinas.[33] Our sensations and physical feelings he thought of as a part of the 'composite' of soul and body, and so necessarily dependent on the existence of the body. But our actively thinking mind does not seem so obviously confined to our bodily organs; on the contrary, it is that by virtue of which we are able to gain knowledge of a world which exists prior to and independently of our bodies, by enquiry into the impressions made on them. As Aquinas saw it, such considerations gave reasons for believing positively that this aspect of the soul does actually survive the death of the body. Duns Scotus said that they did not amount to a demonstration, but rather suggested a possibility whose actuality would have to be established on other grounds, such as divine revelation; and Thomas de Vio Cajetan, who in general was an assiduous follower of Aquinas, agreed with Scotus on this matter. (It is of some interest that it is just those aspects of the mind on which Place and Armstrong disagree, Place preferring a behavioural analysis, Armstrong an explanation in terms of the brain or central nervous system, that Aquinas claims can be shown to survive the dissolution of the body.) Though there is no space to go into the matter at length here, it seems that the view of Scotus and Cajetan, that these considerations do not strictly speaking demonstrate that the aspect of the soul in question will actually survive the death of the body,[34] is at least plausible; given that they are right, if its survival is to be established, it must be on some other ground. This brings us to the third sort of consideration which I said might be relevant to determining whether or not the soul survived death, that which is empirical or quasi-scientific.

When the British and American Societies for Psychical Research were founded in the early 1880s, the question of life after death was at the head of their agenda. This has ceased to be so; probably because this question, for reasons some of which will appear, has turned out to be about the most intractable in an area of enquiry notorious for the intractability of its questions. After more than a century of intensive investigation, one might have expected a few undisputed facts to have been established in the field. Unfortunately, this is not the case. Now, just as at the beginning of the present century, a substantial portion of the intellectual community, both scientists and other scholars, regard the whole business of psychical research as a waste of time, energy and money; but some, and those not the least eminent, have been impressed or even convinced by the evidence. The matter has not been helped by the notorious deception and fakery which seems to dog investigations of this kind; though perhaps one should bear in mind the remark of the sceptic Martin Gardner, that while cheating and self-deception seem commoner in psychical research than in orthodox science, it is not by much.[35] It is also notable that some 'sceptics' have been alleged, circumstantially and by reputable authorities, to be at least as dishonest as believers in their approach to the evidence.[36]

One reason why the question of life after death has tended to be placed on the back burner by psychical researchers over the last few decades is made clear in a classic article by E. R. Dodds.[37] The gist of his argument is that all of those curious phenomena, for which the existence and activity of spirits of the dead have been assumed to account, can be explained at least as plausibly in other ways. Suppose Smith has an Aunt Jemima of whom he is inordinately fond, and the lady dies. A few weeks later he goes to a 'medium', wondering if by any chance he can glean some evidence to the effect that her spirit still exists and is in a fairly happy state. In trance, the medium (with whom neither Smith nor his aunt have previously been acquainted) is apparently 'taken over' by some 'entity' who sounds to Smith like Aunt Jemima, and has some of her characteristic mannerisms of speech. The entity informs Smith that a King Charles guinea is to be found at the bottom of a certain drawer in Aunt Jemima's house which is hardly ever opened. Naturally, Smith can hardly wait to conduct the experiment; when he does so, the King Charles guinea turns up in the very place predicted, and he is jubilant. (This kind of sequence of events, it is worth adding in parenthesis, is a good deal more common than most people would suppose; as anyone may find by leafing through a few volumes of the *Proceedings of the Society for Psychical Research*.) But Smith has a sceptical friend who has made a study of these matters, and is a good deal less enthusiastic. How does Smith know, she asks, that the medium did not have paranormal 'clairvoyant' knowledge about the existence of the guinea and its whereabouts? Could not he himself, again, have had unconscious knowledge about the matter, which was read telepathically by the medium? Smith, of course, is likely to protest that these alternative explanations are extremely far-fetched. But his sceptical acquaintance may well demand in what respect they are more far-fetched than the survival of the spirit of his Aunt Jemima, and her ability and willingness to communicate with him.

It was to obviate difficulties of this kind that a proposal was made early in the twentieth century by two intellectually eminent men, Henri Bergson the philosopher and Sir Oliver Lodge the physicist. They suggested that alleged communications from the spirits of the dead, whether through mediums, ouija boards, 'automatic writing', or any other means, should be treated like travellers' tales; and it should be asked whether there was any consistency between them that could not, at least at all readily, be accounted for by honest error, the wish to deceive, or sheer coincidence. The first person to follow their suggestion was the distinguished English geologist Robert Crookall, who decided to devote his retirement to investigating this matter. I judge his book *The Supreme Adventure*,[38] which appeared in 1961, to be of great and much underestimated importance. Crookall wisely restricted himself to a carefully limited question: what experiences, if any, are undergone by persons of average intellectual and spiritual attainment in the immediate aftermath of death? (Different though related questions are investigated by Crookall in later publications.) From the vast range of material which Crookall collates, a number of results come out which would never have been expected *a priori*. For example, it seems that those who die by violence are apt to be conscious immediately after their death, and sometimes do not know for some time that they have died; whereas those who die naturally or after a long illness usually go through a comatose period which lasts a number of days. (Those who die by explosion constitute yet a third category.) I do not intend here to summarize Crookall's conclusions, which are liable to seem fantastic (though no more so, perhaps, than much of what is maintained by contemporary physicists) unless one takes into account the mass of evidence on which they are based; but I would like to emphasize the appropriateness of his method in approaching the momentous questions with which he deals. He justly concludes that the claim that human conscious subjects survive the death of their bodies is about as well confirmed by the relevant data as the theory of evolution.

Over the last few decades, due to advances in medicine, many persons[39] have returned from the brink of death to report what are known as 'near-death experiences' (NDEs). Raymond Moody has distinguished sixteen such experiences, some of which are apt to be undergone by those who nearly die (I understand that few if any have gone through them all) – impressions of looking down at one's body from above, of being drawn through a tunnel with light at the end, of meeting deceased relatives, of regretting having to return, and so on. NDEs have by now achieved considerable notoriety, and been studied by quite a number of authors.

The case against taking NDEs as evidence for life after death has been made with considerable force and skill by Gerd Hovelmann.[40] He writes that the recurring set of experiences described by Moody and others is just what one might expect from human brains in a state of near-collapse, given the similar nature and structure with which those brains have evolved. Furthermore, it has to be borne in mind that none of those who report these experiences have actually *died*; since it is of the essence of the state of death that it is permanent and irrevocable. It seems to me that the first point is of greater weight than the second. It is surely arbitrary to take permanence, rather than cessation of heartbeat, of respiration, or of electrical activity of the brain, as uniquely diagnostic of death. Up to recent times, these signs of life virtually always ceased nearly together, and did so permanently; this is presupposed by the traditional conception of death. If respiration, heartbeat and brain activity cease temporarily, it appears to me mere conceptual dictatorship to refuse to call the patient concerned 'clinically dead'. Suppose we take all four circumstances mentioned as together characteristic of death; might it not be plausibly argued that when two or three of them obtain, the experiences undergone may be some indication of what would happen when all four of them did so, and the patient was therefore unequivocally dead?

It looks as though both of Hovelmann's points could be contested, if there were grounds of a different sort for believing in the survival of bodily death by human souls; and if the relevant information corroborated what might be inferred about the afterlife from the study of NDEs. It seems to me that both conditions are met by Crookall's work, where both the fact of survival is confirmed, and the apparent information given about the immediate afterlife fits very well with the content of NDEs.[41]

Philosophers sometimes maintain that one cannot really conceive what it would be like either to be aware of oneself as a disembodied spirit, or to come across evidence of the activity of such beings. If people really find difficulty in conceiving either of these things, they should read the numerous available reports of NDEs or of 'out-of-the-body' experiences on the one hand, and of alleged communications from the dead on the other. Those who are 'sceptical'[42] about these matters should be invited to make clear, to themselves as well as to others, whether they are denying that the relevant phenomena occur; or claiming that, even if they do occur, the existence and activity of discarnate spirits is the wrong way of accounting for them. Even if the reports are all due to lying or to honest mistakes of observation, they and the proffered explanations for them make obvious sense at first sight; and those who insist that there is a deeper level of analysis at which they do not make sense after all may be suspected of covertly assuming some philosophical dogma or other, very likely of logical positivist provenance. It was the logical positivists who brought into fashion the practice of alleging that claims with which one is in fundamental disagreement are nonsensical; but in fact, as is by now notorious, the criteria to which they appealed literally made nonsense of their own position.

Over the last few years I have myself come to be convinced, rather against my will, of the truth of the doctrine of reincarnation, the cumulative case for which, from the thousands of convincing reports of 'past-life regressions' which have now been obtained, seems to me as strong as for any kind of life after death. (That some of these reports are clearly bogus, like that of the person who 'remembered' having been Queen Elizabeth I of England on an occasion when she was being entertained by Sir Walter Ralegh on his yacht, is neither here nor there.) The doctrine does not sit too easily with traditional Christianity (though some great Christian thinkers, like Origen, have believed in it); but it will not do for Christians to allow this fact to affect unduly their assessment of the relevant evidence. And it is surely not very plausible to suppose that most persons are fitted for an eternity of bliss or of torment at the end of a single earthly life. It ought to be admitted, too, that there is a certain moral attractiveness in a view which suggests, for example, that those who have been vicious bullies may expect to suffer from the actions of such people in a subsequent lifetime; and that we gradually learn the lessons that we need to learn in a wide variety of human situations and circumstances.

According to Jack MacIntosh,[43] memory is logically dependent on personal identity, and personal identity in its turn on bodily continuity. The first claim seems fair enough; if I have a vivid impression as though of something having happened to me when I was a small boy, and in fact it happened to my brother at a time when I was absent, and not to me, then I do not remember it. The second claim seems to me much more dubious. Our usual conceptions of memory and of personal identity depend, I should say, on certain things *not* occurring which, if a large and ever-increasing body of evidence is to be taken at its face value, often *do* occur.[44] Suppose that, under hypnotic regression, I have a very vivid and detailed impression which seems just like a memory of having been a powder-monkey in one of Admiral Lord Nelson's ships, and having my leg taken off by a cannon-ball. Suppose too that I have previously had no knowledge whatever of the period and the situation, but that careful investigation confirms that an event took place which corresponds in the smallest detail to what I appear to remember. Suppose again (as there is now substantial reason to believe) that the practice of hypnotic regression showed that phenomena of this kind were really rather commonplace; that many or most people had impressions of this kind in appropriate circumstances. In that case, it appears to me that our notions of memory and personal identity would quite properly adapt themselves accordingly, so that the person in my example could truly say 'I was in a former life a powder-monkey serving under Nelson, and I remember having my leg taken off by a cannon-ball'. I submit that it would be sheer pedantry to insist that she or he was not the same 'person' as had undergone the experience in question, or that her or his apparent 'memory' was not a real one.

I used to be convinced that the Buddhist doctrine of 'no-soul' – a theory, reminiscent of the philosophy of David Hume, to the effect that our conscious lives are nothing over and above a succession of sense-impressions, memories and feelings – was really incompatible with any form of expectation of life after death, in spite of the fact that belief in reincarnation is at least equally characteristic of Buddhism. But I now think that I was too hasty. If the series of impressions can continue up to the death of the associated body, there seems no compelling reason why it should not continue after its dissolution, and after a while in association with another body. Perhaps the continuity of the impressions is to be compared with that of an ocean wave, or as one Buddhist classic suggests,[45] with a flame which may be transferred from one torch to another. When a wave crosses an ocean, it is a mere disturbance of the water that travels; the water itself remains relatively stationary. Similarly, when one piece of paper is lit from another, it is a process rather than, strictly speaking, a thing or aggregate of things which is passed on.

I blush to have defended a form of naive interactionism in this chapter; but however much this may wring the withers of the tidy-minded, it is what the relevant evidence appears to demand, so far as I am acquainted with it. As to belief in an afterlife, those who assume unquestioningly that it is mere wish-fulfilment should perhaps be reminded that the prospect is not necessarily a pleasant one. C. D. Broad, after a careful weighing of evidence on both sides of the issue, wrote that he would be rather more annoyed than surprised at finding that he had survived the death of his body.

Notes

1 Buddhists characteristically do not believe in a substantial soul, but contrive to believe in reincarnation all the same.
2 Again, Buddhism is problematic; the ultimate goal of human life may be conceived either as some positive form of bliss, or rather as blessed annihilation.
3 See I. Kant, *Critique of Practical Reason*, trans. L. W. Beck (New York, 1956), pp. 126–30; cf. S. Körner, *Kant* (Harmondsworth, 1955), pp. 163–71.
4 See Shadia B. Drury, *The Political Ideas of Leo Strauss* (New York, 1988).
5 See A. G. N. Flew, 'Death' in A. G. N. Flew and A. C. MacIntyre (eds), *New Essays in Philosophical Theology* (London, 1955), p. 272.
6 See F. C. Copleston, *A History of Philosophy*, vol. III (London, 1960), pp. 221–3.
7 D. C. Stove, *The Plato Cult and Other Philosophical Follies* (Oxford, 1991), p. 83.
8 (New York, n.d.), ch. 6. This book was first published in 1936.
9 See B. F. Skinner, *Science and Human Behaviour* (New York, 1953), pp. 33–6.
10 Skinner, op. cit., pp. 72–3.
11 Ryle, *The Concept of Mind* (Harmondsworth, 1963), pp. 63, 69–70, 87, 302.
12 Paul Churchland, *Matter and Consciousness* (Cambridge, MA, 1988), pp. 26, 36–7, 79, 167.
13 Churchland, op. cit., pp. 172–4.
14 'AI' is short for 'artificial intelligence'.
15 John R. Searle, 'Turing the Chinese Room' in T. Singh (ed.), *Synthesis of Science and Religion: Critical Essays and Dialogues* (San Francisco, 1988).
16 Daniel Dennett, *Consciousness Explained* (Boston, 1991), p. 435.
17 Dennett, op. cit, p. 438.
18 I have not seen the review, but was informed of it by Letitia Meynell.
19 For a similar argument, see Taylor, op. cit., pp. 96–8.
20 John R. Searle, *Minds, Brains and Science* (Cambridge, MA, 1984), pp. 18–23.
21 For a defence of a kind of interactionism, see K. R. Popper and J. C. Eccles, *The Self and Its Brain* (Berlin, 1977).
22 Hilary Putnam has remarked that, while science is incapable of giving an account either of values or of intentionality, it is ineluctably dependent on both. See his *Realism with a Human Face* (ed. J. B. Conant; Cambridge, MA,

1991), p. 138; and *Renewing Philosophy* (Cambridge, MA, 1992), p. 55. After all, science is about things, and the making of scientific discoveries depends on people using their minds well.

23 The conception of epistemology and metaphysics which I am sketching in these paragraphs is developed at length by Bernard Lonergan in *Insight: A Study of Human Understanding* (Toronto, 1992).

24 This leaves open the question of whether 'disembodied souls', if they exist, have some kind of rarefied bodies or quasi-bodies.

25 We must prescind here from the question of the possibility or reality of 'unconscious thoughts', which would lead us too far afield.

26 Searle, *Minds, Brains and Science*, pp. 15–17.

27 *Phaedo*, 72e–77d.

28 *Meno*, 82b–85b.

29 *Phaedo*, 79e–80a.

30 Descartes, *Meditations on First Philosophy* in Descartes, *Philosophical Writings: A Selection*, ed. G. E. M. Anscombe and P. T. Geach (Edinburgh, 1954).

31 A not dissimilar suggestion was made by Sir John Eccles in *The Neurophysiological Basis of Mind* (Oxford, 1956). Having asked, in a delightfully creative misreading of Ryle, 'What kind of machine could a ghost operate?', he thought an answer was to be found in the neural network of the brain. See also Popper and Eccles, *The Self and Its Brain*.

32 The various ways out that have been proposed are clearly and amusingly summarized, with illustrative drawings, in Richard Taylor's *Metaphysics* (Englewood Cliffs, NJ, 1963), chs 1–3.

33 See F. C. Copleston, *Aquinas* (Harmondsworth, 1955), pp. 158–66. Aquinas stresses our knowledge of abstractions and non-physical things.

34 For Scotus, see F. C. Copleston, *A History of Philosophy*, vol. II (London, 1964), pp. 541–4. On Cajetan, see Copleston, *History of Philosophy*, vol. III, p. 340.

35 Quoted by D. M. Stokes in Paul Kurtz (ed.), *A Skeptic's Handbook of Parapsychology* (Buffalo, NY, 1985).

36 Cf. S. Braude, *The Limits of Influence: Psychokinesis and the Philosophy of Science* (London, 1986), 'Introduction'; also the discussion of the Bridey Murphy case in C. J. Ducasse, *Belief in Life After Death* (Springfield, Il., 1961).

37 'Why I do not believe in survival', *Journal of the British Society for Psychical Research* (1934).

38 (2nd edn; Cambridge, 1974).

39 Including, of all people, the late Professor A. J. Ayer. As a result of his experiences, he said he thought that the survival of his consciousness was more probable than he had previously held. This scandalized some of his fellow sceptics, whom he reassured, however, by saying that he was no closer to believing in God than he had been before.

40 'Evidence for survival from near-death experiences? A critical appraisal' in Paul Kurtz (ed.), *A Skeptic's Handbook of Parapsychology* (Buffalo, NY, 1985).

41 The matter is summarized in R. Crookall, *What Happens When You Die* (Gerrards Cross, 1978), pp. 171–2.

42 It is a major source of intellectual mischief that people do not always bother to distinguish between 'scepticism' in the sense of willingness to test all of one's beliefs at the bar of the evidence, and in the quite different sense of dogmatic refusal to believe that certain classes of supposed things or events exist or occur.

43 See J. J. MacIntosh, 'The impossibility of miraculous reincarnation' in J. J.

MacIntosh and H. A. Meynell (eds), *Faith, Scepticism and Personal Identity* (Calgary, 1994).

44 See Hans Ten Dam, *Concerning Reincarnation* (Harmondsworth, 1990); Ian Stevenson, *Twenty Cases Suggestive of Reincarnation* (Charlottesville, VA, 1974); and the references to the work of Helen Wambach in Ian Currie, *You Cannot Die* (New York, 1978).

45 *Questions of King Milinda*.

11

Philosophy and world religions

Julius Lipner

At the outset, we are faced with profound procedural problems. On the face of it, it seems quite reasonable to entitle a chapter in a book on the philosophy of religion 'Philosophy and world religions'. But this is a chapter in a book on the philosophy of religion almost entirely in *Western* contexts, and as such the title may come laden with assumptions. After all, the title makes reference to *world* religions, a number of which are Eastern in origin, so that the prospect of cross-cultural contexts raises its head. Our task then is clearly not as straightforward as it could seem, and we must first enquire into what the title might mean with a due regard for its non-Western referents.

But first let me say how glad I am that such a chapter-heading appears at all in a book like this. Besides quite properly extending the scope of the book, such a chapter might with profit raise issues taken for granted in the rest of the volume. To begin with, how might 'Philosophy and world religions' be interpreted? One interpretation could be: What sense can those Western modes of thought we call 'philosophical' make of the world religions? Underlying this interpretation could be the assumption that the term 'philosophy' is properly applied only to certain patterns of Western thought and that non-Western modes of thinking cannot be properly described as 'philosophical'. In other words, there is no comprehensive sense of 'philosophy' straddling both Western and non-Western modes of thought.

This is by no means a strained interpretation. There is plenty of evidence to show that a number of Western philosophers have held this view. In his book *Reason and Tradition in Indian Thought*,[1] J. N. Mohanty distinguishes three views among Western thinkers who maintain that there is no philosophy proper outside Western thought, that in fact, Western and non-Western intellectual traditions are radically different enterprises. Mohanty regards E. Husserl (1859–1938) as representative of one position. This is the position that philosophy proper is pure *theoria*, and that such thinking is properly, if not exclusively, classically Graeco-Western. Non-Western 'philosophies', e.g. the Indian and Chinese, are really mythical-practical modes of thought whose goal is well-being rather than the disinterested pursuit of truth. As such, 'it is a mistake, a falsification of their sense, for those raised in the scientific ways of thinking created in Greece and developed in the modern period to speak of Indian and Chinese philosophy and science . . .' (quoting Husserl).[2]

The second position, according to Mohanty, is that espoused by R. Rorty. In Mohanty's exposition, this view holds that Western philosophical thought is 'philosophical' in that it developed a unique kind of history informed by certain distinctions (e.g. that between philosophy and theology, and that between philosophy and literature), by particular needs of its exponents, and by specific institutional structures (e.g. Western universities). All these factors combined to make Western philosophy the project it is. But these conditions are not repeatable in other cultures, so that systems of comprehensive thought in other cultures are quite different enterprises. In other words, Western philosophy has been so radically contextualized to become the thing it is, that no other cultural tradition of comprehensive thought can properly be called philosophy by comparison.[3]

The third position considered is that exemplified by M. Heidegger (1889–1976), for whom Western philosophy, beginning with Plato, is a unique metaphysics of subjectivity (that came to an end with Nietzsche). No other culturally defined system of thought compares with this so that '"Western-European philosophy" is in truth a tautology'.[4]

Mohanty goes on to repudiate all three positions. He points out that the three thinkers in question expound their views entirely on an *a priori* basis; none of them has acquired the competence or empathy to study any non-Western tradition in a sustained manner 'from within', and he says sternly:

> It is indeed sickening to find philosophers argue a thesis about a field about which they know almost next to nothing – and so inevitably using arguments that follow a priori from their methodological premisses, expecting that no empirical evidence could show them wrong.
>
> It is only those who know both the traditions from within, who have studied the source material of both, who have learned to think within both traditions, who can judge whether what is being done in the two traditions is similar. (op. cit., p. 288)

As one who, like Mohanty, has studied at least the Western and Indian traditions 'from within' in the manner described, I agree with this judgement on the a-priorists. Husserl was simply insufficiently informed about non-Western traditions; Heidegger's extreme nationalism left him quite prejudiced, and, coupled with lack of relevant knowledge, it led to superimposed conclusions, but does Rorty – also no expert in non-Western traditions – nevertheless make a significant methodological point? If Western and non-Western traditions have different *kinds* of histories of reflective, comprehensive view-making, each defined as the project it is by its own radical contingency, then can we speak of 'philosophy' (which includes the 'philosophy of religion') in some encompassing sense in this regard? I believe that indeed we can, so long as we do not use the term 'philosophy' in some trivially unique sense. If the word is allowed to outstrip its etymology (the so-called Greek love of wisdom[5]) and is taken to refer to a rational, critical and systematic enquiry into the human condition and/or basic human activities and goals such as true cognition, language and right-living, by means of a sustained attempt to ground this enquiry on experience and argument – and this seems to be more or less its current meaning – then I do not see how we can rule out *a priori* that philosophy can be done and indeed has been done in this sense around the world. After all, the term 'philosophy' has been used to cover a disconcertingly wide range of intellectual endeavour in its *Western* context; if this is acceptable, I do not see why the word cannot be applied to sustained intellectual activity of the kind described earlier, outside the Western context.

So, having engaged in one methodological skirmish, we might interpret the title of this chapter in another way: 'What do different forms of philosophies of religion, Western and non-Western' [all this subsumed under 'Philosophy'] 'make of the world religions?' This formulation is intended to homogenize neither 'Western philosophy of religion' nor 'non-Western philosophy of religion', and on the assumption that there are non-Western philosophies in the broad sense of 'philosophy' given above, by 'philosophy *of religion*' I mean the philosophy of religious objects (which include such objects as questions about the nature and scope of religious experience, about the existence and nature of some ultimate reality or God and its relationship with persons and the world; enquiry into the nature of the good life in relationship with either this ultimate being or at least a higher order of being; problems pertaining to the existence of evil; forms of religious language, and so on[6]). The kind reader (and our kind editor who has formulated this daunting chapter-heading in the first place) does not expect, I hope, a potted account of what various philosophies of religion make of different world religions.[7] As but one possible task entailed by our chapter-title, this in itself would involve a mammoth study. But even before such a study could be undertaken, we would have to clarify another large procedural question: what on earth is a world religion? Let us give this question some thought, for its consideration could yield valuable insights.

Does a 'world religion' or faith deserve the qualifier 'world' (we have already commented on 'religion' in note 6) because it has attained some (inevitably arbitrarily determined) (1) minimal geographical global distribution, (2) number of adherents (whose identity as 'religious' would again be subjected to arbitrary criteria) or (3) judicious combination of both?[8] In any event, these are *a posteriori* criteria. There could also be *a priori* criteria for determining a 'world religion', e.g. the universalizability in some way of its proposals for belief and/or practice. Thus it seems that Judaism, which at present has been calculated to have no more than 18 million adherents (which represents a tiny fraction of the global population), by no means evenly or even extensively distributed about the world,[9] has generally been accounted a 'world religion', at least to a significant extent on such *a priori* grounds, namely that its basic theological beliefs are universalizable either on their own terms, or, more to the point I suspect, in so far as they can metamorphose into or act as the basis of Christian belief and practice which constitute the 'ideal' 'world religion', namely Christianity.[10] Would such criteria make Sikhism, which currently may number a million *more* adherents than Judaism (largely in India but also scattered about the world), a 'world religion'?[11] On the analogy of the relationship between Judaism and Christianity, it is not clear which world religion Sikh beliefs and/or practice might act as the propaedeutic to or indeed metamorphose into. And where would New Age religion or spirituality figure? Works are appearing which make New Age religion – generally characterized as individualistic, based on personal experience, often immanentist and optimistic about human development, and as sitting lightly to organized religion, which it regards as preoccupied with external ritual and institutional processes – a discernible movement, in some serious analyses of considerably greater extent in geographical distribution and numbers than such religions as Judaism and Sikhism combined.[12] 'World religion', therefore, though a very popular description, is also a very contentious one, and important questions of academic integrity, religious identity and revisionary history arise in seeking to determine which religions deserve the qualifier 'world'.[13]

But there is an even more important issue involved here: the apparently unitary nature of a phenomenon described as a world religion. What might a 'world religion' be? Consider likely contenders for this description: Christianity, Hinduism, Buddhism, Islam. Is each a unitary or homogeneous reality? Can one, without stumbling methodologically, speak of *the* Christian approach to something, *the* Hindu view of life, *the* Buddhist or Muslim response – as if there were only one in each case? Hardly. Wilfred Cantwell Smith has shown in his study *The Meaning and End of Religion*[14] that our *penchant* for reifying religious traditions in terms of abstract nouns (Hinduism, Buddhism, Christianity, etc.[15]) is only a couple or so centuries old, a legacy of the European Enlightenment which sought to essentialize religious traditions as more or less homogeneous *systems of belief*.

One of the great gains of post-modernist approaches to the study of religion has been the *contextualization* of the object of such study and the consequent realization that in this respect essentialist methodologies are conceptually distortive of 'the reality on the ground'. There is no single thing called 'Christianity' or 'Hinduism'. 'Christianity' and 'Hinduism' are cluster-terms or, perhaps even more correctly, family-names for separate religious traditions that have elements in common in a way analogous to family-resemblances. Such commonalities are not functions of a single homogeneous and homogenizing essence. This allows for a genuine intrinsic plurality to exist *within* the ambit of a family of religious traditions, just as there is extrinsic plurality *between* the families of religions. In other words, just as we can speak, in a duly informed way, of different religious families using the names 'Hinduism', 'Judaism', 'Islam' and 'Christianity', so we must be prepared to speak of different religious traditions within these families of faiths. Hinduism and Christianity are different religious traditions, as are Vaishnavism and Saivism within Hinduism, and Orthodox and non-Orthodox forms of belief and practice within Christianity, not to mention Gaudiya Vaishnavism and Sri-Vaishnavism within Vaishnavism, and Methodism and Anglicanism within non-Orthodox Christianity. And so on – each of the major established religious traditions may be delineated in the form of a quite complex 'family-tree'.

The extrinsic and intrinsic plurality of religions of which I speak are not strictly analogous – at least in an important respect. For we may ask: according to which criterion or criteria can we call the different members of the Hindu family-tree 'Hindu' (as opposed, say, to Buddhist and Christian members) – and vice versa? Is there some objective 'glue' – or, in keeping with our running metaphor, some genetic code – which enables us to do this? Or is our naming purely arbitrary? This is a key question. Without wishing to spend too much time on it, let me say that in the vast majority of cases there do seem to be objective grounds for identifying the various members of the religious family-trees. These grounds would turn on such things as common patterns of discourse informed by key concepts, images, myths and symbols, as well as shared practices, goals, aspirations and approaches to life.[16] But the matter need not be resolved entirely 'objectively'; there could be borderline or perhaps hyphenated cases, e.g. 'Hindu-Christian' traditions, requiring a subjective element of decision to arrive at some conclusion. It is in this rather federated sense, then, of the intrinsic plurality of religions, that one may speak, as Brian Hebblethwaite does, of 'the Anglican tradition' in the philosophy of religion,[17] and though he is quick to point out that 'it can hardly be claimed that philosophy of religion, as undertaken by twentieth-century Anglicans ... constitutes a particular identifiable school', he goes on to say, in a way that undermines his case to some extent, 'we may discern a number of common threads running through these diverse approaches ... [and] at the turn of the century, the leading Anglican philosophers of religion, *could* be described as belonging to a somewhat loose-knit school ... ' (p. 171). The point is that there are different approaches if not kinds of the philosophy of religion within and between the established religious traditions of the world, and one cannot overlook this immensely complicating factor in trying to deal with a project described as 'Philosophy (of religion) and world religions'. By now the kind reader (and our kind editor) must perforce have come to the happy conclusion that a contribution under such a title as ours cannot but be a methodological study – but perhaps a significant one for all that. For such a study could raise and clarify issues propaedeutic to the writing of more specific chapters in works similar to the volume in which this essay appears, chapters which deal severally with the diversity of philosophical or philosophy-of-religion approaches in the context of established religious traditions of the world.

To proceed. Having concluded that we cannot say *a priori* that there is no philosophy (or philosophy of religion) proper in the 'world religions' (or shall we say, the major religious traditions of the world – whatever this might arbitrarily mean), including non-Western religions,[18] we might consider what may be another illuminating interpretation of our chapter-heading, namely, what do the various philosophical strands in the different major religious traditions have to offer us *qua* philosophy of religion? What are their chief concerns, emphases, approaches, conclusions? I have already warned the kind reader (and our kind editor) not to expect potted accounts in response to such questions. Trying to answer this last question is another immense assignment, requiring far more wide-ranging expertise than I can command. For even if we were to agree that Judaism, Christianity, Islam, Hinduism, Buddhism and Sikhism with all their intrinsically plural major strands are 'world religions' (but what about New Age religion, Jainism, Confucianism, and Tao, not to mention many more?[19]), my task would still be too great, and I would hardly be able to do justice to a single one of them. Further, in the light of what I have said, I do not think I could take up the two or three major religions I do know something about in a way that is *representative* of the other world religions, for I hope I have cast enough doubt upon whether such a thing is possible, not only actually but also methodologically.

Rather, let us consider a closely related but more fundamental issue: granted that there may well be philosophies of religion inherently embedded in the world religions, each with its own distinctive identity, can – at this point we are not saying 'should' – can they (or rather, their exponents) engage in dialogue with one another? We need to clarify this question further.

By definition it seems that those philosophies of religion belonging non-controversially to a particular religious family – e.g. 'Christian' (to include, say, Anglican, Roman Catholic and Orthodox approaches), 'Hindu' (to include, say, Vaishnava and Saiva approaches), 'Buddhist' (to include, for instance, Theravada and Madhyamaka approaches) – *can* engage in dialogue with one another, for on what grounds can we say that they cannot? As members of the same family they share the same conceptual and linguistic world, are 'at home' with fundamentally the same or similar symbolic, mythical and doctrinal structures. Vaishnavas and Saivas under 'Hinduism', Roman Catholics and Anglicans under 'Christianity', Theravadins and Madhyamakas under 'Buddhism', can dialogue within the confines of their own religious family-trees – that is, engage in sustained debate and exchange of ideas in pursuit of truth and understanding (even though they may not always have externalized these objectives) – partly because during their protracted histories they *have* done so, producing new meaningful emphases, coherent conceptual structures, significations, outworkings, during the course of their internal development. A crucial feature of what it is to be 'Christian', for example, is to share with others who are identified as Christians the same linguistic-cultural web of patterns of discourse and practice, and long-term goals and aspirations. Since the *differentiae* of the various strands of this web are quantitative rather than qualitative, dialogue – characterized, shall we say, by a cognitive exchange and redintegration of semantic and linguistic content based on mutual understanding – is quite possible. Indeed, even dialogue across overlapping linguistic-cultural webs – those of Judaism, Christianity and Islam, for example, or Hindu and Buddhist systems of thought – is possible, for the reason that they are historically interconnected, structurally commensurable patterns of development. One just needs to call to mind the great and fruitful philosophical interactions between Christianity, Islam and Judaism of the medieval world – if only we could recapture the mutual intellectual respect and appreciation on which these were based! – not to mention the centuries-old exchanges between Hindu, Buddhist and Jain systems of thought.

But, say some, genuine dialogue is not possible across the religio-cultural divides of our world, and any attempt to engage in such dialogue would be doomed to failure. For it would lack the requisite linguistic and semantic commensurability between the religio-cultural matrices involved, and produce results that would remain superficial and worthless at best, and profoundly misguided and misleading at worst. Genuine dialogue cannot take place across the barriers of cultural incommensurability – there are insufficient grounds for the cognitive exchange and redintegration of semantic and linguistic content. According to this 'incommensurabilist' view then, philosophies of religion cannot genuinely dialogue across certain cognitive divides since the linguistic-cultural webs involved do not overlap in a sufficiently significant manner; in this context, philosophies cannot, like spiders, move appropriatively from one web to another; rather, like the fly, they are trapped within the confines of a particular web. So we may ask: commensurabilist spider, or incommensurabilist fly: which?

Much seems to be at stake. If there are structural barriers to free dialogue between philosophies of religion of the world, important consequences for the doing and development of philosophy would follow, not to mention changes in attitude and outlook. Fortunately, I do not think we need abide by the incommensurabilist's view. For a start, there are *a posteriori* reasons to indicate that it is wrong. Consider the origins and growth of some of the major religious traditions of the world. Christianity, a linguistic-cultural web in its own right for the incommensurabilist,[20] is itself a now integral composite of what formerly were culturally very different matrices indeed, including the Hebraic and the Hellenistic. Perhaps the same may be said of Sikhism and Sufism (both of which include Hindu and Muslim – 'non-Semitic' and 'Semitic' – matrices in interestingly different ways), among other faiths. If religious traditions can arise with integrity in this way, then surely dialogue, including philosophical dialogue, can similarly occur in this way. Indeed, the process of thus dialogically constructing new faiths has continued, e.g. Keshab Chandra Sen's religion of the 'New Dispensation' in late-nineteenth-century Bengal *inter alia*.[21]

But there are also analytic reasons to reject the incommensurabilist position, and these have to do with what may be described as the inherently open-ended nature of cognitive structures. We may distinguish two forms of the incommensurabilist stance, the 'weak' and the 'strong'. According to the strong stance, it is not possible even to properly understand the cognitive structures of an alien linguistic-cultural web (where 'alien' means originatively quite other, without historical interconnection or overlap of conceptual matrices), for there is no true common ground on the basis of which one can significantly 'under-stand' the viewpoint of the other. Genuine dialogue, namely exchange and redintegration of semantic and linguistic content preceded by mutual comprehension, in this context is quite impossible. The weak stance concedes the possibility of genuine mutual understanding, but denies the possibility of dialogue on the grounds that cross-cultural cognitive transactions unduly distort and dislocate the contents of these transactions.

We repudiate both stances. However culturally divergent the cognitive structures of 'alien' linguistic-cultural webs may be, they are nevertheless basically human: human in origin and human functionally, and it is a condition of their humanness that such structures be inherently open-ended. This open-endedness, which gives the lie to the incommensurabilist positions, is of two kinds, or rather is manifested in two ways: (1) through the possibility of what we may call empathetic understanding (which militates against the strong incommensurabilist stance), and (2) by way of (substantive) change and growth (which countermands the weak stance).

(1) Empathetic understanding is our well-attested capacity to enter imaginatively into the perspective of another human being, to grasp the other *qua* other (it is this well-attestedness that makes the strong incommensurabilist position an epistemologically myopic one). Empathetic understanding is not a recondite occurrence. At an informal level it is a widespread and much-valued phenomenon of our daily lives, transcending barriers of gender, race and culture. From instances of flashes of empathy or sympathy with the other (where we speak of 'identifying' with the other) to the more sustained identification of parents, lovers and friends, empathetic understanding is integral to the fabric of everyday experience. It is the capacity we have as humans to project ourselves 'into the shoes', to adopt the standpoint, of the human other.

It is a *contextual* capacity: on the one hand we are able to access the other in a way that does not allow the other's particular circumstances of gender, race, age, etc., to act as insuperable obstacles to this access; on the other hand, these very circumstances act as the co-ordinates of the new perspective we adopt. Empathetic understanding, *qua* empathetic, is neither intrusive nor distortive with respect to the reality of the other; rather it is a way of objectively affirming the other in their otherness. At a more formal level, empathetic understanding is familiar to the scholar. It is the scholar's tool to enter the perspective of the subject under scrutiny. As such it involves a rigorous training of the imagination to acquire a disciplined pliability.

As its name implies, empathetic understanding is an act of understanding or cognitive grasping; it is not an act of evaluation (which is a further mental act). Once the other is understood *qua* other to some extent, it is open to the understander to evaluate the other under some aspect or other, and indeed to use this understanding for his or her own ends, good or bad. In so far as an act of empathetic understanding may have been motivated for a moral purpose, or may be used for moral/immoral ends, it has a moral dimension; the act of understanding itself, however, seems to be amoral. Thus we may understand the murderer and his actions in depth, without necessarily approving or condemning his motives.[22]

Though empathetic understanding is a way of identifying cognitively with the other, even when developed to a heightened degree it provides only partial access to the other: one cannot actually become the other in their totality. Nevertheless, it is a mode of *real access*, of really becoming the other. This is confirmed by the fact, which most of us experience at various points of our lives, of being reassured by the other, notwithstanding differences of gender, race or culture, *that they have really been understood.* This is only possible through empathetic understanding. But at the same time this reassurance is a guarantee of the open-endedness of human nature and its cognitive structures. We grasp the human other *qua* other by virtue of our shared humanness, transcending, in so far as we can identify with the other, *differentiae* of the other. And we are more or less successful human beings, the more or less successfully we are able to live and move within the terms of this dialectic. This fundamental commonality and the cognitive access it provides negates the strong incommensurabilist position, and signals the malleability and adaptability of our cognitive structures; it shows that such structures are not inescapable, self-contained webs. Indeed, maintaining this stance – those who argue for the absolute inalienability of context belong to this category – is not to take due account of our cognitive capacities and demands as human beings; it is to be epistemologically myopic.[23]

But we can take empathetic understanding further – into what I have called *constructive empathy.* Elsewhere[24] I have described constructive empathy as follows:

> [It is a] mode of [cognitive] access [that] is *constructive* in two senses. First, it is a means of understanding in the context of *positive* intentions, viz. the desire to open channels of communication in relationships of true reciprocity. Hence it is not an assault on, a destructive attending to, the other. Second, in deploying it one is required to position oneself, in as sensitive, comprehensive, whole-hearted yet focused a manner as possible, in the living situation of the other. As such it is a regulated expression of the creative powers of the imagination.
>
> This mode of access is also *empathetic.* Its goal is no less than to assume the identity of the other by a process of 'becoming' the other ... this method seeks to develop to the full the powers of plasticity of the imagination. This can take place only by a disciplined dialectic of training and implementation ... in so far as it is an ideal to live in relationships of true reciprocity, one must strive to make of constructive empathy an habitual expression of a certain orientation to the world ... [for] people realise instinctively that true understanding of the other requires a passage from egoity to alterity, a transition from self to other.

As described above, constructive empathy is a disciplined process with both a cognitive and moral dimension. Its moral component comes to the fore in the underlying motivation to relate positively with the other on the basis of sustained empathetic understanding. Often this is not easy, but this does not mean that it cannot (or should not) be attempted. Certainly in the area of the philosophy of religion, it is an extension of a *professional* requirement, namely empathetic understanding as a scholarly method. Whether empathetic understanding is deployed then as a professional tool or, by way of constructive empathy, as a means of *dialogic* interaction (with a view to building bridges of understanding and acquiring an appreciation of the other), it is the marker of the significant mutual cognitive access[25] that *is* possible with respect to the other in the philosophical domain, notwithstanding cultural and other divides.

(2) A different but related facet of the cognitive process we have been speaking about, is the fact and mode of the way cognitive structures – concepts, symbols, paradigms, not to mention tropes, beliefs, arguments and doctrines – are susceptible to change and growth. It is their open-endedness that makes this possible within the parameters of a fundamental human commonality. Within these parameters, these cognitive structures are continually undergoing modification, sometimes substantial modification, on the basis of interactive transactions such as conversations, discussions, debates and controversies, which take place both inside and outside a religious tradition (or linguistic-cultural web, if you like).

Consider the Christian doctrine of the Trinity. A watershed in the formulation of this doctrine was the Council of Nicaea in 325. Here, within a conceptual matrix already formed by the integration of Hebraic and Hellenistic elements (not to speak of any other, namely Persian), current concepts of substance, personhood and relation *inter alia* were, on the basis of extensive argument and debate (taking account, historically, of the discussions that led up to the formulation), combined to articulate a particular expression of the doctrine. But debate on this understanding, and development of the doctrine in numerous ways and contexts, have continued over the centuries.[26] In so far as the continuing debates have taken cognizance of basically Christian assumptions, beliefs and objectives, these changes may be regarded as internal to the Christian context. But, as is well known, with the passage of time Christian thinkers, for all sorts of theological and socio-political reasons, have also engaged in debate with those who have eschewed basic Christian tenets, including humanists, atheists and scientists. These 'external' debates have had to take cognizance of new understandings of the concepts of substance, person, relation, causality, etc., which have had to be factored into the on-going process of the reconstructions of the doctrine of the Trinity. In other words, most contemporary understandings of the doctrine of the Trinity are the results of centuries of continuing conceptual change and growth engendered by *intra*-Christian no less than *extra*-Christian debate. It is surprising how on occasion (Christian) incommensurabilists take (*a priori*) exception to dialogue with non-Christian faiths while overlooking the 'dialogue' and its attendant significant changes that *have* occurred (and continue apace) with

321

secular forces nearer home (indeed, many incommensurabilists have fostered such external exchanges).

Unless cognitive structures were inherently open-ended, these substantial changes in the dialectic of the continuity-in-discontinuity of the history of these structures could not take place. For these changes (or certainly enough of them) are based on the assimilation and integration to a significant extent of new external material. There are dozens of similar instances, perhaps with overtly more philosophical content, with regard to Christianity – take, for example, doctrines of the existence and nature of God, creation, and free will – not to mention other religious traditions. It is by virtue of the commonality of their humanness that cognitive structures are thus inherently open-ended and as such susceptible to more or less substantive transactional change. I do not think that the incommensurabilist position (weak or strong) can pass muster, then, and I believe that in a communicationally shrinking world in which thinking people are slowly but surely realizing that there is an increasing demand to interact culturally, religiously, politically, economically, ecologically and in other ways on the basis of converging objectives, the future for 'philosophy and world religions' is not particularly bleak.

Hitherto we have been arguing for the possibility of inter-cultural dialogue in the philosophy of religion. If we now agree that the commensurabilist spider is entitled to fix a beady eye on the incommensurabilist fly, we may ask, *should* such dialogue occur? I hope that enough has been said to indicate that it should. The advantages of such dialogue far outweigh the disadvantages. Any recourse to a *hermeneutic of suspicion* (to use the fashionable jargon) in the interactions between faiths and philosophies is to be severely limited. No doubt it is well to be systematically suspicious of superficial and tendentious resemblances in such encounters,[27] but it is quite another thing, as we have argued, to maintain that dialogic interaction is not viable. Indeed, sensitive, informed and constructive dialogue is highly desirable, a hermeneutic of suspicion in this context being a prerequisite only to ensure a successful outcome, rather than an insuperable barrier. Such dialogue is highly desirable, not only because it is likely to increase knowledge and good will between peoples, but because in its wake philosophy itself will become a far more rigorous and hence beneficial enterprise. I find it hard to avoid the conclusion that confining oneself to debates within particular linguistic-cultural webs or sets of webs risks logical laxity, cultural narrow-mindedness and philosophical complacency. So many basic assumptions and goals would simply be taken for granted; so much impoverishment would result. Comparative philosophy (and comparative philosophy of religion) properly conducted would push forward the barriers of our understanding of the meaning and scope of rationality, truth, faith and evidence (to name but a few seminal concepts), not to mention our appreciation of human nature and its proximate and ultimate goals; it would provide fresh perspectives and salient correctives for life and thought. This will often be a harsh schooling, but it holds out the prospect of a liberative experience. As Scharfstein suggests: 'If, as comparative philosophers, we are bold, imaginative, and precise enough, we shall discover worlds of which we have only imprecise hints at present' (op. cit., p. 97); worlds – if we are to survive as thinking, co-operating beings – that we really cannot afford not to explore and inhabit.

Notes

1 J. N. Mohanty, *Reason and Tradition in Indian Thought: An Essay on the Nature of Indian Philosophical Thinking* (Oxford, 1992); see pp. 282f.
2 E. Husserl, *The Crisis of European Sciences and Transcendental Phenomenology*, ed. and trans. D. Carr (Evanston, 1970); see Mohanty, op. cit., p. 284.
3 Mohanty refers to R. Rorty, J. B. Schneewind and Q. Skinner (eds), *Philosophy in History* (Cambridge, 1985) as defending this view.
4 Here Mohanty (op. cit., p. 288) quotes J. L. Mehta, *Philosophy and Religion: Essays in Interpretation* (New Delhi, 1990) in describing Heidegger's stance.
5 Which Mohanty rightly points out did not originally entail an attitude of pure *theōria*, but included an understanding and active pursuit of the good life.
6 This list is neither exhaustive nor representative (though it is admittedly somewhat circular) for arriving at some general description of 'religion'. How to define religion is itself a highly contentious question. The tendency for Western (and Westernized) scholars is to understand the meaning of 'religion' primarily in terms of categories peculiar (though not necessarily exclusive) to Christian, or at least Semitic, understandings of religion, e.g. salvation (however this may be described), though in that case it is doubtful if this criterion would fit Confucianism – generally understood as a religion with different main objectives – or indeed those forms of Hinduism which advocate recourse to the deity or deities for succour in this world, with ultimate 'salvation' functioning in practical terms as no more than some distant ideal. Provided we are aware of this methodological issue, it will suffice for the purposes of this essay to broadly understand by the word 'religion' a way of life that offers ego-transcending human fulfilment against a horizon of some supra-human ideal or reality. In any event, see the contents of this book for other concerns of the philosophy of religion, mainly in a Western context.
7 In this chapter I do not wish to make a consequential distinction between 'philosophy of religion' and 'philosophical theology'. If we grant that the latter implements a philosophical approach from within the framework and its assumptions of a particular faith, then let us subsume 'philosophical theology' under the former heading.
8 Or does one have to introduce some equally arbitrary criterion of time, e.g. some form of 'axial period' which would be noteworthy only because its

convenient elasticity could stretch to include the origin of any preferred religious tradition?

9 See Ian Markham (ed.), *A World Religions Reader* (Oxford, 1996), pp. 356–7, 218.

10 Markham (op. cit.) seems to suggest this: 'This small minority has had a greater influence on world history than any other comparable group of people . . . they generated the religious outlook that gave birth to Christianity and Islam' (p. 219).

11 G. Larson in his *India's Agony over Religion* (Albany, 1995), p. 19, gives the total number of Sikhs as 16 million, but Markham gives about 19 million (op. cit., pp. 356–7).

12 Such religion is one of the prime focuses of the *Journal of Contemporary Religion*, published thrice a year by Carfax Publishing Company, Abingdon, Oxfordshire.

13 I am assuming, of course, that this epithet is not to be taken in the trivial sense of 'of/in the world', which meaning would apply to *every* religious tradition in the world.

14 Wilfred Cantwell Smith, *The Meaning and End of Religion* (New York, 1962; London, 1978).

15 'Islam' as a descriptive term for the religion of Muslims is relatively recent; the older studies are more revealing of their essentialist methodology in speaking of 'Mohammedanism'.

16 For an attempt to discern the nature of 'Hinduness' with respect to Hinduism, see Julius Lipner, 'Ancient Banyan: an inquiry into the meaning of "Hinduness" ', *Religious Studies* 32 (1996).

17 Brian Hebblethwaite, 'The Anglican tradition' in Philip L. Quinn and Charles Taliaferro (eds), *A Companion to the Philosophy of Religion* (Oxford, 1997).

18 The well-known *Encyclopedia of Philosophy* (8 vols, ed. Paul Edwards; New York/London, 1967), which describes itself as the successor to 'the only previous major philosophical reference work in the English language, J. M. Baldwin's *Dictionary of Psychology and Philosophy* [which appeared in 1901]' (p. ix), has grasped the nettle and without apology or explanation says, 'the *Encyclopedia* treats Eastern and Western Philosophy . . . ' (ibid.); this includes entries treating of non-Western thinkers and traditions and which might well be described as falling under the philosophy of religion, e.g. the articles entitled 'Indian philosophy' and 'History of mysticism' (Ninian Smart), 'Islamic philosophy' (Fazlur Rahman), 'Chinese philosophy' (Wing-Tsit Chan), 'Madhva', 'Ramanuja', 'Sankara' (Ninian Smart), etc. The entry 'Philosophy of religion, History of' (by H. D. Lewis) contains sections on Hinduism, Taoism and Confucianism, and Buddhism.

19 It is noteworthy that in the single-volume *Who's Who of World Religions* (ed. J. Hinnells; London, 1991), no definition is provided of 'world religion'. Since, however, the work seeks to place 'religions in a truly global setting', and 'also seeks to understand individual religions in a world wide perspective' (Introduction), it seems that 'world religion' is understood in an extremely broad yet undefined sense, incorporating not only 'living' but also dead faiths. Thus, besides the religions already mentioned, the list of traditions considered in this work includes 'African Religions . . . Bahai . . . Egyptian religion (Ancient) . . . Gnosticism . . . Meso-American religions . . . Pacific religions, Roman religion . . . [and] Zoroastrianism' (p. xv); 26 categories are mentioned. In *A World Religions Reader* edited by I. Markham (see note 9) there is also no clear

description of what a 'world religion' might be, and the religions considered are Hinduism, Buddhism, Chinese religion, Shintoism, Judaism, Christianity, Islam, and Sikhism.

20 At least of the type of G. Lindbeck; see his *The Nature of Doctrine: Religion and Theology in a Postliberal Age* (London, 1984).

21 On occasion, the New Dispensation has been described as 'superficial', but I have yet to encounter a philosophical justification of this epithet. In this context three points are worth noting: (1) these dialogic constructs can be more or less successful, i.e. more or less coherent, systematic, integral; but variability in this regard is not necessarily proportionate to viability; (2) the longevity of a composite faith (and even the fact that it may have become defunct) is not a necessary indicator of its inherent validity or viability, for extrinsic circumstances (e.g. natural disasters) no less than intrinsic factors can play a crucial role in determining whether a faith survives or not; (3) depending on the nature of the dialogue, the resulting construct may be either individual or collective.

22 Empathetic understanding seems to involve a moral component in another way: the act of 'under-standing', of acknowledging as true what is perceived to be the case, is an act of submitting to the truth, and hence moral as such.

23 For a fine, and I trust complementary treatment, in wider perspective, of the inevitability and desirability of our capacity for continually 'decontextualizing' and 'recontextualizing', see B.-A. Scharfstein's 'The contextual fallacy' in G. Larson and E. Deutsch (eds), *Interpreting Across Boundaries: New Essays in Comparative Philosophy* (Princeton, 1988, and Delhi, 1989). Scharfstein notes: 'Caution slips easily into hypercaution, which deserves the name because it is sterile. For those interested in comparative thought it is therefore important to recognize that an extreme emphasis on context can be unreasonable and intellectually expensive enough to be considered a fallacy [p. 85] ... The parochialism it encourages is itself a form of misunderstanding, intellectually little but myopia raised to the status of virtue [p. 94].'

24 In 'Seeking others in their otherness', *New Blackfriars* 74 (1993).

25 'Cognitive' here must be understood to include the emotional.

26 One may get a sense of the early development by consulting any good relevant reference work; see, e.g., A. Di Berardino (ed.), *Encyclopedia of the Early Church*, vol. II (English version; Oxford, 1992).

27 It is a common narrowness to regard resemblance as the ruling genius of dialogue; constructive dialogue of the kind we have endorsed celebrates and profits from difference as well. Some differences point to ultimate incompatibility, no doubt, forcing reappraisals of one's own stance; other differences turn out to be mutually complementary and encourage new avenues of thought.

12
Science and religion

Dominic J. Balestra

Introduction: situating the question of science and religion today

Sooner or later certain basic, big questions regarding the physical world lead to questions regarding the relationship between science and religion. A minimally complete list of such big questions should address the nature, origins and meaning or significance of the universe. They might well include such questions as: What is the nature of the physical world, i.e. what is it made of and how does it work? How did it, its basic constituents and their patterns of behaviour (laws) originate? And finally there is a question of significance or meaning regarding the universe: for what purpose, if any, does it exist? Is there any significance to the fact that we are a part of the physical universe? We may reasonably and responsibly specify the latter in the following way: Does our presence – the presence of human knowers who act morally and politically, and who sometimes raise questions of truth or justice, especially regarding the pursuit and prospect of their attainment – add yet another dimension of meaning, an eschatological one which transforms an initial question of nature and origins into an emergent question of ends and purpose? Something like the latter form of the question of meanings breaks out of current discussions of the so-called Anthropic Principle of the latest theories of modern physics or the biochemistry of the cell.[1] It has served as an invitation from the side of science to address the question of the relation between science and religion. This more or less salutary opening to religion could only have occurred relatively recently. Before then the prevailing positions in science and philosophy of science were inhospitable toward a positive relation between science and theology.

In the early part of the twentieth century scientific cosmology, though highly mathematical in its structure, was a highly speculative discipline lacking a solid observational ground. Nevertheless, the only accepted scientific, as distinct from philosophical or theological, cosmology had no need to consider the question of origins. In its view on a large scale the universe always was, is and will remain the same. And Darwin's contributions, in the domain of life, removed the last bridge to a theology of nature. Science was at best agnostic and indifferent to religion; but more often outrightly antagonistic toward any hint of a creation that might lead to a creator. The situation in the philosophy of science only reinforced the lack of contact between theology and science. Well into the 1960s a logical empiricist model of science dominated the academic construal of scientific explanation and rationality. In its extreme forms it prohibited metaphysical and theological language as meaningless, and it tried to sustain science as logical and empirically objective. It effectively banished any possible dialogue between science and theology.

Forty years ago the question of science and religion would have been relatively easy to handle. Little was written about the question and even less in response. In contrast the last twenty-five years of scientific discussions about origins, and the new, post-Kuhnian philosophy of science, present a significantly transformed context, a new problem-situation for taking up the question of science and religion at the end of the twentieth century. Long-held and tired conceptions about both science and religion can no longer be presumed. Recognition of the limits of logic in scientific method and the correlate disclosure of the dimension of historicity in scientific rationality recasts the question of science and religion. In particular, it removes an old barrier (the hard demarcation) between science and theology and, thereby, clears a way for new avenues of exchange between these disciplines. The new developments in science and philosophy of science require different answers to the two preliminary questions immediately posed by the question of science and religion today – Whose religion? Which science?

Forty years ago the answer to the first question would have been easy: 'Any religion, it does not matter, since all religion is intellectually unacceptable.' Since most of this book has dealt with questions of God and religion in the Western tradition of Judaeo-Christian theism, in what follows our general use of the term 'religion' will be confined to Judaeo-Christian monotheism. Admittedly one could challenge such a restriction on the referent of religion, especially in light of such works as Fritjof Capra's *The Tao of Physics* or *The Dancing WuLi Masters* by Gary Zukov, which offer intriguing speculative interpretations of the meaning of the least-understood aspects of quantum physics in terms of Eastern religions. The historical fact that the growth of modern science has been a Western European development further supports our constraint on religion. There are also thematic and methodological reasons which counsel caution about moving too easily beyond an only recently emerged critical and historically sensitive Western philosophy of science. The developments of a disciplinary theology and a doctrine of creation in Western monotheism add yet another constraint on our choice of religion.

So much for 'Whose religion?'; what of 'Which science?'? Do we reach back to the origins of Western science in the early Greek cosmologists, from Thales to Empedocles among others, and the initial breaking away from mythic thinking about nature? Or do we simply leap into contemporary discussions of the implications of Big Bang cosmology or the Anthropic Principle for scientific support of a creator-God, all the while ignoring history? Forty years ago both science and Anglo-American philosophy of science would have made the task of identifying 'which science' relatively uncomplicated. Stripped of its seventeenth- and eighteenth-century deistic, if not theistic, sensibility, science entered our century as agnostic and indifferent, if not outrightly antagonistic, toward religion. Religion was often viewed as the enemy of modern science. 'Real science' was clearly understood to be objective, empirical and rational. It bore no relationship to religion, none of any cognitive import – except perhaps to eliminate the latter as contributing toward any understanding of the cosmos. At the time, the portrait of science was dominated by a foundationalist epistemology, i.e. logical empiricism. In the latter's view science aimed to establish empirically testable, generalized explanations of observable but problematic phenomena. Such phenomena might be freely falling bodies or the deviation of a planet from the expected path of its usual orbit. In its view, as the phrase 'logical empiricism' suggests, the objectivity of science rested with an evidential base of empirical facts, facts which were independent of any hypothesized theory under question and available to all through sense observation. And the rationality of science was ascribed to the logical testability, the logic of the hypothetical-deductive method, of its explanatory hypotheses.

In sum, the rationality and objectivity of science were synonymous with, respectively, logicality and empiricism. Only those aspects of science amenable to this model of objective rationality, features internal to what was called the 'context of justification', were of cognitive significance. Social, economic or psychological factors in the genesis of a hypothesis, such as for example, the development of nineteenth-century thermo-dynamic theory as motivated by the central role of the steam engine in the industrial revolution, were considered irrelevant to the question of whether a theory was true or rationally warranted. In general, such social and historical dimensions of science were relegated to a distinct 'context of discovery' which was presumed to be external to science *qua* knowledge. In this way the agnostic or atheist could square with history and acknowledge the role of religious motives in the founding fathers, most notably Galileo, Kepler and Newton, for whom the vocation of the natural philosopher was to read the mind of God in the Book of Nature.

This portrait of scientific knowledge grew out of the modern dogma of a fact/value dichotomy, which located questions of ethics and values in a subjective sphere alien to the fact world of science. Indeed, it reinforced the treatment of questions of ethics as non-rational matters for meta-ethical analysis of feelings and emotions, and it pretty much relegated theology, revealed or natural, to meaningless assertions construed as emotive expressions of 'wish-fulfilment' or the absurdity of our place in the universe. With the exception of Catholic philosophical thinkers and metaphysically minded approaches such as that of process philosophers, like Alfred North Whitehead and Charles Hartshorne, or certain American pragmatists, philosophical treatment of science and religion was quite sparse. And more often than not, philosophy sought to demarcate and exorcize religious thought from science.

A persistent pattern: faith challenged by reason

The road to Rome: out of Athens and Jerusalem

The seventeenth-century scientific revolution did not produce the first challenge to religion on the basis of reason. In our century reason's most powerful form is that of a scientific reason whose uses, applications and technologies are transforming our world into what Francis Bacon dreamed of in his *New Atlantis*, an earthly city of man which has eclipsed St Augustine's *City of God* as an image of a world without end. Inasmuch as our modern science is at the heart of reason today, we may construe the history of the encounters and conflicts between modern science and religion as an important, recent set of episodes in the story of the relation between faith and reason. It is a story that reaches back to Greek mythic religion and the challenge which the early Greek natural philosophies presented to it. The early dialogues of Plato afford us a glimpse into the tensions and struggles generated by the new philosophical ways of thinking. We cannot treat this topic here, but we must consider the incorporation of Greek reason in the medieval Christian mind.

When Greek science emerged as an autonomous authority in Aristotle the notion was continuous with the *theōria* of metaphysics. In its medieval appropriation it was called *scientia naturalis*, which was a 'science' continuous with *philosophia naturalis* and thereby with metaphysics. The philosophical response to the Copernican revolution, from Descartes's metaphysical dualism to Kant's epistemological dualism, breaks this continuity of *theōria*. It should alert us to the significant shift in meaning of the term 'science' before and after the Copernican revolution. Moreover, if modern science is a particular type or mode of reason, then it behoves us to go back to pre-modern 'science'.

Virtually no Greek philosophy, from Thales to Aristotle, could ever accept as rational two themes, creation *ex nihilo* and a real infinite. But the Hebrew scriptures revealed the word of a God, 'he is who is', who created everything *ex nihilo* – not in the manner of an artist sculpting a work out of clay, but by divine command. Accordingly there is nothing, no thing, no chaos, no universe, however formless, prior to God's creative act of genesis, of originating the world. Thus, the world and time have a beginning. God in this sense transcends the created world, God is transcendent. As 'he who is' God came to be understood as existence in and of itself, which is to say, infinite being. In this way the notion of the God of Jerusalem came to be understood as the transcendent, infinite Being who creates the world out of nothing.

In Aristotle's philosophy time is the measure of motion, and real time is that which is the measure of the circular motions of the planets and the stars. Since there can be no motion if there is nothing moving, no temporal beginning of the universe is possible. So, Aristotle concluded that the cosmos is eternal, it simply has always existed with ever-orbiting heavenly bodies. As eternal, always having existed, there is no need for a creation of the universe. Furthermore, the basic structure of time as the measure of the recurring circular motion of the heavenly bodies is cyclical. There is no end of the universe, nor purpose for its historical time as cyclical issues in an eternal recurrence of the same. For early Christian thinkers the cyclical time of Aristotle's universe did not cohere with the linear time and eschatology of a salvation history. Perhaps Augustine more than any other early Christian philosopher and theologian appreciated the challenge that Greek reason presented. For Augustine and other Christian thinkers until the twelfth century the Genesis story provided the occasion for a consideration of nature. Beyond that we do not find much medieval 'science' until well into the twelfth century. In his attempt to reconcile the Genesis account of the origins of the universe Augustine developed a remarkably sophisticated theory of the 'literal meaning' of the biblical texts and the 'intended meaning'.[2] It is an exemplary episode of faith coming to grips with reason.

The roads out of Jerusalem and Athens had for some time merged and led to Rome. The medieval universities had been established by various Roman Catholic orders and were growing. By the twelfth century, the rediscovery of Aristotle through the work of Islamic philosophers had brought his thought into the foreground of discussion in the medieval universities. Philosophers, theologians and students had reconsidered Aristotle and thereby renewed the faith and reason debate, but this time it was between a Platonically minded faith and an Aristotelian reason. In the thirteenth century St Thomas Aquinas and other leading scholars had come to refer to Aristotle as 'the philosopher'. Accordingly the question of faith and reason became that of how to reconcile Aristotle and Christian truths.

To a large extent St Thomas Aquinas succeeded in coherently incorporating significant aspects of Aristotle's philosophy of nature into perhaps the greatest synthesis of Greek thought and Christian revelation to this day. Yet over the question of origins Thomas drew upon the truths of revelation to set the limit to reason. He conceded that reason could not establish that the world had a beginning in time, but then insisted upon deferring to revelation's doctrine of creation to set a limit to what Aristotle's reason could establish.

Fundamental Aristotelian principles of nature[3] – the hylomorphic (matter and form) account of material substances, the 'act, potency and privation' model of change, and the doctrine of the four causes – had to be reworked so as to accommodate a strong sacramental theology of a transcendent, infinite creator. To achieve the needed synthesis Aquinas made his own brilliant contributions. He introduced and developed the key distinction between *esse* and essence, using it to rework a new account of individuation. He developed a powerful doctrine of analogy. The doctrine on *esse* and essence combined with Aristotle's hylomorphic position made talk of an infinite being coherent, and the doctrine of analogy enabled a modest, intelligible talk of the transcendent God of Jerusalem. In regard to the theme of science and religion (as a variant of the theme of faith and reason) it is extremely important to note that Aquinas had reformed an Aristotelian metaphysics of substance which became the received view of the theologian and the natural philosopher for the next three centuries. In addition to the beliefs about God's creation, infinity, and transcendence, Aquinas also provided a way for the theologian to theorize about sacrament, specifically the Eucharist, in terms of a metaphysics of substance. At the same time the natural philosopher (a medieval 'scientist') described, classified and explained nature in terms of the categories and principles of Aristotle's organismic 'naturalism'. Aristotle's hylomorphic view of nature secured a qualitative, teleological physics of motion, a view of nature as constituted by qualitatively higher levels of various kinds of individuals: inanimate mixes of earth, air, fire and water, various plants, animals, and at its summit the living, thinking social human animal. The hylomorphic principles of nature readily provided basic laws of natural motion to explain the powerful geocentric astronomy of Ptolemy. In brief, hylomorphic theory explained the natural free fall of bodies on earth as a function of the dominant inanimate elements whose nature was determined by a qualitative form of the material content of the inanimate thing. Hot air naturally rises and heavy rocks sink to the bottom of the pool. Generalized, the law of natural *terrestrial* motions is that heavy things fall toward the centre of the earth tending by their natural form toward their natural place, and light things ascend away from the centre 'seeking' their natural place within the sphere of the orbit of the moon. The latter is a real boundary marking the other domain of the physical universe, the *celestial* domain of the planets and stars whose real natural motions are *uniform circular motions* as a result of the nature or form of the celestial material, the fifth element.

Quite independent of Christian theology the Aristotelian principles of nature set up and ground a two-domain physics of motion which cuts the universe into two quite distinct and separate realms, the celestial and the terrestrial. Inasmuch as Aristotle's philosophy of nature and its 'physics' are realist, any astronomy which is taken as realist must conform to the fundamental principles of the two domains. This partially explains the failure of the heliocentric theory of the ancient astronomer Aristarchus. This realism must be kept in mind to appreciate the resistance to the Copernican hypothesis. By the end of the thirteenth century Ptolemy's technical astronomy was securely embedded within the hard core of qualitative, teleological Aristotelian laws of motion of two distinct domains – the *celestial* and the *terrestrial*. Together they constituted a quite powerful world system or cosmology, one of the two referred to in the title of Galileo's immortal work *Dialogues on the Two Chief World Systems* (1632). Working from this system in the fourteenth century, Nicholas Oresme at Paris and natural philosophers at Merton College at Oxford developed what many scholars now recognize as a late-medieval 'science' of motion. It was quite sophisticated in its conceptual descriptions and analyses of change and motion in terms of Aristotelian categories of quality, quantity and forms. The latter grew out of a distinctly medieval concern with the manner in which qualities or forms, such as the redness of an apple, varied in intensity. An increase in intensity of the given quality was called an intension, and a decrease in the intensity was called a remission. More specifically, the 'science' of motion developed upon a basic analogy between variable qualities and local motions of a physical body. The natural philosophers had devised ingenious techniques of geometric representation of intension and remission of forms which, when applied to local motion, were remarkably anticipatory of modern kinematics, i.e. the descriptive classical physics of the movement of bodies.

In the early decades of this century when he turned to doing his pioneering studies in the history of science, the late nineteenth-century physicist and philosopher of science Pierre Duhem was taken by surprise at what he discovered in the Paris and Oxford of the fourteenth century. It led him to reconsider the standard thesis regarding the origins of modern science. Though still controversial, Duhem's historical thesis has been sustained and elaborated by the contemporary Benedictine physicist and theologian of science Stanley Jaki, and independent support is provided by the superb scholarship of the Dominican William Wallace on the Aristotelian sources and influences on Galileo's early work. In sum, the general historical claim of the Duhem–Jaki thesis is that, *pace* the still dominant position of a radical seventeenth-century Copernican revolution as at the origins of modern science, the Aristotelian natural philosophers at Merton College in Oxford and Oresme at Paris in the late fourteenth century are the true benefactors of our modern physics of motion. Though still somewhat controversial, Jaki's strengthening of Duhem's original thesis offers a rich, alternative historiography which aids in exposing the prejudices of the standard, somewhat stale portrait with its persistent secularism and accompanying scientism. Clearly, the Duhem–Jaki thesis holds the prospect of a bridge from medieval natural philosophy to early modern physics. But it does not promise any easy way to a *rapprochement* between modern science and Christian theology, even if the Church concedes, as it has today, that it made an error in regard to Galileo. A true *rapprochement* would need to show that the natural philosophy of the new physics was, as understood at that time, consonant with both the Scripture and the systematic theology of the Church.

Galileo and the 'New Science': battle for the heavens

Most of the current discussions are concerned about the modern science which was born of Galileo's battles for the Copernican theory and which reached maturity in Newton's successful synthesis of the earth and the stars under a uniform set of laws of nature integrated by his theory of universal gravitation. Through that period the new physics engaged theistic-minded philosophers from Descartes to Kant in a struggle to reconcile the demands of the new physics and astronomies of an infinite universe for a world-view which could retain a place for an infinite creator whose existence was not beyond the reach of reason. Indeed, members of the eighteenth-century Royal Society, including Isaac Newton, Robert Boyle and Robert Hooke, approached their investigations of nature as explorations of the creator's handiwork – so much so that it grew into a 'physico-theology' which argued from the findings of design in nature by the new science to God's wisdom. The immense popularity of John Ray's *The Wisdom of God Manifested in the Work of Creation* (1691) illustrates how the new science worked its way into a new 'natural theology' which effectively replaced the older one of medieval metaphysics.

The walls of the Stanza della Segnatura in what is today the Vatican Museum are the artwork of Raphael. One wall holds the fresco initially entitled 'The Triumph of the Eucharist'; the other holds the more familiar

'School of Athens'. The two images stand opposite, but not opposed, to each other in lasting witness of a joyful harmony between the sacred and the profane. Not long after Raphael completed the room in 1511, new fissures began to break forth, undermining a too brief *Pax Vaticana* for Christian reason. From within the Church, and its equilibrated theology of nature, burst forth the explosive personality of the passionate Augustinian, Martin Luther, quickly followed by a flurry of dissenting, protesting voices. No longer would history record one holy, catholic Christian Church. No longer would there be one voice, however complex the theology behind it, articulating reason's understanding of the faith. At that same time another thinker, also a Catholic and a cleric, though no explosive theologian and a reformer only of the calendar, Nicholas Copernicus, came forth with no less revolutionary a message for either the sacred or the profane. Quietly underlabouring on the geocentric astronomy of Ptolemy, Copernicus disclosed another fault-line in the landscape of Raphael's medieval cosmos. As Luther had shaken Christian faith's theology – until then a reason seeking to understand its faith – leaving it permanently shattered, Copernicus inadvertently set Greek reason's philosophy of nature on course toward an earth-quaking collision. Any realistic construal of the Copernican thesis would penetrate to the heart of the Aristotelian cosmology, leaving a black hole into which the order of its nature would collapse like a fading star. But what would, what could replace this world system which had stood for some 1,300 years? Which observations had confirmed well enough to meet modern-day methodological standards, which made sense of physical things and their motions, which had served Western civilization with a reliability unsurpassed by any alternative scheme of the world. If this world system was mistaken, then how could anyone be sanguine about prospects for a replacement, for a new science!

So it was that two deeply reverberating shock waves, emanating from two separate sources – science and religion – cracked the sixteenth century, throwing all into a chasm of doubt. This then was the horizon of an uncertain world into which Galileo was born in 1564, the year of Shakespeare's birth and some ten years after the thirteenth session of the Council of Trent. After some years of quiet consideration the Copernican question became pressing. On 5 March 1615 the Sacred Congregation of the Index issued a decree which stated:

> And because it has also come to the attention of the aforementioned Sacred Congregation that the Pythagorean doctrine concerning the mobility of the earth and the immobility of the sun, which Nicholas Copernicus, *De Revolutionibus Orbium Coelestium*, and Diego de Zuniga [in his commentary on Job] also taught, and which is false and altogether incompatible with divine Scripture, is now spread abroad and accepted

by many, as appears from a certain printed Epistle of a certain Carmelite Father [Foscarini] ... therefore, in order that an opinion ruinous to Catholic truth not creep further in this manner, the Sacred Congregation decrees that the said Nicholas Copernicus, *De Revolutionibus orbium*, and Diego de Zuniga on Job be suspended until corrected; that the book of the Carmelite Father Antonio Foscarini be indeed altogether prohibited and damned; and that all other books similarly teaching the same thing be prohibited: as accordingly it prohibits, damns, and suspends them all by the present Decree.[4]

Because Foscarini was head of the Carmelite order in Calabria his defence of the Copernican theory, a long letter sent to his Superior General on 6 January 1615, charged the explosive atmosphere in Rome. Though Galileo is not mentioned in the decree he did meet on his initiative with Cardinal Bellarmine, the Jesuit who was head of the Sacred Congregation. Bellarmine cautioned Galileo not to advocate a realist defence of the Copernican theory. Sixteen years later, after Bellarmine had died and Galileo's friend Cardinal Maffeo Barberini became Pope, Galileo published his famous work which defended the Copernican thesis by arguing for the motion of the earth, *The Dialogues on the Two Chief World Systems*. Shortly after its publication, Galileo was condemned, ordered before the Inquisition, and threatened with excommunication and punishment if he did not abjure.

The common opinion is that the modern warfare between science and religion was initiated in the case of Galileo, and that the initial battle was over the conflict between Scripture and science. In defending Copernicus's thesis, Galileo had pitted himself against the word of God, for the Scriptures say that the sun moves! There is some truth to this view, but it is seriously incomplete, and without the rest of the story it unfolds as a half-truth that distorts. We might be tempted to say that the fateful confrontation is simply explained by a double literalism: too literal a reading of Scripture and too literal a reading of scientific theory (in this case Copernicus) put Galileo and his Church on a collision course. This did play a part in the rhetoric of the ensuing debate, especially given the pressure on the Church from a Reformation that had stressed a more faithful return to the 'Word of God as written'! But this was not the decisive source of the deep tension. Cardinal Bellarmine, the head of the Holy Office, as a theologian was of course quite adept in his Church's sophisticated tradition of interpreting the texts of Scripture, a biblical hermeneutics that went back a thousand years to St Augustine. According to that tradition, if a clear and evident reason demonstrates a truth about nature and that truth conflicts with a literal reading of Scripture, then we may question whether a literal interpretation is intended in the relevant Scripture passages. Though not a theologian, Galileo was mindful of this interpretive tradition. So he knew that he needed a stronger case than so far presented in defence of the Copernican thesis. His telescopic discoveries of the phases of Venus provided strong support for the Copernican theory but not the demonstrative proof required by Bellarmine. However, by the end of 1615 he became convinced that he had a demonstration of the Copernican thesis – this was his argument based on the action of the tides. Basically he reasoned that the action of the tides was due to the combined motions of the earth's daily rotation and its annual revolution about the sun. So confident was Galileo that he believed he could now meet the standards of the Augustinian principles of interpretation. Thus he wrote his famous letter to the Grand Duchess Christina, in which he explains how she might hold faithfully to Scripture while also accepting the truths of the new science. He formulated his position on the relationship between truths of science and truths of faith in three major claims: first, the book of Nature and the book of Scripture complement and cannot contradict one another, since they come from the same Author; second, science is a legitimate path to truth independent of sacred theology; and third, Scripture cannot be used against scientifically established statements.

In sum, Galileo had advocated the separation of theology and science (more accurately philosophy of nature) as autonomous disciplines. Even though Galileo's arguments did not convince Cardinal Bellarmine in 1616 that the Copernican theory was true, Galileo remained confident that the tension between the heliocentric thesis and the Bible was reconcilable in accord with then available hermeneutical principles. But given this, was that fateful warfare between science and religion inevitable? And why has it persisted even into our own decade today?

In *Galileo: Heretic*, Pietro Redondi argues that the deeper source lies with Galileo's atomism which risks Eucharistic heresy. Before the Copernican theory became an issue, the Church at the thirteenth session of the Council of Trent (1561) had made a fateful decision in pronouncing a definitive and combative version of the truth of the Eucharist mystery, the doctrine of transubstantiation. Inasmuch as this dogma was couched in the language of the substance metaphysics of Thomas and Aristotle, the Church had yoked itself to the Aristotelian natural philosophy and its physics of motion. While many scholars do not find Redondi's thesis fully acceptable, Richard Blackwell agrees with the important point that the Church following Trent had made a commitment to Aristotle's natural philosophy. By the end of the sixteenth century Fr Aquaviva, the Superior General of the Jesuits, had decreed for their *Ratio studiorum*: 'In matters of any importance philosophy professors should not deviate from the views of Aristotle ... '[5] Since the Church had committed itself to the truth of the Aristotelian–Ptolemaic world system, and since the Copernican astronomy could not be harmonized with the Aristotelian cosmology, any realistic construal of the

Copernican thesis could be headed for an explosive confrontation on a number of fronts – scriptural theology, systematic theology, and natural philosophy. This cast an uneasy, dark shadow eclipsing the light of Raphael's fading fresco. No longer could nature and grace commingle in peaceful harmony; between science and religion there would be enmity. Seen against the background of Trent, a meaningful case can be made that 'Galileo's crusade' went beyond the Copernican issue, that he sought to keep his Church, for its own good, from the mistake of making an article of faith out of any disputable 'scientific' position.

Once committed there was no turning back. In so choosing, the Church, inadvertently or not, and unaware of the radical implications of Copernicus's treatise (quietly published at his death in 1543), had opted for a realism with respect to *scientia*. This stands in marked contrast to the instrumentalist words of the Lutheran Osiander's famous preface to Copernicus's book *De Revolutionibus*. He says: 'There is no need for these hypotheses to be true, or even to be at all like the truth; rather, one thing is sufficient for them – that they should yield calculations which agree with the observations.' Though quicker than the Catholic Church to prohibit any realist reading of the Copernican theory, the Lutherans and other Protestant churches exploited the instrumentalist understanding of mathematical hypotheses so that the practical uses of the new sciences might be advanced. Because of their long tradition of a sophisticated reading of Scripture and a more recent history of strong interest in a *scientia naturae*, Catholic theologians hesitated to condemn the Copernican thesis. Hadn't the Pope commissioned Copernicus? There was no objection to Galileo's teaching the mathematical theory, so long as he made it clear that its import was only *instrumental*. As Bellarmine had put it:

> Galileo will act prudently ... if he will speak hypothetically, *ex suppositione* ... To say that we give a better account of the appearances by supposing the earth to be moving, and the sun at rest, than we could if we used eccentrics and epicycles, is to speak properly; there is no danger in that, and it is all that the mathematician requires.

Unlike the eighteenth-century Anglican Bishop, George Berkeley, Bellarmine was not a complete instrumentalist in regard to science. But he was astute and saw in instrumentalism one possible way out for both the Church and Galileo. Eventually the Catholic Church too would fall in line with the rest, but not for similar reasons, not for scriptural reasons. The irony is that the Council of Trent had embraced too literal an interpretation of the *scientia naturae*, alongside a much more sophisticated theology of Scripture. Both sides of the confrontation had slipped fatally into an unforeseen pitfall, a naive realism in regard to science. As a scientific realist Galileo did not want Scripture to fall, he only wanted to bring down the

Aristotelian cosmos. But without a compelling, demonstrative argument and given the decision of Trent, the die was cast.

The latter part of the seventeenth century experienced rapid growth in physics that brought to completion in the Newtonian–Keplerian world system the revolution unwittingly initiated by Copernicus. The issue of realism did not rest with the success of Newton. A somewhat invisible philosophical struggle over the question of the realistic import of the abstract, mathematical constructs persisted through the next two centuries to the contemporary impasse on this issue.

Descartes's theory of matter as *res extensa*, and the argument of his *Meditations* (1640) II and VI, was the first and clearest statement of a scientific realism. Moreover, Descartes also made mathematics the distinctive feature, the hallmark that demarcates a modern physics from a classical Greek conception of a science of nature. In so doing Descartes had also disclosed the deeper epistemological problem for a realistic interpretation of modern science: the problem of justifying claims that cannot be strictly proven, *demonstrated* in the language of Bellarmine and Galileo, on the bases of hard empirical evidence. To the extent that a scientific theory postulates the existence of non-observable theoretical entities and mechanisms, the question arises that insofar as the new science is empirical knowledge then by what logic is it entitled to go behind the observable phenomena to the material reality, whether Newton's atomic masses or Bohr's atom? This is a deep and serious problem, for however mathematical our modern physics, its epistemic authority is tied to a base of empirical evidence. Newton gave unequivocal expression to the methodological rule that however logical, however mathematically powerful our hypotheses, each must face the tribunal of observational evidence. But he also recognized that the epistemological price of the empirical security was a limited ontological return. As a result Newton hesitated to give full ontological import to his mass particles, especially that invisible glue that holds them and the world all together – *gravity*.

Berkeley was the first among the modern philosophers to penetrate the new science (by then Newton's physics) and to argue that its realist interpretation was a formidable threat to religious faith and authority. According to him so long as taken realistically the success of the new science was a proof of the power of the human intellect to discover the secrets of the world – to uncover the reality hidden behind the appearances. Such a human power, unaided by divine revelation, brings forth science and its technology as a new Prometheus. Unbound, such a power knowledge unfolds as nothing less than a potential rival to the God of Abraham. For Berkeley, to accept a realistic reading of science was tantamount to eating of the forbidden fruit. Is not the original sin in Genesis that of an arrogance and pride in the power of a human knowledge, a power knowledge that goes further than Thrasymachus to claim that 'might makes truth'?

The dogged empiricism behind Berkeley's instrumentalist criticism boomeranged when it reached the philosopher David Hume, who turned it against all knowledge, whether human or revealed. Neither science nor religion was entitled to cognitive access to a 'hidden reality' beyond the appearances. Kant, who firmly believed both in God and in the truth of Newton's physics, was critically shaken by Hume's assault on both sides of the science/religion divide. In response to Hume, Kant transformed Berkeley's theocentric Idealism into an anthropocentric epistemology which issued a dualistic compromise between faith and reason. Kant himself announced this as the 'delimitation of [scientific] knowledge, that makes room for faith', where the latter includes the realm of both morals and theology. In the Kantian exchange the epistemological insurance for the Newtonian science had a high price tag, that of renouncing any cognitive access to a reality behind the world of empirical appearances. Conversely, if science could no longer be a metaphysics, neither could metaphysics be a science. In sum, no scientific knowledge of any thing-in-itself nor of God is possible. But what is truth if not about the real! The stakes in this epistemological game of realism had achieved their highest risk with Kant. It was a game in which the gamble was all or nothing. There could be no winner on the roll of its dice, for neither science nor religion could give reason a knowledge of the real. The only outcome was knowledge of no real thing but only of appearances, which is to say, nothing.

Darwin and the science of origins: the battle for human nature

The Galileo case has long been viewed as a testament to a close-minded, authoritarian Church opposed to free-thinking, critical enquiry. As the new science matured with Newton and displayed its power in a steadfast progress to the dream of Laplace's superman, peaceful coexistence had been achieved under dualist terms negotiated by Kant. While questions of physical nature belonged to this new, empirical, mathematical science, living nature seemed to remain with philosophy, and human nature ultimately belonged to theology. As long as human beings were a part of the world, the questions of origins remained safely within the sanctuary of religion. But the nineteenth-century turn to history redrew the lines of confrontation as it renewed the warfare. Darwin's naturalistic account of the 'descent of man' once again brought forth the second major battle between science and religion.

Early nineteenth-century theologians construed the intricate structures and variety of nature as unmistakably manifesting God's creative work. William Paley's widely influential *Natural Theology* (1802) traced a providential adaptation of creatures to their world, transforming the naturalist's studies into a type of natural theology. Through an examination of numerous examples of organs marvellously serving their functions, such as that of the hand, the heart, and especially the eye, Paley argued that there was design of means-to-ends in nature. By analogy he argued that just as the design structure exhibited in the watch requires the intelligent watchmaker, the numerous variety of design structure exhibited through-out nature all the more requires an intelligent maker of nature. Paley understood a change occuring 'by chance' to mean that it occurs by the operation of causes without design. Thus, in his view living organisms are so well adapted that their design structure could not be the outcome of 'chance'. Unlike the metaphysical natural theology of Aquinas, Paley's 'naturalist' natural theology proved to be particularly vulnerable to the concept of evolution as later proposed by Darwin. Since the meaning of 'chance' in the Darwinian mechanism of 'chance variation and natural selection' is precisely how Paley understood the term, Darwin's theory of evolution subsequently presented a deep threat to early nineteenth-century natural theology. We have seen that Copernicus's theory challenged in a fundamental way the 'natural science' of Aristotle, and thereby the theo-logy which had yoked itself to Aristotle. Likewise Darwinian theory threatened the biology of natural design and thereby the nineteenth-century natural theology of the design argument. The first indication of the vulnerability was in the excited responses, especially the flurry of scientific and theological opposition to *Vestiges of the Natural History of Creation* (1644), anonymously published by Robert Chambers, which advanced the theme that adaptive development gave rise to new species. Some six years after returning from his five-year voyage (1832–37) as the naturalist aboard the *Beagle*, Darwin found the key to a mechanistic account of gradual modification of species in the economist Malthus's *Essay on Population*, which theorized on population pressures and competition in the human struggle for existence. By this time Darwin had formed the rudiments of his famous theory, but he waited to publish it. In anticipation of a stormy reception, he took further time to study and refine his observations of an astonishing array of additional varieties of biological species. In *Ever Since Darwin*, Stephen J. Gould argues that Darwin delayed publishing his theory so long because it needed a stronger materialist climate of opinion to win acceptance and withstand the bishops' attacks on it. Recall that Spencer had already begun to popularize the idea of a materialist evolution, albeit more Lamarckian, and Marx had already inverted Hegel's dialectical idealism into a dialectical materialism by 1859, the year that Darwin finally published *On the Origins of Species by Means of Natural Selection, or the Preservation of Favoured Races in the Struggle for Life*. Its major theme was twofold: one, that all living things developed from a few relatively simple forms, or perhaps even one; and two, that the development of species is the result of a *gradual* process of descent with modification through a mechanism of 'chance variation and natural selection'. Darwin's argument may be recapitulated as: Populations of animals and plants exhibit *random variations* due to chance (unplanned) environmental events. Some of these variations advantage some organisms over the rest of the population in the *struggle for survival*. Such favourable variations transmit their advantageous features to their progeny. Since populations tend to be more than the environment can support, the proportion of the advantaged population (with the favourable variations) that survive and reproduce will be larger on average than the proportion lacking the favourable variations. This latter constitutes the mechanism of *natural selection*. Thus, as a result of the mechanisms of random (i.e. unplanned) variations and natural selection in the struggle for survival, a proportion of a population may undergo over successive generations continuous, gradual changes which can result in the origin of a new variety, species, or genera, i.e. of a new population at any taxonomic level. In essence, Darwinian natural selection is a differential death rate between two variant sub-classes of a population.

Though Darwin suggested that some variation is due to the action of the environment or effects of use or disuse, he conceded that the 'causes of variation were unknown'. Without a good scientific explanation (i.e. one in terms of scientific law) of the source of variation, Darwin's theory itself might have become extinct. As it happened, a bit ironically, an Augustinian monk and botanist in Austria, Gregor Mendel, solved the puzzle of inheritance and formulated its basic laws in 1864, though this was not known to the scientific community until 1900. Mendel's Laws of genetic inheritance greatly strengthened the Darwinian theory. Today the synthesis of the two theories into a general theory of evolution is called neo-Darwinian population genetics.

Though it did not explicitly include the human species in its account, it was implied. In *The Descent of Man* (1871) Darwin had explicitly extended his natural selection thesis as a completely adequate account of all human origins, including mental and moral capacities as well as physical features. This carried the causality of a natural selection without design into the eschatological sphere, presenting a much more profound threat to theology. Meanwhile, by 1880 the cumulative force of Darwin's argument began to convince many biologists, and the subsequent communication of Mendel's discovery secured Darwinian evolutionary theory in the scientific community. But as the scientific reception grew from healthy criticism to bona fide acceptance, the popular concern with the religious and ideological implications swelled to feverish levels. Oddly, political radicals enthusiastically supported the Victorian Darwin, which only strengthened conservative opposition. While Darwin personally avoided being dragged into the public controversy, the scientist and strong advocate of evolution

Thomas H. Huxley, who proudly proclaimed himself 'Darwin's bulldog', hounded opponents such as Bishop Wilberforce and W. E. Gladstone in public debate. These public spectacles generated images of Darwin as 'monkey lover' or 'enemy of the Bible', and disrupted the peace of demarcation, re-igniting the warfare between science and theology. Unlike Galileo, who was an unwavering theist and Christian, Darwin migrated from a naive acceptance of Christian doctrines in his youth to a reluctant agnosticism, in the end remarking that 'the whole subject is beyond the scope of man's intellect . . . The mystery of the beginning of all things is insoluble by us; and I for one must be content to remain an agnostic.'

Buttressed by Marx's political philosophy as social science, and Freud's translation of belief in God as wish-fulfilment and the assimilation of religion as an illusion, the stakes became apocalyptic. For many Protestants it was war between two fundamentally incompatible ways of seeing the world. For other sincere Christians and scientists, like the physicist Michael Faraday, there was only one way out of their dilemma – a doctrine of mutual exclusion by agreement, a leading of two lives. A kind of schizophrenic life of the mind. In the United States the Scopes Monkey trial of 1925, which found John Scopes guilty of teaching Darwinian evolution in his high-school class, was a poignant reminder that the war was real. A victory short-lived (it was overturned on a technicality) and ambivalent, it would seem vanishingly small and immeasurably distant if not for the recent revival of the issue with the movement called 'creation-science'.

Strong biblical fundamentalism and the US constitutional prohibition of any religious teaching in the public schools have converged to set the stage. In California Christian parents, most of fundamentalist or evangelical convictions, became concerned that the teaching of evolution in public school as the *only* account of the origins of life, especially human life, conflicted with the Christian beliefs about creation. They argued that to present Darwin's theory as the only account was not religiously neutral. The California Board of Education was persuaded in 1969 to allow the creation story of Genesis to be presented as an alternative to the evolutionary theory. Since it was clear this conflicted with the separation clause of the First Amendment, the Genesis story was re-construed as a scientific account which 'creationists' labelled 'creation-science'. Creationists argued that creation-science explains data in the fossil record that Darwinian evolution cannot. Organized creationists successfully lobbied two state legislatures, Arkansas and Louisiana, to enact 'balance treatment' statutes into law in 1981. Outraged with the new law, a coalition of scientists, theologians and some religious leaders filed suit in the US Federal court and the Arkansas 'balance treatment' statute was overturned by a ruling of Federal Judge William Overton. Judge Overton's decision was based on a two-fold claim of demarcation: firstly, that a science can be identified by five 'essential characteristics' (including falsifiability) which creation-science fails to exhibit; and secondly, that creation-science is identifiable as a theological doctrine. But as we shall see later in this chapter, recent philosophy of science shows that this principle of demarcation between science and non-science is not tenable.

Regrettably, the entire affair reinforced an old image of warfare between science and religion. Ironically it occurred at a time when the results of science in cosmology and biochemistry have produced findings salutary to religion, and philosophy of science has removed old walls of separation. It also creates confusion and inhibits responsible discussion about the religious doctrine of creation and scientific theories which bear on it. In the words of Ernan McMullin:

> A particularly unfortunate consequence of the controversy is that the term 'creationist' has been rendered unusable by ordinary Christians, Jews or Muslims in describing their own beliefs. Yet they believe in God as creator; they profess the faith that the universe is God's handiwork. They are all 'creationists' in the most basic sense ... The entire role of creation has been rendered suspect by an ill-advised liberalism that would have seemed out of place in Augustine's day.[6]

Following his highly polemical *Darwin on Trial*, Philip Johnson has argued in *Reason in the Balance* that the real issue in the creationist–evolutionist debate is a metaphysical one over whether naturalism (by which he means a scientific materialism) is the best explanation of everything. Johnson is not altogether off track, but he encumbers the philosophical issue about method and metaphysics with the heated political controversies of the creationist issue. The question of whether there is anything beyond nature, transcendent to nature, cannot be answered by modern science. The web formed by the methodologies and the explanatory structures of modern science does not warrant assertions regarding God. When popularizing scientists like Carl Sagan interject, for example, that 'the Cosmos is all there is or ever was or ever will be', they are making a philosophical claim which is outside the normal warrant of science. In his widely read *Chance and Necessity* the French molecular biologist Jacques Monod interweaves a defence of scientific materialism through his lucid account of molecular evolutionary biology. In his BBC lecture Monod is uncompromising in his thoroughgoing reductionism: 'Anything can be reduced to simple, obvious mechanical interactions. The cell is a machine. The animal is a machine. Man is a machine.' Never mind that such micro-reduction to the mechanistic does not square with quantum theory. He purports to show how biochemistry in eliminating intelligent design at the molecular level explains away purposive behaviour and eventually consciousness in animals and humans. On this basis he concludes that there is no purpose in the cosmos.

Monod's philosophical reasoning is filled with gaps, conflations and, in general, is embarrassingly unsophisticated. Implicit in his argument is a line of reasoning characteristic of all such scientism, namely, a partial knowledge entails knowledge of the whole; if there is a sound science of a given subject matter, it warrants making a metaphysics of the science. Better attempts than Monod's might add the lemma that the sum total of the particular sciences effectively becomes our metaphysics. There is a nest of methodological and epistemological issues which haunt such sopho-moric moves; but such scientistic reasoning is flawed at the outset, for the inference that what is true of the part is true of the whole exhibits the fallacious pattern of the classic logical fallacy of composition. Kant recog-nized this danger in the promising prospects of Newton's physics. For the flip side of Kant's prohibition that 'metaphysics can't be a science' is the lesson that the new, empirical sciences, not even the total set of all the modern sciences, physics plus chemistry, plus biology, and even socio-biology (of Edward O. Wilson), cannot be a legitimate substitute for a metaphysics!

Obviously, there is more to support such a total commitment by such bright thinkers as Sagan, Monod and Wilson. Contemporary philosophers of science (Lipton) believe that the pattern of reasoning characteristic of science, which entitles it to claim our intellectual allegiance, is that of 'inference to the best explanation'. From Aristotle's articulation of such a pattern in his *Posterior Analytics* I, 2, to its modern formulations as 'retroduction' in science (McMullin, 1992), the goal of the best explanation which has withstood severe tests and disciplinary scrutiny is what every science strives for. It is one of the hallmarks of science. Bright thinkers like Monod, Sagan and Wilson recognize this and presume that the best explanation in science is the best explanation for each and every thing, including the cosmos as a totality. Again, compositional reasoning! They even infer more, that scientific explanation is the only intellectually acceptable explanation for anything! Because certain types of explanations (for example, moral duty as an explanation for someone's behaviour) are ruled out of science for methodological reasons, it does not follow that such explanations *tout court* do not contribute to our understanding. Nonethe-less, they rule out any other kind of explanation, metaphysical or theological, of astronomical origins or of biochemical mechanism or of evolutionary development. In general, such scientistic thinking illustrates what the philosopher Alfred North Whitehead has described as 'the fallacy of misplaced concreteness'. The issue of scientism stands in a critical intellectual juncture between science and theology, especially for a modern science as distinct from a premodern *scientia*. Tom Sorrell's *Scientism*, the first rather complete, serious treatment of this topic, will reward the interested reader with a balanced, penetrating critique which is helpful precisely because it does not denigrate science in a postmodern diatribe.

We have criticized scientistic thinking for its extrapolating from particular scientific theories and for its totalizing of scientific method and explanation in its absolute rejection of theology. If we may think of scientism as an inverted physico-theology, then for similar methodological reasons we should be cautious about claims that the recent 'Big Bang' cosmology or the Anthropic Principle proves that a creator-God exists. Another important reason for counselling caution here is due to the tentative or provisional nature of all scientific theories. Nonetheless, it is a fact that some results of the latest scientific cosmology have ignited an astonishing discussion among physicists, philosophers and theologians. An understanding of the wider dialogue about origins followed by a look at the new philosophy of science can help both scientist and theologian, and anyone else, avoid the intellectually narrow and irresponsible standpoints like those behind both creationism and scientism.

Rapprochement

In spite of the continuing enmity, there have also been significant indications of a *rapprochement* between science and religion. Recent developments in science and philosophy of science show that intellectual engagement between science and theology can contribute to a more complete, more intellectually responsible and self-critical appreciation of the 'big questions', and the diverse disciplinary perspectives on them.

Physics and the origins of the cosmos

In the early twentieth century scientific cosmology had little to say about any genesis or evolution of the physical universe. Nor did it have the need to explain any origins. Basically the universe consisted of a virtual infinity of bodies spread through an infinite Euclidean space in an independent homogeneous time-line infinite in both directions, the past and the future. Since it was understood to be infinite in age and size, no question – at least no scientific question – about the nature of its origins arose. But all of the elegance and simplicity of the Newtonian cosmos was lost after the twentieth-century revolution in physics. An extraordinary complexity replaced the elegant simplicity of a cosmos constituted by atoms with electrons neatly orbiting protons and neutrons like planets around their sun. General relativity theory and quantum theory decisively ended clas sical physics and its complacent absence of any account of an early universe. In elaborating his general theory of relativity (GTR) in 1917, Einstein discovered that it predicted an unstable universe – one that would either expand or contract, and not remain stable. Since most cosmologists presumed a static universe, i.e. one that is completely unchanging in time when viewed on the largest scales, Einstein to his later regret inserted a 'correction factor' in his equations so that his first mathematical model would conform to a static model. But Einstein's 'correction' proved to be a mistake, and physicists considered the notion of an *expanding universe*, after Edwin Hubble observed the systematic 'redshift' in the light spectra from all distant galaxies. The redshift can be explained by the recession of all galaxies from earlier positions closer to one another. Since the universe is expanding, it follows that its receding galaxies were closer and closer together in the more and more remote past. Accordingly it would be reasonable to conjecture that a very long time ago the stuff of the stars had been so densely 'compressed' at one singular moment and 'place' as to constitute a unique beginning of the universe. Thus was the Big Bang hypothesis born.

Many scientists, such as physicist Arthur Eddington and the astronomer Fred Hoyle, found the Big Bang hypothesis repugnant because of its intimation of a supernatural event – the creation of the world! Motivated in part by a deep hostility toward the Christian view of a creation by God once and for all, Fred Hoyle sought to avoid the Big Bang by championing a rival theory of the universe, called the Steady State theory. Unyielding, Hoyle reasoned that though the universe is expanding, if the rate of expansion and the density of matter were always the same, then the universe would not be changing its large-scale state. Expansion without a fixed density of matter would result in a thinning out of the universe due to the same amount of matter in a larger and larger space. To keep the density (ratio of matter to space) constant Hoyle proposed a continuous creation of matter, specifically, of the lightest of the elements, hydrogen, *from nothing* and *with no cause*. At Princeton in 1952, when asked about Hoyle's theory, it was reported that Einstein dismissed it as 'romantic speculation'. In 1964 two radio astronomers, Arno Penzear and Robert Wilson, discovered the cosmic background (black body) radiation which had been predicted earlier in 1948 by Alder and Herman on the basis of the Big Bang model. This provided strong corroboration of the Big Bang and a compelling refutation against the Steady State model. The background radiation is like fossil evidence that there was a higher density of the radiation source in the past than in the present. Another triumph of the Big Bang theory is that its prediction of the cosmic abundance of the light elements (75 per cent hydrogen and 25 per cent helium) is very close to the abundances observed so far.

Nuclear processes led to the production of the light elements and then of large-scale structures — galaxies, stars and the solar system, eventually providing the environment in which our life evolved. Our presence on this earth that was spawned in our solar system in the universe today poses what has come to be called the Anthropic Question: Why have conditions in the universe been so ordered that intelligent life can exist? In the popular *A Brief History of Time*, Stephen Hawking underscored the importance of the question by stressing that on the basis of our present theories a universe with the requisites for complex life to evolve was infinitely improbable, given the almost limitless number of equally plausible alternative theories. Because of the improbability of the initial fine-tuning required at the quantum level, as well as later, our universe should not have come to be. Then why does our universe exist? In its simplest language the 'Anthropic Principle' (principle is a misnomer) answers this question 'because we are here'. One formulation is: The universe (and hence the fundamental parameters on which it depends) must be such as to admit the creation of observers in it at some stage. As Ernan McMullin remarks: 'The anthropic principle has unmistakable overtones, once again, of physicotheology. The initial cosmic features that enable a universe to develop in which man could one day evolve are so unlikely according to present theory that it is tempting to invoke the plan of a Creator' (McMullin, 1985, p. 45). Later, McMullin (1993) argues for a shift from an *anthropic principle*, which requires too strong a sense that the universe *had* to be of the sort that would make human observers inevitable, to an anthropic *explanation*: evidence of 'fine-tuning' of the initial conditions ought to be given an anthropic explanation. He then distinguishes between two forms of the *anthropic* explanation: one, a many-universe model where many actual universes co-exist, each realizing different initial conditions such that we are in the one that permits our existence. The other, a theological model, in which the fine-tuning of the initial conditions required by the Big Bang is explained theistically by a creator who could/would have ensured that such fine-tuning would be realized. These are two quite different versions of anthropic explanations; the former is cosmological and the latter is theistic. The cosmological version is marginally scientific in the sense that it is so highly theory-dependent that it is at the boundary between science and metaphysics. The theistic version does not satisfy the expectations of a scientific explanation; it includes a theological frame of reference. We agree with McMullin when he adds '[t]his does not, of course, invalidate it as an explanation unless one were to hold that only science can explain'; but we hasten to add that between theology and science there is philosophical explanation. Science cannot be the only kind of explanation, without becoming scientism. Whether the philosophy between science and theology is primarily epistemological (this is McMullin's position) or primarily metaphysical (as in the work of Stanley Jaki) is a complex matter for another discussion.[7]

Biology and the intelligent origins of life

It is important to distinguish two distinct general claims regarding evolution: one, the theory that evolution occurred (simply stated, this is the general claim of the fact that all organisms have had parents), and two, the theory explaining how evolution occurred. Such as the Darwinian theory of natural selection.

Since the mid-1970s, Darwinian theory has been severely criticized from within the scientific community, and creationists moved quickly to exploit this. Not only did they selectively use scientific criticisms, in a fashion reminiscent of proof-texting in scriptural interpretation, to reject the Darwinian account of the *how* of evolution, they extended their 'proof-texting' to the claim *that* anything like an evolution from a common ancestry took place at all. But the rejection of Darwinian theory does not logically entail the rejection of the claim that evolution occurred. However, it would require an alternative theory of the mechanism of evolution. In the absence of such an alternative mechanism, serious doubts about the fact of evolution would very likely arise. The latter coupled with the 'proof-texting' drove a wedge that created an opening for a return to a literalist reading of Genesis.

Major criticisms of Darwinian theory from different spheres have coalesced to put Darwin 'on trial' today. In the first major scientific criticism aimed at Darwinian gradualism, S. J. Gould and N. Eldridge argued that the fossil record requires that 'evolution is concentrated in very rapid events of speciation'.[8] In effect, evolution by revolution! Gould and Eldridge proceed to explain Darwin's method as a manifestation of the cultural bias of the Victorian English life. 'Phyletic gradualism was an *a priori* assumption from the start – it was never "seen" in the rocks; it expressed the cultural and political biases of nineteenth-century liberalism. Huxley advised Darwin to eschew it as an "unnecessary difficulty." We think it has now become an empirical fallacy.'[9] It may be that the creationists' exploitation of Gould's work made him all the more steadfast in his *a priori* commitment to a materialistic theory of evolution, abhorring anything like intelligent design. Most Christian scientists hold that something like evolution, the common descent of the variety of life, has in fact occurred.

While he might well accept the critical import of Gould's 'punctuated equilibrium' with respect to Darwin, biochemist Michael Behe would severely quarrel with Gould's presumption about the adequacy of any mechanistic materialism, Darwinian or dialectical or otherwise, for explaining evolution. In his recently published *Darwin's Black Box*, Behe adds a new dimension to the scientific challenge in his trenchant questioning of whether the Darwinian mechanism of natural selection working on random variations (genetic mutations) provides an adequate account of the evolution of the molecular biology of the cell. Ironically he argues from the 'same'[10] molecular biology to which Jacques Monod appealed to uphold a basically Darwinian mechanism of 'chance and necessity'. Drawing upon his deft knowledge of the 'Lilliputian world' of molecular biology he argues against the adequacy of the Darwinian mechanism and, more important, for the much bolder thesis that the elegance and complexity of biological systems at the molecular level exhibit the design of a purposeful arrangement of parts. 'Our ability to be confident of the design of the cilium or the intracellular transport rests on the same principles as our ability to be confident of the design of anything: the ordering of separate components to achieve an identifiable function that depends on the components' (p. 204). The inference to design requires the identification of the functioning components of an interacting molecular system, and the determination that the system is not a composite of several separable systems.

The inference to design is an argument by analogy. Behe builds his argument through a succession of detailed examinations of the biochemistry of vision, of blood-clotting, cellular transport and more. It results in a strong enough analogy to warrant the pivotal claim that '[t]he laboratory work of graduate students piecing together bits of genes in a deliberate effort to make something new is analogous to the work that was done to cause the first cilium' (p. 205). He insists that the finding of intelligent design is as momentous as the discovery that disease is caused by bacteria or that radiation is emitted in quanta. He acknowledges that the concept of design is new in molecular biology and that a host of questions will no doubt be raised (Mon Dieu! What would Monod say?) and need to be answered before the notion of design can carry forward a significant research programme. But he also recognizes that a lingering prejudice still resident in the scientific community generates a strong reticence toward design. In his words the reticence is due to the dilemma of the elephant: 'while one side of the elephant is labelled intelligent design, the other side might be labelled God'. It is the fear of proposing the supernatural as an explanation for a natural event. Behe believes the scientist should follow the physical evidence to wherever it leads, even to the other side of the elephant! This may well be reasonable, but many would insist it is not scientific. Similar to the situation regarding the anthropic explanation, Behe's proposed explanatory hypothesis of 'intelligent design' is at the boundaries between science and metaphysics. But unlike the heavily theory-laden access to the existence of the initial parameter conditions in the Big Bang cosmology, 'through a maze of theories obliquely', Behe has a more direct access through the bridge of a very strong, concrete analogy.

The infinitely large and the infinitely small of the highly abstract and mathematical field equations of GTR and the wave equations of quantum theory pose deep philosophical difficulties for ensuring the existence of the unimaginable world they posit. But the reality of the Lilliputian world of Behe's explorations may withstand the philosopher's scrutiny if the analogy is strong enough. Of course, this is not the first time that a turn to analogy is being made to establish a bridge to a reality not immediately available. Where Aquinas had used it so that reason could say something about the reality of a transcendent God, our latest scientific cosmology struggles to touch an ever-receding reality. Between theology and cosmology Behe's turn to a biology of intelligent design holds the prospect of a quasi-scientific way to the other side of the elephant. Whether it proves to be a bridge too far, it is too soon to foresee.

Another line of criticism, and a once potentially devastating one, focuses on the nature of Darwinian explanation. Philosopher Karl Popper charged that Darwinian theory is not empirically falsifiable. And since empirical falsifiability is an essential feature of a genuinely scientific theory, which demarcates a scientific theory as scientific, Darwinian theory is not bona fide scientific. This does not mean that it does not offer an explanation nor that its merits cannot be critically and rationally debated. According to Popper it can be discussed and debated but only as a 'metaphysical research programme'.[11] Had Popper been able to consider the paper of Gould and Eldridge mentioned above he might have been convinced that Darwin is 'empirically refutable'. But it does not matter now, for today it is generally conceded that the attempt to formulate an effective Popperian 'principle of demarcation' has not succeeded. (Ironically Judge Overton had based his decision on the expert testimony, that a bona fide scientific hypothesis could be demarcated by Popperian falsifiability, and that Darwinian theory is falsifiable while 'creation-science' is not!) Most philosophers of science have abandoned the quest of demarcation, yet few would conclude that there is no disciplinary difference between theology and science. However, pressed to articulate the difference they might appeal to sociological as well as methodological features, and risk demarcating science by something like a Rorty solidarity society.

Methodological demarcation: a waning wall

Until recently the received position in academia was that science had a privileged status as distinctive in its objectivity and rationality. For many educated individuals and in the public understanding of science this view still persists. It rests upon two closely related themes in the philosophy of science: one, the thesis that rationality is logicality; and two, the demarcation thesis, which asserted that as a result of the rationality thesis, science

is distinctive as an intellectual enterprise. All other intellectual disciplines
— ethics, history, political theory and social sciences (but not theology,
which was usually excluded as intellectually unacceptable) — were considered more or less rational to the extent that they could exhibit the
pattern of scientific rationality as understood according to these two theses.
As a result of the work of Toulmin, Kuhn, the later Popper and Lakatos,
these two themes collapsed under the weight of much more historically
minded, critical scrutiny of the theory of science. The collapse of the
disciplinary dividing wall and the insufficiency of an algorithmic method
of theory choice removed the old portrait of 'real' science from a distinctive
hegemony in the spectrum of disciplinary rationality.

The first thesis, that rationality is logicality, asserts that the rationality
of science ultimately rests with its methodology, the so-called hypothetical-deductive method of modern science. And this method is a means
of logically testing a scientific hypothesis (proposed as a universal explanatory theory of a problematic phenomenon) by reference to a firm, objective
base of empirical fact. The second, the demarcation thesis, held that such
logically empirical testability essentially distinguishes a scientific hypothesis from a non-scientific one.

Insofar as scientific theories include universal statements, inductive logic
(as Hume had argued) cannot establish scientific laws and theories as true;
logically speaking, even the best-confirmed and long-established theories
could be false. This logical feature of induction, combined with the fact
that the history of science exhibits confirmed theories which subsequently
come to be rejected, provides a strong case that the theories of science are
fallible and so only provisional or tentative. Early in his work Karl Popper
recognized and argued for such fallibility of all scientific theories. Accordingly, he asked, whence the rationality of science?

Having rejected the inductivist construal of the method of science,
Popper exploited a basic feature of deductive logic, namely, though a
universal statement cannot be demonstrated as true on the basis of a finite
number of experimental confirmations, a universal assertion (All S are W)
could be proven false by a single, contradictory statement (Some S is not
W). Armed with this fact of logic, Popper developed the theme that
although science is at best conjecture, it is rational conjecture precisely
because it submits its plausible, conjectured theories to severe attempts at
falsification by critical experiment. In Popper's own words, 'only the falsity
of the theory can be inferred from empirical evidence, and this inference is
a purely deductive one'.[12] Accordingly, the rationality of science consists in
a critical process of bold conjecture and critical refutation. Having interpreted the hypothetical-deductive method of scientific testing as a logic of
falsification, Popper then revised the demarcation thesis to read: 'the
criterion of the scientific status of a theory is its falsifiability, or refutability,

or testability' (Popper, 1963, p. 37). In spite of this strong statement of falsifiability, Popper argued for other theses which reveal a much more subtle falsifiability, one which Lakatos called sophisticated methodological falsificationism. Two of these theses are: one, the primacy of theory over observation (this is akin to the Kuhnian thesis that all observations are theory-laden, there are no theory-neutral facts); and two, the logic of the problem-situation, which maintains that the critical method of conjecture and refutation only has significance in the context of a clearly formulated and shared problem-situation. Thus, science conjectures theories as proposed solutions to problems, and to the extent that the conjecture survives critical attempts to refute it, we may rationally accept the theory, at least until the next test.

A major line of argument against falsifiability originates with Pierre Duhem's thesis of the non-falsifiability of isolated scientific hypotheses. In his words: 'In sum, the physicist can never subject an isolated hypothesis to experimental test, but only a whole group of hypotheses; when the experiment is in disagreement with his predictions, what he learns is that at least one of the hypotheses constituting this group is unacceptable and ought to be modified; but the experiment does not designate which one should be changed.'[13] The 'whole group', to which Duhem refers, involves a complex network which includes: background knowledge, 'hard core' theories (e.g. Aristotle's two-domain laws of motion or the three laws of motion in Newton), auxiliary hypotheses (such as explain the workings of the radio telescopes in astronomy and legitimate the 'observed results' as evidence), and the hypothesis under test. The logic of falsification cannot target the hypothesis under consideration nor compel its rejection. The logic can guarantee only that somewhere something is amiss. It does not tell us where to look, or how to locate the source of the trouble. Indeed, one could introduce new auxiliary hypotheses in order to absorb the shock of failure and to immunize against the otherwise fatal effects of a recalcitrant experiment. For example, consider one of the objections to the Copernican theory which requires the earth to rotate at about one thousand miles per hour. Remember, in 1632 no human experienced travelling nearly so fast relative to the earth, at least none that lived to report it! Galileo responded to this by conjecturing his (mistaken) theory of circular inertia. This same auxiliary hypothesis was used to respond to the tower argument. The sequence of such auxiliary hypotheses is designed to 'protect' some fundamental theoretical principles. The latter is similar to Kuhn's paradigmatic theory or Lakatos's 'hard core' of the research programme. Sooner or later the series of auxiliary hypotheses, which Lakatos appropriately named the 'protective belt', must exhibit some corroborated empirical results, otherwise it risks being judged as *ad hoc*. The subsequent development of the protective belt generates, in programmatic response to various problems for the 'hard core' and possibly subsidiary principles, a complex historical series of subsidiary theories which retains the 'hard core'. Lakatos named this historical series a scientific research programme. In the case of scientific cosmology, the 'hard core' of Hoyle's research programme is the Steady State theory in contrast to the Expanding Universe theory of the Big Bang proponents. As we have seen above, Hoyle responded to Hubble's observation of the redshift, and its *prima facie* support of an expanding universe, with an auxiliary hypothesis of the constant ratio of the rate of expansion to the density of matter. In effect, the Steady State theory and the Big Bang theory emerged as rival research programmes, and in time the Big Bang exhibited the empirical results that have made it the accepted theory today. The case of the eventual acceptance of the Big Bang theory exhibits two important features of the rationality functioning in the methodology of a scientific research programme: one, that no logically simple test from one result decided the question; and two, that the 'rational acceptance' is the outcome of a programmatic, historical sequence of conceptual and experimental results. In effect, today's philosophy of science recognizes that there is no ahistorical instant rationality of an abstracted hypothetical-deductive logic of testing. It is in the retrospect of history that the rationality of the theory choice can be judged. Moreover, given the provisional status of any theory and the theory-laden nature of all empirical observations, it becomes clear that the rational judgement, even in the light of history, is not exclusively due to a logic of testing the research programme against a pure empirical evidential base. It does not follow that a logic of experiments is not an essential part of rational theory choice, only that logic is not enough. Despite its brilliance, Lakatos's development of methodological falsificationism does not succeed in eradicating the subject's judgement in the rational appraisal and choice of theories. The judgement of the experienced scientist, like Aristotle's *phronēsis* in the judgement of the moral individual, is an essential aspect of scientific rationality.

Since Duhem first argued his thesis, subsequent philosophers of science (most notably W. V. O. Quine, Thomas Kuhn and Imre Lakatos) have both developed its argument and expanded its thesis. And even Karl Popper, the champion of falsifiability, has successively revised his position in response to Duhemian criticisms such that it closely resembles that of Lakatos. The clear result is that the distinctive advantage of *modus tollens* is lost and the Popperian programme of falsification is no longer tenable. Its sharp demarcation thesis wanes, and history enters into its rationality. Kuhn and Quine, Lakatos and Laudan, Newton-Smith and even Feyerabend, have each in their respective way developed a Duhemian philosophical programme for enlarging the functioning unit of rational appraisal from a single isolated hypothesis to a complex, programmatic network of theories variously characterized as paradigm, conceptual scheme, research programme, research tradition, and even a Wittgensteinian 'form of life'.[14]

Even if we were to distinguish between an isolated test statement and a contextualized test statement, and identify the latter as the potential 'falsifier', the rational import gained could not be restricted to a sharply demarcated scientific context. For as conjectural, such theory-laden statements are fallible and therefore provisional. Accordingly any demarcation of science predicated upon falsifiability can only be a matter of degree and in terms of its historical situation. *Now* we see that the rationality of science is a highly complicated, historically situated process of critical discussion among enquirers in an open communication, something more like the kind of rationality Popper has always recognized as operative in good philosophy, the rationality of critical realism (Popper, 1963, ch. 8). Others have called this 'critical rationality'. In its view, even in the wake of demarcation there still survives an unmistakable feature always at the heart of Western rationality: that a rationally acceptable theory, thesis, doctrine, or whatever appropriate unit of the disciplinary enquiry, is one which has withstood the critique of the discipline as a proposed answer to the questions posed by the problematic shared by members of the discipline. Like Alasdair Mac-Intyre's notion of a 'tradition', somewhere between one and only one rationality and 'anything counts', this issues in a pluralism of many rational disciplines of enquiry. Thus, what we may call 'rational pluralism' is a major salutary effect of the collapse of demarcation.

Obviously, though Popper did not anticipate it, this opens the academy to reconsidering the disciplinary rationality of theology, revealed or natural. In *Theology in an Age of Scientific Reasoning*, Nancy Murphy argues that the pattern of the development of a theological doctrine as an answer to a core question, for example the question of Christ's death as an atonement, exhibits a pattern of a theological research programme not unlike that of Lakatos's account of scientific rationality as a 'methodology of scientific research programmes'. One major effect of the demise of demarcation is that science and its rationality is not so distinctive in its logic and objectivity as to legitimately claim a privileged status as rational enquiry. Murphy's work provides an excellent illustration of the salutary effect that the methodological debate in recent philosophy of science has had for disciplines like theology. Murphy never asserts that there is no important difference between theology and science, but that the disciplinary distinction is not hard-and-fast. Rather, as we have seen in the case of scientific rationality, the judgement of the experienced theologian is ineradicable.

Concluding unscientific remarks

An important corollary to the preceding discussion of rationality and demarcation is that in intellectual questions regarding theology and science the judgement of the experienced scientist and the experienced theologian is ineradicable. It then follows that the judgement of the individual who is experienced as both scientist and theologian is specially desirable in the dialogue between theology and science. Methodological results of the philosophy of science have removed a thick wall which divided modern science and theology. No doubt its recent fallout has helped create a climate much more hospitable to moving across disciplines in dialogue about the big questions. And the recent revival of such big questions in physics and biology has charged the atmosphere with some exciting prospects for shared understanding. At the same time, these developments when set in a larger historical context advise caution. Theology should remember the legacy of Galileo's struggles with a theology which had yoked itself with the science of Aristotle. Today philosophy of science is virtually unanimous about the fallible and so provisional status of all scientific theories. This methodological finding underscores the lessons of history. Does this mean that science as provisional knowledge and theology as 'eternal' revelation can only meet in the end with nothing to exchange now?

Theologian and physicist Ian Barbour offers a useful classification which helps develop a critically reflective answer to the latter question. In brief, Barbour partitions the possible relationships between science and theology into four basic types: Conflict, Independence, Dialogue, and Integration. Jacques Monod's scientific reductionism and Edward Wilson's sociobiology represent instances of a 'scientism' which inevitably leads to a conflict with theology. By excluding any other knowledge as valid, and adding the *a priori* lemma that there is no God (because the web of science cannot recover any God), then there can be no rational room for any theology, revealed or natural. On the side of religion, as we have seen in the case of 'creationism', naive literalist readings of Scripture invade the disciplinary integrity of the sciences. There can be no tolerance from either perspective, for from naive literalism in theology, and naive realism and methodological chauvinism in the sciences, conflict must arise.

The demarcation between the language of science and the language of theology was initiated by Galileo and eventually developed into Kant's epistemological dualism. It is a good illustration of the Independence type of relationship between science and theology: each discipline with its respective autonomy with nothing to say to each other. But for Kant it was at the price of either discipline laying claim to a truth about reality in itself, whether it would be about the starry skies above us or the word of God within! In an interesting way both of these types share a naive realist perspective regarding reality and our knowledge of it. Both presuppose that the metaphysics of science or theology is all or nothing, that it ensures complete and final knowledge of reality or that all enquiry is in vain. There is no in-between. But recent philosophy of science says, with virtual unanimity, that our science is by its very nature provisional and incomplete. Accordingly, we find both the Conflict view and the Independence view unacceptable because of the metaphysical dogmatism each presupposes. This conclusion may not be obvious in the case of the Independence view. For one might subscribe to disciplinary autonomy without claiming complete or permanent knowledge, conceding that our current science is provisional and incomplete. But what would this imply? A pluralism, one which is itself provisional and for which the possibility of convergence between science and theology, in the long run, cannot be excluded.

The Christian tradition has always struggled to bring faith and reason together. In light of its doctrine of creation there is a presumption that human reason, the intellect as distinct from the will, is reliable. As a part of God's creation reason is adequate as an instrument to study nature. In our modern times, ever since Galileo met with Bellarmine, the struggle between faith and reason has unfolded as that between science and religion. In this chapter we have traced out major aspects of this struggle, exposing the mistakes and errors from human beings on both sides of the elephant. This trace signifies that the Christian thinker today, especially the theologian, cannot rest with the dogmatisms of yesterday whether they be those of the Conflict view or the momentary truce of the Independence view. Thus, for both philosophical reasons and for religious reasons we reject the first two categories as acceptable accounts of the relation between science and theology today.

The last two categories, Dialogue and Integration, represent positions more in line with that tension-filled road out of Rome, of a *fides quaerens intellectum*. Because of the provisional and incomplete nature of the findings of science, the Dialogue view cautiously restrains from any premature integration at either a substantive level or a methodological level. It recognizes sufficient parallels between the disciplines to warrant a dialogical relation between science and theology. In this relation it is usually theology reformulating its understanding of a basic doctrine, such as creation, in light of the best current knowledge from science. But it also recognizes disciplinary differences which require respecting the integrity of the distinct disciplines. Representatives of the Dialogue view are Wolfgang Pannenberg among Protestant authors, and Ernan McMullin among Catholic authors. Whether the quantum physicist and Anglican priest John

Polkinghorne falls into this category or the Integration view is difficult to determine. But this may be due to an inadequacy in Barbour's taxonomy, for Professor Polkinghorne cautiously holds out for the possibility of some convergence for a dialogical theology of nature.

The last category, Integration, holds that some sort of integration between the content of science and theology is possible. Barbour distinguishes three versions of Integration. One version is a 'natural theology' which claims that the existence of God can be inferred, at least as a plausible hypothesis (Richard Swinburne), from the evidence of design in nature which science discovers. Like the eighteenth-century 'physico-theology' which it resembles, this natural theology is vulnerable to unexpected findings in science which might conflict with the basic theological claims. The second version is a 'theology of nature' which in appropriating scientific theories within its otherwise distinctly theological concepts may reformulate its understandings of basic theological doctrines, such as that of creation. The Jesuit palaeontologist Teilhard de Chardin's *The Phenomenon of Man* readily comes to mind as an example of a theology of nature. More recently the current theologian and biochemist Arthur Peacocke works a critical realist approach to develop a theology of nature. A major issue for the theology of nature is the nature of God's creative action: is it a continuous creation with God as remote but primary cause? Or, is it a deistic-like plan initiated and implemented into a proximate chain of secondary causality, the domain of scientific study? The third version of Integration, 'systematic synthesis', is a comprehensive metaphysics which incorporates contributions from both science and theology into a coherent world-view. The process metaphysics of Alfred North Whitehead exemplifies this version of integration. It is interesting to note that each version of integration represents a standpoint which works the integration respectively from science to theology, from theology to science, and from both science and theology into an 'overriding' metaphysics. In every case theology is affected by science; in the 'natural theology' even the data of theology may be construed as derived from the findings of science. In the latter two versions, theology's understandings of the data of theology may be affected by science. But are the concepts or theories of science ever reformed as a result of theological developments? No example comes readily to mind. A way may be through an indirect route, made possible by theology's subsumption within the more comprehensive, integrative metaphysics. A way which seems quite Hegelian and which places philosophical metaphysics in a privileged position *vis-à-vis* science and theology.

In September 1987 on the occasion of the three hundredth anniversary of the publication of Newton's *Philosophiae Naturalis Principia Mathematica*, Pope John Paul II hosted a week-long working conference on the theme of 'Our Knowledge of God and Nature: Physics, Philosophy and Theology',

Dominic J. Balestra

The following June, as George Coyne SJ prepared the conference papers for publication (*Physics, Philosophy, and Theology*), the Pope wrote a lengthy letter (which George Coyne includes with the conference papers) encouraging, at moments urging, an open pursuit of a relational, dialogical unity between science and theology. As relational, the encouraged unity insists upon respecting the integrity of the distinct disciplines. Accordingly, he insisted that the unity is not that of an identity between science and theology, nor is it the unity of a reduction of one discipline to the other. Rather, it is the unity of a shared relationship upon which dialogue can proceed, a Dialogical Unity. His letter indicated a sophisticated awareness of the recent themes in science and philosophy of science, many presented in this chapter. He holds up Aquinas's accomplishment in respect to Aristotle as the benchmark to be surpassed. But Aquinas could rely upon a *scientia naturalis* that transcended the particularities of time. The task for the theologian today is even more daunting, for history has entered into the bloodstream of science and its epistemology. John Paul's letter acknowledges this dimension of modern science in his observation that 'physicists possess a detailed though incomplete and provisional knowledge of elementary particles'.

The Pope's perspective is a cautious one which seems to fall between Barbour's categories of Dialogue and Integration. Though an alternative set of categories, for example, one which added 'convergence' as a distinct one somewhat between dialogue and integration, might be proposed, Barbour's taxonomy provides enough perspective to appreciate a closing caution. Whether Dialogue or Integration or Convergence, any substantive contact between the content of scientific knowledge and theology will require a critical realism which accommodates the historicity of science as well as theology. The truths of revealed theology may be eternal but our understandings of those revelations hopefully are still improving.

Notes

1 George Ellis, *Before the Beginning: Cosmology Explained* (London, 1993) provides a succinct, reliable, highly readable presentation of twentieth-century scientific cosmologies of the physical universe. Michael Behe, *Darwin's Black Box: The Biochemical Challenge to Evolution* (New York, 1996) argues that a survey of the best scientific literature on the biochemistry of the cell, essential to all living organisms, leads to the conclusion of 'intelligent design' which can not be explained by the gradualist Darwinian mechanisms of chance variation and naturally necessitated selection.

2 See St Augustine, *The Literal Meaning of Genesis* (2 vols; New York, 1982) and E. McMullin's excellent 'Introduction' to *Evolution and Creation* (Notre Dame, 1985).

3 See St Thomas Aquinas, 'The Principles of Nature' in Robert P. Goodwin,

Selected Writings of St. Thomas Aquinas (Indianapolis, 1965). This work is an excellent illustration of Aquinas's elucidation and summary of Aristotelian ideas about nature which could be of use to a theologian.

4 Quoted in Richard J. Blackwell, *Galileo, Bellarmine, and the Bible* (Notre Dame, 1991), p. 122. This is an excellent account of the infamous first confrontation between the Church and Galileo over the latter's defence of the Copernican theory. It provides the reader with a reliable, rich understanding of the historical situation in 'science', astronomy and theology in order to set up the question of 'truth' in science and religion. It also is an invaluable resource for locating original sources; a number of primary text documents are included as appendices.

5 Quoted ibid., p. 141, ch. 6. 'The Jesuit dilemma: truth or obedience?' The Jesuits at the Collegio Romano were at the forefront of the leading work in mathematics and astronomy entering the seventeenth century. In this chapter Blackwell explains how in a very short time the special Jesuit pledge of obedience to the Pope in the atmosphere of the Counter-Reformation led to the virtual disappearance of the 'scientist' in the relatively new order.

6 Ernan McMullin, 'Evolution and creation' in E. McMullin (ed.), *Evolution and Creation* (Notre Dame, 1985).

7 See W. Stoeger in R. J. Russell, W. R. Stoeger and G. V. Coyne (eds), *Physics, Philosophy and Theology* (Vatican City, 1988).

8 Stephen Jay Gould and Niles Eldridge, 'Punctuated equilibrium: the tempo and mode of evolution reconsidered', *Paleobiology* 3.2 (Spring 1977).

9 Ibid.

10 In quotes, because whether, after subsequent debate, it *is* the same remains to be seen!

11 K. Popper, 'Darwinism as a metaphysical research program', *Methodology and Science* 9 (1976).

12 Karl Popper, *Conjectures and Refutations* (New York, 1963), p. 55.

13 P. Duhem, *The Aim and Structure of Physical Theory*, trans. from 1914 French edn by P. Wiener (New York, 1954), II, ch. 6, pp. 180–90.

14 See W. H. Newton-Smith, *The Rationality of Science* (Boston and London, 1980), chs 3–6 for a critical examination of this development in Popper, Lakatos, Kuhn and Feyerabend. A more recent, but briefer, presentation of the development of the unit of scientific rationality is provided by Ernan Mc-Mullin, 'The shaping of scientific rationality' in E. McMullin (ed.), *Construction and Constraint: The Shaping of Scientific Rationality* (Notre Dame, 1990).

Further reading

Note: The following bibliography is intended to provide a solid working tool for anyone seriously interested in philosophy of religion, especially those approaching the subject for the first time. Divided into sections which more or less correspond to sections of the preceding text, it aims to be fairly comprehensive, and to point its users to writings representing a wide range of positions, not just those of contributors to this book.

General works on philosophy of religion

William Abraham, *An Introduction to the Philosophy of Religion* (Englewood Cliffs, NJ, 1985)

Baruch Brody (ed.), *Readings in the Philosophy of Religion* (2nd edn; Englewood Cliffs, NJ, 1992)

Steven M. Cahn and David Shatz (eds), *Contemporary Philosophy of Religion* (Oxford, 1982)

W. Norris Clarke SJ, *Explorations in Metaphysics: Being–God–Person* (Notre Dame and London, 1994)

Brian Davies, *An Introduction to the Philosophy of Religion* (2nd edn; Oxford, 1993)

J. C. A. Gaskin, *The Quest for Eternity* (Harmondsworth, 1984)

R. Douglas Geivett and Brendan Sweetman (eds), *Contemporary Perspectives on Religious Epistemology* (New York and Oxford, 1992)

John Hick, *Philosophy of Religion* (4th edn; Englewood Cliffs, NJ, 1990)

H. D. Lewis, *Philosophy of Religion* (London, 1965)

John Mackie, *The Miracle of Theism* (Oxford, 1982)

Basil Mitchell (ed.), *The Philosophy of Religion* (Oxford, 1971)

Anthony O'Hear, *Experience, Explanation and Faith* (London, 1984)

Michael Peterson, William Hasker, Bruce Reichenbach and David

Basinger, *Reason and Religious Belief: An Introduction to the Philosophy of Religion* (Oxford and New York, 1991)

Michael Peterson, William Hasker, Bruce Reichenbach and David Basinger (eds), *Philosophy of Religion: Selected Readings* (New York and Oxford, 1996)

Louis P. Pojman (ed.), *Philosophy of Religion: An Anthology* (3rd edn; Belmont, CA, 1998)

Philip Quinn and Charles Taliaferro (eds), *A Companion to Philosophy of Religion* (Oxford, 1997)

William L. Rowe, *Philosophy of Religion* (Encino and Belmont, CA, 1978)

William L. Rowe and William J. Wainwright (eds), *Philosophy of Religion: Selected Readings* (3rd edn; New York and London, 1997)

Patrick Sherry (ed.), *Philosophers on Religion* (London, 1987)

Note

Several contemporary journals either specialize in philosophy of religion or often contain much that is relevant to the subject. These include:

Faith and Philosophy
International Journal for Philosophy of Religion
International Philosophical Quarterly
New Blackfriars
Religious Studies
Sophia
The Thomist

Religious issues have been staple fare for philosophers from the dawn of time, so those approaching philosophy of religion will benefit from reading, and following up what they find in, some standard histories of philosophy. Especially to be recommended is F. C. Copleston, *A History of Philosophy* (9 vols; London, 1946–75).

1. Philosophy and religion

General

Jack A. Bonsor, *Athens and Jerusalem: The Role of Philosophy in Theology* (New York, 1993)

Stuart Brown (ed.), *Reason and Religion* (Ithaca and London, 1977)

M. J. Charlesworth, *Philosophy of Religion: The Historic Approaches* (London, 1972)

J. Collins, *The Emergence of the Philosophy of Religion* (New Haven, CT, 1967)

C. F. Delaney (ed.), *Rationality and Religious Belief* (Notre Dame and London, 1979)

Etienne Gilson, *Reason and Revelation in the Middle Ages* (New York, 1938)

Anthony Kenny, *What Is Faith?* (Oxford and New York, 1992)

J. Pelikan, *Christianity and Classical Culture* (New Haven, CT, 1993)

Terence Penelhum, *Reason and Religious Faith* (Oxford, 1995)

Alvin Plantinga and Nicholas Wolterstorff (eds), *Faith and Rationality* (Notre Dame and London, 1983)

John E. Smith, *Reason and God: Encounters of Philosophy with Religion* (New Haven and London, 1961)

Richard Swinburne, *Faith and Reason* (Oxford, 1981)

Ancient and early medieval thinking

A. H. Armstrong (ed.), *The Cambridge History of Later Greek and Early Medieval Philosophy* (Cambridge, 1967)

Jonathan Barnes (ed.), *The Cambridge Companion to Aristotle* (Cambridge, 1995)

Peter Brown, *Augustine of Hippo* (London, 1967)

Henry Chadwick, *Augustine* (Oxford, 1986)

Mary T. Clark, *Augustine* (London, 1994)

Brian Davies, *The Thought of Thomas Aquinas* (Oxford, 1992)

Brian Davies and G. R. Evans (eds), *Anselm of Canterbury: The Major Works* (Oxford, 1998)

G. R. Evans, *Old Arts and New Theology* (Oxford, 1980)

G. R. Evans, *Anselm* (London, 1989)

G. R. Evans, *Philosophy and Theology in the Middle Ages* (London, 1993)

L. P. Gerson, *God and Greek Philosophy: Studies in the Early History of Natural Theology* (London and New York, 1990)

Terence Irwin, *Classical Thought* (Oxford and New York, 1989)

Werner Jaeger, *The Theology of the Early Greek Philosophers* (Oxford, 1947)

Richard Kraut (ed.), *The Cambridge Companion to Plato* (Cambridge, 1992)

Norman Kretzmann, Anthony Kenny and Jan Pinborg (eds), *The Cambridge History of Later Medieval Philosophy* (Cambridge, 1982)

Norman Kretzmann and Eleonore Stump (eds), *The Cambridge Companion to Aquinas* (Cambridge, 1993)

David Luscombe, *Medieval Thought* (Oxford, 1997)

John Marenbon, *Early Medieval Philosophy* (London and New York, 1983)

John Marenbon, *Later Medieval Philosophy* (London and New York, 1987)

C. F. J. Martin, *An Introduction to Medieval Philosophy* (Edinburgh, 1996)

Armand A. Maurer, *Medieval Philosophy* (New York, 1962)

Eric Osborn, *The Beginning of Christian Philosophy* (Cambridge, 1981)

G. L. Prestige, *God in Patristic Thought* (2nd edn; London, 1952)

John M. Rist, *Augustine* (Cambridge, 1994)

Colette Sirat, *A History of Jewish Philosophy in the Middle Ages* (Cambridge, 1985)

R. W. Southern, *Saint Anselm: A Portrait in a Landscape* (Cambridge, 1991)

Jean-Pierre Torrell, *Saint Thomas Aquinas: The Person and His Work* (Washington, DC, 1996)

From the thirteenth century to the twentieth century

V. C. Chappell (ed.), *The Cambridge Companion to Locke* (Cambridge, 1994)

John Cottingham (ed.), *The Cambridge Companion to Descartes* (Cambridge, 1992)

Don Garrett (ed.), *The Cambridge Companion to Spinoza* (Cambridge, 1996)

J. C. A. Gaskin, *Hume's Philosophy of Religion* (2nd edn; London, 1988)

Stuart Hampshire, *Spinoza* (Harmondsworth, 1951)

M. J. Inwood, *Hegel* (London, Boston, Henley and Melbourne, 1983)

Nicholas Jolley (ed.), *The Cambridge Companion to Leibniz* (Cambridge, 1995)

David Fate Norton (ed.), *The Cambridge Companion to Hume* (Cambridge, 1995)

Bernard M. G. Reardon, *Kant as Philosophical Theologian* (London, 1988)

Barry Stroud, *Hume* (London and New York, 1977)

Ralph C. S. Walker, *Kant* (London, Henley and Boston, 1978)

Philosophy, religion and twentieth-century theologians

James Barr, *Biblical Faith and Natural Theology* (Oxford, 1993)

Karl Barth, *Church Dogmatics* (Edinburgh, 1936–69)

Rudolf Bultmann, *Theology of the New Testament* (2 vols; London, 1952, 1955)

William V. Dych, *Karl Rahner* (London, 1992)

David Ford (ed.), *The Modern Theologians* (2nd edn; Oxford, 1997)

Alasdair Heron, *A Century of Protestant Theology* (Cambridge, 1980)

Gerald McCool SJ, *From Unity to Pluralism: The Internal Evolution of Thomism* (New York, 1989)

Gerald McCool SJ, *The Neo-Thomists* (Marquette, 1994)

Alister McGrath (ed.), *The Blackwell Encyclopedia of Modern Christian Thought* (Oxford, 1993)

John Macquarrie, *Twentieth Century Religious Thought* (4th edn; London, 1988)
John O'Donnell, *Hans Urs von Balthasar* (London, 1992)
Karl Rahner, *Foundations of Christian Faith* (London, 1978)
Paul Tillich, *Systematic Theology* (3 vols; Chicago, 1951, 1957, 1963)
Hans Urs von Balthasar, *The Glory of the Lord* (Edinburgh, 1982–91)

Wittgenstein and philosophy of religion

Cyril Barrett, *Wittgenstein on Ethics and Religious Belief* (Oxford, 1991)
Robert J. Fogelin, *Wittgenstein* (2nd edn; London, 1987)
Hans-Johann Glock, *A Wittgenstein Dictionary* (Oxford, 1996)
Paul L. Holmer, 'Wittgenstein and theology' in Dallas M. High (ed.), *New Essays in Religious Language* (New York, 1969)
W. Donald Hudson, *Wittgenstein and Religious Belief* (London, 1975)
Alan Keightley, *Wittgenstein, Grammar and God* (London, 1976)
Fergus Kerr, *Theology After Wittgenstein* (Oxford, 1986)
Norman Malcolm, *Wittgenstein: A Religious Point of View* (Ithaca, NY, 1994)
Gareth Moore, *Believing in God* (Edinburgh, 1989)
D. Z. Phillips, *The Concept of Prayer* (London, 1965)
D. Z. Phillips, *Faith and Philosophical Enquiry* (London, 1970)
D. Z. Phillips, *Death and Immortality* (London, 1970)
D. Z. Phillips, *Religion Without Explanation* (Oxford, 1976)
D. Z. Phillips, *Belief, Change and Forms of Life* (Atlantic Highlands, NJ, 1986)
D. Z. Phillips, *Faith After Foundationalism* (London and New York, 1988)
D. Z. Phillips, *Wittgenstein and Religion* (London, 1993)
D. Z. Phillips (ed.), *Rush Rhees on Religion and Philosophy* (Cambridge, 1997)
Patrick Sherry, *Religion, Truth and Language-Games* (London, 1977)
Hans Sluga and David G. Stern, *The Cambridge Companion to Wittgenstein* (Cambridge, 1996)
Ludwig Wittgenstein, *Philosophical Investigations* (trans. G. E. M. Anscombe; Oxford, 1958)
Ludwig Wittgenstein, *Tractatus Logico-Philosophicus* (trans. D. F. Pears and B. F. McGuinness; London, 1961)
Ludwig Wittgenstein, *Zettel* (trans. G. E. M. Anscombe; Oxford, 1967)
Ludwig Wittgenstein, *On Certainty* (trans. Denis Paul and G. E. M. Anscombe; Oxford, 1974)
Ludwig Wittgenstein, *Culture and Value* (trans. Peter Winch; Oxford, 1980)

Ludwig Wittgenstein, *Philosophical Occasions 1912–1951* (ed. James C. Klagge and Alfred Nordmann; Indianapolis, 1993)

Foundationalism and philosophy of religion

Thomas Aquinas, *Commentary on the Posterior Analytics of Aristotle* (trans. F. R. Larcher; Albany, NY, 1970)

Aristotle, *Posterior Analytics* (trans. Jonathan Barnes, 2nd edn; Oxford, 1994)

Robert Audi, 'Direct justification, evidential dependence, and theistic belief' in Robert Audi and William Wainwright (eds), *Rationality, Religious Belief, and Moral Commitment* (Ithaca, NY, 1986)

Robert Audi and William Wainwright (eds), *Rationality, Religious Belief, and Moral Commitment* (Ithaca, NY, 1986)

Herman Bavinck, *The Doctrine of God* (trans. William Hendricksen; Grand Rapids, MI, 1951)

John Calvin, *Institutes of the Christian Religion* (trans. Lewis Battles Ford; Philadelphia, 1960)

Scott MacDonald, 'Theory of knowledge' in Norman Kretzmann and Eleonore Stump (eds), *The Cambridge Companion to Aquinas* (Cambridge, 1993)

D. Z. Phillips, *Faith After Foundationalism* (London and New York, 1988)

Alvin Plantinga, 'Reason and belief in God' in Alvin Plantinga and Nicholas Wolterstorff (eds), *Faith and Rationality* (Notre Dame and London, 1983)

Alvin Plantinga, 'The foundations of theism: a reply', *Faith and Philosophy* 3 (1986)

Alvin Plantinga, *Warrant and Proper Function* (Oxford, 1993)

Alvin Plantinga and Nicholas Wolterstorff (eds), *Faith and Rationality* (Notre Dame and London, 1983)

Philip Quinn, 'In search of the foundations of theism', *Faith and Philosophy* 2 (1985)

Eleonore Stump, 'Aquinas on the foundations of knowledge', *Canadian Journal of Philosophy*, Supplementary Volume 17 (1992)

Nicholas Wolterstorff, 'Can belief in God be rational if it has no foundations?' in Plantinga and Wolterstorff (1983)

Nicholas Wolterstorff, 'The migration of the theistic arguments: from natural theology to evidentialist apologetics' in Robert Audi and William Wainwright (eds), *Rationality, Religious Belief, and Moral Commitment* (Ithaca, NY, 1986)

Linda Zagzebski (ed.), *Rational Faith: Catholic Responses to Reformed Epistemology* (Notre Dame, 1983)

2. Arguments for God's existence

General

Peter Angeles (ed.), *Critiques of God* (Buffalo, NY, 1976)
Bernadino M. Bonansea, *God and Atheism* (Washington, DC, 1979)
Mark Corner, *Does God Exist?* (Bristol, 1991)
Brian Davies, *Thinking About God* (London, 1985)
Clement Dore, *Theism* (Dordrecht, 1984)
Antony Flew, *God and Philosophy* (London, 1966)
Antony Flew, *The Presumption of Atheism* (London, 1976)
Alfred J. Freddoso (ed.), *The Existence and Nature of God* (Notre Dame, 1983)
Richard M. Gale, *On the Nature and Existence of God* (Cambridge, 1991)
John Hick, *The Existence of God* (London, 1964)
John Hick, *Arguments for the Existence of God* (London, 1971)
Hans Küng, *Does God Exist?* (London, 1980)
H. D. Lewis, *Our Experience of God* (London, 1959)
J. L. Mackie, *The Miracle of Theism* (Oxford, 1982)
Hugo Meynell, *God and the World* (London, 1971)
Alvin Plantinga, *God and Other Minds* (Ithaca and London, 1967)
Alvin Plantinga, *God, Freedom and Evil* (London, 1975)
Robert Prevost, *Probability and Theistic Explanation* (Oxford, 1990)
James F. Ross, *Philosophical Theology* (2nd edn; Indianapolis, 1980)
J. J. C. Smart and J. J. Haldane, *Atheism and Theism* (Oxford, 1996)
Richard Swinburne, *The Existence of God* (Oxford, 1979; rev. edn, 1991)
Richard Swinburne, *Is There a God?* (Oxford, 1996)
F. R. Tennant, *Philosophical Theology* (Cambridge, 1930)
Peter Vardy, *The Puzzle of God* (London, 1990)

Cosmological arguments

G. E. M. Anscombe, '"Whatever has a beginning of existence must have a cause": Hume's argument exposed' in *Collected Philosophical Papers*, vol. I (Oxford, 1981)
Timothy McDermott (ed.), *Thomas Aquinas: Selected Philosophical Writings* (Oxford, 1993), sections 2–6; 20–22; 27–28
G. E. M. Anscombe and P. T. Geach, *Three Philosophers* (Oxford, 1961)
David Braine, *The Reality of Time and the Existence of God* (Oxford, 1988)
William Lane Craig, *The Kalam Cosmological Argument* (London, 1979)
William Lane Craig, *The Cosmological Argument from Plato to Leibniz* (London, 1980)

William Lane Craig and Quentin Smith, *Theism, Atheism and Big Bang Cosmology* (Oxford, 1993)

Herbert A. Davidson, *Proofs for Eternity, Creation and the Existence of God in Medieval Islamic and Jewish Philosophy* (Oxford, 1987)

Brian Davies, *The Thought of Thomas Aquinas* (Oxford, 1992)

Germain Grisez, *Beyond the New Theism* (Notre Dame and London, 1975)

Anthony Kenny, *The Five Ways* (London, 1969)

Norman Kretzmann, *The Metaphysics of Theism: Aquinas's Natural Theology in 'Summa Contra Gentiles' I* (Oxford, 1997)

Bernard Lonergan, *Insight* (New York, 1957)

Herbert McCabe, *God Matters* (London, 1987), Part 1

Herbert McCabe, 'The logic of mysticism I' in Martin Warner (ed.), *Religion and Philosophy* (Cambridge, 1992)

Scott MacDonald, 'Aquinas's parasitic cosmological argument', *Medieval Philosophy and Theology* 1 (1991)

Hugo Meynell, *The Intelligible Universe: A Cosmological Argument* (London, 1982)

Barry Miller, *From Existence to God* (London and New York, 1992)

Milton K. Munitz, *The Mystery of Existence* (New York, 1965)

Bruce R. Reichenbach, *The Cosmological Argument: A Reassessment* (Springfield, IL, 1972)

William Rowe, *The Cosmological Argument* (Princeton and London, 1975)

James Sadowsky, 'The cosmological argument and the endless regress', *International Philosophical Quarterly* 20 (1980)

John J. Shepherd, *Experience, Inference and God* (London, 1975)

Ontological arguments

G. E. M. Anscombe, 'Why Anselm's proof in the *Proslogion* is not an ontological argument', *The Thoreau Quarterly* 17 (1985)

G. E. M. Anscombe, 'Russellm or Anselm?', *The Philosophical Quarterly* 43 (1993)

Jonathan Barnes, *The Ontological Argument* (London, 1972)

Clement Dore, 'Ontological arguments' in Philip Quinn and Charles Taliaferro (eds), *A Companion to Philosophy of Religion* (Oxford, 1997)

G. R. Evans, *Anselm* (London, 1989)

D. P. Henry, *Medieval Logic and Metaphysics* (London, 1972)

John Hick and Arthur McGill (eds), *The Many Faced Argument* (London, 1967)

Graham Oppy, *Ontological Arguments and Belief in God* (Cambridge, 1995)

Alvin Plantinga, *The Nature of Necessity* (Oxford, 1974)

R. W. Southern, *Saint Anselm: A Portrait in a Landscape* (Cambridge, 1991)

C. J. F. Williams, *What Is Existence?* (Oxford, 1981)

C. J. F. Williams, *Being, Identity and Truth* (Oxford, 1992)

C. J. F. Williams, 'Russelm', *The Philosophical Quarterly* 43 (1993)

Nicholas Wolterstorff, 'In defence of Gaunilo's Defense of the Fool' in C. Stephen Evans and Merold Westphal (eds), *Christian Perspectives on Religious Knowledge* (Grand Rapids, 1993)

Design arguments

J. D. Barrow and F. J. Tipler, *The Anthropic Cosmological Principle* (Oxford, 1986)

F. Burtola and U. Curi (eds), *The anthropic principle: The Conditions for the Existence of Mankind in the Universe* (Cambridge, 1990)

W. L. Craig, 'Barrow and Tipler on the anthropic principle vs. divine design', *British Journal for the Philosophy of Science* 38 (1988)

Brian Davies, 'Mackie on the argument from design', *New Blackfriars* (September 1983)

Brian Davies, *An Introduction to the Philosophy of Religion* (Oxford; new edn 1993), ch. 6

P. Davies, *The Mind of God* (Harmondsworth, 1992)

R. Dawkins, *The Blind Watchmaker* (Harlow, 1986)

G. Doore, 'The argument from design: some better reasons for agreeing with Hume', *Religious Studies* 16 (1980)

J. C. A. Gaskin, *Hume's Philosophy of Religion* (2nd edn; London, 1988)

R. D. Geivett and B. Sweetman (eds), *Contemporary Perspectives on Religious Epistemology* (Oxford, 1992), Part IV

L. P. Gerson, *God and Greek Philosophy: Studies in the Early History of Natural Theology* (London, 1990)

N. C. Gillespie, 'Divine design and the Industrial Revolution: William Paley's abortive attempt to reform natural theology', *Isis* 81 (June 1990), pp. 214–29

E. Gilson, *From Aristotle to Darwin and Back Again* (trans. John Lyon; Notre Dame, 1984)

R. Hambourger, 'The argument from design' in Cora Diamond and Jenny Teichman (eds), *Intention and Intentionality: Essays in Honour of G. E. M. Anscombe* (Brighton, 1979), ch. 8

J. F. Haught, *The Cosmic Adventure: Science, Religion and the Quest for Purpose* (Ramsey, NJ, 1984)

J. Hick, *Philosophy of Religion* (4th edn; London, 1990), ch. 2

J. Horigan, *Chance or Design?* (New York, 1979)

David Hume, *Dialogues Concerning Natural Religion* (ed. Martin Bell; Harmondsworth, 1990)

R. H. Hurlbutt, *Hume, Newton, and the Design Argument* (Lincoln, 1965)

S. Jaki, *God and the Cosmologists* (Edinburgh, 1989)

Anthony Kenny, *Reason and Religion* (Oxford, 1987), ch. 5

J. Leslie, *Physical Cosmology and Philosophy* (New York, 1990)

Thomas McPherson, *The Argument from Design* (London, 1972)

H. Montefiore, *The Probability of God* (London, 1985)

R. A. Oakes, 'Is probability inapplicable – in principle – to the God-hypothesis?', *The New Scholasticism* 44 (1970), pp. 426–30

A. Peacocke, *Creation and the World of Science* (Oxford, 1979)

M. Peterson *et al.*, *Reason and Religious Belief: An Introduction to the Philosophy of Religion* (New York, 1991), ch. 5

A. Plantinga, *God and Other Minds: A Study in the Rational Justification of Belief in God* (Ithaca, NY, 1967), chs 4 and 10

G. Priest, 'The argument from design', *Australasian Journal of Philosophy* 59 (1981)

N. Rescher (ed.), *Current Issues in Teleology* (Lanham, MD, 1986)

J. Sadowsky, 'Did Darwin destroy the design argument?', *International Philosophical Quarterly* 28 (1988)

W. C. Salmon, 'Religion and science: a new look at Hume's *Dialogues*', *Philosophical Studies* 33 (1978), pp. 143–76

G. Schlesinger, *New Perspectives on Old Time Religion* (Oxford, 1988), ch. 5

Richard Swinburne, 'The argument from design', *Philosophy* 43 (1968)

Richard Swinburne, 'The argument from design: a defence', *Religious Studies* 8 (1972)

F. R. Tennant, *Philosophical Theology*, vol. II (Cambridge, 1930), ch. 4

R. C. S. Walker, *Kant* (London, 1978), ch. 12

M. Wynn, '*A priori* judgments and the argument from design', *International Journal for Philosophy of Religion* 39 (1988)

M. Wynn, 'Some reflections on Richard Swinburne's argument from design', *Religious Studies* 19 (1993)

God and religious experience

W. P. Alston, *Perceiving God: The Epistemology of Religious Experience* (Ithaca, NY, 1991)

Timothy Beardsworth, *A Sense of Presence* (Oxford, 1977)

John Bowker, *The Sense of God* (Oxford, 1973)

Roderick M. Chisholm, *Theory of Knowledge* (2nd edn; Englewood Cliffs, NJ, 1977)

Caroline Franks Davis, *The Evidential Force of Religious Experience* (Oxford, 1989)

Peter Donovan, *Interpreting Religious Experience* (London, 1979)

N. Horsburgh, 'The claims of religious experience', *Australasian Journal of Philosophy* 33 (1957)

William James, *The Varieties of Religious Experience* (the 1901–02 Gifford Lectures; New York, 1982)
Steven T. Katz (ed.), *Mysticism and Philosophical Analysis* (London, 1978)
Anthony Kenny, 'Mystical experience: St John of the Cross' in Anthony Kenny, *Reason and Religion* (Oxford, 1987)
C. B. Martin, *Religious Belief* (Ithaca, NY, 1959)
T. R. Miles, *Religious Experience* (London, 1972)
William L. Rowe, 'Religious experience and the principle of credulity', *International Journal for Philosophy of Religion* **13** (1982)
Richard Swinburne, *The Existence of God* (Oxford, 1979)
Illtyd Trethowan, *Mysticism and Theology* (London, 1974)
William Wainwright, *Mysticism* (Brighton, 1981)

3. The attributes of God

General

J. Collins, *God in Modern Philosophy* (Chicago, 1959)
Brian Davies, *Thinking About God* (London, 1985)
Steven T. Davis, *Logic and the Nature of God* (London, 1983)
R. Garrigou-Lagrange, *God: His Existence and Nature* (2 vols; St Louis, 1934)
Gerard Hughes, *The Nature of God* (London and New York, 1995)
Anthony Kenny, *The God of the Philosophers* (Oxford, 1979)
H. P. Owen, *Concepts of Deity* (London, 1971)
E. L. Mascall, *He Who Is* (London, 1945)
Thomas V. Morris (ed.), *The Concept of God* (Oxford, 1987)
Thomas V. Morris, *Our Idea of God* (Notre Dame and London, 1991)
Ronald H. Nash, *The Concept of God* (Grand Rapids, MI, 1983)
Edward R. Wierenga, *The Nature of God* (Ithaca, NY, 1969)

Simpleness

Robert Adams, 'Divine necessity' in Robert Adams, *The Virtue of Faith* (Oxford, 1987)
Thomas Aquinas, *Summa Theologiae* Ia, 2–11 (trans. Timothy McDermott; London, 1964)
Timothy McDermott (ed.), *Thomas Aquinas: Selected Philosophical Writings* (Oxford, 1993), sections 21–25
David Burrell, *Aquinas, God and Action* (London, 1979)
David Burrell, *Knowing the Unknowable God* (Notre Dame, 1986)
David Burrell, *Freedom and Creation in Three Traditions* (Notre Dame, 1993)

Brian Davies, 'Classical theism and the doctrine of divine simplicity' in Brian Davies (ed.), *Language, Meaning and God* (London, 1987)

Lloyd Gerson, *God and Greek Philosophy* (London, 1990)

Sara Grant, *Towards an Alternative Theology: Confessions of a Non-dualist Christian* (Bangalore, 1991)

Pierre Hadot, *Plotinus: The Simplicity of Vision* (Chicago, 1993)

Christopher Hughes, *On a Complex Theory of a Simple God* (Ithaca, NY, 1980)

Moses Maimonides, *Guide of the Perplexed* (trans. S. Pines; Chicago, 1963)

William Mann, 'Divine simplicity', *Religious Studies* 18 (1982)

William Mann, 'Simplicity and immutability in God', *International Philosophical Quarterly* 23 (1983)

Barry Miller, *A Most Unlikely God* (Notre Dame, 1996)

Thomas V. Morris, 'On God and Mann: a view of divine simplicity', *Religious Studies* 21 (1985)

Alvin Plantinga, *Does God Have a Nature?* (Marquette, 1980)

Fazlur Rahman, 'Essence and existence in Avicenna', *Mediaeval and Renaissance Studies* 4 (1958)

Robert Sokolowski, *God of Faith and Reason* (Washington, DC, 1994)

Eleonore Stump and Norman Kretzmann, 'Absolute simplicity', *Faith and Philosophy* 2 (1985)

Kathryn Tanner, *God and Creation in Christian Theology* (Oxford, 1988)

Eternality

Timothy McDermott (ed.), *Thomas Aquinas: Selected Philosophical Writings* (Oxford, 1993), section 22

St Augustine, *Confessions* (trans. Henry Chadwick; Oxford, 1991), Book XI

Karl Barth, *Church Dogmatics* (Edinburgh, 1936–69)

Boethius, *The Consolation of Philosophy* (trans. V. E. Watts; London, 1969)

F. H. Brabant, *Time and Eternity in Christian Thought* (London, 1937)

John B. Cobb and David Ray Griffin, *Process Theology: An Introductory Exposition* (Belfast, 1976)

Michael J. Dodds, *The Unchanging God of Love: A Study of the Teaching of St Thomas Aquinas on Divine Immutability in View of Certain Contemporary Criticism of this Doctrine* (Fribourg, 1986)

Paul Helm, *Eternal God* (Oxford, 1987)

Norman Kretzmann and Eleonore Stump, 'Eternity', *Journal of Philosophy* 79 (1981)

Brian Leftow, *Time and Eternity* (Ithaca, NY, 1991)

William Ockham, *Predestination, God's Foreknowledge, and Future Contingents* (trans. and ed. Marilyn McCord Adams and Norman Kretzmann; New York, 1969)

Alan G. Padgett, *God, Eternity and the Nature of Time* (London, 1992)

Nelson Pike, *God and Timelessness* (London, 1970)

Richard Sorabji, *Time, Creation and the Continuum* (London, 1983)

Richard Swinburne, *The Christian God* (Oxford, 1994), ch. 4

Thomas G. Weinandy, *Does God Change?* (Still River, MA, 1985)

Nicholas Wolterstorff, 'God Everlasting' in Steven M. Cahn and David Shatz (eds), *Contemporary Philosophy of Religion* (Oxford, 1982)

John C. Yates, *The Timelessness of God* (Lanham/New York/London, 1990)

Omnipotence

Timothy McDermott (ed.), *Thomas Aquinas: Selected Philosophical Writings* (Oxford, 1993), section 26

Harry H. Frankfurt, 'The logic of omnipotence', *The Philosophical Review* 74 (1964)

P. T. Geach, *Providence and Evil* (Cambridge, 1977)

Charles Hartshorne, *Omnipotence and Other Theological Mistakes* (Albany, NY, 1984)

Gerard J. Hughes, *The Nature of God* (London and New York, 1995), ch. 4

Anthony Kenny, *The God of the Philosophers* (Oxford, 1979)

J. L. Mackie, 'Omnipotence', *Sophia* 1 (1962)

J. L. Mackie, 'Evil and omnipotence', *Mind* 64 (1955)

George I. Mavrodes, 'Some puzzles concerning omnipotence', *Philosophical Review* 72 (1963)

Lawrence Moonan, *Divine Power: The Medieval Power Distinction up to Its Adoption by Albert, Bonaventure, and Aquinas* (Oxford, 1994)

Richard Swinburne, *The Coherence of Theism* (Oxford, 1977), ch. 9

Linwood Urban and Douglas N. Walton (eds), *The Power of God* (New York, 1978)

G. van den Brink, *Almighty God: A Study of the Doctrine of Divine Omnipotence* (Kampen, 1993)

Edward R. Wierenga, *The Nature of God: An Inquiry into Divine Attributes* (Ithaca and London, 1989), ch. 1

Omniscience

Timothy McDermott (ed.), *Thomas Aquinas: Selected Philosophical Writings* (Oxford, 1993), sections 24, 25, 30

Boethius, *The Consolation of Philosophy*, Book V

Hector Neri Castaneda, 'Omniscience and indexical reference', *Journal of Philosophy* 64 (1967)

William Lane Craig, *The Only Wise God* (Grand Rapids, 1987)

P. T. Geach, *Providence and Evil* (Cambridge, 1977)

Gerard Hughes, *The Nature of God* (London and New York, 1995), ch. 3

Anthony Kenny, 'Divine foreknowledge and human freedom' in Anthony Kenny (ed.), *Aquinas: A Collection of Critical Essays* (London, 1969)

Norman Kretzmann, 'Omniscience and immutability', *Journal of Philosophy* **63** (1966)

Jonathan L. Kvanvig, *The Possibility of an All-Knowing God* (London, 1986)

Luis de Molina, *On Divine Foreknowledge* (Part IV of the *Concordia*, trans. and ed. Alfred J. Freddoso; Ithaca, NY, 1988)

John C. Moskop, *Divine Omniscience and Human Freedom* (Macon, GA, 1984)

Nelson Pike, 'Divine omniscience and voluntary action', *Philosophical Review* **74** (1965)

Alvin Plantinga, 'On Ockham's way out', *Faith and Philosophy* **3** (1986)

Alvin Plantinga, 'Divine knowledge' in C. Stephen Evans and Merold Westphal (eds), *Christian Perspectives on Religious Knowledge* (Grand Rapids, MI, 1993)

A. N. Prior, 'The formalities of omniscience' in A. N. Prior, *Papers on Time and Tense* (Oxford, 1968)

G. van den Brink, *Almighty God: A Study of the Doctrine of Divine Omnipotence* (Kampen, 1993)

Robert Young, *Freedom, Responsibility and God* (London, 1975)

Linda Zagzebski, *The Dilemma of Freedom and Foreknowledge* (New York, 1991)

Personal

R. M. Adams, *The Virtue of Faith* (New York, 1987)

R. M. Adams, *Leibniz* (Oxford, 1994)

W. Alston, 'Functionalism and theological language', *American Philosophical Quarterly* **22** (1985)

Peter A. Bertocci, 'The person God is' in G. N. A. Vesey (ed.), *Talk of God* (London, 1969)

Boethius, *Tractates, De Consolatione Philosophiae* (trans. H. F. Stewart, E. K. Rand, S. J. Tester; Cambridge, MA and London, 1978)

M. Buber, *I and You* (trans. W. Kaufman; New York, 1923)

E. S. Brightman, *Persons and Reality* (New York, 1958)

R. Chisholm, *Persons and Object* (La Salle, IL, 1976)

B. Davies, 'Classical theism and the doctrine of divine simplicity' in B. Davies (ed.), *Language, Meaning and God* (London, 1987)

R. J. Feenstra and C. Plantinga Jr (eds), *Trinity, Incarnation and Atonement* (Norre Dame, 1989)

H. Frankfurt, 'Freedom of the will and the concept of a person', *Journal of Philosophy* **68** (1971)

P. Geach, *God and the Soul* (London, 1969)

C. Hansen, *A Daoist Theory of Chinese Thought* (New York, 1992)

J. Hick, *Disputed Questions in Theology and the Philosophy of Religion* (New Haven, CT, 1993)

G. Jantzen, *God's World, God's Body* (London, 1984)

I. Kant, *Groundwork of the Metaphysic of Morals* (trans. H. J. Paton; New York, 1964)

C. S. Lewis, *The World's Last Night and Other Essays* (New York, 1960)

J. Locke, *An Essay Concerning Human Understanding* (ed. P. H. Nidditch; Oxford, 1975)

J. L. Mackie, *The Miracle of Theism* (Oxford, 1982)

M. Martin, *Atheism* (Philadelphia, 1990)

N. Rescher, *Pascal's Wager* (Notre Dame, 1985)

D. N. Robinson, *Aristotle's Psychology* (New York, 1989)

J.-P. Sartre, *Being and Nothingness* (trans. H. Barnes; New York, 1992)

R. Swinburne, *The Coherence of Theism* (Oxford, 1977)

R. Swinburne, *The Existence of God* (Oxford, 1979)

R. Swinburne, *The Evolution of the Soul* (Oxford, 1986)

R. Swinburne, *The Christian God* (Oxford, 1994)

C. Taliaferro, *Consciousness and the Mind of God* (Cambridge, 1994)

C. Taliaferro, 'Taking philosophy personally', *The Cresset* **57** (1994)

A. Thatcher, 'Christian theism and the concept of a person' in A. Peacocke and G. Gillet (eds), *Persons and Personality* (Oxford, 1987)

T. Tur, 'The "person" in law' in A. Peacocke and G. Gillet (eds), *Persons and Personality* (Oxford, 1987)

Keith Ward, 'Is God a person?' in Gijsbert van den Brink, Luco J. van den Brom and Marcel Sarot (eds), *Christian Faith and Philosophical Theology* (Kampen, 1992)

C. C. J. Webb, *God and Personality* (London, 1971)

A. N. Whitehead, *Process and Reality* (New York, 1978)

4. Religious language

William P. Alston, *Divine Nature and Human Language* (Ithaca and London, 1989)

Thomas Aquinas, *Summa Theologiae* I, 13, in Volume 3 of the Blackfriars edition of the *Summa Theologiae* (ed. Herbert McCabe OP; London, 1964)

Thomas Aquinas, *Summa Contra Gentiles* I, 29–36. English translation: *Saint Thomas Aquinas, 'Summa Contra Gentiles', Book One: God*, trans. with an introduction and notes by Anton Pegis (Notre Dame, 1975)

Timothy McDermott (ed.), *Thomas Aquinas: Selected Philosophical Writings* (Oxford, 1993), sections 20–24, 27–30

Karl Barth, *Church Dogmatics* (Edinburgh, 1936–69)

R. B. Braithwaite, *An Empiricist's View of the Nature of Religious Belief*, reprinted in Basil Mitchell (ed.), *The Philosophy of Religion* (Oxford, 1971)

Stuart Brown, *Do Religious Claims Make Sense?* (London, 1969)

David B. Burrell, *Aquinas: God and Action* (London and Henley, 1979)

Cajetan (Thomas de Vio Cardenalis Cajetanus), *De Nominum Analogia* (English translation: E. A. Bushenski and H. J. Koren [trans.], *The Analogy of Names* [Pittsburgh, 1953])

Brian Davies, *Thinking About God* (London, 1985)

Colm Luibheid and Paul Rorem (trans. and eds), *Pseudo-Dionysius: The Complete Works* (London and Mahwah, NJ, 1987)

Frederick Ferré, *Language, Logic and God* (London and Glasgow, 1970)

Oswald Hanfling, *Logical Positivism* (Oxford, 1981)

R. S. Heimbeck, *Theology and Meaning* (London, 1969)

John Hick, *Faith and Knowledge* (London, 1974)

D. High, *Language, Persons and Belief* (New York, 1967)

H. Lyttkens, *The Analogy Between God and the World* (Uppsala, 1952)

John Macquarrie, *God-Talk* (London, 1967)

Moses Maimonides, *The Guide for the Perplexed* (trans. M. Friedlander; London, 1936)

E. L. Mascall, *Existence and Analogy* (London, 1966)

Kai Nielsen, *Scepticism* (London, 1973)

Humphrey Palmer, *Analogy* (London, 1973)

I. T. Ramsey, *Religious Language* (New York, 1963)

Paul Ricoeur, *Time and Narrative* (3 vols; Chicago, 1984–85)

Paul Ricoeur, *The Conflict of Interpretation* (3 vols; Chicago, 1984–88)

James Ross, *Portraying Analogy* (Cambridge, 1981)

James Ross, 'Semantic contagion' in A. Lehrer and E. Kittay (eds), *Frames, Fields and Contrasts* (New Jersey, 1992)

Patrick Sherry, *Religion, Truth and Language-Games* (London, 1977)

Janet Martin Soskice, *Metaphor and Religious Language* (Oxford, 1985)

A. C. Thiselton, *New Horizons in Hermeneutics* (London, 1992)

D. Tracy, *The Analogical Imagination* (London, 1981)

Ludwig Wittgenstein, *Philosophical Investigations* (trans. G. E. M. Anscombe; Oxford, 1958)

5. Creation, providence and miracles

Timothy McDermott (ed.), *Thomas Aquinas: Selected Philosophical Writings* (Oxford, 1993), sections 3–6, 20–33
William Lane Craig and Quentin Smith, *Theism, Atheism, and Big Bang Cosmology* (Oxford, 1993)
Thomas P. Flint, *Divine Providence: The Molinist Account* (Ithaca, NY, 1998)
Alfred J. Freddoso, 'The necessity of nature', *Midwest Studies in Philosophy* 11 (1986)
Paul Gwynne, *Special Divine Action* (Chicago, 1997)
Brian Hebblethwaite and Edward Henderson (eds), *Divine Action* (Edinburgh, 1990)
Paul Helm, *The Providence of God* (Leicester, 1993)
Herbert McCabe, *God Matters* (London, 1987), Part 1
Herbert McCabe, 'The logic of mysticism I' in Martin Warner (ed.), *Religion and Philosophy* (Cambridge, 1992)
Luis de Molina, *On Divine Foreknowledge* (Part IV of the *Concordia*; trans. with intro. and notes Alfred J. Freddoso; Ithaca, NY, 1988)
Thomas V. Morris (ed.), *Divine and Human Action* (Ithaca, NY, 1988)
Philip L. Quinn, 'Creation, conservation, and the Big Bang' in John Earman *et al.* (eds), *Philosophical Problems of the Internal and External Worlds* (Pittsburgh, 1993)
James F. Ross, 'Creation', *The Journal of Philosophy* 77 (1980)
James F. Ross, 'Creation II' in Alfred J. Freddoso (ed.), *The Existence and Nature of God* (Notre Dame and London, 1983)
Richard Swinburne, *The Concept of Miracle* (London, 1970)
Richard Swinburne (ed.), *Miracles* (London and New York, 1989)
Kathryn Tanner, *God and Creation in Christian Theology* (Oxford, 1988)
James E. Tomberlin (ed.), *Philosophical Perspectives*, vol. V: *Philosophy of Religion* (Atascadero, CA, 1991)

6. The problem of evil

Marilyn McCord Adams and Robert Merrihew Adams (eds), *The Problem of Evil* (Oxford, 1990)
M. B. Ahern, *The Problem of Evil* (London, 1971)
Thomas Aquinas, *The Literal Exposition on Job* (trans. and ed. Anthony Damico and Martin D. Yaffe; Atlanta, GA, 1989)
Timothy McDermott (ed.), *Thomas Aquinas: Selected Philosophical Writings* (Oxford, 1993), sections 27–33

James L. Crenshaw, *Theodicy in the Old Testament* (Philadelphia and London, 1983)

Brian Davies, *The Thought of Thomas Aquinas* (Oxford, 1992)

Brian Davies, 'How is God love?' in Luke Gormally (ed.), *Moral Truth and Moral Tradition: Essays in Honour of Peter Geach and Elizabeth Anscombe* (Dublin and Portland, OR, 1994)

G. R. Evans, *Augustine on Evil* (Cambridge, 1982)

A. Farrer, *Love Almighty and Ills Unlimited* (London, 1961)

Antony Flew, *The Presumption of Atheism* (London, 1976), chs 6 and 7

P. T. Geach, *Providence and Evil* (Cambridge, 1977)

John Hick, *Evil and the God of Love* (2nd edn; London, 1975)

Daniel Howard-Snyder (ed.), *The Evidential Argument from Evil* (Bloomington and Indianapolis, 1996)

Herbert McCabe, *God Matters* (London, 1987), Part 1

C. F. J. Martin, *Thomas Aquinas: God and Explanations* (Edinburgh, 1997)

Nelson Pike (ed.), *God and Evil: Readings on the Theological Problem of Evil* (London, 1971)

Alvin Plantinga, *God, Freedom and Evil* (London, 1975)

D. Z. Phillips (ed.), *Rush Rhees on Religion and Philosophy* (Cambridge, 1997), sections 1–7, 13–14, 21 and 25

George N. Schlesinger, *New Perspectives on Old-Time Religion* (Oxford, 1988), ch. 2

Kenneth Surin, *Theology and the Problem of Evil* (Oxford, 1986)

Richard Swinburne, *The Existence of God* (Oxford, 1979; rev. edn, 1991), ch. 11

Peter Vardy, *The Puzzle of Evil* (London, 1992)

Barry L. Whitney, *What Are They Saying About God and Evil?* (New York/ Mahwah, NJ, 1989)

7. Faith and revelation

Thomas Aquinas, *Summa Theologiae*. See especially part II-II, questions 1–9

Maurice Cranston, *John Locke: A Biography* (New York, 1957)

Justo L. González, *The Story of Christianity*, vol. II: *The Reformation to the Present Day* (San Francisco, 1985)

John Jenkins, *Knowledge and Faith in Thomas Aquinas* (Cambridge, 1997)

J. N. D. Kelly, *Early Christian Doctrines* (rev. edn; San Francisco, 1978)

John Locke, *An Essay Concerning Human Understanding* (ed. Peter H. Nidditch; Oxford, 1975)

Alasdair MacIntyre, 'The relationship of philosophy to its past' in Richard

Rorty, J. B. Schneewind and Quentin Skinner (eds), *Philosophy in History: Essays on the Historiography of Philosophy* (New York, 1984)

Alasdair MacIntyre, *Whose Justice? Which Rationality?* (Notre Dame, 1988)

Richard Swinburne, *Faith and Reason* (Oxford, 1981)

Charles Taylor, 'Philosophy and its history' in Richard Rorty, J. B. Schneewind and Quentin Skinner (eds), *Philosophy in History: Essays on the Historiography of Philosophy* (New York, 1984)

Jean-Pierre Torrell, *Saint Thomas Aquinas*, vol. I: *The Person and His Work* (Washington, DC, 1996)

Nicholas Wolterstorff, 'The migration of the theistic arguments: from natural theology to evidentialist apologetics' in Robert Audi and William J. Wainwright (eds), *Rationality, Religious Belief, and Moral Commitment* (Ithaca, NY, 1986)

Nicholas Wolterstorff, 'What is Cartesian doubt?', *American Catholic Philosophical Quarterly* 67 (Autumn 1993), pp. 467–95

Nicholas Wolterstorff, *John Locke and the Ethics of Belief* (Cambridge, 1996)

8. Philosophy and Christianity

Peter Abelard, 'Exposition of the Epistle to the Romans' in E. R. Fairweather (ed.), *A Scholastic Miscellany* (Philadelphia, 1956)

William J. Abraham and Steven W. Holtzer (eds), *The Rationality of Religious Belief* (Oxford, 1987)

William Alston, *Perceiving God: The Epistemology of Religious Experience* (Ithaca, NY, 1991)

Matthew Arnold, *Literature and Dogma* (London, 1876)

St Augustine, *On the Trinity* in *Augustine: Later Writings* (ed. J. Burnaby, Library of Christian Classics, vol. VIII; Philadelphia, 1955)

Michael D. Beaty (ed.), *Christian Theism and the Problems of Philosophy* (Notre Dame and London, 1990)

William Charlton, *Philosophy and Christian Belief* (London, 1988)

Brian Davies, *An Introduction to the Philosophy of Religion* (Oxford, 1993)

C. Stephen Evans and Merold Westphal (eds), *Christian Perspectives on Religious Knowledge* (Grand Rapids, 1993)

A. G. N. Flew and A. C. MacIntyre (eds), *New Essays in Philosophical Theology* (London, 1955)

Thomas P. Flint (ed.), *Christian Philosophy* (Notre Dame, 1990)

A. Van Harvey, *The Historian and the Believer* (Philadelphia, 1968)

C. S. Lewis, *Undeceptions: Essays on Theology and Ethics* (London, 1971)

Hywel D. Lewis, *Jesus in the Faith of Christians* (London, 1981)

Bernard Lonergan, *Insight: A Study of Human Understanding* (Toronto, 1992)

Herbert McCabe, *God Matters* (London, 1987)

Hugo Meynell, *The Theology of Bernard Lonergan* (Atlanta, 1986)

Hugo Meynell, *Is Christianity True?* (London, 1994)

Thomas V. Morris, *The Logic of God Incarnate* (Ithaca and London, 1986)

Thomas V. Morris (ed.), *Philosophy and the Christian Faith* (Notre Dame, 1988)

Alan G. Padgett (ed.), *Reason and the Christian Religion* (Oxford, 1994)

E. Stump and T. Flint (eds), *Hermes and Athena: Biblical Exegesis and Philosopical Theology* (Notre Dame, 1993)

Richard Sturch, *The Word and the Christ: An Essay in Analytic Christology* (Oxford, 1991)

Richard Swinburne, *Faith and Reason* (Oxford, 1981)

Richard Swinburne, *Responsibility and Atonement* (Oxford, 1989)

Richard Swinburne, *Revelation* (Oxford, 1992)

Richard Swinburne, *The Christian God* (Oxford, 1994)

Gijsbert van den Brink, Luco J. van den Brom and Marcel Sarot (eds), *Christian Faith and Philosophical Theology* (Kampen, 1992)

Peter van Inwagen, *God, Knowledge and Mystery* (Ithaca and London, 1995)

Nicholas Wolterstorff, *Reason Within the Bounds of Religion* (Grand Rapids, 1984)

9. Morality and religion

Robert M. Adams, 'Moral arguments for theistic belief' in Robert M. Adams, *The Virtue of Faith and Other Essays in Philosophical Theology* (Oxford, 1987)

Jonathan Barnes (ed.), *The Complete Works of Aristotle* (Princeton, NJ, 1984)

Jonathan Barnes (ed.), *The Cambridge Companion to Aristotle* (Cambridge, 1995)

Philip Bricker and R. I. G. Hughes (eds), *Philosophical Perspectives on Newtonian Science* (Cambridge, MA, 1990)

J. Burnaby, *Amor Dei* (London, 1947)

Roger Crisp and Michael Slote (eds), *Virtue Ethics* (Oxford, 1997)

Philippa Foot (ed.), *Theories of Ethics* (Oxford, 1967)

P. T. Geach, 'Plato's Euthyphro' in P. T. Geach, *Logic Matters* (Oxford, 1972)

J. C. B. Gosling, *Plato* (London, 1973)

Paul Helm (ed.), *Divine Commands and Morality* (Oxford, 1981)

W. D. Hudson, *A Century of Moral Philosophy* (Guildford and London, 1980)

Richard Kraut (ed.), *The Cambridge Companion to Plato* (Cambridge, 1992)

Anthony J. Lisska, *Aquinas's Theory of Natural Law* (Oxford, 1996)

A. MacIntyre, *After Virtue* (London, 1981)

J. L. Mackie, *Hume's Moral Theory* (London, 1980)

W. G. MacLagan, *The Theological Frontier of Ethics* (London, 1961)

David Melling, *Understanding Plato* (Oxford, 1987)

Richard Norman, *The Moral Philosophers* (Oxford, 1983)

H. P. Owen, *The Moral Argument for Christian Theism* (London, 1965)

D. Z. Phillips (ed.), *Religion and Morality* (New York, 1996)

Plato, *The Collected Dialogues* (ed. Edith Hamilton and Huntington Cairns; Princeton, NJ, 1961)

P. L. Quinn, *Divine Commands and Moral Requirements* (Oxford, 1978)

Ian Ramsey (ed.), *Christian Ethics and Contemporary Philosophy* (London, 1966)

D. D. Raphael, *Moral Philosophy* (Oxford, 1981)

Illtyd Trethowan, *Absolute Value* (London, 1970)

J. O. Urmson, *Aristotle's Ethics* (Oxford, 1988)

10. People and life after death

Timothy McDermott (ed.), *Thomas Aquinas: Selected Philosophical Writings* (Oxford, 1993), sections 18 and 19

D. M. Armstrong, *A Materialist Theory of the Mind* (London, 1968)

Paul Badham and Linda Badham, *Immortality or Extinction?* (London, 1982)

David Braine, *The Human Person* (London, 1993)

C. D. Broad, *Religion, Philosophy and Psychical Research* (London, 1953)

Peter Carnley, *The Structure of Resurrection Belief* (Oxford, 1987)

Paul Churchland, *Matter and Consciousness* (Cambridge, MA, 1988)

R. Crookall, *The Supreme Adventure* (Cambridge, 1974)

R. Crookall, *What Happens When You Die* (Gerrards Cross, 1978)

I. Currie, *You Cannot Die* (New York, 1978)

Steven T. Davis (ed.), *Death and Afterlife* (London, 1989)

D. C. Dennett, *Consciousness Explained* (Boston, 1991)

E. R. Dodds, 'Why I do not believe in survival', *Proceedings of the Society for Psychical Research* (1934)

C. J. Ducasse, *Belief in Life After Death* (Springfield, IL, 1961)

J. C. Eccles, *The Neurophysiological Basis of Mind* (Oxford, 1956)

J. C. Eccles and K. R. Popper, *The Self and Its Brain* (Berlin, 1977)

Paul Edwards (ed.), *Immortality* (London, 1992)

Paul Edwards, *Reincarnation: A Critical Examination* (London, 1996)

Antony Flew (ed.), *Body, Mind, and Death* (New York, 1964)

P. T. Geach, *God and the Soul* (London, 1969)

John Hick, *Death and Eternal Life* (London, 1979)

Anthony Kenny, *The Metaphysics of Mind* (Oxford, 1989)

Anthony Kenny, *Aquinas on Mind* (Oxford, 1993)

Hans Küng, *Eternal Life* (New York, 1984)

P. Kurtz (ed.), *A Skeptic's Guide to Parapsychology* (Buffalo, NY, 1985)

H. D. Lewis, *The Self and Immortality* (London, 1973)

H. D. Lewis, *Persons and Life After Death* (London, 1978)

Herbert McCabe, 'The immortality of the soul' in Anthony Kenny (ed.), *Aquinas: A Collection of Critical Essays* (London, 1969)

J. J. MacIntosh and H. A. Meynell (eds), *Faith, Scepticism and Personal Identity* (Calgary, 1994)

R. Moody, *Life After Life* (New York, 1973)

R. Moody, *Reflections on Life After Life* (New York, 1977)

Terence Penelhum, *Survival and Disembodied Existence* (London, 1970)

John Perry (ed.), *Personal Identity* (Berkeley, Los Angeles and London, 1975)

U. T. Place, 'Consciousness and perception', *Proceedings of the Aristotelian Society*, Supplementary Volume (1966)

U. T. Place, 'Burt on brain and consciousness', *Bulletin of the British Psychological Society* (1969)

Bruce R. Reichenbach, *The Law of Karma* (London, 1990)

Gilbert Ryle, *The Concept of Mind* (Harmondsworth, 1963)

Richard Swinburne, *The Evolution of the Soul* (Oxford, 1986)

Richard Taylor, *Metaphysics* (Englewood Cliffs, NJ, 1963)

Richard Warner and Tadeusz Szubka (eds), *The Mind–Body Problem: A Guide to the Current Debate* (Oxford, 1994)

11. Philosophy and world religions

S. Biderman and B. Scharfstein (eds), *Rationality in Question: On Eastern and Western Views of Rationality* (Leiden, 1989)

William Christian, *Oppositions of Religious Doctrines* (London, 1972)

F. C. Copleston, *Religion and the One: Philosophies East and West* (London, 1982)

F. C. Copleston, *Philosophies and Cultures* (Oxford, 1989)

John Hick, *An Interpretation of Religion: Human Responses to the Transcendent* (London, 1989)

J. Kellenberger (ed.), *Inter-Religious Models and Criteria* (London, 1993)

G. J. Larson and E. Deutsch (eds), *Interpreting Across Boundaries: New Essays in Comparative Philosophy* (Princeton, 1988; Delhi, 1989)

B. Matilal, *Logical and Ethical Issues in Religious Belief* (Calcutta, 1982)

J. N. Mohanty, *Reason and Tradition in Indian Thought* (Oxford, 1992)

Alvin Plantinga, 'A defence of religious exclusivism' in Louis P. Pojman (ed.), *Philosophy of Religion: An Anthology* (2nd edn; Belmont, CA, 1994)

S. Sutherland, L. Houlden, P. Clarke and F. Hardy (eds), *The World's Religions* (London, 1988)

Keith Ward, *Religion and Revelation: A Theology of Revelation in the World's Religions* (Oxford, 1994)

Keith Ward, *Religion and Creation* (Oxford, 1996)

12. Science and religion

Ian G. Barbour (ed.), *Science and Religion: New Perspectives on the Dialogue* (New York, 1968)

Ian Barbour, *Religion in an Age of Science* (San Francisco, 1991)

Michael Behe, *Darwin's Black Box* (New York, 1996)

Richard J. Blackwell, *Galileo, Bellarmine, and the Bible* (Notre Dame, 1991)

Paul Davies, *God and the New Physics* (New York, 1983)

Stanley Jaki, *The Road of Science and the Ways to God* (Edinburgh and Chicago, 1978)

Peter Lipton, *Inference to the Best Explanation* (London, 1991)

Ernan McMullin (ed.), *Evolution and Creation* (Notre Dame, 1985)

Ernan McMullin, *The Inference that Science Makes* (Milwaukee, 1992)

Ernan McMullin, 'Indifference Principle and Anthropic Principle in cosmology', *Studies in the History and Philosophy of Science* 24 (1993)

Jacques Monod, *Chance and Necessity* (New York, 1972)

Wolfhart Pannenberg, *Theology and the Philosophy of Science* (London, 1976)

John Polkinghorne, *One World* (Princeton, 1987)

Holmes Rolston III, *Science and Religion: A Critical Survey* (New York, 1987)

Robert J. Russell, William R. Stoeger SJ and George V. Coyne (eds), *Physics, Philosophy and Theology* (Vatican City, 1988)

Edward O. Wilson, *On Human Nature* (Cambridge, 1978)

Zygon: Journal of Religion and Science. (A *sine qua non* for work in science and religion)

Index of names

Abelard, Peter   81, 239–40
Adams, Robert   146–51
Alston, William P.   67, 173, 177, 214, 220, 231–2; *author of Chapter 2(d)*
Anaxagoras   7, 107–8, 256
Anscombe, Elizabeth   32
Anselm of Canterbury, St   8–9, 22–3, 54–6, 75, 228, 241, 243
Aquinas, St Thomas   2, 5, 9–10, 13, 23–5, 32, 35, 39–40, 43–5, 49–52, 55, 59, 71–3, 79, 87–92, 97, 108–27 *passim*, 131–3, 137, 143, 169, 174–5, 181–9 *passim*, 202–24, 243–6, 270–2, 288, 303, 331, 336, 340, 350, 358
Aristotle   5–8, 24–5, 35–6, 39–40, 43–7, 51–2, 59, 70–4, 88–91, 97–8, 108–14 *passim*, 118–27 *passim*, 132–4, 182, 187–8, 194, 215, 218, 255, 264–72, 288–9, 299, 301, 329–40 *passim*, 344, 352–5, 358
Armstrong, D. M.   291, 303
Augustine of Hippo, St   8, 14, 75, 79, 81, 98, 109–10, 169, 182, 237, 243, 329–30, 335–6, 343
Averroës   71, 288
Avicenna   71–4
Ayer, A. J.   117, 289

Balestra, Dominic J.   4; *author of Chapter 12*
Barbour, Ian   355, 357–8
Barrett, Cyril   31
Barrow, John D.   139
Barth, Karl   22–5, 77
Bavinck, Herman   37–8
Beardsworth, Timothy   66

Behe, Michael   348–50
Bentham, Jeremy   272–4
Bergson, Henri   304
Berkeley, George   337–9
Billingham, Richard   13
Blackwell, Richard   336
Bloch, Ernst   26
Boethius   75, 78–9, 89–91, 96–8
Braine, David   48, 51; *author of Chapter 2(a)*
Braithwaite, R. B.   117–18
Brentano, Franz   243
Brightman, E. S.   96
Broad, C. D.   308
Bruno, Giordano   14–15
Buber, Martin   100
Bultmann, Rudolf   24
Burrell, David B.   *author of Chapter 3(a)*
Butler, Joseph   98

Cajetan, Thomas de Vio   111–12, 118, 303
Calvin, John   38, 79
Cantwell Smith, Wilfred   314–15
Capra, Fritjof   327
Carnap, Rudolf   117
Carson, D. A.   144
Chambers, Robert   340
Chisholm, Roderick M.   68, 98
Churchland, Paul   291–3
Clarke, Norris   112
Clarke, Samuel   16, 143
Copernicus, Nicholas   334–8, 340, 352
Coyne, George   358
Craig, William Lane   3, 45–6; *author of Chapter 5*
Crombie, Ian   229

383

Index of names

Crookall, Robert 304–5

Darwin, Charles 60–2, 267–9, 282, 327, 340–2, 348–50
Davey, F. N. 241
Davidson, Donald 130, 205
Dennett, Daniel 293–5
Descartes, René 12–15, 37, 54–6, 98, 101, 110, 266–7, 289, 290, 294, 301–2, 329, 333, 338
Dionysius, Pseudo-Dionysius 9, 109, 187
Dodds, E. R. 303–4
Duhem, Pierre 332–3, 352–3
Dummett, Michael 229–30
Dyson, Hugo 240

Eccles, John 110
Eddington, Arthur 346
Eddy, Mary Baker 169
Einstein, Albert 298, 346
Eldridge, N. 348, 350

Flew, Antony 82, 84, 229, 289
Flint, Thomas 147, 151
Foot, Philippa 274
Frankfurt, Harry 98
Frege, Gottlob 25, 43
Friedman, Alexander 139

Galileo 332–39, 342–56 passim
Gardner, Martin 303
Gassendi, Pierre 55
Geach, Peter 99, 178, 243
Gould, Stephen J. 340, 348, 350
Greco, John 213; author of Chapter 1(e)
Grisez, Germain 48
Groves, Peter author of Chapter 1(c)

Haldane, John 48
Hambourger, R. 61
Hartshorne, Charles 125, 329
Harvey, A. Van 236, 238
Hasker, William 146–7, 150–1
Hawking, Stephen 139–41, 347
Hebblethwaite, Brian 245, 315–16
Hegel, Wilhelm Friedrich 12, 14–15, 18–20, 26, 357
Heidegger, Martin 24–5, 312
Helm, Paul 185; author of Chapter 3(b)
Hick, John 102, 118, 172–3, 179, 245
Hobbes, Thomas 16, 97
Holcote, Robert 13

Hovelmann, Gerd 305–6
Hoyle, Fred 346, 353
Hubble, Edwin 346, 353
Hughes, Gerard J. author of Chapter 3(d)
Hume, David 5, 12, 15–19, 32, 37, 50–1, 60–1, 63, 98, 117, 156–7, 237, 246, 277, 283, 307, 339, 351
Husserl, E. 311–12
Huxley, Thomas H. 341–2, 348

Irenaeus of Lyon, St 172

Jaki, Stanley 333, 348
James, William 65–6, 101, 103
Jantzen, Grace 97
Jaspers, Karl 81
Jenkins, John author of Chapter 7
Jesus Christ 10, 22, 25, 102, 110, 156–7, 203, 213, 218, 229–31, 237–46 passim, 354
John Paul II, Pope 357–8
Johnson, Philip 343
Jüngel, Eberhard 26

Kant, Immanuel 5, 12, 15–16, 17–18, 19, 21, 25, 42, 44, 45–6, 48–9, 54, 55–6, 99, 101, 103, 132, 246, 283, 287, 329, 333, 339, 344, 355–6
Kenny, Anthony 32, 84
Kerr, Fergus 32
Kierkegaard, Søren 20, 22
Koterski, Joseph author of Chapter 1(b)
Kretzmann, Norman 78
Kuhn, Thomas 351–3
Küng, Hans 26
Kvanvig, Jonathan 147

Lakatos, Imre 351–4
Leibniz, Gottfried Wilhelm 18, 45, 47–8, 54, 101, 110, 143
Levinas, Emmanuel 100
Lewis, C. S. 105, 239–40
Lindbeck, George 26
Lipner, Julius author of Chapter 11
Locke, John 16, 98, 202–24
Lodge, Sir Oliver 304
Lonergan, Bernard 25–6, 48, 243–4
Lorenz, Konrad 241
Luther, Martin 209, 334

McCabe, Herbert 31–2, 177, 184–5, 193
MacIntosh, Jack 289, 307

Index of names

Index of subjects

Index of subjects

Index of subjects